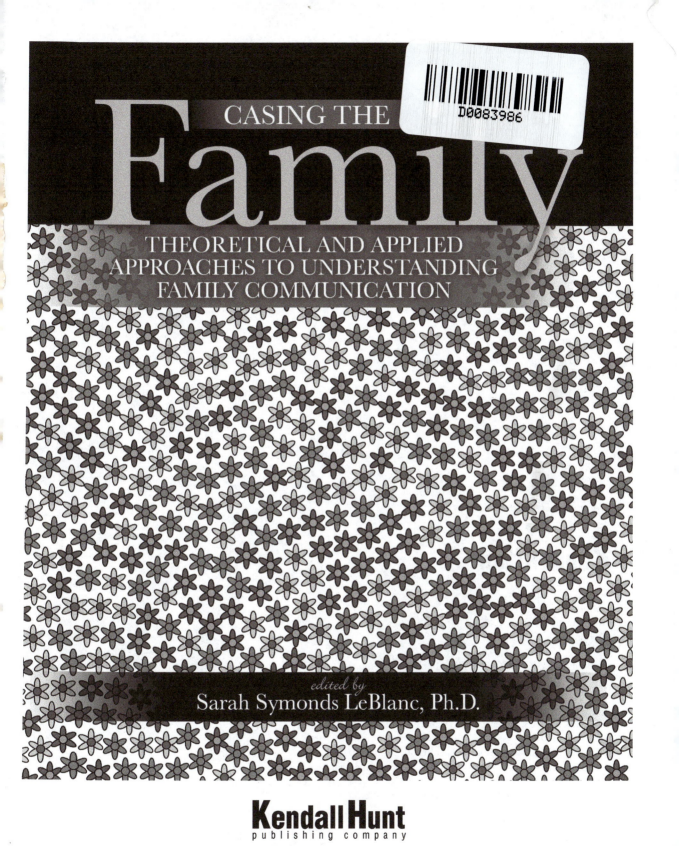

CASING THE

Family

THEORETICAL AND APPLIED APPROACHES TO UNDERSTANDING FAMILY COMMUNICATION

edited by

Sarah Symonds LeBlanc, Ph.D.

Kendall Hunt
publishing company

Cover image © Shutterstock.com

www.kendallhunt.com
Send all inquiries to:
4050 Westmark Drive
Dubuque, IA 52004-1840

Copyright © 2019 by Kendall Hunt Publishing Company

ISBN 978-1-5249-8943-9

Published in the United States of America

CONTENTS

ACKNOWLEDGMENTS

I was 42 years old when I first saw the film *Milo and Stitch*. I went in blind, only knowing it was about a little girl and her odd-looking pet. While I wasn't necessarily impressed with the film, one line stood out as I watched—"*Ohana* means family. No one gets left behind . . . no one is forgotten."

No one gets left behind.

I was 42 years old when my mother died. Her death, our estrangement, and reading the case studies for this book had me contemplating family more than I usually do when conducting my research. Peeling the layers off of the word family confirmed what I teach my students: there is no one definition of family and all families are not the same. Everyone has a family.

No one gets left behind.

The idea for this book was stewing in my head since I first started teaching family communication. The more stories that were shared during class time, the more it seemed like class was becoming a therapy/counseling session and less about seeing communication in action. I want my students to be introduced to the concepts and theories, see how they are present within a family, and then be able to apply what they have learned to their own lives. Reaching that goal seemed like a long way to travel.

Not all students are comfortable sharing their personal lives within the safe confines of a classroom. But not all students watch the same television shows, attend the same movies, or even read the same books, so finding culturally relevant examples of family became a chore. Wouldn't it be nice if all students could discuss the same family?

I proposed this book more as a side comment. I actually said, "But you don't have a case study book for family communication?" I was asked, "Are you interesting in developing one?" My response…maybe. Maybe quickly became yes. It is needed.

Having this book become a reality is surreal. It would not have happened without the support of the contributing authors, students from my Fall 2018 Family Communication and Communication Theory courses, my graduate advisees, and my editor and the staff at Kendall Hunt.

It wouldn't be a family communication book if I also didn't thank my family: my husband, Matt, my daughters, Caroline and Evangeline, my in-laws, Kathy and Mike, and my siblings, Jennifer, Abby, Emily, and Andrew. I dedicate this book to my deceased parents, Peter and Dolly. Without them, I would not have had experiences to critically analyze and want to study.

No one gets left behind…or forgotten.

CONTRIBUTING AUTHORS

Jordan Atkinson (PhD, West Virginia University) is an assistant professor in the Department of Communication and Journalism at Missouri Western State University.

Maria Brann (PhD, University of Kentucky; MPH, West Virginia University) is a full professor of communication studies at IUPUI who studies communication surrounding health vulnerabilities.

Kerry Byrnes-Loinette (PhD, West Virginia State University) is a professor of communication studies at Collin College who studies communication in families and in the teacher-student relationship.

Peter Clarke (PhD, University of Minnesota) is a professor at the USC Annenberg School for Communication and Journalism and at USC's Keck School of Medicine, and a coinvestigator of the VeggieBook study.

Deborah Neffa Creech (MA, University of North Carolina Chapel Hill) is a doctoral candidate at the USC Annenberg School for Communication and Journalism and a research assistant for the VeggieBook study. She researches how interpersonal communication and technology use at home influence health behaviors.

Jocelyn M. DeGroot (PhD, Ohio University) is an associate professor in the Department of Applied Communication Studies at Southern Illinois University Edwardsville. Her research interests include computer-mediated communication and communicative issues of death and dying. She also examines dynamic tensions in interpersonal relationships such as MIL/DIL relationships, motherhood, and online catfishing.

Katherine J. Denker (PhD, University of Missouri) is an associate professor at Ball State University. Her work centers on issues of power and voice in both the instructional and interpersonal context, with a further focus on couples' co-constructions of work-life concerns. Her work has appeared in multiple book chapters as well as recently in journals including the *Journal of Family Communication, Women & Language, Computers in Human Behavior,* and *Communication Teacher.*

Tim Dun (PhD, University of Iowa) is associate professor of communication at Brock University in Canada. His recent scholarship examines new parents' relationships with their parents, researching changes surrounding the birth of a new generation. His work has appeared in the *Journal of Family Communication, Qualitative Communication Research,* and the *Journal of Social and Personal Relationships.*

Kristina Wenzel Egan (PhD, University of Missouri) teaches courses related to communicating in close relationships and has interviewed more than a hundred individuals who identify as members of eldercare families. Her research focuses on how family relationships communicatively navigate health and illness experiences. Specifically, her scholarship uses interpretive methods to examine how familial caregiving relationships communicate during late-life health issues, including parental caregiving, end-of-life communication, and stories of dying.

Susan H. Evans (PhD, University of Michigan) is a research scientist at the USC Annenberg School for Communication and Journalism and coinvestigator of the VeggieBook study.

Sean Fourney (MA, West Chester University) is a PhD candidate at the University of Southern Mississippi's School of Communication. His main focus is on risk communication with an emphasis on collaborations within and beyond organizational boundaries. In the summer of 2018, he worked as a public engagement intern at New Orleans Homeland Security and Emergency Preparedness where he helped inform the city's diverse audiences about mitigation measures during hurricane season. Before entering higher education, Sean worked in broadcasting as a producer and on-air host in both his hometown of Easton, PA and West Chester, PA.

Eletra S. Gilchrist-Petty (PhD, The University of Memphis) is an associate professor of communication arts at The University of Alabama Huntsville. Her program of research focus on human communication as situated in the domains of instructional, interpersonal, and intercultural communication.

Joanna Glovinsky (MA, University of Southern California Annenberg) was field director for the VeggieBook study before founding Fruitstitute, a fruit tree care and education company for backyard growers in Southern California.

Jayne R. Goode (PhD, University of Missouri) is an associate professor of communication at Governors State University. She is the graduate program director and basic course director. Her research and teaching interests concern political communication, identity, and activism.

Maria Hannah (BA, Indiana University South Bend) is pursuing graduate work in communication studies. She is looking to focus largely on organizing and relating with a focus on instructional communication.

Haley Kranstuber Horstman (PhD, University of Nebraska–Lincoln) researches communicated sense-making in the context of family diversity and adversity. She grounds much of her work in narrative theorizing and methodology. Currently, she is working on several grant-funded projects studying family communicated sense-making of difficult experiences, such as miscarriage and racial discrimination. Her work has been published in top-ranked peer-reviewed journals such as *Communication Monographs, Journal of Applied Communication Research, Health Communication, Personal Relationships, Journal of Social and Personal Relationships,* and *Journal of Family Communication.*

Elizabeth Jenkins (M.A., Ball State University; formerly Tobin) is a PhD student in the School of Communication Studies at Ohio University. Her research examines the light and dark sides of interpersonal relationships as communicated through computer-mediated communication (CMC). Specifically, she is interested how the same CMC processes (e.g., telling white lies via text message) are interpreted as positive (e.g., communicated a white lie intending to be kind to a sibling) or negative (e.g., the sibling believes the white lie lacks kindness) depending on the relational context. Ms. Jenkins seeks to understand mediated sexual communication, specifically sexting between intimate partners. Further, she studies communication between teens and parents concerning mediated and non-mediated sexual behaviors and consent. Ms. Jenkins also conducts formative health campaign intervention research surrounding sexting. Moreover, she investigates white lie deception within various interpersonal relationships from linguistic, motivational, and deception detection perspectives.

Falon Kartch (PhD, University of Wisconsin-Milwaukee) is an assistant professor in the Department of Communication at California State University, Fresno. Her research focuses primarily on family types and experiences which have historically been "on the margins" of family communication research, including post-divorce nonresidential parenting, nonresidential motherhood, and coming out to family members.

Anne Kerber (PhD, Ohio University) is an assistant professor in the Department of Communication Studies at Minnesota State University, Mankato. Her research focuses on the intersections of health and organizational communication, and has appeared in journals such as *Health Communication*, *Women & Language*, and *Management Communication Quarterly*.

Mary E. King (PhD, Rutgers University) is currently an associate professor at Bloomsburg University of Pennsylvania. Her research examines close, personal relationships with a focus on how romantic couples navigate transitions in their relationship. Dr. King's research has been published in the *Journal of Family Communication*, *The Wiley Blackwell Encyclopedia of Family Studies*, *Communication Quarterly*, the *Journal of Social and Personal Relationships*, and the *Western Journal of Communication*.

Michael W. Kramer (PhD, University of Texas) is professor and chair in the Department of Communication at the University of Oklahoma. His research focuses on the socialization/assimilation process of people joining and leaving organizations, along with leadership and decision making. His work examines both employees and volunteers.

Sarah S. LeBlanc (PhD, University of Missouri) is an assistant professor of interpersonal communication and research methods at Purdue University, Fort Wayne. Her research intersects between health and family communication. She is currently exploring a link between supportive communication, postpartum depression, and the infant mortality rate. In addition to a few book chapters and co-authoring one book, LeBlanc's work has appeared in *Death Studies*, *The Journal of Loss and Trauma*, and *Health Communication*.

Corey Jay Liberman (PhD, Rutgers University) is an associate professor in the Department of Communication and Media Arts at Marymount Manhattan College. His research spans the interpersonal communication, group communication, and organizational communication worlds, and he is currently interested in studying the social practices of dissent within organizations, specifically the antecedents, processes, and effects associated with effective employee dissent communication, as well as risk and crisis communication. He is currently working on a coauthored book entitled *Risk and Crisis Communication: Communicating in a Disruptive World*, as well as a coedited case study book focusing on mediated communication. He is coauthor of *Organizational Communication: Strategies for Success (2nd Edition)*, editor of *Casing Persuasive Communication*, and coeditor of *Casing Crisis and Risk Communication*, all published by Kendall Hunt. He has a coedited volume, *Casing Communication Theory*, which will be out in the spring of 2019.

Anthony Machette (MA, Purdue University Fort Wayne) is a graduate student at the University of Oklahoma. His research focuses primarily on how culture, gender, and biological sex affects communication in the interpersonal relationships. Having lived in the United States, Australia, and Taiwan, much of his research examines the differences between cultures and how these differences continue to communication.

Andrea L. Meluch (PhD, Kent State University) is an assistant professor at the University of Akron. Much of her research focuses on cancer patient experiences of social support. She has published articles and book chapters in a variety of outlets, including the *Journal of Communication and Healthcare* and *Southern Communication Journal.*

Courtney Waite Miller (PhD, Northwestern University) is a professor of communication at Elmhurst College. Her recent research focuses on conflict in close relationships and the role this plays in relational, mental, and physical health. She has published in a variety of outlets such as *Communication Yearbook, International Journal of Conflict Management*, and *Argumentation and Advocacy.*

Aimee E. Miller-Ott (PhD, University of Nebraska-Lincoln) is an associate professor of communication at Illinois State University. Her overarching research interest focuses on how people in romantic and family relationships manage their private information and identities. She has published numerous articles on the role of cell phones in romantic, family, and platonic relationships and how these devices impact attentiveness and face needs in interactions. She also studies relationships (e.g., foster families, families with parents with Alzheimer's disease, work spouses) that rely on their discourse to define, explain, and defend their relationships as legitimate.

Shaye Morrison (MS, Texas Christian University) is currently a PhD student in interpersonal/family communication at the University of Missouri. She studies the communication surrounding infertility. In particular, Shaye is interested in how social network members influence the construction of conversations surrounding infertility, as well as personal and relational outcomes of those conversations.

Scott A. Myers (PhD, Kent State University) is a professor and Peggy Rardin McConnell endowed chair of communication studies in the Department of Communication Studies at West Virginia University.

Kaitlin E. Phillips (PhD, University of Nebraska-Lincoln) is an assistant professor of communication studies at Utah State University where she researches the interplay between family and personal identity focusing on how people create family identity and solidarity, and the perceptions of difference in relational quality across family members. Her work has been featured in journals such as *Journal of Communication, Communication Monographs, Journal of Family Communication, Western Journal of Communication*, and *Southern Communication Journal.*

DeAnne Priddis (PhD, University of Wisconsin-Milwaukee) is an assistant professor in the Department of Communication at Middle Tennessee State University (Murfreesboro, TN). Her research includes conflict in families and organizations, with a primary emphasis on how family members cope with another's addiction. Her work has been published in *Health Communication, SAGE Research Methods Cases*, and *Pennsylvania Communication Annual.*

Narissra Maria Punyanunt-Carter (PhD, Kent State University) is an assistant dean of international affairs and an associate professor in the department of communication studies at Texas Tech University where she teaches interpersonal communication, gender, nonverbal, and romantic relationships. Dr. Punyanunt-Carter's research interests include romantic relationships, computer-mediated communication, father-daughter communication, and mass media portrayals of romance.

Sarah E. Riforgiate (PhD, Arizona State University) is an assistant professor of communication at University of Wisconsin, Milwaukee. Her research concentrates on communication pertaining to public/paid-work and private-life. Her work has been published in *Communication Monographs, Journal of Family Communication*, and *Management and Communication Quarterly.*

Kristina M. Scharp (PhD, University of Iowa) is an assistant professor of communication at the University of Washington and a director of the Family Communication and Relationships Lab. She researches difficult family transitions such as parent-child estrangement and the processes by which family members cope with their distress. Featured in journals such as *Communication Research, Human Communication Research, Family Relations*, and the *Journal of Family Communication*, she is particularly interested in ways people navigate entering and exiting the family. Her research has won top papers at both the international and national communication associations and has garnered attention from outlets such as *The New York Times, Forbes-India, PBS, NPR*, and the *Wall Street Journal.* She currently serves on the editorial board for journals such as *Communication Teacher, Family Relations, Journal of Family Communication, Journal of Social and Personal Relationships*, and *Personal Relationships.*

Amy M. Smith (PhD, Bowling Green State University) is an associate professor of media and communication at Salem State University. Her research interests are varied and include issues of family communication, community building, gender and media, and diversity in pedagogy. In the classroom, Amy uses the guiding principle of "meet them where they are" to foster meaningful relationships with students and help them achieve their highest potential. Amy regularly presents her research at the National Communication Association Annual Conference, where she also serves as reviewer and respondent to multiple divisions and interest groups. Her publications include *Tracing family lines: The impact of women's genealogy research on family communication* (2012), *Family genealogy and family communication: Finding common ground* (2016, Genealogy), and her forthcoming book, titled *Fiber spaces: Knitting community together* (McFarland Press).

B. Liahnna Stanley (BA, University of South Florida Tampa) is a second-year master's student in the Department of Communication at University of South Florida. She researches how people living with opioid addiction communicate and make meaning of addiction, health, and identity. Her research explores the interplay between these phenomena and developing ways in which we can improve the health of underprivileged populations. Keeping to a reflexive ethos, she listens to the narratives that emerge between herself as researcher and the participants to better understand how they communicate about their experiences with addiction. In her spare time, she volunteers with SafeExchange Tampa, an NPO devoted to mobilizing harm reduction strategies to minimize the negative consequences associated with drug use.

Shawn C. Starcher (PhD, Kent State University) is an assistant professor at Muskingum University. His research interests are interpersonal communication, family communication, and health communication. More specifically, he examines how families discuss mental health issues and how that impacts their relationships in the family environment.

Anne M. Stone (PhD, University of Illinois Urbana-Champaign) is an associate professor of communication at Rollins College, Winter Park, FL. Her research focuses on the role of communication in improving health and relationships across the lifespan. She published an article in *Journal of Applied Communication Research* that explored how nurses communicate with patients and families coping with Alzheimer's disease. Other projects have examined the role of uncertainty and information management for pre and posttransplant patients, which culminated in an article published in the journal *Qualitative Communication Research* and examined the experiences of uncertainty in a surgical waiting room, which was published in *The Permanente Journal*.

Lindsay Timmerman (PhD, University of Texas) is an associate professor in the Department of Communication Studies at Texas State University. Her research centers around close relationships, specifically focusing on stigmatized disclosure, long-distance relationships (including military marriage), family secrets, and under-studied close relationships.

Lynn H. Turner (PhD, Northwestern University) is professor of communication studies and director of the interdisciplinary family studies minor at Marquette University. Her research areas include interpersonal, gendered, and family communication. She is the co-author or coeditor of over 12 books as well as multiple articles and book chapters. Her articles have appeared in a variety of journals including: *Management Communication Quarterly, Journal of Applied Communication Research, Women & Language, Journal of Family Communication,* and *Western Journal of Communication.*

Tennley Vik (PhD, Ohio University) is an Assistant Professor in the Department of Communication Studies at the University of Nevada, Reno. Her research interests include privacy and disclosure dilemmas as well as how families and interpersonal dyads communication about sex and sexuality.

Phillip E. Wagner (PhD, University of Kansas) is a faculty member of the Department of Communication Studies, director of General Education, and chair of the Chancellor's Advisory Council on Diversity, Equity, and Inclusion at the University of South Florida at Sarasota-Manatee. Phil's research explores the intersections of health, identity, and gender and he has been published in journals such as the *Journal of Applied Communication Research, Communication, Women & Language, The International Journal of Men's Health, Communication Quarterly,* and *Communication Teacher.* Phil has also given a TED talk on his work on masculinity and fitness.

Sydney O'Shay Wallace (MA, Eastern Michigan University) is working on a doctoral degree and is also a fellow at the Merrill Palmer Skillman Institute for Child and Family Development. Her research interests are grounded in the study of stigma communication in family and health contexts. Sydney's current research projects include a study of how families communicate and manage stigma when experiencing substance abuse within the family, and a study of nurses' experiences caring for patients with substance use issues. The overarching goals of Sydney's research involve helping better understand how families communicatively cope with the presence of substance abuse, in efforts to inform an intervention aimed at helping families experiencing substance use issues.

Tiffany R. Wang (PhD, University of Nebraska-Lincoln) is an associate professor of communication studies at the University of Montevallo where she explores communication surrounding college transition within instructional and family contexts. Her work has been featured in journals such as *Communication Education, Communication Reports, Communication Teacher, The Journal of Continuing Higher Education, Journal of Divorce & Remarriage*, and *Journal of Family Communication*.

Savaughn Williams (MA, Ball State University) researches the intersection of interpersonal relationships, media depictions, and race. Her current work centers on interracial friendships and she has recently presented work at the Organization for the Study of Communication, Language, and Gender.

Brendan Young (PhD, University of Iowa) is an associate professor of communication at Western Illinois University-Quad Cities. He earned his PhD at the University of Iowa where he studied the sponsorship in Alcoholics Anonymous. He subsequently worked at the Department of Veterans Affairs where he researched barriers to mental health services among rural veterans. He conducts grant-funded research on mutual help groups like A.A. and Al-Anon, focusing on their impact on veterans and their families. His work has appeared in *Alcoholism Treatment Quarterly, Substance Use & Misuse*, the *Journal of Social Work Practice in the Addictions*, the *Journal of Groups in Addiction and Recovery*, the *International Journal of Mental Health and Addiction, Addiction Research and Theory*, the *Journal of Family Communication*, the *Journal of Veterans Studies*, the *Journal of Rural Health*, and *Patient Education and Counseling*.

Valerie J. Young (PhD, University of Arizona) is an associate professor in the Department of Communication at Hanover College. Her research interests include intimate relationship maintenance and interpersonal health communication and social influence.

Diana G. Zulli (PhD, University of Utah) is an assistant professor of public relations and political communication at Purdue University. Her research focuses on the interaction of communication theory, political and military rhetoric, and digital technology. In particular, she is interested in how communication theories function in, and are affected by, the rapidly changing digital communication environment, how news media shapes understandings of political and military events, and how digital technology affects political processes. Diana has industry experience in public relations, and she teaches a wide range of strategic communication topics, including public relations, advertising, and integrated marketing.

INTRODUCTION

On any given weekday, I encounter two of my families. I have the family I created when I married my husband and we had two children. My "created" family is a mix of "voluntary," as I chose to marry my husband and we chose to have children, and "involuntary," as I did not choose my husband's parents.

My second family is my work family. This is a voluntary family type as I chose to accept this job. There are no assigned roles, but we are bound by the same goals and sometimes work toward the same outcome. My colleagues have been a constant in my life since my oldest was three months old. They are defacto aunts and uncles to my children.

They were there when my daughter was admitted to the children's hospital because she couldn't put on weight. They were there when my father died during my first spring break at the institution. They were there when I announced my second pregnancy. They were when I learned the news of my mother's passing. They have watched my children grow and they have accepted my family into the department's family.

With the completion and publication of this book, I have a third family, my contributing authors and the individuals at Kendall Hunt Publishing. The supportive communication I have received has gotten me through some dark moments during this process.

Now that you have purchased this book for your course, you are volunteering to become a part of our family communication family. The book and the included case studies were designed and written with you, the student, in mind. During the course of your lifetime, you have witnessed the changing nature of your own family. Additionally, you have noticed the changing nature of family around the world and have observed how many people across the United States, as well as in various countries around the world, define family.

My teaching experience brought to life how many of my students do not like discussing their family. I implemented the Harry Potter series into my family communication courses and quickly became known as the Harry Potter professor. However, with each new incoming class, I realize that not every student has read, or was allowed to read and see, Harry

Potter. It was in those moments when I knew a family communication case study book was needed.

Just like every snowflake is unique and different, so is each family. That is the beauty about this book. You are able to examine various family types and scenarios in the United States. By examining the family and the scenario from each case study, you and your classmates will be able to critically analyze and discuss a "safe" family.

The first section of this book highlights the Changing Nature of Family. Atkinson and Myers start you off with a piece examining four classmates and how each one represents a different quadrant of the family communication patterns theory. The second case study, by Electra Gilchrist, highlights the uncertainties that influence a family as a result of transracial adoption. King focuses on how family changes once all the children leave home while Punyanunt-Carter focuses on culture's impact on multicultural children. Wang and Phillips explore how first-generation college students struggle with family communication while Zulli concludes the section on how military couples struggle during deployments. Each case study features a different type of family illustrating how much the definition of family has changed within our culture.

The second section of the book focuses on three influences on family: Relationships, Parents, and Culture. Kartch and Timmerman explore how a 16-year-old girl handles communication with and between her divorced parents. Machette dives into how couples handle traditions in an intercultural relationship. Miller explores the impact of differing opinions among generations when it comes to spanking, and Smith brings to light how much impact inheritance has on family communication. Vik and DeGroot portray how much moms conform to societal expectations to hide how hard mothering can be. Wagner explores how parents communicate about fat and fitness. Finally, Williams and Denker conclude the section by examining how one young lady handles portraying her race and gender based on things she learned from her mother and grandmother.

The expanding boundaries of family is the theme of the third section Negotiation of Boundaries within the Family. DeGroote and Young provide three vignettes about handling the involuntary in-law relationship through three aspects of the communication privacy management theory. Dun provides a picture of how the birth of a child influences events leading up to the birth of the child and relationships between the birth parents and grandparents afterwards. Jenkins examines parent-teen communication about the sexting habit through an attachment theory perspective. Kramer examines the dialectics the middle generation face when they are both parents and grandparents, but they also need to care for their aging parents. Wenzel Egan explores how adult siblings share information on an aging parent care.

As a scholar of dark family communication, no case study book would be complete without a Dark Side of Family section. Neffa-Creech and colleagues highlight how a mobile app can influence how families discuss food. Goode brings many dinner conversations to light when she explores how bipartisan parents' communication impacts their children's beliefs. Riforgiate and Turner explore how being bullied in the workplace influences life at home, while Scharp uncovers how family estrangement impacts family get-togethers. Starcher tackles communication between parents and children on when they should talk about adolescent depression.

Exploring one dark issue in particular, the fourth section highlights the growing problem of Addiction within Families. Byrnes-Loinette and Brann explore narratives of adult children of alcoholics. Priddis continues with the alcohol theme by exploring the impact a parent's drinking has on the entire family. O'Shay-Wallace explores how one daughter's drug addiction impacts her relationship with her parents, her parents' relationship with each other, and her relationship with her sister. Stanley takes an autoethnographic approach by sharing how her family has handled addiction. Young concludes the section by examining how families handle addiction going public and what they encounter during recovery.

Health issues is the theme of the final section, Health and Family. Fourney starts things off by examining his life with a sibling with mental disabilities. Kerber explains how family members handle their "chronic illness identity" when inheriting the family business. Liberman introduces us to the emotional regulation theory and how it comes into play when dealing with a skin cancer diagnosis. Meluch and Hannah take us behind closed doors when they share how families handle life after a breast cancer diagnosis. Miller-Ott illustrates how children can lose a parent twice—once to Alzheimer's and then to death. Morrison and Horstman shed light on how couples communicate about miscarriage. Stone's piece highlights the experiences of uncertainty associated with changing roles of family members, navigating healthcare and treatment decisions, and family conflict when adult children have to make healthcare decisions about their parents.

THE THIRD CLASS

As the first week of classes ended and the syllabus and expectations had been communicated to my students in the family communication course, I could not help but panic over how to teach and illustrate the definition of family, communication, and family communication during the next class period. This anxiety resulted from a conversation I had with a colleague as we noticed that no one reads the same books or watches the same shows.

"Well maybe focus on something you watch and/or read."

"Seriously?" I responded. "I watch Disney Jr. and PBS Kids. My reading is all chick-lit. I doubt that would help."

"Then I can't help ya," my colleague responded.

Our conversation floated across my mind as I lay in bed, unable to sleep, staring at the ceiling. As an assistant professor, I teach and study family communication. Family communication is my passion, the thing other than my children and husband, that gets my blood pumping in the morning and adds to the excitement of going to work.

"Okay," I thought, "I need to figure out how I could teach college students what family is and show them different examples. I need them to move beyond the 2.5 kids with a white picket fence. But how?" I contemplated this dilemma as my body succumbed to sleep.

When my alarm went off, I rolled over, hit snooze, and then it hit me. I decided to teach "what is family" by using Daniel Tiger (Santomero, 2018). I was excited to put this plan into motion and family communication could not come quick enough.

"For today, you had to read the first chapter of your family communication text. By the end of today's class, I want you to be able to define family, define communication, and define family communication."

The class broke into their small groups to discuss the reading and the questions they derived to spark discussion amongst them. I walked amongst the groups, occasionally playing devil's advocate, asking a question to have them think deeper, or even challenging them on their responses. As I picked up bits and pieces of their conversations, I would take notes and then head to the white board to jot down key words and phrases I overheard.

"Now that you had time to discuss the reading in your small groups, let's come together and discuss today's three questions."

I pause, point to the white board, and ask "What is family?" Answers started flying at me so fast that I had a hard time keeping up with the writing.

"Come together"

"Close, trust, care"

"Maintain relationships"

"Support system"

"Constant, go-to"

"Self-defined"

"Voluntary"

I stop, examine the list, turned to the class and ask, "Do these terms define family or do they represent family?"

Silence. Slowly one hand shot up.

"Yes, Josh."

"Most of the terms represent what families should do. The last two terms, self-defined and voluntary, I would argue go more towards the definition of family."

"Who agrees with Josh?" I glance at some of the hands that have come up. "Why, Margaret?"

"Because the definition of family is foggy, according to our reading today."

"Okay, so why is the definition of family foggy, to use the term Margaret used?"

Some may argue that even communication scholars can't agree on the definition of family. Thomas-Maddax and Blau (2013) use the U.S. Census Bureau's definition of family. The Census Bureau (2010) defines family as "a group of two people or more related by birth, marriage, or adoption, and residing together." Turner and West (2018) define family as

> A self-defined group of intimates who create and maintain themselves through their own interactions and their interactions with others; a family may include both voluntary and involuntary relationships; it creates both literal and symbolic internal and external boundaries; and it evolves through time: it has a history, a present, and a future (p. 4).

"Anyone?" Silence fills the classroom. "Do you think we define family differently because of how we see or perceive family?"

"What do you mean?" Phyllis asked from the front row.

I turn back to the board and write: nuclear, extended, immediate, adopted, and step.

"What do these words have in common?"

"They are all families," Phyllis declared.

"That's right, but do these types define family? Think of it this way, as a mother of a couple of preschoolers who love PBS, I watch a lot of Daniel Tiger." I pause as I flash a picture of Daniel Tiger's family on the board. Daniel is a member of an immediate or nuclear family. He has Dad Tiger, Mom Tiger, and baby Margaret. Sometimes his Grandpere visits. The Grandpere would be extended family."

"But we could argue that they are an immediate family or nuclear family because they are all related by blood," a student shouts out from the back.

"That's true. But then, one of Daniel's friends is Oh the Owl," I say as the next picture comes on the screen. "Oh lives with his uncle, who is his primary guardian. How do they fulfill the Bureau's definition of family? Josh?"

"Well," Josh begins. "They are related by blood, but they are not immediate. Enough information isn't given to determine if the uncle adopted Oh. They are a family because they reside together?" he asks hesitantly.

"But what if the uncle isn't related by blood? What if Oh's parents are incarcerated or incapable of fulfilling their parental roles? Just because they reside together shouldn't make them a family. Having the uncle volunteer to take Oh in would make them more of a family for me," MaryJane inserts.

"But why, MaryJane?"

"It goes back to Turner and West's definition. We have voluntary kin, such as parents having children. Parents are not required to have children but rather they volunteer to," MaryJane begins. "The uncle volunteers to take Oh in. Oh is a voluntary member of his family. Now if Oh had a sibling, that would be an involuntary family member."

"Now we are getting somewhere," I continue. "Families are made up of involuntary and voluntary family members. But also, we could assume that Oh and his uncle share a past and are working through the present. Now, let's look at Daniel's friend, Prince Wednesday. Now Wednesday has an older brother, an involuntary member of the family from Wednesday's perspective. But what is also unique about Wednesday is that his parents, King Friday and Queen Sara Sunrise are older parents." The third picture appears.

"Wait. If they are older parents, couldn't we assume that both Wednesday and his older brother were adopted? Then that would add another type of family into the neighborhood," Beatrice contributes.

"We could assume, Beatrice, but we don't really know. What is interesting about Prince Wednesday's family is that the show also introduced his cousin, Chrissie, who has braces on her legs. This introduction highlights how some families have members with disabilities."

"Do you think the viewers get this, though?" Judy asked from the front row. "I mean you have studied this, but do the three- to five-year-old viewers who watch this understand the types of families that are present? And are their other types present in this neighborhood?"

"To your first question, I hope that I can use this information to teach diversity to my children and don't expect them to see all these examples. To your second question, yes, other family types are present. The neighborhood also has a single-parent family (Katerina the Cat)

and a biracial family (Miss Elena's family). Interracial marriages only became legal in 1967 in our country. Most recently, the creators introduced Jodi, a platypus whose family is multigenerational and without a father. Jodi lives with her mom, her grandmother, and a pair of twin brothers. What else is unique about Jodi is that her mother works fulltime as a doctor, so her grandmother is the primary caregiver during the day."

"But that's becoming less unique," Josh points out. "My cousins watch Doc McStuffins (Nee, 2012–2019) and her mother works also as a doctor, and the father stays home."

"That is true, as that is another favorite show of my children. What both of these shows, Daniel Tiger and Doc McStuffins, can teach young children is how they may encounter different family types or structures. But given that there are different types of structures, how does this impact communication? Lindsay, how did your group define communication?"

"We said," Lindsay began, "communication is an exchange between two or more people."

"Well technically," I began, "communication can also take place within yourself and that is intrapersonal communication. But, yes, communication is the exchange between two or more people. But what is exchanged and how? Judy?"

"We exchange information or messages through nonverbal and verbal signals," she replied.

"Thomas-Maddox and Blau (2013) define communication as "the process of generating meaning in the mind of another" (p. 4). Turner and West (2018) define it as "the process of meaning-making between people" (p. 12). But as you discussed in your groups, communication is also the exchange of symbols, signs, and words."

"But communication is also dependent on the context, right?" Beatrice asks.

"Yes, if we go back to the models of communication, what we say and how we say it is dependent on the context. For example, I will say 'we need to use our indoor voices' to my children when they are yelling in public, but when we are at home, I am more likely to say 'take it down a notch' or 'stop yelling'. The meaning of the messages are the same but different symbols are used depending on the context. This leads to our last question: what is family communication? Josh?"

"We said family communication is how families are formed and kept together."

"But it is more than that," Margaret begins to argue. "Family communication is organized, and we use it to inform or warn."

"Okay, wait a minute, both of your groups are correct. But what would happen if we combine our two definitions from family and communication?"

"It is the exchange of information through verbal and nonverbal means between individuals who self-define as family," Josh states.

"Good start, Josh," I begin. "What we need to remember is that there is no one strict definition of family communication, because each family is different. Throughout the next 14 weeks, we will look at factors that impact the exchange of information between those who define themselves as a family. But before we go there, first we will discuss theories. See you next time."

DISCUSSION QUESTIONS

1. How do you define family?
2. How has the evolution of family types impacted the definition of family?
3. How do you define communication? How does your membership in a family impact how you define communication?
4. What is family communication?

REFERENCES

Nee, C. (Creator/Producer). (2012–2019). Doc McStuffins. [Television Series]. Los Angeles, CA: Disney.

Santomero, A. (Creator/Producer.). (2012–2019). Daniel Tiger's neighborhood. [Television Series]. New York, NY: PBS.

Thomas-Maddox, C., & Blau, N. (2013). Family communication: Relationship foundations. Dubuque, IA: Kendall Hunt.

Turner, L. H. & West, R. (2018). Perspectives on family communication (5th ed.). New York, NY: McGraw Hill Education.

U.S. Census Bureau. (2010). Current population report, 2010. Retrieved from www.census.gov

Part I

THE CHANGING NATURE OF DEFINING FAMILY

CHAPTER 1

Family Communication Influences in the College Classroom: A Case Study

Jordan Atkinson – *Missouri Western State University*
Scott A. Myers – *West Virginia University*

ABSTRACT

As part of an undergraduate family communication course, four students are tasked with completing an oral in-class presentation about their family communication patterns. According to family communication patterns theory (FCPT), families have a level of conversation orientation and a level of conformity orientation. These two orientations intersect to form four family types: protective, consensual, pluralistic, and laissez-faire. In this case study, these four students (i.e., Stephanie, Jack, Becky, and Nathan) discuss their respective families and the communication within their families as it relates to the two orientations and four family types. Following their presentations, each of the students have a one-on-one conversation with their instructor, Dr. Garcia, about how their family communication patterns affect their communication with others and their communication in the classroom. Through their conversation with Dr. Garcia and through self-reflection, the four students are able to recognize the influence of family communication patterns on their own communication patterns with individuals outside the family unit.

CASE STUDY

On a warm September morning at Mountainview State University, students rush to get to their first class of the day. With her Starbucks coffee and bag in hand, Dr. Stacy Garcia enters the room where her family communication class meets. Comprised mostly of junior and senior students, family communication is a required course for every student majoring in communication studies at Mountainview State University. In Dr. Garcia's class, there are 15 students enrolled, which is a typical class size at this small, liberal arts university. Dr. Garcia is coming off a stellar year as she was recently awarded the esteemed "Professor of the Year" award. Typically, students really enjoy Dr. Garcia and her classes, as she goes above and beyond to make their class experience enjoyable and to help them be successful. Besides the typical weekly readings, two exams, and three journal article abstracts, the major assignments in this family communication course include (a) an oral presentation in which students apply FCPT to their own families by discussing how communication behaviors in their family relate to the two orientations (i.e., conversation orientation and conformity orientation) and four family types (i.e., protective, consensual, pluralistic, and laissez-faire), (b) an oral debate about a family communication issue, and (c) a research proposal using a family communication construct or theory.

Most of the 15 students in the course know each other from previous courses and other activities; however, four of them are close friends. These four students are Stephanie, Jack, Becky, and Nathan. Stephanie is a strong student with aspirations of pursuing a Master's degree in communication studies after graduation. Jack is an average student who is involved with numerous clubs and activities, including the Student Government Association. Becky is a four-year member of the Mountainview State University dance team and the president of the Communication Studies Club. Nathan is a quiet student, but is motivated to do well academically.

Dr. Garcia is lecturing about family communication patterns theory (FCPT) on the second day. She has already discussed the two orientations as well as the four family types (Koerner & Schrodt, 2014). While discussing the students' first major assignment of the semester, Dr. Garcia explains, "So for the next week, you will be working on your first major assignment in the course. This assignment is an oral presentation in class about your family communication. Specifically, you will need to use the information from FCPT that we discussed in class and from your readings and then apply that information to your own family communication. You can talk about your current family communication and also how your parents communicated with you when you were younger. I want you to discuss your family's level of conversation orientation and conformity orientation and provide examples for both. I also want you to discuss which family type best describes your family and why. Feel free to contact your family members to ask them their opinions about your family communication. Your presentation should last between three and five minutes and should follow the rubric that I have provided. We will present these in class next Friday. Do you have any questions?"

"Do we need to cite sources in the presentation?" Becky asked.

Dr. Garcia replied, "Not necessarily. They are not required; however, you are welcome to make references to the book and articles we have read, if you think it will enhance your presentation."

Jack asked, "So should I just talk about my parents or should I discuss other family members as well?"

"You should talk about your family as a whole. Remember, FCPT involves the whole family," answered Dr. Garcia. "If you have any other questions, please feel free to email me or stop by my office. Have fun with this assignment!"

As class was dismissed, Stephanie, Jack, Becky, and Nathan left the classroom together and started walking to the cafeteria. As they were walking, they started to talk about the assignment Dr. Garcia just announced. Becky, who was excited about the assignment, said, "I'm actually looking forward to this presentation. I mean, who doesn't love talking about their family?"

Nathan answered, "Me! My family might be the most dysfunctional family I know."

Becky laughed, "Oh, don't be dramatic. You don't have to give every detail about your family situation."

"I know. But Dr. Garcia said she wanted an honest assessment including the good, the bad, and the ugly," Nathan reminded her.

Jack replied, "Dude, you'll do just fine. At least you will have to talk in class with this assignment. I don't think you have talked in class all semester yet."

Stephanie and Becky chuckled.

"I just don't like speaking up in class. That's all. I like Dr. Garcia, but I'm just shy. Anyway, I'll catch you all later. I am going back to my dorm to take a nap," Nathan replied.

Over the next few days, students prepared their presentation and spent much time studying the two orientations and four family types to apply to their family. On the day of the oral presentations, Becky was the first to volunteer. She started her presentation by showing a picture of her family, which included her parents and brother. She said, "I'm excited to tell you about what communication is like in my family. First, according to FCPT, I would classify my family as a pluralistic family. This means we are high in conversation orientation but low in conformity orientation. Sometimes we have conflicts, and when we do, we all have our respective opinions. For example, my dad is very conservative and I am very liberal so we disagree a lot when it comes to politics." At this point in her presentation, Becky showed a picture of herself at a recent Democratic rally and noted how her dad did not agree with her, but encouraged Becky to have her own views on issues. "They have always encouraged me to have my own opinion and make my own decisions. I would say communication is very open in our family as well. As traditional as it may sound, we still eat dinner together as a family, and during these dinners, we talk about our day and what is going on in our lives. When I am here at school, I talk to my mom about three times a week. I am really lucky to have great parents who do their best to support me. Growing up, my parents would always encourage me to make friends and to communicate with others outside of our family unit. One thing I always appreciated about my parents was that when they had to make a family decision, they asked me and my brother for our opinions as well." Becky then showed a picture of her family on a Florida beach. "My dad was offered a job in Florida last year. Even though he really wanted to take up the job, he asked for our opinion and we decided together, as a family, that he should not take up the job because my mother, my brother, and I did not want to move from our hometown. I realize that in some families, the parents would have never even asked the children about their opinion (Koerner & Fitzpatrick, 1997). I have always been grateful that my parents value my input."

"Nice job, Becky!" commented Dr. Garcia. "I like how you discussed the various levels of conversation orientation and conformity orientation in your presentation. Your family sounds similar to my family because we handle conflict situations the same way."

"Yes, it can get interesting sometimes," replied Becky.

"I'm sure it does. What a good start to our presentations! Who would like to go next?" asked Dr. Garcia.

Nathan raised his hand and replied, "I guess I'll go next. I'll be glad to get this over with."

Dr. Garcia encouraged him to do a good job and reminded him to address as many aspects of his family type as possible.

Nathan seemed hesitant as he shuffled his feet to the front of the room. As he began his presentation, he displayed a picture of his mom, his dad, his grandmother, his two brothers, and himself. "I should probably start with a little family history. What you see here in this picture is a happy family. You can obviously tell that this is an older picture. I was only 11 years old in this picture, so that was about 10 years ago. Since then, my father left us. That happened when I was about 13. About five years ago, my grandma passed away. My mom has been remarried a couple of times but neither of those marriages survived. While my family story might not be as picturesque and perfect as some, I love my mom and brothers dearly. However, my family type would be classified as laissez-faire, according to FCPT. The laissez-faire family type is low in both conversation orientation and conformity orientation. The people in my family do not engage in much conversation with each other. I know we care about each other, and we talk sometimes, but not very often. On an average, my mom will call me about once a week to check on me. She works really hard though. She actually has two full-time jobs to support our family. She works as a beautician during the day and as a waitress in the evenings and on weekends. As for conformity orientation, my brothers and I have never been forced to believe the same way as our mother. We actually just avoid confrontation, and when we do have differences, we just do not talk about it. One of the articles we read about FCPT was about interpersonal closeness and it was discovered that laissez-faire families are not usually as close as the other three family types (Ledbetter, 2009). I completely agree with the article because my family is simply not that close. Sometimes I think my family would fall apart if I didn't make the effort to hold us all together. I wish I had more family pictures to share with you all, but honestly we haven't taken one in many years."

As Nathan made his way back to his seat, the rest of his classmates clapped for him. Dr. Garcia replied, "Thanks, Nathan, for your honest assessment of your family communication. It seems like you nailed the family type based on what you shared about your levels of conversation orientation and conformity orientation. You gave a nice presentation!"

Nathan replied, "Thank you! I was nervous."

Dr. Garcia reiterated, "You did well. Okay, who is presenting next?"

Stephanie stood up as she said, "I'll go next!"

"Great, Stephanie!" exclaimed Dr. Garcia.

As she took a deep breath, Stephanie made her way to the front of the room. She started, "So my family seems to be a little different in their communication compared to the other families that have been discussed. First of all, I would classify my family as the protective type. This means they are low in conversation orientation but high in conformity orientation. So when I was growing up, my parents were strict with me. I remember in middle school when my friends would go camping or to the movies, my parents would rarely let me go. Even today, they are still pretty strict. Obviously I'm an adult now and I can make my own decisions, but I still listen to them. I basically never questioned their authority because I would be disciplined if I did. They always made the decisions and I had to roll with them. We do not have a lot of conflict in my family, but when we do, we mostly avoid it and do not talk about it. For example, about a year ago, my older brother told our family that he was gay. Unfortunately, my parents did not react well. They did not talk to him about it or ask any questions. Basically, they shunned him because, as they said, he went against their values. It is a sad situation actually. I am the only person in the family that my brother currently talks to regularly. The article that we read in class that resonated with me was the one about privacy orientations that found that protective families have a stronger trait-like orientation to privacy compared to other family types (Bridge & Schrodt, 2013). That is so characteristic of my family because my parents, and even me to an extent, are very private people. We rarely share a lot of information about ourselves to people outside our family."

At this point, Stephanie shows a picture of her family. She commented, "This is a picture from a few years ago in Nebraska. I was born and raised in Nebraska and this picture was right before we moved to Georgia. My brother and I really miss Nebraska but we were forced to move and we had no voice in the matter. I guess it worked out though because I wouldn't have made it here to Mountainview with you all had I not moved."

Stephanie's classmates applauded after she concluded her presentation. "Wonderful presentation, Steph. I like how you discussed conflict avoidance and privacy, because those are common characteristics of protective families. Wow! We have had such an array of families discussed so far in our presentations. Who is presenting next?" asked Dr. Garcia.

At this point, Jack takes a gulp of water, grabs his speaking notes, and heads to the front of the room. Jack enthusiastically started his presentation, "My family is high in conversation orientation and high in conformity orientation, which makes my family type consensual. I'm actually an only child. My family consists of my parents and me, but my grandpa also lives with us. Our communication style is open as we share lots of things with each other. On an average, I talk to my mom and dad twice daily when I'm here at school. Yes, they call way too much! At first, I wanted to go to a bigger university farther away from home, but they would not let me. As far as making decisions in the family, my parents have the final word. They might listen to what I have to say, but ultimately it is their call. When we were reading the different articles about FCPT in class, the one about how families manage conflict was really interesting. My family type uses the obliging and integrating styles of conflict management, which is exactly what the article found (Shearman & Dumlao, 2008). And in that same article, it was discussed that the consensual family type was the most common in the United States. My family is open with each other, which is probably why I am so open with them, my friends, and my coworkers. I've always been an 'open book' basically."

At the conclusion of all of the presentations, Dr. Garcia complimented the students on a job well done. "I'm quite pleased with the presentations. It was neat to see how each of you took this theory and applied it to your own families. Hopefully, you can see how your family communication may influence the ways in which you communicate now as an adult. Instead of having our class on Tuesday, I would like for each of you to sign up for a short, 10-minute meeting with me in my office. I just want to spend some time with you personally to discuss your presentations and how you think FCPT influences your communication with others, specifically in the classroom. How's that? Any questions?"

Over the next few days, students signed up for a time to meet with Dr. Garcia. The first student to meet with Dr. Garcia was Becky.

"Hi Becky, come on in!" said Dr. Garcia.

Becky replied, "Thanks! How are you today?"

"I'm doing well. I just wanted to talk to each of you individually about your presentations. How do you think yours went?" asked Dr. Garcia.

"It was a fun activity and I feel like I did a great job. I made sure to cover many elements of my family type while thoroughly describing the communication in my own family."

"I agree. I think you did a great job as well. So you picked the pluralistic family type. How do you think your family communication environment affects your communication now as an adult?" Dr. Garcia asked.

"Well, with both my friends and in class, I'm pretty talkative. I have never been afraid to speak up or to make new friends. Also, my parents have always given me some level of autonomy in decision making, so I think that has helped me make good decisions in college. In the classroom, I'm not afraid to disagree with someone and to be vocal about it. Of course, I'm always respectful of other people's opinions as they should be with mine."

"Yes, I think that is an important quality to have," Dr. Garcia replied.

"Absolutely! Thank you for making us do this assignment. It was really helpful and I had some good conversations with my family about it."

"That's wonderful! I'm glad you enjoyed it. Tell your parents they did a great job raising you. I hope I can meet them when you graduate in May."

Becky answered, "Thank you. Yes, I will let them know. Have a nice day, Dr. Garcia!"

Becky grabbed her backpack and walked out of Dr. Garcia's office. As she was leaving, Nathan was outside the office door.

"Hey Nathan! I think Dr. Garcia is ready for you," Becky said.

"Thanks. I am dreading this," Nathan said quietly. "I'm afraid about what she's going to say about my presentation. I don't think I did very well."

"You've got this," Becky said reassuringly. "Text me and let me know how your meeting went."

"Nathan! Are you out there?" asked Dr. Garcia. "Come on in!"

Nathan took a sip of his energy drink and hesitantly walked into Dr. Garcia's office. "Good morning!"

"Good morning! Let me first say that I was really pleased with your presentation."

Nathan let out a huge sigh of relief, "Thank you. I actually enjoyed it. I didn't think I would enjoy it at first, but it was almost therapeutic to talk about my family."

"That's great! I appreciated your level of honesty with regard to your family," Dr. Garcia commented. "How do you think your family communication has influenced your communication as a young adult now?"

"So I've been thinking about this. Because laissez-faire families are lower in conversation orientation, I don't think I am as talkative as some of my peers. In class, I am almost afraid to speak up. I know our next assignment in your class is an oral debate and I'm actually really nervous about it. I am not that good at arguing, either," Nathan said.

"Well, I'm glad you brought that up because I did want to address your participation in class. I really would like to hear you speak more. You have only said a couple things so far this semester and, as you know, participation is 25% of the grade. When you do say something, it is intelligent and meaningful, but I just need to hear more," Dr. Garcia said with a smile.

"Absolutely! It's hard, but I will push myself to get out of my comfort zone and speak up."

"Wonderful! I'm glad to hear it. Again, nice job on your presentation, Nathan."

Nathan replied, "Thanks, Dr. Garcia. Have a good day."

Stephanie was the next student to visit Dr. Garcia's office. As she was approaching the office, Stephanie could feel her heart pounding as she was nervous about her oral presentation feedback.

"Come on in, Stephanie!" Dr. Garcia said enthusiastically.

"Thanks. How was your weekend?" asked Stephanie.

"It was really good. My family and I went to the football game and that was a lot of fun! So I just wanted to talk to you for a few minutes about your presentation. Thank you for being so honest and descriptive about your family communication. I think your examples accurately described the protective family style. Thank you for sharing the story about your brother. Do you think he is getting the support he needs right now?"

"I do. He has some really great friends where he lives. I wish my parents were more supportive of him. I think my mom wants to be more supportive and encouraging toward my brother, but my dad will not let her. My dad doesn't agree with it and instead of talking about it, he just ignores it. Adhering to family values is really important to my dad."

Dr. Garcia thought to herself for a few seconds and then replied, "How do you think taking a class in family communication is helping you in your own family communication?"

"I'm glad you asked. So as I was preparing for this assignment, I called my parents and they did not want me to share the story about my brother. But what they don't know won't hurt them. I actually explained to them how we were the protective family type and they disagreed with me. They think we are much more conversational with each other than we are, and they also think that we are much lower in conformity orientation then we are. It is almost like they are in denial. I also called my brother and told him about this assignment. He completely agreed with me about our family type," Stephanie said as she chuckled. "He knows that we, as a family, do not have many open conversations and that we typically avoid conflict because that's how our parents raised us."

Dr. Garcia nodded in agreement. She continued, "So how do you think your family type and upbringing have influenced your communication with friends and classmates?"

"Well, I'm a work in progress. I used to be a lot quieter than I am now. I still have trouble speaking up, though; when I disagree with someone, I usually just keep it to myself. I see how elements of my upbringing influence my current communication, but I am getting better at communicating. I love my parents dearly, but I am starting to recognize that how they handle situations and communication is not always ideal," Stephanie commented.

"Well, it sounds like you are learning a lot about yourself and your family so far."

Stephanie replied, "I am! Thank you for the feedback and the questions, Dr. Garcia. I'm really enjoying this class so far. It is my favorite this semester!"

"Well, that is good to hear. I will see you on Thursday, Stephanie."

With a smile on her face, Stephanie departed from Dr. Garcia's office. As she left, Jack was waiting for his meeting to begin.

Jack asked Stephanie, "Are we still meeting tonight at 7:00 p.m. to work on our group project for Dr. Jackson's class?"

"Yes, I'll be there. Have a good meeting!" Stephanie said.

Dr. Garcia walked out of her office and greeted Jack, "Welcome, Jack! How are you today?"

"I'm good. I am little tired from working on my newspaper articles most of the night, though."

"Oh wow. I'm sure you are tired then. Be sure to get some rest," Dr. Garcia encouraged. "The reason I wanted to chat today was to ask a couple of questions about your presentation. First of all, how do you think you did?"

"I think I did pretty well. I like that I implemented the research articles in my presentation."

"Yes, I think you did a nice job on that part of the presentation. So you described your family as having a consensual family type. How do you think your family communication influences the way you communicate with people outside of your family?" asked Dr. Garcia.

"My parents are very communicative. They talk a lot. Like I said, they call me multiple times a week and they want to hear all the details about my day. I can see how this has influenced me to be extremely communicative with my friends and my classmates. I'm never afraid to speak up and ask questions. As you know, I'm usually one of the first people to participate when you ask a question in class."

"That is true. I do appreciate your level of participation. What about conformity orientation?"

Jack answered, "I don't want to say they are controlling, but they do interject themselves into several aspects of my life. I have always been accustomed to them making most of my decisions for me. So, when it comes to my friends and my girlfriend, I do not think I always handle conflict effectively."

"I understand. I'm glad you brought up in your presentation that consensual families are the most common types of families in the United States. So, what do you think you've learned from this assignment?"

"This has been very eye-opening for me. I have learned a lot about my family and I've also learned that there is no perfect family. Sure, the research says some types of communication are better than others, but no family is perfect. I have gained insight on how my parents socialized me and it has also helped me realize the ways I might socialize my children in the future."

Dr. Garcia smiled and said, "Very nice! I'm glad to hear you found this assignment helpful. Well, thanks for stopping by. Keep up the good work and I'll see you Thursday, Jack!"

Thursday quickly came and the students were eager to begin their next unit in Dr. Garcia's class. Once everyone arrived, she started the class saying, "I would like to thank you all for stopping by my office earlier this week. I found each conversation both enjoyable and productive. I hope you did as well. Collectively, I think you did a nice job on this assignment. It was interesting to hear about the wide range of family types represented in this class. I hope this activity helped your understanding about family communication and how that influences communication in young adulthood. Okay, I guess we should get started on our next unit in class. Let's start with another important theory in family communication, Communication Privacy Management Theory!"

DISCUSSION QUESTIONS

1. How helpful was Dr. Garcia's assignment to the students in her family communication class in understanding and applying FCPT to their own families? Is this assignment one which you would be comfortable completing?
2. Would you classify your family as being protective, consensual, pluralistic, or laissez-faire? Why?
3. Aside from conversation orientation and conformity orientation, in what other ways can family communication patterns influence how young adults communicate with both their instructors and their classmates in their courses? How do family communication patterns influence young adults' communication with their instructors out of class?
4. Based on their respective family types, what recommendations would you offer to Becky (i.e., pluralistic family type), Nathan (i.e., laissez-faire family type), Stephanie (i.e., protective family type), and Jack (i.e., consensual family type) to improve their in-class communication in Dr. Garcia's class?

REFERENCES

Bridge, M. C., & Schrodt, P. (2013). Privacy orientations as a function of family communication patterns. *Communication Reports, 26*, 1–12. doi:10.1080/08934215.2013.773054

Koerner, A. F., & Fitzpatrick, M. A. (1997). Family type and conflict: The impact of conversation orientation and conformity orientation on conflict in the family. *Communication Studies, 48*, 59–75. doi:10.1080/10510979709368491

Koerner, A. F., & Schrodt, P. (2014). An introduction to the special issue on family communication patterns theory. *Journal of Family Communication, 14*, 1–15. doi:10.1080/15267431.2013.857328

Ledbetter, A. M. (2009). Family communication patterns and relational maintenance behavior: Direct and mediated associations with friendship closeness. *Human Communication Research, 35*, 130–147. doi:10.1111/j.1468-2958.2008.01341.x

Shearman, S. M., & Dumlao, R. (2008). A cross-cultural comparison of family communication patterns and conflict between young adults and parents. *Journal of Family Communication, 8*, 186–211. doi:10.1080/15267430802182456

CHAPTER 2

"You Don't Know What You Don't Know": Mitigating Uncertainty in Transracial Adoption

Eletra S. Gilchrist-Petty – *The University of Alabama Huntsville*

ABSTRACT

While families have long been viewed as complex and interrelated entities, many factors, such as transracial adoption, can add compounding layers to family dynamics. Transracial adoption represents a process that can be affected by many layers of uncertainty because not only do the adopted child(ren) and adoptive parents not look similar, their cultural experiences and backgrounds are often shaped and communicated differently. Also, according to the major tenets of uncertainty reduction theory (URT), human engagement can be mired by many unknowns, which can create feelings of anxiety and dissonance within the individuals. This case study expounds upon the multifaceted nature of transracial adoption through the theoretical lens of uncertainty reduction. An analysis of the Smith family explores how unknowns permeated the family's journey through transracial adoption. The case study lends particular attention to how the family has used a mix of passive, active, and interactive strategies to reduce cognitive and behavioral uncertainties and construct a redefined, racially mixed family structure.

CASE STUDY

Most of us are predictable creatures of habit. We often take the same routes to work or school each day, use similar rhetorical phrases when greeting people, religiously watch our favorite television shows, and even interact with our family members in predictable ways. Why? Well, predictability is familiar and, therefore, comfortable. In contrast, uncertainty can create feelings of stress and anxiety because we do not know what to expect. Uncertainty reduction theory (URT) posits that people often feel uncertain about people or situations they do not know and, thus, engage in uncertainty reduction to make sense of the unknown, minimize dissonance, and foster a more predictable state (Berger & Calabrese, 1975).

As the premier and most enduring relationship type, the native family typically provides a secure sense of certainty and predictability. It is customary for family members to participate in collective traditions and beliefs, enjoy common social activities, share a blood connection, and look similar. Transracial adoption reflects the antithesis of the traditional biological family because the adopted child(ren) represent a different race or ethnicity than the adoptive parents. While compelling evidence presupposes that race and racial identity are social constructs (Martinez, 1998), racial differences among people are generally glaringly apparent, especially within the same nuclear family. Hence, much uncertainty can define transracial adoption because not only do the adopted children and adoptive parents not look similar, their cultural experiences are often shaped and communicated differently.

This case study explores the breadth and depth of complex uncertainties that can define the multifaceted nature of transracial adoption. The case involves the Smith family who live in a large southern city in the United States. The upper-middle-class family is of Euro American descent and was initially comprised of four members: mom, Karen; dad, Gabe; son, Lance; and daughter, Julie. In 2014 this family began the process of adopting two young African American boys: Zeb, aged three , and Kris, aged two, who are also biological siblings. In less than two years the Smith family formally adopted Zeb and Kris, becoming a blended transracial family. Through the theoretical lens of uncertainty reduction, this case study addresses various layers of the unknown that precipitated challenges during and following the transracial adoption. The case study lends particular attention to describing how the family reduced uncertainty and constructed a redefined conjugal family.

A Case Study of the Smiths and Transracial Adoption

The author became aware of the Smith family's navigation through the transracial adoption process from her collegial relationship with Karen, the mother in the Smith family. Hence, to better understand the nuances of the family's experience with transracial adoption, the author conducted an hour-long, in-depth, and semistructured telephone interview with Karen. The interview structure was designed so as to elicit and encourage the interviewee to use rich language to describe the transracial adoption experience through storytelling (Lindlof & Taylor, 2011).[1] The ensuing represents salient segments from the interview transcript.[2]

Author: Growing up, how many children did you want to have?

Karen: Zero. I did not want any children whatsoever. Growing up I wanted to be a Broadway star. My grandmother was an open feminist, so I got a lot of interesting insights from her.

Author: How did you go from not wanting any children growing up to now being the mother of four children?

Karen: I married Gabe when I was 22, and he was eight years older than me. He literally turned 30 the day after we got married. So he was in a different life-place than I was. He definitely wanted children—he came from a much bigger family than me. When we had our son, Lance, and our daughter, Julie, I wanted to stop because I hated being pregnant. I pretty much puked nonstop. So after we had the two I was done.

Author: So, what made you consider adoption, especially transracial adoption?

Karen: I got pregnant right away, so it wasn't a fertility thing. We just felt like we could love kids we didn't physically give birth to. It was actually Lance, who instigated going into foster care.

Author: Tell me about that. How did Lance persuade you to expand your family?

Karen: Lance comes to us around the age of 12 or 13 and says—and this is the exact quote—"I feel like I have a little brown brother out there." So, I said to him that it sounds like he would be open to adoption. Then, he said a really profound thing. He said that "if we don't do this quickly, by the time I'm 16 I'll only care about myself and I won't want to help you." Gabe and I talked about it and said, let's do it; let's help here in our community. We immediately went and got training.

Author: What happened once you received the training?

Karen: It took about three months to get the training done, and within 24 hours of our training being done Zeb and Kris were there with us.

Author: Wow! That was fast. So, you now have two little black boys living in your home agedtwo and three. What were some of the biggest challenges you encountered?

Karen: Oh my God! Well first, you don't know what you don't know. As someone who has been living under white privilege my entire life, I assumed it would be the same with the boys.

Author: What are some examples of how your life experiences differed from the boys?

Karen: Hair! Both my boys have different hair textures. Three years later I'm still not sure I've figured it all out. I now know you buy different products based on the hair texture. The other thing I didn't realize is that you can't have just anybody cut their hair. This whole

---

1. To protect the family's confidentiality, all names reflect pseudonyms.

2. To aid in readability and flow, vocal disfluencies (e.g., pauses) and discourse markers (e.g., "uhm") have been deleted from the transcript.

edging thing is a huge deal. The white community is so oblivious to this hair thing. Oblivious! They don't know what to do at all. They don't know that there is any kind of difference and that there are different products. I had a friend tell me that as a white mother of brown children you will be judged on your ability to keep their skin healthy and their hairlines up. So I had to find a hairdresser, thinking that a barbershop is a barbershop, right? No it's not. I had an old white man destroy my son's hair, after telling me he could do it. They basically came out looking like little old men because their hairline was backed up so far. So I asked a friend, and that's how I found a black barbershop. Whenever I took Lance, if I ever had to wait more than 20 minutes to get my little boy's hair cut, it was on! I take Zeb and Kris, and it was a two-hour long process! So I had to learn the rituals—that guys hung out at the barbershop and it was cultural. So yes, the hair thing was really hard.

Author: Were there any other challenges besides hair?

Karen: Skin. As a white person, I don't ever remember putting lotion on my skin unless it itched, hurt me, or was sunburned. The importance of taking care of their skin was another part of learning about the co-culture. It was very much a 'you don't know what you don't know' kind of thing, but by the way, you will be judged on it. So, that was very difficult for me.

Author: Do you encounter any unique verbal or nonverbal messages when you are out in public with your sons?

Karen: I have not had one person come up and say anything racist to me, ever. Where we live I feel like there is way more acceptance than there would be in other parts of the Deep South. From a nonverbal standpoint, I've learned there is a novelty to it. Basically we've become those people—the white parents with the black children. When we go places I see people look and they're trying to figure out what's happening. There's cognitive dissonance happening and they're reaching for some attribution to explain it. When I am with them I get approached significantly more, and people will ask just about anything—just like they do when you're pregnant. It's like we've become a bit of a freak show.

Author: What are some of the questions they ask you?

Karen: The first question is almost always what country they are from. The assumption is that I have been benevolent and gone to some country in Africa and rescued these children from being child soldiers. I've started getting a little sassy about it (and say the country they are from with an African accent) just to exploit how stupid it is that that's the first thing they would think. I feel like I want them to see they have been biased, but I don't want to alienate them to the point where they feel like they can't ask me questions.

Author: Aside from where they are from, are there any other questions people tend to ask?

Karen: It's very common for people to ask me where the real parents are. I hear the title "real parents" a lot. I always say, "You're looking at their real parents." There's literally nothing fake about me. The correct term is birth parents. I've learned you have to teach people because, again, you don't know what you don't know. People are very brave to ask questions, and they are not usually rude, but it's nothing I would have ever encountered with my two white children. No one would say, "Julie you are so beautiful. Who is your birth father?"

Author: Are the verbal and nonverbal messages about the same with both boys or have you noticed a difference between the two?

Karen: Often they come up and say how cute they are—cute is always the word. They tend to talk specifically to Kris, who is by far the lighter of the two. I have no clue if that is a subconscious bias, but when people comment on cuteness or sweetness it is always, always to Kris who's lighter.

Author: Along those lines, do you have authentic conversations with your sons about race in general and the racial difference within your family?

Karen: I'm fully aware that though I took them out of a dangerous physical situation, I've also complicated their lives by bringing them into a culture they are going to have a harder time identifying with. We openly talk about how this is going to be confusing to people, and it's not usually out of hatred or anger, but you're going to have to get really comfortable with the fact that this is going to be confusing. Your teacher is always going to assume when I come in for a parent–teacher conference that I'm black—always. This does not make us wrong, right, good, or bad—just different.

Author: How do you plan to prepare them for some challenges that they as black boys may encounter, such as racism?

Karen: I surround them with lots of people of color from all walks of life in order to expose them to the fact that there is a rainbow. We are also close to their birth family. It is the best-case scenario that we have because now we have a family group that we can go to as a touch-point to learn more about their background. They invited us to the family reunion and came to Zeb's birthday party last year. We actively reached out and said we wanted to keep in touch. Here's the thing, I know a lot about communication and I read a lot, but I will never know what it's like to be a black man in America—never. Will they live under white privilege simply by being my kids? Yeah, but they are black children, and as many people I can surround them with of their race, I will do.

Author: Is there anything else you do to prepare them for potential challenges?

Karen: We have already had the police talk. I go out of my way to introduce them to every police officer, and we've talked about what to do and say if you are ever pulled over. I never had that conversation with my white son, not one time until he started driving. But I'm thinking ahead. And I've told them that a lot of people only have a media representation of a black male. So don't be mad if you see someone lock the door—it's their ignorance, not yours. We've had these conversations when the boys were three, four, and five years old. I don't want it to be a situation where they come back later and say, "Why didn't you teach me that?"

Author: What do you say to people who would say your story is reflective of the "white savior complex"?

Karen: The funny thing is whenever I encounter someone who says something similar to that, I always say, "Well, let me know how that works out because I ain't saved anybody yet." I don't feel the need to save them. I didn't go into foster care saying, "Let me find a person of color and lift them out of poverty." It just so happened that two black boys were placed into my family. It could have been anyone—Latino, Caucasian—anybody, and our souls connected with these children. We knew we were supposed to parent these children, regardless of their race. In the foster care world, kids are just kids. Regardless of their race, they are coming with a set of trauma if they are coming out of the foster care world. So we are trying to parent from trauma, not race.

Author: I know when the adoption was finalized you had your sons' last names legally changed to Smith. Other than changing their last names what were some of the strategies you used to negotiate a new racially mixed family structure?

Karen: It's really interesting because it just kind of happened. Part of it is that I have friends who are people of color. Some people live in a homogenous world where they wouldn't know where to go for help. I've always been very intentional about having a varied group of friends. So I had a village that could help me. I have friends where early on I could go to and say, "give me some insight on this."

Author: What is the overall message about transracial adoption that you would want others to know who may be considering it?

Karen: The big advice I would give is that you need to be intentional about the fact that you don't know what you don't know. So be intentional about finding people as a point of reference that can teach you things and partner with you to become part of your village to help you raise the kid, because you can't raise them in your own little circle. You have to be intentional.

DISCUSSION

The Smith family's journey with transracial adoption has been riddled with unknowns. As a white upper-middle-class family, their lives have been shaped and housed in privilege—a decisively different story from Zeb and Kris, two young black boys who had faced layers of trauma from infancy. Uncertainty reduction theory (URT) offers a conceptual lens to examine the unknowns as experienced through transracial adoption. Berger and Calabrese (1975) conceptualized URT as a theoretical guide for explaining how strangers use communication in initial interactions to reduce uncertainties. URT posits that there are two types of uncertainty in initial encounters: cognitive and behavioral. Cognitive concerns the degree of uncertainty associated with thoughts, beliefs, and personalities, whereas behavioral considers ambiguities surrounding actions or interactive practices (Berger, 1979; Berger & Bradac, 1982). The Smith family encountered many behavioral uncertainties, but black hair ranked among the most salient.

Black hair is a rhetorical construction reflective of *body politics*, which signifies that the human body is enriched with constitutive meanings that situate the body as a site of privilege and/or struggle (Gilchrist & Jackson, 2012). Karen's statement that "this whole edging thing is a huge deal" indicates that she quickly learned that hair in the black community is much more than cells and fibers that sprout from the scalp. Hair in the black community serves a rhetorical function (White, 2005) and is used to influence perceptions of self and others. Gilchrist and Jackson (2012) conjectured that black hair is an identity marker and symbol of status that reflects not only acceptable grooming practices, but beauty, acceptance, and power. In the Smith family, hair was simply hair that could be groomed by essentially anyone, as reflected in Karen's statement that "a barbershop is a barbershop." However, after having an unsuccessful barbershop experience with Zeb and Kris, Karen promptly realized that cutting and styling black hair is both a science and an artform that is unknown to many white people. With much passion and conviction, Karen exclaimed, "The white community is so oblivious to this hair thing. Oblivious!"

The Smith family's uncertainty about black hair was complicated even further when they transracially adopted sons with different hair textures. The textures and curl patterns of black hair are so diverse that a black hair typing system has been developed that classifies black hair based on four main types (Walker, 2018). Type 1 refers to straight hair with a fine to coarse texture that is difficult to hold curls, whereas Type 2 is wavy hair that encompasses fine and thin to coarse and frizzy hair. Type 3 concerns curly hair defined by loose to corkscrew curls, and Type 4 represents tightly coiled or kinky hair accentuated by either soft or wiry coils (Walker, 2018). The variations in black hair were unknown to the Smith family, and hence, the parents were unaware of the necessity of choosing haircare products based on the type of black hair. Once Karen became educated on the varied black hair textures, she could properly maintain her sons' hair: "I now know you buy different products based on the hair texture," she said. However, Karen unapologetically admitted that "three years later I'm still not sure I've figured it (black hair) all out"—suggesting that she still has some levels of uncertainties when it comes to caring for her transracially adopted sons' hair.

Akin to hair, Karen identified skin as another uncertainty encountered from transracial adoption. First, based on experiences of only previously caring for white skin, the family was unaware that differences abound in skin types. As noted by Karen, she only moisturized her skin when there was an issue with it, such as sunburn. In contrast, when she adopted Zeb and Kris, it became starkly apparent that moisturizing black skin is part of the daily grooming ritual needed to prevent the skin from being dry or having an "ashy" appearance. Along with moisturizing the skin, Karen spoke of becoming cognizant to the constitutive meanings attached to black skin tones. Research by Gilchrist and Jackson (2012) argued that contemporary connotations of beauty in the black community have historically aligned with Eurocentric standards of beauty that privilege lighter skin tones.

Karen expressed an awareness that her son with the lighter skin tone always gets the most compliments from strangers: "When people comment on cuteness or sweetness it is always, always to Kris who's lighter," she recalled with a sense of puzzlement. While no one even loosely associated cuteness with skin color with her two white children, the link between skin color and attraction has been blatantly obvious with Karen's two black sons, supporting research findings that claim, comparable to black hair, skin color can signify privilege, beauty, value, and identity (Blay, 2010).

While the Smith family encountered an array of behavioral uncertainties that stemmed primarily from black hair and skin, the transracial adoption also birthed cognitive uncertainties. As a reminder, cognitive uncertainties concern our cognitions, thoughts, and beliefs (Berger, 1979; Berger & Bradac, 1982). According to Karen, her racially mixed family creates uncertainty in others: "It's like we've become a bit of a freak show," she said, while remembering the countless times people look at her racially mixed family and try to understand its atypical composition. Individuals have an innate desire to maintain consistency and predictability, as presumed through Festinger's (1957) cognitive dissonance theory. Thus, when individuals grow up living in and witnessing racially homogeneous families, they come to expect this as the norm. Therefore, the novelty of encountering a racially diverse family can spark disharmony or dissonance, which explains the nuanced nonverbal messages received by the Smiths.

Cognitive uncertainties also abound regarding Zeb and Kris' biological parents, who are often referred to as the "real parents" by onlookers. Scholars have long reasoned that the United Sates is an extremely race-conscious society (Holling, Moon, & Nevis, 2014), and race represents the most salient identity marker (Gilchrist-Petty, 2018). Hence, when people observe the skin tone and racial distinctions of Zeb and Kris compared to other members in the Smith family, people quickly conclude that the two black children have different parents, and their natural tendency is to minimize the uncertainty surrounding Zeb and Kris' biological parents through inquisitions about their "real parents." Interestingly enough, people do not automatically presuppose that either Lance or Julie is adopted. Hence, whether it is a correct or incorrect assumption, the racial likeness shared between the white parents and the white children in the Smith family breeds a sense of certainty and predictability that supports our potentially false assumptions of what it means to be a family.

A major assumption underlying URT is that uncertainty is an aversive state of existence that fosters stress; thus, when individuals experience uncertainty their primary concern is to reduce uncertainty and increase predictability through the use of passive (e.g., observation), active (e.g., asking others about a particular person or situation), or interactive (e.g., direct communication) strategies (Berger & Bradac, 1982). The Smith family engages a mix of strategies to mitigate uncertainty in transracial adoption. For example, the family has become more aware of the constitutive meanings of black hair and skin by observing (i.e., passive strategy) the verbal and nonverbal emphases placed on hair and skin in the black community. According to Karen, she has acquired an acute awareness that hair and skin are major commodities from which her sons are judged. Dovetailing the passive uncertainty reduction strategy is the active strategy of seeking out information. Karen's statements about having a diverse group of friends she can go to and ask questions reflect her use of an active strategy to minimize uncertainty with transracial adoption. In Karen's own words, she has "a village [of] . . . friends where . . . [she can go] and say, give me some insight on this." Lastly, the Smith family relies on interactive strategies to guide the boys in negotiating the intricacies of their racial identity. "I will never know what it's like to be a black man in America," Karen acknowledged. Hence, she is vigilant about providing her sons with opportunities to directly engage an array of co-cultures, including members from their birth family. Interview data from transracial adoptees confirm the importance of providing black and brown adopted children with opportunities to directly communicate and interact with successful role models who look like them (Cradle Staff, 2018). In other words, mitigating transracial adoption uncertainties and cultivating a well-adapted new family structure requires "intentionality," as urged by Karen. Parents of transracial adoptees must intentionally seek out people who look like their children to serve as reference points for them and examples of distinction for their children.

CONCLUDING THOUGHTS

The family has historically been viewed as a collective unit or system, whereby it is seen as a complex, interdependent, and dynamic entity. Adding to the complexities of the modern-day American family is the growing rate of adoption, where one out of every 25 U.S. families with children have at least one adopted child, and 40% of adopted children are of a different race, culture, or ethnicity than the adopted parents (Adoption Network Law Center, 2018). These figures suggest that racial diversity is a growing factor in families who adopt. Given that "race is an ongoing and unfolding dynamic process" (Holling et al., 2014, p. 3), uncertainties can obfuscate transracial adoption, as experienced by the Smith family examined in this case study. A prevailing theme that emerged from Karen's interview was "you don't know what you don't know," suggesting that the Smith family confronted a mix of uncertainties resulting from the cultural and racial differences of its members. Though uncertainties continue to unravel, the Smith family is traversing unpredictable terrain via a mingling of passive, active, and interactive uncertainty reduction strategies. Through intentionality, or the deliberate engagement with cultural influencers, the family members have not only erected a redefined family, but fostered a well-adapted and diversified environment for their transracially adopted sons comprised of individuals who look like them. Even though it has only been a few years since Zeb and Kris were adopted into the Smith family, the author asked Karen if it was safe to assume that she could not imagine life without them. Her response was definitive and unequivocal: "Oh yes, they are our kids."

DISCUSSION QUESTIONS

1. What were the major cognitive and behavioral uncertainties the Smith family experienced through transracial adoption?
2. What is uncertainty reduction theory, and what were some strategies that helped the Smith family mitigate uncertainty in transracial adoption?
3. What role does intentionality play in cultivating a redefined conjugal family following transracial adoption?

REFERENCES

Adoption Network Law Center. (2018). *Adoption statistics*. Retrieved from https://adoptionnetwork.com/adoption-statistics

Berger, C. R. (1979). Beyond initial interaction: Uncertainty, understanding, and the development of interpersonal relationships. In H. Giles & R. St. Clair (Eds.), *Language and Social Psychology* (pp. 122–144). Oxford, England: Blackwell.

Berger, C. R., & Bradac, J. J. (1982). *Language and social knowledge: Uncertainty in interpersonal relations.* London, England: E. E. Arnold.

Berger, C. R., & Calabrese, R. J. (1975). Some explorations in initial interaction and beyond: Toward a developmental theory of interpersonal communication. *Human Communication Research, 1,* 99–112.

Blay, Y. A. (2010). Pretty color 'n good hair: Creole women of New Orleans and the politics of identity. In R. Spellers & K. Moffitt (Eds.), *Blackberries and redbones: Critical articulations of black hair/body politics in Africana communities* (pp. 29–52). New York, NY: Hampton Press.

Cradle Staff. (2018, June 15). What we learned from our children: Raising black children across racial lines roundtable. *The Cradle Blog.* Retrieved from https://www.cradle.org/blog/what-we-learned-our-children-raising-black-children-across-racial-lines-roundtable

Festinger, L. (1957). *A theory of cognitive dissonance.* Stanford, CA: Stanford University Press.

Gilchrist, E. S., & Jackson, R. S., II. (2012). Articulating the heuristic value of African-American communication studies. *Review of Communication, 12*(3), 1–14. doi:10.1080/15358593.2012.666670

Gilchrist-Petty, E. S. (2018). *Deviant communication in teacher-student interactions: Emerging research and opportunities.* Hershey, PA: IGI Global.

Holling, M. A., Moon, D. G., & Nevis, A. J. (2014). Racist violations and racializing apologia in a post-racism era. *Journal of International and Intercultural Communication, 7,* 1–27. doi:10.1080/17513057.2014.964144

Lindlof, T. R., & Taylor, B. C. (2011). *Qualitative communication research methods.* Thousand Oaks, CA: Sage Publications, Inc.

Martinez, G. A. (1998). African-Americans, Latinos, and the construction of race: Toward an epistemic coalition. *Chicana/o Latina/o Review, 19,* 213–222. Retrieved from https://escholarship.org/uc/item/45r88575

Walker, A. (2018). *Do you know your hair type?* Andre Walker Hair. Retrieved from https://www.andrewalkerhair.com

White, S. B. (2005). Releasing the pursuit of bouncin' and behavin' hair: Natural hair as an Afrocentric feminist aesthetic for beauty. *International Journal of Media and Cultural Politics, 1,* 295–208. doi:10.1386/macp.1.3.295/1

CHAPTER 3

Just the Two of Us: The Ups and Downs of an Empty Nest

Mary E. King – *Bloomsburg University of Pennsylvania*

ABSTRACT

The empty-nest phase of marital relationships is characterized as the period of time when the last child leaves the home, whether to attend college, join the military, move in with a romantic partner, or move out independently (Harkins, 1978; Junge & Maya, 1985). For parents this can often be a time of newfound freedom as the constraints of childrearing are lessened and the opportunities for more personal time and time spent with one's spouse increase. However, research suggests that the empty-nest relationship is also riddled with frustrations and challenges. Thus, this case study will highlight the transition to the empty-nest phase of marriage by exploring positive experiences (the empty-nest experience) and the darker side of this time for spouses (the empty-nest syndrome). Questions for discussion are presented for consideration.

CASE STUDY

Romantic relationships are constantly in a state of flux (Baxter, 1993; Baxter & Montgomery, 1996; Werner & Baxter, 1994), which is a good thing because relationships tend to work out best when they are dynamic and changing, as opposed to stagnant, stuck, and dull. However, when people in committed relationships, namely couples who have been married for years, find themselves in a state of transition it can be a scary time, riddled with uncertainty and anxiety. For instance, when a married couple transitions to the empty-nest phase of their relationship, they might experience some frustrations and ambiguity, or they could rekindle their romantic relationship in light of their newfound freedom from the everyday stressors of raising and taking care of their children. In fact, some studies show that the empty-nest phase of marriage is a time of increased conflict and high rates of separation and divorce (Brubaker, 1985; Kreider, 2005; Radina, Hennon, & Gibbons, 2008), perhaps as a result of the low levels of marital satisfaction compared to other life stages (Anderson, Russell, & Schumm, 1983).

The *empty-nest experience* occurs when parents find joy and satisfaction in their relationship and new roles without their children in the home (Raup & Myers, 1989). For example, individuals may rekindle their romantic relationship by having more date nights with their spouse, spending more time enjoying leisure activities with their spouse, or even just by reducing the amount of daily stressors taking care of a family and children entails (e.g., cleaning up after others, preparing meals, serving as the family chauffeur, participating in their children's activities and sports, etc.).

But sometimes when the kids leave the home, individuals and couples evaluate their new relationship, their spouse, and their own roles and find they are not as happy as they once were. This phenomenon is known as the *empty-nest syndrome*. Sometimes the absence of children in the home can be highlighted by *not* having regular family dinners or outings. Moreover, individuals whose roles were primarily defined as the child's caretaker (i.e., a stay-at-home-mom; Black & Hill, 1984) may find additional struggle in redefining their role and identity (Borland, 1982; Raup & Myers, 1989), resulting in feelings of grief, sadness, or depression (Kahana & Kahana, 1982). Additionally, empty-nesters might also find that their positive experiences could contribute to the empty-nest syndrome (White & Edwards, 1990; Umberson, Williams, Powers, Chen, & Campbell, 2005); if parents are *so* relieved that their children are *finally* out of the house, this might manifest as feelings of guilt that they are so relieved by their children's absence.

Communication Issues in the Face of the Empty-Nest Transition

When communication scholars examine close, personal relationships, they often focus on the emotional, cognitive, and behavior antecedents and outcomes of individual experiences and the relationship as a whole. For example, researchers explore how transitions in relationships present an opportunity for upheaval due to increased relational uncertainty and interference from partners (Solomon & Knobloch, 2004; Solomon, Knobloch, Theiss, & McLaren, 2016). The relational turbulence theory (RTT; Solomon et al., 2016) highlights transitional periods romantic couples go through as especially challenging. When faced with new situations, roles, or episodes, individuals may experience heightened anxiety or ambiguity about the state of their romantic relationship. According to Solomon and Knobloch (2001, 2004) this uncertainty, or *relational uncertainty*, is comprised of three interrelated sources of ambiguity: *self-uncertainty* (the uncertainty individuals feel about their own involvement in a romantic relationship), *partner uncertainty* (the uncertainty individuals have about their partner's involvement in a relationship), and *relationship uncertainty* (the uncertainty individuals have about the stability and future of a relationship as a whole).

Relational uncertainty, coupled with *partner interference* (to what extent a partner helps or hinders goal achievement) are both mechanisms that can contribute to more intensified emotional, cognitive, and communicative experiences. For example, Nagy and Theiss (2013) identified four themes of relational uncertainty empty-nesters experience during their transition to this stage: (a) new roles and identities, (b) dependency anxiety, (c) love and intimacy, and (d) growing older; and four themes of partner interference: (a) relationship facilitation, (b) guilt, (c) forced activity, and (d) household chores. Additional research found that relational uncertainty and partner interference contribute to indirectness, topic avoidance, and withdrawal in conflict interactions between spouses (King & Theiss, 2016) and interference also predicted criticism in conflict with a spouse. Moreover, the same study identified avoidant communicative patterns (indirectness, topic avoidance, and withdrawal) as conflict behaviors that contribute to a more rapid decrease of the stress hormone, cortisol, whereas approach conflict behaviors (criticism and demandingness) contribute to an increase in cortisol for empty-nesters.

Beyond the management of uncertainty and ambiguity during the transition, empty-nesters are also faced with the challenge of redefining their identity, both individually and as a couple. For example, with the children gone from the house, empty-nesters must re-establish dialectical tensions in their relationship that were once well coordinated, such as new ways of finding autonomy and still maintaining connectedness with a spouse (Harkins, 1978; Nagy & Theiss, 2013).

A Hypothetical Case Study: Ben and Olivia

Let us consider the transition to the empty-nest phase of marriage through the lenses of two hypothetical couples, Olivia and Ben, and then Marcus and Julie.

Olivia and Ben met in high school and quickly became high school sweethearts. After graduation they both got jobs in the same town that they grew up in. They worked hard and saved up some money; after a few years they were able to get married and buy a house together just a few miles across town from their families' homes. They worked hard and it wasn't always easy, but they had each other.

In fact, Olivia and Ben were *really* there for each other. They were always showing each other how much the other meant to them. For example, Olivia would always surprise Ben by picking up his favorite candy when she went grocery shopping. Ben would get up early before work sometimes to fold a load of laundry to help out around the house. They really, truly loved each other and showed it as often as they could. They loved to do things together, too. They would go to backyard barbeques, take walks in the park, and open a bottle of wine in front of the fireplace after a long week at work. Olivia and Ben craved spending time with one another; nothing made them happier.

Nothing made them happier, that is, until Olivia became pregnant. Then, all of a sudden with the birth of their only child, Jack, their love grew. It was like that scene in *How the Grinch Stole Christmas*—their hearts seemed to literally burst with love. Olivia quit her job at the local supermarket to stay home and take care of Jack. They spent the next few years changing diapers, buying book bags for school, cheering on the sidelines of soccer games, and proudly teaching Jack how to drive a stick shift. Life was *great*.

One day in high school, Jack started to get some mailings from colleges. Neither Olivia nor Ben had ever been to college, but this was always their dream for their son. Jack was smart, dedicated, and would undoubtedly go far in life, and Olivia and Ben would do anything to make his dreams come true. They had always squirreled away money whenever they could, and now the time had come to send their only son off to college, the first in the family to ever do so.

As the day approached, reality started to set in—Jack was about to leave the house. He wasn't going far away, but still, he was moving out of the house. Olivia and Ben were buzzing with excitement for him, and were excited, too, to be able to rekindle their romantic relationship. After all, with Jack out of the house, they could take more vacations (now that they didn't have to plan things around soccer practices), relax a bit at dinnertime, and even check out some binge-worthy Netflix while cozied up on the couch with each other. They were both genuinely looking forward to spending more quality time with one another and getting back to a routine where they didn't have to be caregivers and "mom and dad," just Olivia and Ben.

But after a few weeks of life as an empty-nester, and even though they had been expecting this for years and planning for months, Olivia and Ben start to face some challenges they hadn't expected. For example, Olivia, a stay-at-home mom, no longer has Jack at home to care for. She used to make family meals and enjoy cleaning the house and taking care of her family. She regularly drove Jack to visit friends, supported him at athletic events, and loved hearing about how his day was. Now that Jack is out of the house, Olivia has more time for her personal hobbies (she loves to garden and exercise), which is fun and fulfilling, but she feels as though she's struggling to really "find herself." In fact, she doesn't really know who she is, anymore. After all, with Jack out of the house, is she really still a "stay-at-home mom"?

Olivia also can't understand why Ben isn't doting on her the way he used to before Jack was born. She enjoys her personal space, time, and activities, but still wants to talk to Ben about things. In fact, she really wants to talk about things with Ben, like for example taking a trip, planning for retirement, and how they can spend their newfound "couple-time." But every time she brings this up to Ben he's always "late for a tee time" or "held up at work." This frustrates Olivia because she feels like every time she tries to talk to Ben he's just brushing her off to do other things.

Ben is also experiencing some highs and lows associated with the empty nest. He enjoys being able to spend more time golfing with his friends but gets annoyed regularly with Olivia because she's constantly asking him to do things with her. He wants to spend time with Olivia, but he feels as though she's always pestering him to help out around the house or to go shopping. He just can't help but think, "Why won't she just leave me alone? Can't she just go to yoga?" He also gets annoyed when she complains that he works too much, but he's always worked this much in the past, so why is it bothering her now? When he tries to talk with Olivia about their retirement plans and financial planning there is almost always an argument because Olivia wants to stay in their home (closer to where Jack is attending school), but Ben would love to retire to Florida and buy a boat. They just can't seem to get back to the way their relationship used to be before having Jack.

The Empty-Nest Case of Marcus and Julie

As Olivia and Ben are going through this rough time and trying to get back on track, their friends down the road are just starting to gear up for some big moves themselves. Marcus and Julie are a few years younger than Olivia and Ben, but they have children in the same school district, Marcus works at the same company as Ben, they attend the same church, and they all enjoy having the families spend time together. Marcus and Julie love each other as much as Olivia and Ben, and they had an amazing time dating and forming their romantic relationship before their twins were born.

Actually, the twins were a bit of a surprise, but still, a welcome surprise. Marcus and Julie met in college and successfully landed pretty good jobs shortly after. They were happy in their life, and then . . . surprise! Julie found herself pregnant...with twins! This was a happy little twist in life, and so they got married and settled down just a few blocks away from their soon-to-be new friends, Olivia and Ben. Julie and Marcus both kept their jobs after having their twins, Nia and Nala (after all, childcare is expensive and, well, college loans . . .). Nia and Nala just entered high school, so although college is still a few years off in the distance, it has come up in conversations. The whole family has started planning for it and it's something Marcus and Julie, along with their good friends, Olivia and Ben, regularly talk about when they're hanging out.

Marcus and Julie know that when the girls leave for college it's going to be a big change for everyone. They both saw their parents go through all the emotions when they themselves left for school, so they're expecting some challenges to arise as everyone figures out their new roles. They talk with each other a lot about things they are excited about doing when the twins leave, but also a lot about what worries them. They anticipate being lonely at times, so they start planning some trips and things to do, and they start doing this before they become empty-nesters. For example, they met with a travel agent to plan a road trip to several national parks they've never been to, booked a cruise, and bought season tickets for their favorite football team. Marcus and Julie anticipate things might be really different, and probably sad and hard at times, but they're okay with that because they try to be flexible and roll with whatever challenges come their way. Life is full of unexpected moments, after all, and they just do their best to anticipate change and work through the tough times together.

***

As you reflect on the discussion questions that follow, consider what communication researchers have uncovered about the challenges and benefits of the empty-nest phase of marriage. Keep in mind what Olivia and Ben are going through as well as their good friends, Marcus and Julie. As communication scholars we know people can take active steps in altering their communication with their spouse, and we know slight relationship adjustments are necessary to maintain relationships. That said, consider where research suggests Olivia and Ben, and then Marcus and Julie, could make adjustments in their relationship with their spouse to perhaps set themselves up for the empty-nest experience as opposed to the empty-nest syndrome.

DISCUSSION QUESTIONS

1. Ben and Olivia are having a bit of a rough time figuring out how to manage their new roles. As much as they are enjoying their individual space, it seems as though their lives are completely separate and boring....
   - What might our knowledge on dialectical tensions say about this aspect of the empty-nest phase of marriage?
2. Recall that Olivia *wants* to talk with Ben about their future (e.g., retirement, traveling), but every time she initiates a conversation Ben avoids her. She thinks these things are important, so she keeps pushing, and he continues to avoid the subject.
   - What might our knowledge about conflict communication and empty-nesters suggest about their situation?
3. The RTT highlights times of transition as moments in a relational couples' life that are confusing and sometimes challenging. As couples begin to navigate "new waters" with their romantic partners, some bumps and bruises can result.
   - How might the RTT explain Olivia and Ben's empty-nest relationship? As a communication scholar, what might you suggest they do to try to get their relationship back on track?
4. Olivia and Ben are already experiencing some not-so-great things about the transition to the empty-nest stage. However, their friends, Marcus and Julie still have some time to prepare.
   - As a communication scholar, what advice would you give to Marcus and Julie to help them prepare for their impending transition? How are Marcus and Julie's experience of the empty nest likely to be different from Olivia and Ben's? Why?
5. Consider the identities of Olivia (a stay-at-home mom) and Julie (a college-educated working mother).
   - How might their identities be challenged by becoming empty-nesters, and what effect might this have on their experience of this new phase of life?

REFERENCES

Anderson, S. A., Russell, C. S., & Schumm, W. R. (1983). Perceived marital quality and family life-cycle categories: A further analysis. *Journal of Marriage and the Family, 45*, 127–139. doi:10.2307/351301

Baxter, L. A. (1993). The social side of personal relationships: A dialectical analysis. In S. Duck (Ed.), *Social context and relationships* (pp. 139–165). Newbury Park, CA: Sage.

Baxter, L. A., & Montgomery, B. M. (1996). *Relating: Dialogues and dialectics*. New York, NY: The Guilford Press.

Black, S. M., & Hill, C. E. (1984). The psychological well-being of women in their middle years. *Psychology of Women Quarterly, 8*, 282–292. doi:10.1111/j.1471-6402.1984.tb00637.x

Borland, D. C. (1982). A cohort analysis approach to the empty-nest syndrome among three ethnic groups of women: A theoretical position. *Journal of Marriage and the Family, 44*, 117–129. doi:10.2307/351267

Brubaker, T. H. (1985). *Later life families*. Beverly Hills, CA: Sage.

Harkins, E. B. (1978). Effects of Empty-Nest Transition on self-report of psychological and physical well-being. *Journal of Marriage and the Family, 40*, 549–556. doi:10.2307/350935

Junge, M., & Maya, V. (1985). Women in their forties: A group portrait and implications for psychotherapy. *Women and Therapy, 4*(3), 3–19. doi:10.1300/J015v04n03_02

Kahana, B., & Kahana, E. (1982). Clinical issues of middle age and life. In F. M. Berardo (Ed.), *The annals of the American academy of political and social science: Middle and late life transitions* (pp. 140–161). Beverly Hills, CA: Sage.

King, M. E., & Theiss, J. A. (2016). The communicative and physiological manifestations of relational turbulence during the empty-nest phase of marital relationships. *Communication Quarterly, 65*, 495–517. doi:10.1080/01463373.2015.1129353

Kreider, R. M. (2005). Number, timing, and duration of marriages and divorces: 2001 (pp. 70–97). *Current Population Reports*. Washington, DC: US Census Bureau.

Nagy, M. E., & Theiss, J. A. (2013). Applying the relational turbulence model to the empty-nest transition: Sources of relationship change, relational uncertainty, and interference from partners. *Journal of Family Communication, 13*, 280–300. doi:10.1080/15267431.2013.823430

Radina, M. E., Hennon, C. B., & Gibbons, H. M. (2008). Divorce and mid- and later life families: A phenomenological analysis with implications for family life educators. *Journal of Divorce & Remarriage, 49*, 142–170. doi:10.1080/10502550801973146

Raup, J. L., & Meyers, J. E. (1989). The empty-nest syndrome: Myth or reality? *Journal of Counseling & Development, 60*, 180–183. doi:10.1002/j.1556-6676.1989.tb01353.x

Solomon, D. H., & Knobloch, L. K. (2001). Relationships uncertainty, partner interference, and intimacy within dating relationships. *Journal of Social and Personal Relationships, 18*, 804–820. doi:10.1177%2F0265407501186004

Solomon, D. H., & Knobloch, L. K. (2004). A model of relational turbulence: The role of intimacy, relational uncertainty, and interference from partners in appraisals of irritations. *Journal of Social and Personal Relationships, 21*, 795–781. doi:10.1177%2F0265407508090869

Solomon, D. H., Knobloch, L. K., Theiss, J. A., & McLaren, R. M. (2016). Relational turbulence theory: Explaining variation in subjective experiences and communication within romantic relationships. *Human Communication Research, 42*, 507–532. doi:10.1111/hcre.12091

Umberson, D., Williams, K., Powers, D. A., Chen, M. D., & Campbell, A. M. (2005). As good as it gets? A life course perspective on marital quality. *Social Forces, 84*, 487–505. doi:10.1353/sof.2005.0131

Werner, C. M., & Baxter, L. A. (1994). Temporal qualities of relationships: Organismic, transactional and dialectical views. In M. L. Knapp & G. R. Miller (Eds.), *Handbook of interpersonal communication* (2nd ed., pp. 323–379). Newbury Park, CA: Sage.

White, L., & Edwards, J. N. (1990). Emptying the nest and parental well-being: An analysis of national panel data. *American Sociological Review, 55*, 235–242. doi:10.2307/2095629

CHAPTER 4

Dealing with the Development of Children's Ethnic Identity in Interracial Marriages (with an Asian Parent and non-Asian Parent)

Narissra Maria Punyanunt-Carter – *Texas Tech University*

ABSTRACT

This specific case study deals with a couple (an Asian wife and American husband) who have two young biracial kids. The husband, Mark, feels that since the children are born in the United States, they should be raised with American values. The Asian wife, Ling, would like to expose the kids to Asian beliefs, language, and customs. Although Ling was born in China, she has been living in the United States for over 20 years. She has developed an appreciation for both cultures. Ling is torn between respecting her husband's perspectives and accommodating her parents' heritage. Mark thinks that the children will be confused and is worried that other children will mock their cultural differences. He does not want to confuse his children and feels that they are too young to learn about other cultures. Mark feels that Ling is Americanized, and he does not see the need to have the kids learn about their mother's culture, language, or viewpoints.

CASE STUDY

Ling is an only female child of two wealthy Chinese parents, born and raised in Beijing. When she is eight years old, her parents decide to move to Ohio to open a Chinese restaurant. Ling learns to adapt to the culture shock, but her parents instill Chinese ideals and cultural pride in her. She also learns to appreciate American culture. Even though she was born in China, she also feels very American.

As a child, she attends an all-Chinese church and her parents enroll her in Chinese language classes. Her parents surround her with Chinese people living in Ohio. Her school consists of mainly Caucasian students, but she builds friendships with mainly other Asian girls who attend her school. After high school, she attends college where she meets Mark. Ling and Mark are in the same residence hall. They see each other often in the cafeteria and the college library.

Mark was born and raised in Ohio. Mark is an all-American high school football player and was raised in a very white conservative area. He has never traveled anywhere outside of the state of Ohio. Both his parents are middle-class hard-working individuals. He meets Ling in a required college math course. They become study partners and quickly begin dating. Mark has never met anyone like Ling. He loves her fun personality and her charm. He falls in love with her immediately. Both Mark and Ling decide to attend graduate school together. They continue dating for six years. Initially, they talk about getting married. Mark is concerned about getting married because he does not want any children. However, Ling has always wanted to have children. She grew up as an only child, so she longs to have a big family.

When talking about marriage to Ling's parents, they do not approve. Ling's parents do not like Mark. They feel that Mark is ethnocentric and racist because he refuses to learn Chinese and does not want to visit China. Ling's parents are upset that their daughter doesn't want a traditional Chinese wedding. They have always been concerned about Mark's personality and how it will influence their future grandchildren.

Despite not having her parents' blessing, Ling and Mark marry and are very happy as a childless couple. Eventually, they have two children. They have argued about whether to teach their kids Chinese or not. This problem is causing grief in their relationship. The kids would like to make their mother happy by learning her native language but do not want to make their father upset by learning a language that he does not understand. Ling's parents do not speak English proficiently and would like to communicate with their grandchildren in Chinese and feel that the children should learn Chinese because it would be an asset to their professional development. Mark thinks it is unnecessary because they live in a small town and there are very few people who speak Chinese. He would prefer that his kids picked a language that they will use more frequently like Spanish.

Ling sings Chinese kid songs and says some words in Chinese to her kids. Mark does not like anything associated with China. He feels that they are not living in China and do not need to learn anything about China, because Ling has been living in the United States for a long time. Ling was born in China and she wants to share a part of her upbringing with her own kids. She wants her kids to appreciate two different cultures because they are biracial kids.

Ling's parents believe that exposing the children to two different cultures will help them develop cultural appreciation and awareness. They want to be able to communicate with their grandchildren in their native tongue so that they can share more of their cultural beliefs. They have been trying to teach the children Chinese subtly when they babysit the children. These behaviors have truly upset Mark. He can appreciate diversity and his wife's ethnicity. However, he feels that it is unnecessary to speak Chinese and learn about Chinese culture because they are living in a predominantly Caucasian neighborhood. The kids have taken his surname, so Mark believes that others will see the kids as American and not Chinese.

Ling's parents believe that even though the kids were born in the United States and have American names, they still physically appear as mixed-race children. They believe that Chinese is a notable language and it can help the kids in the future. They also think that it can make the kids smarter if they are bilingual.

Ling feels torn. She wants to please her husband, but she also wants to please her parents. She loves her parents and her husband. She appreciates the difference in perspectives and viewpoints regarding whether or not to teach the kids Chinese. However, she also feels that it is more than just teaching the kids Chinese. Ling feels that this would impact the children's cultural identity. Ling has made Chinese food and has introduced the kids to Chinese characters.

Mark is a child psychologist. He has seen how different environments can cause confusion and depression in children. He has also seen how it can impact the child's self-esteem. Hence, Mark believes that it is important to just keep things "normal." He feels that the kids will be more accepted and appreciated if they fit in with other kids similar to them. He believes that the other children at school do not speak other languages, and so his children should only speak English. He also believes that since the kids were born in America, they only need to focus on and learn about American culture and history. Moreover, he fears that his children will be ridiculed for being "different." He is trying his best to protect his children from being bullied by others.

Ling is also a psychologist. She believes that differences can be beneficial to a child's upbringing. She believes that children need to appreciate their family background and understand who they truly are. She believes that kindness can be taught at a young age if children are taught about tolerance and diversity. Hence, she believes that teaching them cultural awareness, especially about the intercultural differences between China and the United States will help them be better citizens.

Mark's parents do not wish to get involved in Mark and Ling's argument. They believe that this is an issue that Mark and Ling need to figure out themselves about what works best for their family. They adore Ling and respect her cultural background. They have never been outside of Ohio either and they know very little about China.

Mark and Ling refuse to compromise on the situation. Ling has been accommodating Mark's requests to not teach the kids Chinese and to not expose them to Chinese influences. Mark knows that this is important to his wife, but he doesn't see any other solution to this problem. Ling and Mark realize that they need to make a decision soon because their kids will only be little for a short time. As psychologists, they both know how culture can impact children's ethnic identities and shape their personalities in the future. Deciding what would be the best thing to do is one of the hardest decisions in their marriage.

To conclude, the development of children's ethnic identities is crucial in interracial marriages. The result of two different cultures has an impact on the child(ren) and their ethnic identities, which affects their professional and personal lives. Parents should pay more attention to this process and know more details about this process. Parents influence their children's ethnic identity, and it is developed through time. Several factors are important in the process of developing an ethnic identity. Parents should know how to utilize these factors to help their children develop their ethnic identities in an effective and beneficial manner.

DISCUSSION QUESTIONS

1. What would be the best way for Ling to please her husband and her parents?
2. Which communication theories explain this case study?
3. How should Ling communicate her culture to her kids so that it doesn't upset Mark?
4. What factors do you think influence a child's ethnic identity?
5. Do you think there are any negative or positive consequences of exposing a child to just one culture? How so?
6. Do you believe that language maintenance and festival maintenance are necessary to maintain the minority group's ethnic identity? Why or why not?
7. What do you think would be the best way to accommodate both parents' concerns?
8. Do you think that a father's ethnic identity has a stronger impact on biracial children's ethnic identities than the mother's ethnic identity? Why or why not?
9. Do you think it would be different if one of the parents was another race besides Asian? Why or why not?
10. What would be the best advice that you could give to either parent in this case study?
11. How do children who have one Chinese parent and one white parent develop their ethnic identity in a family?
12. What factors might impact children's ethnic identities in interracial marriages that have one Chinese parent and one white parent?

CHAPTER 5

Becoming the First in the Family to Graduate from College: First-Generation Students and Family Identity

Tiffany R. Wang – *University of Montevallo*
Kaitlin E. Phillips – *Utah State University*

ABSTRACT

This case study follows the story of Brandon, an 18-year-old first year social work major and psychology minor, as he reflects upon his first semester in college in a series of blog posts that comprise his First Year Experience Seminar Blog. Although Brandon knows he wants to help others and make the world a better place by becoming a social worker, he experiences some challenges learning the ropes of college because he is the first in his family to pursue a college degree. In his first blog, he explores his value, place, and purpose as a college student. In Brandon's second blog, he discusses what he expects from himself and from his time in college. In his third blog, he discusses how he plans to make new connections on campus and maintain connections back home. This case study concludes with discussion questions focused on memorable messages, identity, and turning points.

BRANDON'S FIRST-YEAR EXPERIENCE SEMINAR BLOG

About me. My name is Brandon. I'm an 18-year-old first-year social work major and psychology minor who wants to help others and make the world a better place. I'm a people person who is excited to be the first in my family to pursue a college degree. I've always enjoyed working with children and teens through my volunteer work at the Boys and Girls Club, and I hope to be able to continue to work with people in the future as I pursue my dream of becoming a social worker. My hobbies include playing basketball, volunteering in my community, and singing in my church choir. I'm looking forward to blogging about my first semester in college as a part of this first year experience seminar class. If you're interested in learning more about me, feel free to reach out to me on Facebook, Instagram, or Snapchat. #ClassOf2023

Who are you? blog. Over the past few weeks in my first year experience seminar, my professor has asked me to explore my own interests, desires, and needs while reflecting on how these attributes relate to my life as a college student. In this blog, I will discuss my value, place, and purpose and reflect on where I come from, why I am here, what my values are, and what my purpose is.

I have lived in a small town my entire life with my mom, dad, sister, and brother. I have always dreamed that I would attend college and I am working hard to make that dream a reality. When I think about what it takes to be the first in my family to graduate from college, it means being financially stable and able to attend college. Although my family is moving toward being financially stable and able, there is still a lot of pressure on me to support my family and pay for my college expenses on my own. Growing up in a small town, I went to a high school that was a good school, but it was not anything like some of the larger schools in the bigger cities nearby, where almost all of the graduating seniors go on to college. My small town had a population of about 2700 people and my graduating class that included half the students in the county was about 100 students. I think the area where someone is from can determine whether someone decides to attend college. At those larger schools, high school seniors know they want to go to college because people who live in those areas have four-year degrees or even higher degrees, and many of those students' parents went to college and completed four-year degrees. Where I live, very few people have degrees. Most of my high school classmates graduated high school and went straight into the workforce. My parents and most of my friends' parents didn't go to college.

During high school, while many of my friends were participating in extracurricular activities and doing homework for their classes, I chose to get a job in a fast-food restaurant to help my family pay our bills. Although I started at the bottom there, I worked hard and eventually worked my way up to crew trainer where I worked 30 plus hours a week to try and help my family pay our bills. For the past few years, my mom has been trying to make enough money working as a letter carrier to support our family of five, because my dad has been between jobs and unable to hold down a job for more than three months. Only having one income made our household income really low and made it difficult to pay all of our bills. My sister, my brother, and I got part-time jobs to help support my mom while my dad wasn't working. The lack of family finances made it really hard for my sister, my brother, and me to balance work and trying to help support our family with school and trying to focus on getting into college. Although my mom and dad have always told me I shouldn't worry about adult concerns like paying the bills, I can see how my dad's inability to hold down a job affected my mom and our family. My dad and I didn't really communicate a lot in high school because I was really angry that he was not working and was just sitting at home all day and allowing my mom to go out and work and try to support the whole family on her own. I always thought my dad should have been more responsible for being the breadwinner and shouldn't have left it all up to my mom to support our family. When I saw that he was not working and wasn't putting in the effort to look for a new job, it was difficult for me to look up to him as a role model because I felt like he wasn't fulfilling his responsibility to our family. There were definitely things I wouldn't talk to him about or ask him about because I thought less of him. Don't get me wrong. I love my dad, but I just never understood how he couldn't hold down a job when I was just in high school and able to hold down a steady job while going to school full time. In the future, I don't want to have to worry about whether the bills are going to be paid on time. That's why I'm here in college. I want to be able to hold down a job, support my family, and help other people someday by pursuing a career as a social worker.

Although I have always taken school seriously and worked hard to achieve my dreams, I began to value higher education more when I applied and was accepted to the Upward Bound program at my high school. This program is a college readiness program that helps students like me prepare for college. I firmly believe that the Upward Bound program is the reason I am here. I give them a lot of credit for helping me find the financial resources I needed to pay for college. My high school experience didn't prepare me very well for the ACT exam that I had to take to get into my dream college and qualify for on-campus scholarships that would help me pay for college. I knew that I would need a score of 18 on the ACT exam to get into my dream college. I took the ACT exam nine times and my ACT score still stayed at 17.

From the beginning of my senior year, I knew that I wanted to be a social worker and I knew that I really wanted to come here because I did the Upward Bound program here. As a result, it was very discouraging when I received a letter in November of my senior year that said the university had put my application on hold because of my ACT score. When I took the ACT exam again in December and my score still didn't improve, I called the admissions counselor here and she told me about a program that allowed me to be conditionally admitted if I took specific English and math classes during my first semester. I was excited that I could prove that I belonged here and gain full admission if I made a C or better in my English and math classes.

Although I eventually got conditionally admitted here and am currently participating in the conditional admission program with the goal of making the grades I need to be fully admitted here, it has been frustrating for me that your ability to fulfill your purpose is so dependent on an ACT score. I had a 3.5 GPA and a 17 ACT score in high school while working 30 plus hours a week and I'm really doing well in my English and math classes so far this semester. Not everyone is capable of doing well in timed testing situations and I wish colleges took other criteria into account so that your ACT score alone didn't determine where you went in life or whether you had enough scholarship money to pay for your college education.

In high school, many of my friends' parents were very involved with their college application process because they had college degrees and knew what it would take to get into college. I didn't really talk to my parents about the college application process until I was admitted into college. I didn't even tell them that my application to my dream college was on hold. Once I was conditionally admitted, I just told them I was admitted. Both of them were glad I had gotten in because that would allow me to apply for different scholarships so I could try and pay for school on my own.

I always knew that I would take my education seriously especially if I was able to get a scholarship that would make attending college financially possible. I believe that everyone should take college seriously because it is very expensive and the chance to graduate college is a huge opportunity that not everyone has the opportunity to pursue. I have friends in my residence hall who have to go to the cashier's office on campus all the time and talk with the staff there because there are all sorts of tuition and fee costs that make paying for college difficult. They're not able to afford the textbooks they need for their classes and they're having to take out loans that they'll have to pay back later after they graduate from college. I'm trying my best to keep my grades up this year so I can keep my scholarship, because I know that it's on me to pay for school and I can't afford to not succeed at school. Paying for school myself has made me grow into an adult quickly because I know that I can't really depend on my family for financial support anymore, because my mom needs all the money she can get to pay the bills. I really want to be able to take care of myself and be independent throughout my time in college and after I graduate college so that my parents don't have to worry about financially supporting me when they're already stressed about financially supporting our family on just one income.

Personal expectations blog. Building upon my last blog that focused on my value, place, and purpose, in my second blog I will discuss my personal expectations for college including what I expect from my time in college. I think this blog will be a little bit shorter than my first blog, because I'm still not sure what to expect in college.

Although a lot of people find college to be an intimidating place, because they haven't experienced it before, I believe that I won't have as many issues with transitioning to college socially because I'm a talkative and friendly person who tends to fit right in quickly. In high school, I was treasurer of my senior class, was a part of senior elite, and was in Relay for Life. I loved working with my classmates to plan picnics, design t-shirts, and organize fund-raisers that benefited nonprofit organizations back home. I think my leadership experiences in high school and my experiences doing the Upward Bound program on campus will make the college transition easier. Being part of the Upward Bound program allowed me to know the feel of the campus and what was expected here so there wouldn't be as many surprises. I've always gone to small schools so coming to a small liberal arts university seemed like the right fit for me. I can imagine that transitioning from my small school to a large public school would have been much more difficult for me because I wouldn't have been able to meet new people and make connections with professors as easily. So far, I like being away from home and adulting. Although there have been good and bad days so far, I haven't had any really, really legit bad days. Hopefully this string of good days and positive experiences in college will continue for me throughout the course of this semester.

Learning and wellness blog. As a social work major and psychology minor, I have been most looking forward to this blog because it directly relates to the fields I am studying in college and hope to pursue professionally post my graduation. In my third blog, I will discuss how I personally learn and study; how mental health, self-care, and overall wellness impact my learning; and how campus resources can help me maintain my wellness for maximum learning.

As a people person, I perform best when I can learn and study with others. In class, that might mean I collaborate with my classmates through GroupMe to prepare for an exam. Outside of class, that might mean I go to free TRiO tutoring where I can meet with staff members and peer tutors who can help me maximize my learning. The best advice I would give to other students who are first year students like me would be to utilize your resources. You have to do everything you can to support yourself even if that means asking for help. I don't believe that there's a limit to anything you can do if you keep pushing toward achieving your goals.

As I think about how I prioritize my overall wellness so that I can be a successful learner, I like to surround myself with positive people who will strengthen me and help me grow. Because I've moved away from home, I need to find a new family because I'm not around my family every day and I don't go home to my family every day. Right now, I really rely on my family in the TRiO program here as well as my new church family. They help me to not let my disappointments get me down. I'm learning to let these disappointments just roll off me so that I can roll with the punches and move forward toward achieving my goals.

In addition to seeking out academic and community resources, I am also glad that I can take advantage of free on-campus resources like student health services and counseling services if I need additional support. I also like to go outside and explore different recreational spaces if I need a short break from the stress of college, homework, and classes. I've joined an intramural basketball team this semester. When I'm not studying or going to class, I enjoy going to the student activity center to practice for our weekly games. I also like hiking and kayaking at the university lake when I need time to recharge.

Campus and home connections blog. As I discussed in my personal expectations blog, I'm a talkative and friendly person who tends to fit in quickly. Although I tend to be an outgoing person, I have still faced some challenges making new connections on campus and maintaining connections back home. In this blog, I will discuss the challenges and opportunities I have experienced connecting with my peers, my faculty, and my family this semester.

On move-in day, I was excited to move into my residence hall. Moving away from home felt like an opportunity to forge my own path and start my adult life with the independence and freedom I didn't have back home. I've always had to balance school with supporting my family financially, so it's been quite different to be able to focus fully on school. As I've gotten to know my peers in my residence hall and in my classes, I've begun to realize that many of my peers have very different backgrounds than me. When they're unsure about how to be successful in college, they can just call their parents and their parents are able to provide them with specific advice on what they need to do to be successful. For example, my roommate's parents went to this university, so they know exactly where he needs to go and what he needs to do when he needs help. My parents do their best to support me when I experience challenges, but they're unable to give me specific advice. They just tell me to work hard and reassure me that they're proud of me. Recently, I've begun to rely more on my peers and faculty members for the advice and guidance my parents can't give me because they've never experienced college before.

Taking college classes with faculty members who have doctoral degrees in their fields has been really intimidating so far. Even though I am taking classes like English and math that I also took in high school, my college classes have been much more challenging than my high school classes so far. At times, I feel like an imposter when I sit in class. It seems like my peers already know where they belong, what decisions they are making, and what opportunities they want to pursue in the future. College just seems to come easily to my peers. Sometimes, it seems like there are words that I'm unfamiliar with like general education requirements, degree plans, and credit hours. I understood that I needed some sort of plan to graduate on time in four years, but I wasn't sure how to put this type of plan together. As part of this first year experience seminar class, I was required to meet with my academic advisor to put together an academic plan. Although I was very intimidated to contact my academic advisor who I hadn't met yet because I'm not taking any classes in my major this semester, I found the courage to email her to set up an appointment. She replied the same day and we set up an appointment.

As I entered her office, I was pleased to see a plaque on the wall that said she had won our university's Academic Advising Award. I figured that this must mean that she would be a good advisor for me and would be able to help me answer the questions I had for her about my major and academic plan for graduation with my social work degree. As I started talking to her, my advisor came across as relaxed, calm, and nurturing. I felt comfortable talking to her and didn't feel rushed. She understood that I didn't yet understand the requirements for my degree and that I would have a lot of questions. My advisor opened the conversation by asking me about how my semester was going so far and asking me if I had any questions and concerns. She also gave me a really helpful card that included information on graduation requirements, her contact information, and a list of tips for making the most of college. My advisor told me that it was her goal to make the best possible advising experience for each of her advisees and to provide the most accurate information so that we would know what we needed to do to graduate on time. Although we had only scheduled a half-hour appointment, she assured me that she would spend whatever time was necessary to assist me. In contrast to my parents who gave me general advice about succeeding in college, my advisor was able to give me personalized, targeted advice and guidance that was drawn from her experiences in college. I left the appointment happy that I had met with my advisor. She was able to provide me with the information I needed regarding university requirements, policies, and procedures so I could more clearly understand what was expected from me as a social work student. I also liked that my advisor had an understanding and positive attitude that allowed me to feel at ease with her rather than intimidated by her. She seemed to want to do whatever it took to help me pursue my interests and passions. After meeting with my advisor, I feel more confident that I can talk to some of my other faculty members when I have questions about their classes.

After this positive meeting with my academic advisor, I was excited to go home for the weekend and share all of my college experiences with my family. Although I enjoyed being home for the weekend, I began to feel greater pressure to be successful in college after spending time with my parents, my siblings, and my church community. My mother spent all weekend cooking for me and spending time with me because she hadn't seen me since the beginning of the semester. When I went to church with my family on Sunday, my pastor welcomed me home and made a special point of telling me how proud he was of me and the young man I was becoming. After the church service ended, many of the children and teens I had mentored in high school wanted to talk to me to see what college was like. Although I enjoyed the attention at first, I realized that with this attention came a responsibility to represent my community back home to the best of my ability. I can tell that my parents, my siblings, and my community are counting on me to make it in college and succeed. As I return to campus, I am determined to make my friends and family back home proud. I know that others look up to me and I know that I have no choice but to keep going despite the obstacles I am facing so that I can finish my four-year degree and start a new legacy of college completion for my family.

DISCUSSION QUESTIONS

1. Wang (2014b) discusses the memorable messages[3] first-generation students receive from their parents. Brandon mentions that there were differences between him and his roommate who had parents who graduated from college. How do these differences in student status influence the types of memorable messages Brandon received versus the types of memorable messages students like his roommate might have received?

2. Orbe (2004) and Orbe (2008) discuss how first-generation students vary in how salient they see their first-generation student status in their daily interactions. To what extent is Brandon's first-generation student status a part of his identity as a college student and family member? Does it change as a function of who he is talking with?

3. Jung and Hecht (2004) discuss the identity gaps that emerge from the various layers of identity in communication theory of identity (CTI).[4] Orbe and Groscurth (2004) discuss how first-generation students negotiate their identities on campus and at home. What relationships and groups on campus and at home are important to Brandon? How has Brandon's identity been shaped by these relational partners and group members?

4. Wang (2014a) discusses formational turning points[5] in the transition to college that occur within relationships with college teachers. How would you characterize Brandon's relationship with his academic advisor? What aspects of this relationship resemble a role relationship[6]? What aspects of this relationship resemble an interpersonal relationship[7]? How do you think Brandon's relationship with his academic advisor will change over time?

5. Wang and Nuru (2017) explore turning points first-generation students experience in high school and college. What turning points did Brandon experience during high school and his first semester of college? How have they shaped his identity?

---

3. Memorable messages are short messages that are told to us by someone who is an authority figure. Although we receive lots of messages every day that we may forget quickly, memorable messages can be easily recalled even years after they are shared with us.

4. Identity layers are personal (how one views oneself), enacted (how one behaves), relational (how one sees oneself in the context of relationships), and communal (how one views oneself as part of the collective). These identity layers are connected, and when there is a discrepancy between any of the layers an identity gap occurs—this is where the layers diverge.

5. Turning points are specific moments or conversations where there was a change in the relationship. Turning points are indicative of change and the ongoing process that are relationships.

6. In a role relationship, a student and a professor perform the duties that might be expected of a student and a professor.

7. If a student and a professor decide that they want to build upon their role relationship to develop a relationship that is more personal and long-lasting, the role relationship may transform to an interpersonal relationship that may more closely resemble a mentor and mentee relationship.

REFERENCES

Jung, E., & Hecht, M. L. (2004). Elaborating the communication theory of identity: Identity gaps and communication outcomes. *Communication Quarterly, 52*, 265–283. doi:10.1080/01463370409370197

Orbe, M. P. (2004). Negotiating multiple identities within multiple frames: An analysis of first-generation college students. *Communication Education, 53*, 131–149. doi:10.1080/03634520410001682401

Orbe, M. P. (2008). Theorizing multidimensional identity negotiation: Reflections on the lived experiences of first-generation college students. *New Directions for Child and Adolescent Development, 120*, 81–95. doi:10.1002/cd.217

Orbe, M., & Groscurth, C. R. (2004). A co-cultural theoretical analysis of communicating on campus and at home: Exploring the negotiation strategies of first generation college (FGC) students. *Qualitative Research Reports in Communication, 5*, 41–47.

Wang, T. R. (2014a). Formational turning points in the transition to college: Understanding how communication events shape first-generation students' pedagogical and interpersonal relationships with their college teachers. *Communication Education, 63*, 63–82. doi:10.1080/03634523.2013.841970

Wang, T. R. (2014b). "I'm the only person from where I'm from to go to college": Understanding the memorable messages first-generation college students receive from parents. *Journal of Family Communication, 14*, 270–290. doi:10.1080/15267431.2014.908195

Wang, T. R., & Nuru, A. K. (2017). "He wanted me to achieve that for our family and I did too": Exploring first-generation students' experiences of turning points during the transition to college. *Journal of Family Communication, 17*, 153–168. doi:10.1080/15267431.2016.1264401

CHAPTER 6

Conflict and Coping in Military Families: Expectation Violations During Wartime Deployments

Diana G. Zulli – *Purdue University*

ABSTRACT

The effects of military life extend beyond service members. Military spouses experience a variety of psychological, communicative, and emotional impairments as a by-product of wartime deployments. Yet, the media still promulgates themes, myths, and expectations about military life and deployments that hide the sacrifices of military and spousal service. This case study details the expectations of three military spouses who experienced at least one deployment. In particular, this case study shows how married spouses navigate the discrepancy between expectations and reality in the context of military deployments, providing insight into expectancy violations theory. Discussion questions are offered for further deliberation into expectancy violations theory, conflict, and coping in high stress careers.

INTRODUCTION

More than 2.7 million service members have been deployed to Iraq or Afghanistan since 2001 (McCarthy, 2018), and approximately 1.1 million service members have died in combat since the Revolutionary War (Crigger, 2015). This statistic has unfortunately increased in recent years and does not include the countless mental and physical wounds incurred by military service (Mansfield et al., 2010). The effects of military life are not exclusive to the service members. Wiens and Boss (2006) argue that families also experience variations of psychological impairments as a by-product from their military members' service. Yet, the media still promulgates themes, myths, and expectations about military life, deployments, and spousal service that hide the emotional, psychological, and sometimes physical sacrifices of military service for all parties involved (Howard & Prividera, 2015). Myths such as nationalism, the warrior myth, the returning home myth, and the dutiful spouse myth frame military service and spousal support as honorable, noble, and worth the potentially damaging effects of military life (Howard & Prividera, 2008, 2015; Newsinger, 1997; Parker, 1985). Because of these dominant discourses in the media, military/spousal service and deployments are riddled with expectations that might not match reality. Using the experiences of three military spouses, this case study engages expectancy violations theory (Burgoon, 1993, 2016) as a framework for understanding spousal expectations, conflict, and coping during military deployments.

EXPECTANCY VIOLATIONS THEORY AND MILITARY DEPLOYMENTS

Expectancy violations theory is concerned with what people expect in their interpersonal interactions (Burgoon, 2016). Every person holds an enduring cognition about how others should act in a given situation and context. These expectations can be at the cultural or individual level. For instance, the military is a specific culture that is known as tough, masculine, and hierarchical (Boyce & Herd, 2003). For those joining the military, there is an expectation of deployments, hard work, and sacrifice in the name of national security. Similarly, the military spouse culture emphasizes loyalty, family values, and support for the service member (Howard & Prividera, 2015). Individual differences also create expectations for interpersonal interactions. People come to interactions with a variety of factors that affect the expectations of those interactions, such as demographics, communication patterns, personality traits, physical appearance, age, gender, etc. For instance, how one grows up undoubtedly affects the language and nonverbal behaviors that one uses to communicate. If a couple's language and nonverbal habits deviate too much, there is a possibility for increased conflict because the expectations derived from personal preferences and experiences are violated. Taken together, the culture of the military and individual differences can affect spousal expectations, conflict, and coping during wartime deployments.

MEDIATED MYTHS AND MILITARY EXPECTATIONS

Mediated representations of the military are one explanation for how and why these expectations of military life become dominant in society (Althaus & Coe, 2011; Coe, 2015; Howard & Prividera, 2008, 2015). War and the military have long been topics of interest in popular culture. America as a culture likes to see the heroic military member, the doting and supportive wife, and the perfect coming home story. The media is filled with images of soldiers returning from remote assignments, standing in formation, being relieved from duty, running to their families, and surprising their children in schools, all of which reinforce myths of what military life is "supposed" to be like.

Because the military, foreign policy, and war issues are too complex to fully unpack in a two-hour movie or television series, these stories and this context are often subject to certain widely understood frames. One prominent frame deployed in the media is nationalism. The nationalism frame involves a strong sense of loyalty to a particular nation and the mindset that a nation's interest must be protected at all costs, often justifying military action and service member sacrifice (Howard & Prividera, 2008). As an extension of nationalism, the myth of the warrior hero is used to imply certain characteristics and behaviors held by soldiers and their spouses. The warrior hero is heterosexual, white, male, nationally superior, and morally good (Newsinger, 1997; Parker, 1985). Military service is perceived as sacred and noble; service members are the ultimate heroes, in life and in death (Coe, 2015). The military spouse, by extension, is portrayed as an equally honorable role. The spouse "holds down the home front" and dutifully supports the service member. The spouse never questions the service member's job or gets upset when his or her partner is absent or unable to communicate. Instead, the spouse understands the sacrifices and acknowledges his or her part in defending the country.

DEPLOYMENT EXPECTATIONS: THE CASE OF THREE SPOUSES

To better understand how unfulfilled expectations create conflict between spouses during wartime deployments, this case study focuses on three military spouses: Molly, Alexis, and

Leslie (names changed for anonymity). Molly, Alexis, and Leslie are military spouses who have experienced at least one military deployment. All three women expressed that their expectations going into their first deployment did not match the reality of the situation. These expectancy violations created conflict in their relationships. To manage this conflict, Molly, Alexis, and Leslie had to reframe their expectations and develop clear communication boundaries with their service member spouse. These experiences are detailed below.

Molly

Molly is a new military spouse. Having only been married three weeks, Molly is getting used to her life in the marine corps. Although Molly and her husband are newlyweds, her husband, Jason, has already been twice deployed during their relationship. Jason works on an aircraft carrier in the Pacific Ocean. Molly is aware of Jason's job title, but due to the nature of his work, she is unable to know all the details of his deployments (e.g., location, specific duties, risks involved).

Molly anticipates that her military life will include long distance and deployments. However, she does not anticipate the extent to which her communication patterns with Jason will change during his first deployment. Due to technology, Molly is used to frequent communication with Jason. They are connected all day, every day, which makes the long distance more bearable. When Jason leaves for his first deployment, Molly expects this same level of access to her spouse. Jason expects this as well and promises their communication will continue. Unfortunately, technology on the aircraft carrier is unreliable and in high demand. Jason is not able to connect with Molly, and they often go days without speaking. When Molly and Jason do talk, those conversations are consumed with fights about their lack of communication. Molly is often left to worry about where Jason is in the world and whether or not he is safe. The silence not only causes Molly fear and anxiety over Jason's well-being, but also anger toward him for not fulfilling her expectations and adhering to the communication patterns they established. Jason is frustrated because he feels Molly does not understand the nature of his job.

Molly also expects support from the marine corps during this deployment. Molly recalls seeing movies and television series that show military wives gathered on bases sharing information about their service members and the deployments. At the onset of her marriage, the marine corps reaches out to Molly promising to keep her updated on any developments with the deployment. She is also given a list of resources and spousal groups to help her during this time, further supporting the communal expectations and images she sees in the media. Unfortunately, the marine corps only sends out impersonal emails if there are updates to a service members' status during their deployment. No one from base services reaches out to Molly. Without reliable communication from her spouse and support from others in her situation, Molly is often left feeling uncertain and alone during this deployment.

Molly realizes that she resents Jason for not upholding the communication expectations during the first deployment. During the second deployment, Molly and Jason work to better establish realistic expectations. Jason provides as much information about the deployment as possible but tells Molly they probably will only be able to speak once a week. From the last deployment, Jason knows that email is the mode of communication that is most accessible and reliable. Jason and Molly agree that email will be their primary mode of communication and commit to being as detailed and clear as possible while emailing each other. Jason and Molly also agree to have the more challenging and personal conversations over the phone to eliminate any potential miscommunication. Setting the expectations low alleviates some of the conflict they experienced during the first deployment. Similarly, heading into this second deployment, Molly no longer expects the marine corps to facilitate spousal support. Molly now works to establish her own community of marine wives.

Alexis

Alexis is a military spouse of three years. Alexis' husband, David, has been deployed once and is preparing for his second deployment with the air force. These deployments last approximately eight months and are located in the Middle East. David is part of the security forces and is tasked with providing force protection and guarding air bases.

Alexis anticipates frequent deployments but is shocked with how little time she has to prepare for them. The air force only gives Jason and Alexis two weeks' notice before his first deployment. Both Alexis and Jason are in shock as they scramble to make arrangements for his departure. Alexis suddenly has to learn how to take over Jason's household duties in addition to her full-time job as a teacher and part-time status as a graduate student. Although Alexis recalls seeing movies and hearing stories about service members being deployed with little notice, she does not anticipate these intense feelings of shock and chaos. Initially, Alexis believes she will be able to handle the unpredictability of deployments, like the spouses in mediated representations. She quickly realizes that she needs more time in order to properly cope and prepare for a deployment, time she is often not granted.

During this first deployment, Alexis is in frequent communication with David. He is stationed at a well-established base in Afghanistan, and so he and Alexis talk every day. Alexis is aware of David's responsibilities and expects him to be honest with her about the nature of his deployment, which is very dangerous. David obliges and discusses several close calls his unit has while on patrol. During one phone conversation, the line is suddenly cut off due to a base-wide emergency. Understandably, Alexis is unnerved by these events. Alexis and David begin to quarrel over his job and status in the military. Alexis wants to be in contact with David but is struggling to handle the dangerous realities of his job. The stress of his job begins to weigh emotionally on her, and she starts to lose satisfaction with her role as a military spouse.

Alexis realizes that very little can prepare you for a deployment other than time. However, since she and David cannot guarantee how much time they will have before the next deployment, they begin to have the "what if" conversations. What if David deploys to a location without reliable technology? What if the next deployment violates the expectations established with the first deployment? What if the next deployment lasts longer than a year? What if Alexis becomes pregnant before a deployment? Answering these questions and more help Alexis and David manage the uncertainty of how much time they will have before the next deployment, while also establishing an expectation for how she and David will respond to these "what if" scenarios.

Similarly, the first deployment teaches Alexis that just because she and David can have open communication, that does not mean that she welcomes that disclosure. Alexis and David thus create boundaries for their communication moving forward. She will be open and honest with David, but David will be mindful of how the details of his job affect Alexis. In this sense, the communication becomes somewhat one-directional. Although Alexis is aware of the dangers of military service, this agreement to keep discussions of close calls at bay allows Alexis and David to focus on their relationship and the benefits of military service, rather than the risks. Alexis sees an improvement in her relational satisfaction and is better able to survive the next eight-month deployment.

Leslie

Leslie is an experienced military spouse. She and her husband, Kevin, have been in the air force for over 10 years. Together they have experienced three deployments and one remote station to Korea, which consisted of a year-long separation between her and Kevin. Besides the one-year remote station, the average length of Kevin's three deployments is seven months. Kevin works as a chaplain's assistant and is rarely in harm's way during these deployments. Leslie and Kevin have four children, and Leslie works part-time as a protestant religious education coordinator. Deployments put an enormous strain on Leslie, and she often struggles with how to manage all her responsibilities alone.

Leslie has romantic notions and expectations of deployments at the beginning of her time as a military spouse. In fact, Leslie recalls being a bit excited about the deployment because it was new and different. This romanticism largely stems from the scenes depicted in movies where the service member goes away, the spouse sends letters, and then the service member returns to a grateful country and warm homecoming. Before her first deployment,

Leslie knows that the separation is going to be difficult, but she expects Kevin's return to be worth the wait and sacrifice.

This expectation does not match Leslie's reality. Instead, Leslie quickly learns that there is no backup for when she is stressed, tired, and overwhelmed from juggling her new role as a single mother. She realizes that she alone has to manage the kids when they wake up at 3 a.m.. She knows that she is the only one who can get the kids ready for school every day, even though she needs to head to work herself. She knows that she can never take a break or check out for an afternoon because she alone is running the household. For Leslie, there is no mental or physical relief. Instead of writing love letters to her husband and longing for the day he returns, their communication consists of short emails discussing the kids, house, and other nonromantic life responsibilities. Leslie tries to keep Kevin involved in the decision making, but his absence makes it challenging for Leslie to get things done in a timely manner. Leslie becomes the main decision maker, which frustrates Kevin. Leslie and Kevin's communication grows increasingly strained. As the kids become comfortable with Leslie as the only parent in their lives, both Leslie and Kevin grow concerned over Kevin's homecoming. Yet, Leslie is still hopeful that Kevin's return will be as romantic and effortless as the ones portrayed in popular culture.

Once again, Leslie's expectations about this part of deployments are violated upon Kevin's return. The first greeting is indeed romantic and emotional. The kids are excited to see their dad and the whole family is ready to "get back to normal." Unfortunately, this brief moment of euphoria is short-lived as Leslie, Kevin, and the kids are faced with the realities of reintegration. Leslie is used to managing the finances, home, and assuming the roles of both mom and dad for the kids. As Kevin returns, he expects to step right back into his role in the home, which creates conflict between him and Leslie. The kids are also hesitant to perceive Kevin in the authoritative status he once held. Also unexpected is the post-traumatic stress that Kevin is now dealing with after deployment. At first, Kevin does not recognize that he needs emotional help, and Leslie is ill-equipped to manage this new-found trauma. The two grow apart. Leslie and Kevin struggle to develop a routine and this conflict unfortunately lasts for quite some time.

Leslie realizes that her romantic expectations contributed to the conflict she and Kevin faced during and after his deployment. She realizes that she was juggling too much in Kevin's absence and decides to establish a stronger support system for the next deployment. Doing so not only allows her to better manage being a single, working mom, but having the extra support also diminishes some of the resentment she feels toward Kevin's career. Leslie works to include Kevin in decision-making processes, which enables him to feel more connected to his family and home. Upon return from a deployment, Leslie and Kevin now anticipate a few months of readjustment instead of expecting relationships and roles to automatically go back to normal. This readjustment includes being open to shifting responsibilities, giving the kids grace in rediscovering their relationship with their dad, and being understanding of any post-deployment trauma. Even though each deployment is accompanied with fear and uncertainty, Leslie and Kevin are now honest with themselves about the harsh realities of military deployments. They no longer expect this context to be romantic or glamorous. Reframing these expectations enables Leslie and Kevin to better cope with deployments.

SUMMARY

The problem that framed this case study is that military deployments are riddled with un-realistic expectations that the media spreads to promote nationalism and service member buy-in. By examining the lived experiences of three military spouses, this case study reveals that expectations of deployments often do not reflect reality. For Molly, Alexis, and Leslie, coping started with and marital satisfaction increased by reframing communication, the romanticism of deployments, and the coming-home narrative.

DISCUSSION QUESTIONS

1. How might couples best manage expectations or expectation violations when one or both members have high-uncertainty careers?
2. How might disclosure, or the lack thereof, be a tool to manage relational expectations?
3. How might parents in high-uncertainty, high-stress careers help to manage the expectations of their children?
4. How might couples anticipate expectancy violations before they experience a high-stress situation?
5. How might expectancy violation theory be used as an instructional guide for couples in high-uncertainty, high-stress careers (e.g., military, police, firefighter)?

REFERENCES

Althaus, S. L., & Coe, K. (2011). Priming patriots: Social identity processes and the dynamics of public support for war. *Public Opinion Quarterly, 75*, 65–88. doi:10.1093/poq/nfq071

Boyce, L. A., & Herd, A. M. (2003). The relationship between gender role stereotypes and requisite military leadership characteristics. *Sex Roles, 49*(7–8), 365–378. doi:10.1023/A:1025164221364

Burgoon, J. (2016). Expectancy violations theory. In C. R. Berger & M. E. Roloff (Eds.), *The international encyclopedia of interpersonal communication* (pp. 1–9). Hoboken, NJ: John Wiley & Sons.

Burgoon, J. K. (1993). Interpersonal expectations, expectancy violations, and emotional communication. *Journal of Language and Social Psychology, 12*(1–2), 30–48. doi:10.1177/0261927X93121003

Coe, K. (2015). Honoring the dead, supporting the war: Media eulogies and the possibilities of patriotic discourse. In E. S. Parcell & L. M. Webb (Eds.), *A communicative perspective on the military: Interactions, messages, and discourses* (pp. 237–254). New York, NY: Peter Lang.

Crigger, M. (2015, May 24). How many Americans have died in US wars? *PBS News Hour.* Retrieved from https://www.pbs.org/newshour/nation/many-americans-died-u-s-wars

Howard, J. W., & Prividera, L. C. (2008). "Freedom isn't free!:" A critical analysis of militarism, patriarchy, and the ideal solider. *Texas Speech Communication Journal, 30*, 134–145. doi:10.1080/07491409.2008.10162544

Howard, J. W., & Prividera, L. C. (2015). Nationalism, and soldiers' health: Media framing of soldiers' returns from deployments. In E. S. Parcell & L. M. Webb (Eds.), *A communicative perspective on the military: Interactions, messages, and discourses* (pp. 217–236). New York, NY: Peter Lang.

Mansfield, A. J., Kaufman, J. S., Marshall, S. W., Gaynes, B. N., Morrissey, J. P., & Engel, C. C. (2010). Deployment and the use of mental health services among U.S. Army wives. *New England Journal of Medicine, 362*, 101–109. doi:10.1056/NEJMoa0900177

McCarthy, N. (2018, March 20). 2.77 Million service members have served on 5.4 million deployments since 9/11. *Forbes.* Retrieved from https://www.forbes.com/sites/niallmccarthy/2018/03/20/2-77-million-service-members-have-served-on-5-4-million-deployments-since-911-infographic/#65541ee750db

Newsinger, J. (1997). *Dangerous men: The SAS and popular culture.* London, England: Pluto.

Parker, T. (1985). *Soldier, soldier.* London, England: Heinemann.

Wiens, T. W., & Boss, P. (2006). Maintaining family resiliency before, during, and after military separation. In C. A. Castro, A. B. Adler, & T. W. Britt (Eds.), *Military life: The psychology of serving in peace and combat* (Vol. 3: The military family, pp. 13–38). Westport, CT: Praeger Security International.

Part II

RELATIONSHIPS, PARENTS, AND CULTURE

CHAPTER 7

Flying Under the Radar:
Finstas and Nonresidential Parenting

Falon Kartch – *California State University, Fresno*
Lindsay Timmerman – *Texas State University*

ABSTRACT

This case examines the relationships between 16-year-old Cordelia and her recently-divorced parents, Mae and Mark. Based on their visitation agreement, Cordelia lives with her dad (in their original family home) during the school week, and with her mom (in her mom's new house) from Friday through Monday morning. In an effort to keep up regular interactions with her mom during the week, Cordelia uses phone calls, FaceTime calls, texting, and social media to stay in touch — but her dad has started monitoring these conversations in a way that makes Cordelia uncomfortable. He seems envious of the relationship Cordelia has with Mae, and has become frustrated and a bit hostile. In an effort to continue communicating with Mae outside of Mark's prying eyes, Cordelia establishes a second set of social media accounts that her dad won't know about. The case examines issues of nonresidential parenting, privacy rules and privacy management, and social media use in families.

"Ugh! What a complete bummer!" Cordelia thought to herself as she hung up the phone with her mom Mae, feeling completely dissatisfied with their conversation. She isn't dissatisfied with her relationship with her mother—in fact, Cordelia and Mae have a great relationship. At 16 years old, Cordelia can honestly say that she is close to her mother and enjoys her company a great deal. While Mae can be strict when she needs to be, Cordelia is, for the most part, a well-behaved teenager. As a people-pleaser and an only child, Cordelia has what she would consider an easy, open relationship with her mom. There isn't much to hide in that relationship and she looks forward to the time she can spend talking and being with Mae. Her father, Mark, is a slightly different story.

Cordelia and Mark used to have a similarly close relationship. Of course, they didn't talk about certain things—like boys and makeup; she reserved those kinds of topics for conversations with her mother—but she and her dad both loved hockey and shared a great deal of the same interests including music, trying new foods, and marathon running. But while they have always been pretty close and have a history of sharing these interests and experiences together, Cordelia's relationship with her dad has been slowly declining over the past year and a half, starting right about the time of Mae and Mark's divorce. Cordelia did as well as could be expected when her parents announced that they were divorcing. It did not come as a surprise. Mark and Mae are what Cordelia's therapist used to refer to as a "high-conflict couple." They argued a lot and their arguments included yelling, name-calling, and criticism. Part of Cordelia was actually relieved when they announced their divorce, as she was hopeful that this would make it easier for them to be cordial with one another. In part, this was true, because Mae and Mark argue a lot less now than they used to. Cordelia is thankful for this, yet the divorce also brought about new challenges—Mae and Mark started to hash out their conflicts in new and creative ways, and much of that had to do with Cordelia by proxy.

For example, their visitation agreement was a point of contention. Mae and Mark split custody of Cordelia 50/50, but in terms of time spent in each home, she spent Monday afternoon through Friday morning at her father's house and Friday morning through Monday morning at her mother's house. Cordelia knew this was a somewhat "nontraditional" arrangement. All of her other friends with divorced parents spent the week living with their mothers, and the weekends (or in some cases, every other weekend) with their fathers. Sometimes people even asked her what was "wrong" with her mother. This always angered Cordelia because there was nothing "wrong" with her mom at all. Mae works long hours during the week, whereas Mark, who works from home, is around more during the week. It was Cordelia's understanding that this was the basis for the visitation agreement in her family, and from what she saw as a then 14-year-old girl, it was an easy agreement to make. Both of her parents had attorneys, and they had some other person (her mom told her he was a trained mediator) to help them negotiate the parameters of this agreement.

As she thinks about that period of time, Cordelia begins to feel a flood of familiar anxiety in her chest and stomach. While it was relatively easy for her to focus on the positive aspects of her parents not being married anymore, it was much more difficult for Cordelia to find the silver lining in not living with both her parents all the time. Her friends with divorced parents talked about having two of everything: two homes, two beds, two cats, two Christmases—you name it, they had two of them. Some of her friends talked about how great it was to have "double everything" and how they used it to their advantage to obtain more than they would if they only had one of everything, but none of this ever appealed to Cordelia. She didn't want two of anything, expect two parents, that she could have unlimited access to whenever she wanted.

When Cordelia was told about the final visitation agreement, she wasn't surprised by it. In many ways, it felt similar to how her life already was—she was used to seeing her father more during the week and then having mother-daughter time over the weekends because of her parents' work schedules. But back then, she still got to see her mom in the evenings and usually talked to her about her day before she went to bed, and Cordelia and her dad would go running in the mornings, short ones during the week and longer ones in the weekends. These patterns were changing now, and change made Cordelia anxious, especially when it came to changes in her relationships with her parents. As an only child, she didn't have a sibling to lean on during the transition, like many of her friends did. While she never forgot that Mae and Mark were her parents, not her siblings or friends, she still felt she could talk to them about most things and that they were there for her.

After her mom established a new residence in a charming little home across town, Cordelia and Mae worked on setting up her bedroom and decorating other parts of the house together to make it feel like their home. Her dad stayed in their family home, so there wasn't much to be done there. It felt different without her mom's things in the house, but most of the furniture and decorations stayed the same, so in many ways the house did not look any different, and Mark and Cordelia didn't do much with it together. It just was what it was. Cordelia and Mae also developed a schedule for when they would communicate with each other during the week. This helped to ease Cordelia's anxiety a little because she wanted to feel like she had access to both parents no matter what day of the week it was. Cordelia and her mom worked out a schedule for regular telephone and FaceTime calls throughout the week, and Mae was very good about responding to text messages throughout the day, even when she was at work. On the weekends, Cordelia had a similar arrangement with her dad. They had regular times they would call to "touch base," and if she ever needed her father she knew he was only a call or text away.

At the very start, Cordelia was hopeful that this arrangement would end up being okay for everyone, but soon that felt like a silly fantasy. It started with Mark asking a lot of questions about the time Cordelia spent with her mother: "What did you do?" "What is she up to?" "What does the inside of the house look like?" "Is she still hanging out with so and so?" "Is she dating anyone?" Then it spread to Mark trying to sit near Cordelia when she was on the phone with her mom during the week. Cordelia tried to counteract this by going into her room when she called Mae, but her dad always seemed to find an excuse to come into her bedroom—to put away laundry, or to check on batteries in her smoke detector, or just to see "what's up" because he "didn't know she was on the phone." Things quickly escalated to the point where Cordelia could no longer enjoy these phone calls because she knew her father was monitoring them, and then he would question her later about these interactions.

One time, after hanging up with her mom, she walked into the living room to find Mark seated in his chair, arms folded, and angry. He pointedly asked, "Why didn't you tell me you were having conflicts with your friends at school?" Cordelia was shocked. She had just been talking to her mom about some 'mean girls' stuff that was going on with the girls in her high school. She and Mae brainstormed some ways she could try to manage that conflict without getting sucked into it herself. In all honesty, this just wasn't the kind of thing she thought to talk to her father about. She loved him and told him lots of things, but some things felt like "mom's territory" and other things (like whether the Ducks were going to make the playoffs) were "dad's territory."

"I don't know," Cordelia responded, even though she did know. She just didn't want to tell her father that issues with her female friend group were things she would rather talk about with mom because mom gets it.

"You can talk to me about your problems, too, you know," Mark responded. "In fact, I am a better person to talk to than she is. She doesn't know the first thing about how to deal with conflicts; all she knows is how to start them." This felt like a punch to Cordelia's stomach. She was used to her parents saying mean things to one another, but she was not used to them saying things behind each other's backs to her, and the way Mark said "she" with so much disgust made her feel sad and protective of her mom. Soon a pattern developed of Mark asking questions, monitoring any mother-daughter communication that he could, and making rude remarks about Mae to Cordelia. He did not seem to monitor her communication with anyone else, just her mom. While Cordelia was thankful that she did not experience this weird behavior from her dad when she talked to or hung out with her friends, it also made her more upset that her dad seemed to be singling out her mom.

One day, Cordelia came home from school and her dad began to question her about a conversation she and her mom were having on Cordelia's Facebook wall about a viral reaction video. A blogger, that Mae and Cordelia both like, films himself watching people cooking and commenting on it. They share these videos back and forth and have seen some of them so much they have started to quote him as inside jokes. Cordelia was surprised by her dad's questions, because while she knew he had a Facebook account (and they were friends), he really never used it. He went through a "show me what this whole Facebook thing is about" phase that only lasted about a week. Her mother, though, was an avid user of social media. In fact, Cordelia not only interacted with her mom on Facebook, but they also used Twitter, Instagram, Snapchat, and a new app called TikTok to share pictures and videos, make jokes, and just stay in contact. This was already a pattern in their relationship before the divorce, but they started using the apps even more afterward, as it created an easy way for Cordelia to stay in contact with her mom during the week.

"How often are you Facebooking with your mother?" Mark asked.

"Umm… I'm not sure, really," Cordelia responded.

"Well, from the looks of this wall thing, it looks like it is quite frequent. You are supposed to be in school. Your mother is distracting you from your studies and God knows what kind of content people are sharing here. This is not appropriate."

Cordelia protested, "Dad, I have had a Facebook account for years—"

"Yes you have," Mark interrupted. "And if I remember correctly, it was your mother that helped you set all of that up. Isn't that right?"

"Well, yes," Cordelia said. "She did." Cordelia remembers this vividly. She had been talking about wanting her own social media accounts, and her mom agreed—as long as they set them up together, and her mom was able to access them. Cordelia found it annoying, but it's not like she had anything to hide, and she understood that her mother was just trying to protect her from "all the weirdos in cyberspace." It was at that time that her mom opened up her own social media accounts too, and started experimenting with them. They had been communicating on them ever since. This angry conversation about the Facebook wall was a real turning point for Cordelia and Mark. It felt like the "last straw" for Cordelia, and she decided something had to give.

Cordelia wanted to be able to communicate with her mother without her father eavesdropping, monitoring, or asking a bunch of questions. She did not think this was too much to ask. The next day after school, Cordelia went to the mall with her best friends Mariah and Kristi, and recounted the conversation with her father from the day before: "It is just not fair. I am 16 years old and this is my mother. My mother, for goodness sake! I should be able to talk to her about whatever I want, whenever I want, and I should be able to goof off with her on social media without getting the third degree about it. I don't even want to be around my father anymore because all he is doing is violating my privacy. I mean, I don't even have any privacy when it comes to my mom anymore unless I am actually with her and my dad isn't around. It is so lame!"

"Your dad is out of control," Mariah responded.

"Absolutely," Kristi agreed.

"I don't even know how you have put up with this for so long," added Mariah.

"Me neither," Cordelia agreed, "but I am done with it now. I need to do something because I need my privacy back. My relationship with mom isn't about my dad and he should not have access to that information about me. It is mine!"

Cordelia went home that night thinking about what she could do to preserve her ability to speak to her mother during the week. It was not enough to only have access to her during the weekends. The thought of just suspending conversations with her mother until Friday every week made Cordelia anxious; and, honestly, it also made her dislike her father, because it was an invasion of her privacy and it was pointless. Just because he cannot get along with her does not mean I am going to allow him to get in the way of my relationship, Cordelia thought to herself. So while she had never wanted two of anything, besides two parents, she decided if she was going to be able to communicate with her mother without her father's ever-watchful eye, she was going to start having two of some things, starting with two social media accounts.

That weekend when Cordelia was at her mom's house, she set up second Facebook, Twitter, and Instagram accounts. Because her father did not even know what TikTok was, at least not yet, she figured having only one account would be fine, at least for now. But Mark knows she is on the other three regularly, and he knows that Mae is too. Cordelia also had to explain this to her mother, which was a little bit tricky because she had not really told her mom the extent to which her father had been monitoring their communication and asking questions.

"Oh my God! Are you serious?" Mae exclaimed. "That's terrible! I cannot believe you have been feeling anxious about talking to me! I feel horrible and I am about ready to drive other there and have it out with him over this! He has always been envious of me. He is envious of me because of my relationship with you. He is envious about my job. He is angry that, unlike other women we know, I was able to move out and into a house without any financial support from him. He wants to be needed and it just burns him up that I don't need him, and I raised a daughter who doesn't need him either!"

Cordelia was not surprised by her mother's strong reaction. She had seen her mother react strongly to a variety of her father's behaviors for 16 years now. It was a little difficult for her to hear her mother say that her father was envious, but Cordelia had also been so angry at him and so confused about this behavior that she did not feel any urge to protect her dad. In fact, all she really cared about in that moment was getting her mom on board with her idea to create multiple social media accounts.

"I don't know about that," Mae said, "it feels dishonest and it is something else to manage. I can call my attorney and have her scare your dad out of monitoring our conversations—and not just via social media, but our telephone calls, and FaceTime chats as well!"

"No, mom, that is going to be so much drama, and it might make the whole thing worse. The last thing I need is for him to start actually going through my stuff or trying to make it harder for us to communicate. It will be just like having two holidays. It is just two different ways to be present on social media. I will continue to use the old accounts and I can give you, Mariah, and Kristi the information for the new ones. It will be a way for us to keep any real 'girl talk' private, and then we can goof off like we always do without dad trying to butt in. What do you say?" Cordelia pleaded with her mother.

"Well…" Mae hesitated for a moment, but the look on her daughter's face said it all. Cordelia was always prone to anxiety, ever since she was a little girl, and as her mother, she knew darn well that one way Cordelia coped with her anxiety was making sure she had access to her close family and friends if she needed reassurance or support. There really is no real downside to this, Mae thought to herself. "Okay," Mae finally agreed, "what are the usernames of the new accounts? I will friend and follow you right now."

Two months later, it had become routine for Cordelia to check ALL of her social media accounts each day. Her mother would still hop on to "like," "heart," and "retweet" things posted to her old accounts. They did not want Mark getting suspicious, and his social media behavior had only been increasing. He tried to comment on Cordelia's wall posts, and he posted pictures to his own accounts more regularly. Perhaps it was a way for him to reach out to her, but Cordelia didn't care. She didn't have much motivation to communicate with him on social media or otherwise. When she was at her mom's house, she no longer called her dad—she would just see him on Monday. She responded to his texts when he sent them, but that was about it. She might have two houses, but she really only had one home. Meanwhile, Cordelia actually liked having these second accounts. She was very selective about who knew about them. She was not going to allow her father to find out about them; it would blow the whole thing. This meant she restricted knowledge of these accounts to only her mom and her closest friends, and was explicit with all of them about her rules around this information.

"You can never, under any circumstances, talk about these accounts or even mention these accounts to anyone who is not already able to view them," Cordelia told her friend Kathy. Then Cordelia listed who those people were, by name, and asked, "Do you have any questions about this?"

"No," Kathy said. "Geez, your dad is weird. I cannot believe he is this crazy about you talking to your mom. It's your mom!"

"Oh trust me, I know," Cordelia replied. "But you know, another good thing about this is that I can also interact with guys on there and my dad doesn't know anything about it. That part is pretty cool. If my dad saw that I had been chatting with Kevin, he would have all these questions, and he would want to meet him, and I don't want him knowing anything about this. He lost access to my private life when he started acting like a psycho about me, mom, and some silly viral videos."

"Well, that is pretty great, as long as you are okay with your mom seeing that," Kathy said.

"Oh, for sure. My mom is cool and she isn't going to get crazy or embarrass me," Cordelia responded.

Of course, there was also some daily management of these accounts that Cordelia had to do that was annoying. Sometimes it was a matter of remembering on which account she posted certain things, other times it was a matter of having to log in using her laptop because her original logins were still set in all of the apps on her phone. This got really annoying sometimes because instead of just picking up her phone and checking things out, she had to get her laptop out, make sure her father wasn't close enough to her to see she was looking at accounts he did not recognize, and then post, comment, like, etc. Another unforeseen consequence of having these second accounts was concealing them from other people. Cordelia found she wanted more and more of her friends to have access to her new accounts, because in a lot of ways those were starting to feel like the "real" her. These were her true mediated presence, but the more people that she told, the harder it was for her to conceal from other friends. One day, between classes, her friend LaDonna approached her and asked, "So Cordelia, word is you have another Instagram account. Is that true?"

"Where on earth did you hear that?" Cordelia asked. Whoever told LaDonna is going to be in big trouble!, Cordelia thought to herself as she started going through her followers list in her mind and considered who might have violated her privacy rules in this way.

"Oh, I don't think that is the real question," LaDonna replied. "I think the real question is, is it true—and, if so, then why?" Cordelia froze. LaDonna was her friend, but not a close friend. And to make matters worse, LaDonna's mom knows Mark from a running club they both belong to. LaDonna is not someone Cordelia ever would have told about her drama with her father, and she never would have told her about those secondary accounts; but now she knows, and Cordelia had to say something.

"No, it's not true," Cordelia replied. She hated lying, but she did not know what else to do. She would rather lie to keep her secret than reveal it to someone she only casually hung out with. Cordelia hoped it was the right decision.

DISCUSSION QUESTIONS

1. How does Cordelia manage her mutually coordinated privacy rules around the creation of her second accounts? Is this effective? Why or why not? Is there something she could have done differently?
2. What risks does Cordelia take when she creates additional co-owners of her private information?
3. How does social media (and other mediated communication) complicate one's ability to conceal private information from certain parties?
4. Describe the boundary linkages that are created here and the boundary turbulence that results from these links.
5. How permeable would you say Cordelia's boundaries are around her private information? Did this lead to the boundary turbulence? If so, how? If not, why not?
6. How appropriate is it for Cordelia to keep these social media accounts from her father? Why do you feel that way?
7. What do you think Cordelia should do about her situation? How can she best manage this conflict?

SUGGESTED READINGS

Child, J. T., & Petronio, S. (2011). Unpacking the paradoxes of privacy in CMC relationships: The challenges of blogging and relational communication on the internet. In K. B. Wright & L. M. Webb (Eds.), *Computer-mediated communication in personal relationships* (pp. 21–40). New York, NY: Peter Lang.

Child, J. T., & Westermann, D. A. (2013). Let's be Facebook friends: Exploring parental Facebook friend requests from a communication privacy management (CPM) perspective. *Journal of Family Communication, 13*, 46–59. doi:10.1080/15267431.2012.742089

Kartch, F., & Timmerman, L. (2015). Nonresidential parenting and new media technologies: A double-edged sword. In C. Bruess (Ed.), *Family communication in the age of digital and social media* (pp. 447–468). New York, NY: Peter Lang.

Petronio, S. (1991). Communication boundary management: A theoretical model of managing disclosure of private information between marital couples. *Communication Theory, 1*, 311–335. doi:10.1111/j.1468-2885.1991.tb00023.x

Petronio, S. (2002). *Boundaries of privacy: Dialectics of disclosure*. Albany, NY: State University of New York Press.

Petronio, S. (2010). Communication privacy management theory: What do we know about family privacy regulation? *Journal of Family Theory and Review, 2*, 175–196. doi:10.1111/j.1756-2589.2010.00052.x

Petronio, S. (2013). Brief status report on communication privacy management theory. *Journal of Family Communication, 13*, 6–14. doi:10.1080/15267431.2013.743426

Petronio, S., & Bantz, C. (1991). Controlling the ramifications of disclosure: "Don't tell anybody, but...." *Journal of Language and Social Psychology, 10*, 263–269. doi:10.1177/0261927X91104003

Petronio, S., & Caughlin, J. P. (2006). Communication privacy management theory: Understanding families. In D. O. Braithwaite & L. A. Baxter (Eds.), *Engaging theories in family communication: Multiple perspectives* (pp. 35–49). Thousand Oaks, CA: Sage.

Rollie Rodriguez, S. (2014). "We'll only see parts of each other's lives:" The role of mundane talk in maintaining nonresidential parent-child relationships. *Journal of Social and Personal Relationships, 31*, 1134–1152. doi:10.1177/0265407514522898

Rollie, S. S. (2006). Nonresidential parent-child relationships: Overcoming the challenges of absence. In D. C. Kirkpatrick, S. Duck, & M. K. Foley (Eds.), *Relating difficulty: The processes of constructing and managing difficult interactions* (pp. 181–201). Mahwah, NJ: Erlbaum.

Serewicz, M. C. M. (2013). Introducing the special issue on communication privacy management theory and family privacy regulation. *Journal of Family Communication, 13*, 2–5. doi:10.1080/15267431.2013.743424

CHAPTER 8

Lost in Translation:
The Challenges of Intercultural Families

Anthony T. Machette – *University of Oklahoma*

Globalization and immigration have empowered individuals of different cultures to interact with one another more often than ever before (Mok, 1999). Consequently, there has been a growing trend of mixed culture relationships in the United States. In the year 2017, nearly 20% of newlyweds were married to someone of a different race or ethnicity (Livingston & Brown, 2017). Additionally, over 21% of married couple households have at least one foreign-born spouse (Larsen & Walters, 2013).

Scholars have been researching monocultural romantic relationships for decades (Burgoon, & Hale, 1984; Knowles, Manusov, & Crowley, 2015). Yet, it is imperative to identify the difference of cultures within a relationship as no two cultures are the same. The term culture has many definitions but "scholars agree that culture is pervasive in human life and governs people's behaviors" (Liu, Volcic, & Gallois, 2014, p. 57). For this case study, culture is defined as "shared practices and values between the people of a group" (Kaur & Noman, 2015, p. 1795).

Regardless of culture, every relationship experiences challenges (Thomas-Maddox & Blau, 2013). Yet, intercultural families deal with unique tensions in addition to the challenges of monocultural relationships. For example, most intercultural relationships consist of at least one partner speaking another language as well as their native language (Cools, 2006). Additionally, each member of the relationship brings "different viewpoints with regard to gender roles, values, disclosure, norms, traditions, and many other aspects" (Cools, 2006, p. 262). These differences in customs and traditions are often a source of destabilization within the growing number of intercultural marriages (Levkovitch, 1990). The young couple, Mung Yu and Ethan, are an example of this ever-increasing trend of cross-cultural relationships in the United States.

Mung Yu Lin was born in the Hunan Province in China. At age 16, she moved to the Fort Collins, Colorado to attend high school as an exchange student. During her senior year, Mung Yu decided that she wanted to obtain her college education in the United States as well. Her parents were very supportive and recommended that she start looking for colleges to attend.

To start her college career, Mung Yu enrolled in classes at St. Cloud Technical Community College in Minnesota. She didn't know much about Minnesota before moving there but soon fell in love with how friendly everyone was in her new city. After spending one year at the community college, Mung Yu decided to pursue a bachelor's degree at the University of Minnesota. It was at this university that Mung Yu would meet her future husband, Ethan Butler.

Ethan grew up in Peoria, Illinois. He always knew he wanted to go into business. His dad was a successful salesman for a local company specializing in automotive parts throughout the Midwest. Ethan was raised in a loving home with two parents who truly loved each other as well as their son. While things were never bad in Ethan's childhood, he always liked the idea of moving away for the college experience, freedom from his parents, and to escape his hometown.

To achieve this freedom, Ethan worked hard during his last couple of years in high school to earn himself the opportunity to choose from multiple colleges to attend. He was drawn to the University of Minnesota as it wasn't in the same state as his parents. This gave him the chance to be on his own.

Eventually, one fall semester, Mung Yu and Ethan walked in for the first day of their consumer behavior course. While they didn't initially sit together, they were randomly assigned to a group during the icebreakers on the first day of class. Ethan was fascinated by Mung Yu's perspective on marketing. She shared stories of how marketing is done differently in China compared to the United States.

The two often found themselves working together in class. They eventually became friends, relying on each other for help. English was Mung Yu's second language so Ethan would proofread Mung Yu's papers. Ethan was a business major in a psychology class so Mung Yu would share concepts and theories that she had learned from previous courses with him. After the semester finished, the two realized that they still wanted to hang out. This eventually led to them dating.

Mung Yu and Ethan began to realize challenges when they first started dating. For example, a few months into their relationship, Ethan began to notice that Mung Yu did not disclose her feelings much to him. Instead, she often just talked about trivial topics and allowed Ethan to talk about his feelings, his past, and his plans for the future. This behavior confused Ethan. He thought back to his past relationships and couldn't remember his ex-girlfriends being so reserved.

After noticing Mung Yu's tendencies, Ethan began to struggle with knowing if he wanted to self-disclose or keep some of his feelings to himself. He was afraid to say too much. He wondered if saying how he felt would push Mung Yu away. Ethan certainly didn't want to be seen as moving too fast. On the other hand, he wanted to tell Mung Yu how much he cared about her and that he saw a future with her.

What Ethan did not realize was that Mung Yu was observing similar challenges. Mung Yu was raised in China, a culture which does not expect individuals to express their feelings. In the United States, Ethan was taught to be expressive when he loves someone. Conversely, Mung Yu was raised with the understanding that if someone needs to express their deep emotional feelings, they do it rarely and in an indirect, nuanced way.

Mung Yu had been in the United States long enough to know that Americans were more direct with expressing their feelings than most Chinese. Even though she recognized this, she did not know how to handle it. She felt like Ethan kept telling her the same thing when he would express how he felt. She didn't know how to respond. When Ethan would say "I love you" multiple times a day, Mung Yu would question why he needed to keep reminding her. She already knew he loved her, but she didn't see the point in him telling her every day.

This challenge highlights the cultural difference between high-context and low-context cultures. Mung Yu was raised in a high-context culture where, "meaning is indirectly implied rather than directly stated" (Thomas-Maddox & Blau, 2013, p. 114). Ethan, on the other hand, was raised in a society that individuals are encouraged to be direct and explicit while saying exactly what is on their mind (Samovar, Porter, & McDaniel, 2010).

The biggest challenge for Mung Yu and Ethan was the attempt to find the best way to handle the involvement of Mung Yu's parents in the relationship. This is not uncommon for intercultural families. In fact, research has found that some of the most significant stressors for intercultural couples come in the form of in-laws and extended family (Graham, Moeai, & Shizuru, 1985).

Growing up in Illinois, Ethan was always surrounded by the notion that people married due to romantic love. However, in many countries around the world, including China, people marry for a variety of other reasons. In many cases, individuals marry because their parents have determined that a potential suitor would make a good spouse. Even with her parents still in China, Mung Yu's parents were extremely involved in her life, especially when compared to Ethan's parents, who were just a short flight away.

Parental influence does not end after the individual has been married. Instead, the parents are often very involved in decisions such as where the new couple will live, when the couple will start a family, and how the couple should spend their money. While her parents were very involved, they were also very supportive of Mung Yu and Ethan. For example, it was Mung Yu's parents who helped the young couple afford the down payment on their first home, and her parents were always willing to contribute financially if the pair needed it.

This involvement of his in-laws is an example of the difference between individualist and collectivist cultures. Growing up in the United States, an individualist society, Ethan always thought that once he turned 18, he was essentially free to make his own decisions. After he moved out of state for college, his parents had very little influence on his daily life and especially on how he handled his finances. Ethan openly appreciated the help he and Mung Yu received from her parents but struggled with the feeling that he was missing out on the feeling of seclusion within the relationship. He sometimes wondered if there would ever be a time that he and his wife would be able to make a significant life decision just between the two of them. Ethan often felt like when he married Mung Yu, he married her parents too.

The more serious Mung Yu and Ethan's relationship became, the more Ethan began to notice how much Mung Yu talked with her parents. Most evenings while Mung Yu and Ethan would finally get the opportunity to catch up, Mung Yu's parents would call. While this annoyed Ethan at times, he would try to remember that there was a time difference, with China being approximately 12 hours ahead of Minnesota. This meant that evenings and mornings were the only times that Mung Yu could talk with her parents. Ethan always attempted to be understanding but certainly felt that his in-laws were intruding into his alone time with Mung Yu.

Mung Yu would notice that Ethan seemed irritated that she was speaking with her parents in the evenings. She didn't understand why someone would be upset to see their partner being a good child. Filial piety was a cornerstone of Mung Yu's education and she could not comprehend what the issue was with her talking to her parents most nights. Mung Yu also didn't understand why Ethan would be uncomfortable when she would share details with them about the couple's daily life.

Mung Yu and Ethan were very different in their approaches to sharing aspects of their relationship with their parents. Mung Yu tended to reveal most of the details of their relationship with her parents. It is expected in many cultures, including in China, that children share most aspects of their life with their parents well after they have moved out. While many western cultures view getting married as starting your own family, cultures such as those in China view marriage as merely adding to the existing family. Therefore, Mung Yu didn't see any reason to stop being a daughter just because she started a relationship with Ethan.

Often the conversation would include plans for the upcoming week, how much their paychecks were, and if they had plans for getting married and having children together. Ethan, on the other hand, would speak with his parents occasionally, only about when they were going to visit next or to text a family member a happy birthday. He often didn't feel that there was anything in particular about his and Mung Yu's relationship that needed to be discussed with his family.

After graduating, Mung Yu and Ethan got married and settled down in the suburb of Eden Prairie, Minnesota. It was in this town that Ethan landed his dream job, hired by a marketing firm where he had interned during his last few semesters at the University of Minnesota. While both Mung Yu and Ethan were happy to have settled down and started a life together, relational tensions did not disappear.

Shortly after moving to Eden Prairie, Mung Yu and Ethan discovered they were expecting a child. During the pregnancy, both Mung Yu and Ethan recognized there were even more cultural differences that they hadn't expected. Later that year, the young couple welcomed their son, Thomas, into the world. The addition of Thomas was exciting for Mung Yu and Ethan.

The most significant difference and point of contention between the two was the expectation of Mung Yu's mother, Su Yen, that she would stay with the new parents for at least two weeks before Mung Yu was due to give birth and at least a month after Thomas was born. This idea immediately caused tension between Mung Yu and Ethan.

The practice of a grandmother moving in with new parents is standard practice in China. Traditionally, a new father would invite his mother to live with him and his wife to take care of the newborn baby. This allows the new mother to rest and the new father to continue to work on building a career and making money.

With Ethan being an American, his mother was not expected to move in for an extended period of time to help the new parents take care of Thomas. During the pregnancy, Ethan's mom, Anne, offered to fly up to Minnesota to help once Thomas was born. She was excited to help the young couple learn how to change diapers, feed Thomas, and teach them anything else that they didn't know about caring for a newborn. When Ethan explained that Mung Yu's mother was planning on moving in at the end of the pregnancy and staying with them for at least a month after Thomas was born, Anne was hurt.

Su Yen, however, was not attempting to step on anyone's toes. Instead, she was fulfilling her role as the mother of a new parent. Approximately two weeks before Thomas was born, Su Yen flew to Eden Prairie to move in with Mung Yu and Ethan. The moment she stepped foot into the young couple's house, she assumed all the duties of the home.

First, Su Yen began searching through the kitchen, looking for ingredients. She quickly made a list of supplies that Ethan needed to retrieve from the grocery. While Mung Yu was translating the list, Su Yen began to lecture Mung Yu about the importance of eating traditional meals while pregnant. Ethan was annoyed and was happy to get out of the house.

When Ethan returned home, he quickly noticed that the temperature in the house was set uncomfortably high. After unloading the groceries, he adjusted the thermostat to a more manageable temperature. At that moment, Su Yen pulled Ethan away from the thermostat and began lecturing Mung Yu that they need to keep the house warmer or else she and the baby will be sick. Being June in Minnesota, Ethan agreed to disagree.

In the days leading up to Thomas' birth, Ethan became increasingly frustrated. He felt that he had lost his home to his mother-in-law. While he was always understanding of Mung Yu's culture, he didn't want to forfeit his own. He often would vent to Mung Yu about her mother's behavior and her "random rules." Mung Yu would be defensive and tell him he needed to be more open-minded.

Once Thomas was born, the tension rose. Ethan expected that Su Yen would help with cooking and cleaning while Mung Yu and Ethan attended to their new son. Instead, Ethan soon discovered that the plan was for Su Yen to do all of the cooking, cleaning, and caring for Thomas. When Ethan would attempt to hold his son, Su Yen would watch over him and quickly take Thomas out of his arms. She also had rules for Mung Yu.

For example, she demanded that Mung Yu stay in bed for the first month after Thomas' birth. Mung Yu wasn't even supposed to get her hair wet until at least four weeks after giving birth. This is common in Chinese culture, but Ethan didn't care. He felt like Mung Yu was bailing on parenting while leaving him to continually battle with his mother-in-law with whom he didn't even speak the same language.

Su Yen also was very strict about Mung Yu's meals after Thomas was born. One day, on Ethan's way home from work, he stopped and got Mung Yu a pint of her favorite ice cream. Su Yen was distraught to see that Ethan brought this home for his wife. She began to lecture Mung Yu about the dangers of eating cold food within weeks of giving birth. To Su Yen, cold food would cause Mung Yu to not only get sick at the time but to stay unhealthy for the rest of her life.

The most frustrating of all of Su Yen's "rules" was one that Ethan could not understand. He noticed that Su Yen would continually worry about Thomas' belly button. Any time he had the opportunity to practice changing Thomas' diaper, Sun Yen would rush over and cover Thomas' belly button with a small towel. She, like many traditional Chinese, believed that leaving a baby's belly button uncovered would cause the child to become ill.

During Su Yen's lecture, she reminded Mung Yu and Ethan that they needed to be healthy. Su Yen explained that good health was vital for Mung Yu because she not only needed to take care of Thomas as he grew up but also take care of Su Yen and her husband when they got older. The idea of his in-laws permanently moving in with his young family made Ethan nervous about his future.

Ethan had imagined that over the next couple of decades, Thomas would grow up and move away to college. During that time, he assumed he would have earned a few promotions and be financially stable. Ethan imagined that after their son had moved away, he and Mung Yu could enjoy having the house to themselves again and be able to do whatever they wanted, whenever they wanted to. Having two in-laws moving in until their death threw a wrench into these plans.

During the six weeks that Su Yen was living with Mung Yu and Ethan, the young couple struggled. Ethan felt that he lost control of his life, with his mother-in-law having taken over. Mung Yu, on the other hand, could not understand why Ethan was being so ethnocentric. He knew she was Chinese, and she didn't understand why he suddenly was so surprised that her mom wanted to do things differently. Both Mung Yu and Ethan just wanted the other to be normal.

The combination of Thomas' birth and Su Yen's stay created a tension that Mung Yu and Ethan desperately needed to address. Mung Yu wanted to be sure that Thomas was raised with a strong Chinese influence. She trusted her mother and expected Su Yen to play a large role in Thomas' life.

Ethan agreed that Thomas should have strong Chinese roots but didn't want to sacrifice his privacy with Mung Yu and Thomas to get it. Ethan preferred that he and Mung Yu make the parenting decisions. He wanted both sets of grandparents to play a role in Thomas' life but also wanted them to respect that Thomas was ultimately his and Mung Yu's responsibility.

This was a tension that neither Mung Yu nor Ethan had ever expected to experience. Mung Yu felt that she needed to choose between her family and Ethan. Ethan, however, thought that he needed to convince Mung Yu to be with him instead of her parents. Once Thomas was born, both Mung Yu and Ethan leaned heavily on their cultural upbringings, thus creating a tension between both cultures.

This experience highlighted what was in store for Mung Yu and Ethan's young family. While every family has different expectations about specific topics, the differences in cultural expectations affected Mung Yu and Ethan's young family. From self-disclosure about the relationship to sharing their home with in-laws, the challenges that they faced were often compared to other, monocultural, families. Furthermore, the birth of Thomas reminded Mung Yu and Ethan that being in an intercultural family meant that their family would always be unique.

At times, Mung Yu struggled with understanding why their young family was so different from her best friends' families. Mung Yu had watched her Chinese friends, as well as her American friends, navigate life's biggest events with their young families without nearly half the struggles that she and Ethan experienced. When comparing her friends' families to hers and Ethan's, Mung Yu felt that those relationships were so ordinary in comparison. Sometimes she felt that Ethan "just didn't get it."

Mung Yu, Ethan, and Thomas are like any other family in many ways. They're navigating the complexities of creating a household. They're attempting to balance their needs and desires with those of their loved ones. Mung Yu, Ethan, and Thomas, however, are an intercultural family. This leads to unique challenges that families who come from the same culture do not face. As with any family, they will continually be navigating their relationships. Their added cultural elements will offer additional benefits as well as challenges.

DISCUSSION QUESTIONS

1. Do you think that intercultural families experience more challenges than mono-cultural families?
2. Do you think there are challenges unique to intercultural families?
3. Do you think certain cultures can coexist within families better than others?

REFERENCES

Burgoon, J. K., & Hale, J. L. (1984). The fundamental topoi of relational communication. *Communication Monographs, 51*(3), 193–214.

Cools, C. A. (2006). Relational communication in intercultural couples. *Language and Intercultural Communication, 6*(3–4), 262–274.

Graham, M. A., Moeai, J., & Shizuru, L. S. (1985). Intercultural marriages: An intrareligious perspective. *International Journal of Intercultural Relations, 9*(4), 427–434.

Kaur, A., & Noman, M. (2015). Exploring classroom practices in collectivist cultures through the lens of Hofstede's model. *The Qualitative Report, 20*(11), 1794–1811. Retrieved from http://nsuworks.nova.edu/tqr/vol20/iss11/7

Knowles, J. H., Manusov, V., & Crowley, J. (2015). Minding your matters: Predicting satisfaction, commitment, and conflict strategies from trait mindfulness. *Interpersona: An International Journal on Personal Relationships, 9*(1), 44–58.

Larsen, L. J., & Walters, N. P. (2013, September). Married-couple households by nativity status: 2011. Retrieved from https://www.census.gov/

Levkovitch, V. P. (1990). Marital relationships in binational families. *The Soviet Journal of Psychology, 11*, 26–37.

Liu, S., Volcic, Z., & Gallois, C. (2014). *Introducing intercultural communication: Global cultures and contexts*. Los Angeles, CA: Sage.

Livingston, G., & Brown, A. (2017, May 18). Intermarriage in the U.S. 50 years after Loving v. Virginia. Retrieved from http://pewresearch.org/

Mok, T. A. (1999). Asian American dating: Important factors in partner choice. *Cultural Diversity and Ethnic Minority Psychology, 5*(2), 103.

Samovar, L. A., Porter, R. E., & McDaniel, E. R. (2010). *Communication between cultures*. Boston, MA: Wadsworth.

Thomas-Maddox, C., & Blau, N. (2013). *Family communication: Relationship foundations*. Dubuque, IA: Kendall Hunt Publishing Company.

CHAPTER 9

Parenting Styles Across Generations and Use of Physical Punishment

Courtney Waite Miller – *Elmhurst College*

ABSTRACT

In this case study, grandparents are watching their grandsons while their parents are on vacation. The children do not react well to their grandparents' style of disciplining and misbehave. The grandparents respond with physical punishment, a reaction that upsets the children's parents and fractures family relationships.

WHILE THEIR PARENTS ARE AWAY, THE KIDS ARE AT PLAY

John and Stacy were eagerly awaiting their three-day vacation to celebrate their tenth anniversary. It would be their first time traveling as a couple since having children. John's dad and stepmom offered to stay with the boys while they went on the trip. They arrived early in the morning on the day John and Stacy left. Brandon and Zach were already awake and seemed apprehensive about their parents leaving. Zach was running around wildly, refusing to get dressed. Brandon was sulky and withdrawn. John warned Steve and Flora that the boys had been a handful recently.

"Don't hesitate to give them a time-out if they get out of control. It's better to stop it before it really gets going," John said.

"It's okay to take away a privilege," added Stacy. "If they really aren't listening, I take away screen time or dessert. Sometimes I send them to their rooms for a few minutes."

"Don't worry," Steve said. "You forget I raised John and his brother. We'll keep them busy at the pool and outside."

"And I raised two boys too. That's four between us!" Flora laughed.

After John and Stacy left, Flora cooked a big breakfast with the boys. She let them help make the pancake mix and asked Brandon to set the table. Brandon was not used to doing chores at home. His mom always did everything for him. He quietly did his best to set the table. When he finished, Steve gave him a high five. Zach wanted one too so Brandon reached over the table to Zach. He accidentally knocked over a plate of toast. Zach laughed and grabbed the toast, making a lot of crumbs.

Steve was irritated and smacked a spatula down on the table in front of Brandon. "We're not going to have this kind of messing around. I won't stand for this behavior," he yelled.

The loud slap scared the boys. Their parents never acted like this, especially about an accident. The boys were quiet during breakfast, wondering what these days without their parents were going to be like. When they finished eating, Steve told them to clean up the dishes and toast crumbs.

"My mom cleans up for us," Zach said.

Steve replied, "Not when I'm here. Get working."

Zach stayed in his seat while Brandon started to clean up. Brandon cleared the dishes and Flora put a bottle of 409 on the table for him. While no one was looking, Zach sprayed it all over the table and the floor. Zach thought, *What could it hurt? I never get to use this stuff and it smells good.*

On the way back to the table, Flora slipped in the spray. She caught herself before she fell, asking "What's on the floor?"

Zach laughed and pointed at the 409. Brandon joined in too. Steve was furious. He yelled at both boys and told them to go to their rooms for an hour.

"An hour?! Our parents say five or ten minutes, not an hour," Brandon whined.

"I don't care," Steve said. "Get up there before something worse happens to you."

The boys ran upstairs to their rooms. They were both in their own rooms for about 10 minutes when Zach quietly tiptoed into Brandon's room. They played with some Legos and were about to get out a game when Flora found Zach in Brandon's room. She called for Steve.

"I cannot believe you would disrespect us by not staying in your rooms like I told you to do. We were thinking of taking you to the pool today, but now we are staying home all day. You need to learn some respect," Steve yelled.

Flora added, "When my boys acted like this, they got a good spankin'. Maybe that is what you two need."

The boys were quiet for a second and then started laughing. She had to be kidding. No one had ever hit them or even threatened to do anything like that. *They wouldn't really hit us, would they?* Brandon started to worry as he abruptly quit laughing. The boys spent the rest of the day inside trying to entertain themselves.

"Mom would never make us stay home all day like this," Brandon said.

Zach agreed. "Not even Dad would have ruined a whole day! Good thing I have a baseball game tonight. At least we'll get outside then."

Flora made dinner before Zach's game. Stacy said the boys liked macaroni and cheese so Flora made it from scratch with two types of grated cheese and big noodles. She was hoping for a reset so they could all have a pleasant evening at Zach's game. "Dinnertime, kids! Wash your hands," she called.

"Wait, you just made our dinner? My mom always asks us what we want and *then* makes it. She doesn't *choose* for us!" Brandon complained.

"This isn't macaroni and cheese!" Zach cried. "What is this? My mom makes it from the Kraft box! I'm not eating this."

Flora gritted her teeth silently and thought: *What spoiled brats. They should be grateful for the food I cooked for them. I don't let my own grandchildren talk to me this way, let alone Steve's!*

Steve growled, "That is not how things work when we're here. Eat it or you'll go hungry tonight."

The boys ate a few bites begrudgingly. After dinner, they cleaned up as they were asked to. They learned from breakfast. Steve drove them to Zach's baseball game. As soon as they pulled up, Zach ran out to meet his team. He couldn't wait to get away from his grandparents. Steve set up the two camp chairs they had. One for him and one for Flora.

"Where am I going to sit?" Brandon asked.

"Sit on the cooler," Steve answered.

"No, my parents say not to sit on it and I want a seat for the game! My dad usually stands while he helps with the team and I sit in this seat."

"It's the cooler or nothing," Flora replied. "We're using the chairs."

Brandon grumbled under his breath and spent the next two hours roaming the park. He talked with a few people he knew and ate some snacks. *This is miserable. I cannot wait for my parents to get home*, he thought.

Even though Zach's team won and he played well, everyone was quiet on the ride home. The boys quickly showered and went to bed. They were ready for the day to be over. Maybe tomorrow would be better. Steve mentioned going on a bike trail nearby.

A NEW DAY

The boys woke up around 6:30 a.m. as they usually did. They went down to the kitchen hungry for breakfast. Steve and Flora were sleeping.

"Should we wake them up?" Zach wondered.

"No. We can get our own breakfasts. We'll have cereal." Brandon replied.

They boys served themselves cereal and milk, only spilling a few Cheerios. They finished eating while Steve and Flora were still asleep. Zach wanted some juice and tried to pour himself a glass. The bottle was too full for him to pour and he spilled a lot. Deep purple cranberry-grape juice ran off the counter top, on to the chair cushion and floor. Both boys quickly tried to clean up the mess. Just as they were getting the paper towels, Steve came downstairs. He took one look at the mess and began yelling.

"What in the world is this? Is this all you two do—make messes?"

"It was an accident," Brandon replied. "The container was too full."

"Then you should have waited for us!" Steve roared. "Clean this mess up!"

The boys did their best to wipe up the mess, but the juice was sticky and hard to clean. Brandon thought: *We were trying to take care of ourselves. You were sleeping and now you're mad at us for making a mess? It was only an accident.*

"This isn't good enough! I want this floor and countertop to sparkle!" Steve bellowed.

Flora came downstairs and surveyed the mess. She didn't sleep well the night before and wasn't looking forward to another day with Steve's grandsons.

"Get over here and help them clean up this mess," Steve barked at her.

Brandon could not believe how Steve was treating everyone. His parents never acted like this. "Why do you have to be such a jerk?" he said to Steve.

That was it. Steve lost his temper and flew at Brandon. "You've been just begging for a spanking since the minute your parents left. I've had it."

Brandon quickly scampered to his room. He slammed the door and locked it before Steve made it upstairs.

"Good! You can just stay in there all day for all I care," Steve yelled.

Zach was shocked but it was also kind of funny to watch Grandpa chase Brandon. *Would they really hit us? What would my parents say?* he thought. "My parents don't hit us. I'm calling my mom."

He ran to get the phone, but Flora grabbed him roughly by the arm. "Oh no, you don't! You're not calling your parents. They are trying to get a break from you!" she screamed as she dug her fingernails into Zach's arm.

"Ouch! You're hurting me!" Zach cried.

Flora replied angrily. "Good, maybe that will teach you something."

Once again, the boys spent the whole day at home. No bike trail. They played a few games of Uno and Monopoly to pass the time. They quietly ate the chicken Flora cooked for dinner and went to bed without incident. Zach's arm hurt and Brandon knew he had narrowly escaped a spanking.

While the kids were asleep Steve said to Flora, "We taught them something. They went to bed easily. No trouble at dinner either. John and Stacy need to crack down on these kids. They're spoiled rotten."

"I agree," Flora said. "I really would like to see that bike trail. Can we try to make it there tomorrow? It's not fun for us to stay home all day either." They went to bed tired, but relieved thinking they were getting somewhere with the boys.

ONE LAST CHANCE

The next morning Steve and Flora set their alarm so they were in the kitchen when the boys came downstairs. They had a peaceful breakfast and the boys cleaned up the dishes without being asked.

"Let's get ready to go to the bike trail," Flora said brightly.

The boys were thrilled and got dressed quickly. They loved riding bikes and couldn't wait to race down the nice smooth path. On the way to the bike trail, Steve laid out the rules.

"You ride behind me and Flora. No racing and no passing or we will go home."

The boys agreed. They got on their bikes excitedly the minute they arrived. They started out slowly biking behind Steve and Flora, but they really wanted to go fast like they usually did. "Go for it, pass 'em," Zach said to Brandon.

"OK, here we go!" Brandon called.

The boys whizzed past Steve and Flora. They cheered and rode even faster, narrowing missing another rider. A lady with a baby stroller quickly stepped off the path and out of their way.

"Stop this instant!" Steve yelled down the path.

Brandon and Zach acted like they didn't hear Steve and kept riding. When they were tired, they stopped to play in a water fountain. Steve and Flora found them soaking wet and having a wonderful time. This incensed Steve. "We're going home *right now*," Steve snarled. "That was dangerous and you're going to learn never to do that again."

The boys walked their bikes to the minivan. Steve loaded up the bikes and then gave Brandon a hard slap on his bottom. Before Zach knew what was happening, Steve slapped him too.

"Ow, that hurt!" Zach cried.

"My parents are going to be so mad at you," Brandon added.

"Get in the car and shut up!" Steve roared.

They rode home in silence. The boys were stunned and afraid. They didn't know they would get in so much trouble just for trying to have fun on their bikes. *What's the point of riding if you can't go fast?* Zach wondered. Brandon worried that he would be in trouble with his parents now too. He promised to be good while they were gone. They were coming home this evening after dinner and it couldn't be soon enough for anyone.

HOMECOMING

John and Stacy had a wonderful time on their trip. They heard little from Steve and Flora while they were away. Stacy worried things were not going well and texted Steve several times. Steve replied that everyone was fine and texted a few pictures. When they arrived home, Stacy ran inside. She was so excited to see the boys and realized how much she missed them. Zach came tearing down the stairs to greet her.

"They were so mean to us," he whispered.

Stacy noticed Brandon coming out from under the table where he had been hiding. He hugged Stacy tight.

"They were mean to you? I've known them more than 10 years and they've never been mean," Stacy said.

"They spanked us and Flora grabbed me so hard I have scratches on my arm," Zach said.

Brandon nodded in agreement. Stacy was speechless. It couldn't be. John heard part of the conversation as he came in behind Stacy with the luggage. He couldn't believe what he was hearing. By now, Steve was downstairs too and Flora was coming up from the basement with tears in her eyes.

John asked, "Dad, did you spank them?"

"Yes, we did. And it really seemed to help their behavior," Steve responded.

Stacy was so shocked and angry that it took her a moment to speak. She calmly found a way to say, "It's clear this did not go well. We do not believe in spanking our children and are very upset you hurt them. I would like you to leave our home."

"And do not come back tomorrow to celebrate my birthday," John added.

"They were so disrespectful to us," Flora said through tears.

"We're sorry they did not behave, but we do not hit our children," John said. "These are good kids. They've never been in trouble at school, practice, or camp. I cannot understand why they behaved this poorly for you. Why didn't you call us?"

AFTERMATH

Steve and Flora left John and Stacy's home surprised at John and Stacy's reaction. *I spanked John and so did his mother. He turned out fine. What's wrong with it?* Steve wondered. After they left, Zach showed his parents his arm. There were bruises and small half-moon shaped cuts on it. It broke Stacy's heart to see these marks on her child. This was bordering on child abuse for her. It was a lot to process and difficult for her to handle. She truly didn't know what to say.

By now it was past the boys' bedtime. "We are so sorry they hurt you. They should not have done that. Let's go to bed now and we will talk about all of this in the morning, including your behavior," Stacy said.

The boys went to bed and John and Stacy tried to figure out what to do. "Certainly they were not perfect and needed some discipline," John said.

"But this? What gives them the right to hurt our children?" Stacy replied.

"And Flora is not even their grandmother. My mom spanked me growing up, but she would never spank Brandon and Zach. I'm so sorry they did this."

"I'm just still so shocked. This is going to take me a long time to get over, John. I'm going to need some space from your dad and Flora."

"I know. We'll talk with the kids tomorrow and figure out what to do. So much for our relaxing vacation!" John added sarcastically.

In the morning, the boys described their days with Steve and Flora. Nothing they did seemed too terrible. "I never want to see Flora again," Zach said as he looked at his arm.

As a family, they decided they would not see Steve and Flora for a while. John told the boys he was disappointed in how they behaved while they were out of town. John and Stacy thought about additional punishments for the boys but decided they had been through enough. They felt guilty about leaving them with Steve and Flora, but they never thought something like this would happen.

Several weeks later Flora called asking if the four adults could talk. She sounded genuinely sorry for hurting the boys. Steve was indignant and putting all of the blame on Brandon and Zach for misbehaving. "I will apologize to them but I want them to apologize to me first," he said.

"Dad, we trusted you with our kids. We never thought you would hit them. We're especially upset that Flora scratched Zach," John said.

The called ended without a resolution. "He's not sorry," Stacy said. "I really don't know how to move forward with this."

"I know, he's not. He still thinks what he did was right. I want to send him a column from the Trib about corporal punishment and how wrong it is (Stevens, 2018). There's a bunch of studies on it (Gershoff & Grogan-Kaylor, 2016)."

"I don't even know if he would understand that, John. He's pretty set in his ways and for many in his generation, it's acceptable to spank children. Times have changed and it's different where we live. I certainly hope the boys don't tell anyone at summer camp. Someone might call DCFS after hearing this story."

"You're right. We all just need more space from each other. The boys need to be ready to see them again and feel safe being around them too. We'll certainly never leave them alone with my dad and Flora, not even for a minute. I am not going to force the boys to apologize. And I will tell them not to talk about this outside of the house."

EPILOGUE

Over a year went by and Brandon and Zach did not interact at all with Steve and Flora. John and Stacy saw Steve once while visiting a relative. John and Stacy were polite but guarded and said as little as possible to him. They were relieved Flora stayed home. It seems that the relationship will never be the same again.

DISCUSSION QUESTIONS

1. Using Fitzpatrick and Ritchie's (1994) four types of families, what type of family most accurately describes the Smiths? Why did you select this type?
2. What parenting style does Stacy use? What about John? Refer to Baumrind's (1966) parenting styles, if applicable.
3. What parenting style do Steve and Flora use? How do you think this affects Brandon and Zach's behavior?
4. What role does power play in this situation?
5. How does Steve's marriage to Flora affect John, even as an adult?
6. How is systems theory evident in this example?
7. Do you consider what Steve and Flora did to be physical abuse? Or discipline?

FOR FURTHER THOUGHT

1. How would you feel if you were John and Stacy? Would you be able to forgive and forget?
2. How would you feel if you were Steve and Flora? Do you think they have a right to be upset with John, Stacy, and the boys?
3. What do you think about the boys' behavior? Would you parent them differently?
4. What is your view on physical punishment? Would you spank your children?

REFERENCES

Baumrind, D. (1966). Effects of authoritative parental control on behavior. *Child Development*, *37*, 887–907.

Fitzpatrick, M. A., & Ritchie, L. D. (1994). Communication schemata within the family: Multiple perspectives on family interaction. *Human Communication Research*, *20*(3), 275–301.

Gershoff, E. T., & Grogan-Kaylor, A. (2016). Spanking and child outcomes: Old controversies and new meta-analyses. *Journal of Family Psychology*, *30*(4), 453–469. doi:10.1037/fam0000191

Stevens, H. (2018, January 14). Nothing wrong with spanking? Think again. *The Chicago Tribune*, Section 6, 3.

CHAPTER 10

Treasure or Trouble: The Impact of Inherited Artifacts on Family Communication[*]

Amy M. Smith – *Salem State University*

ABSTRACT

This case study examines family artifacts as communicative of family history. I am particularly interested in determining the positionality of the artifact: Does the artifact tell the family story, or does it become the story? Using autoethnography, narrative inheritance, memory, and family story to investigate inherited artifacts passed on in my own family, this case study uses treasured family pieces as a pathway of communicating family narrative and identity. This case study follows the trail of two inherited artifacts within my own family: an antique table passed from my great-grandmother to my paternal grandmother to me, and various china pieces once belonging to my great-grandmother that are now in the possession of two cousins-once-removed. The table works to shape the recent family communication, as it represents a source of tension between my uncle and I over the division of my grandmother's possessions upon her death. The China tells a more distant story that shapes our global and extended family narrative, reaching back to loss during the Great Depression and coming full circle back into our family's possession in the mid-2000s.

[*]An earlier version of this research was presented at the Third International Congress of Qualitative Inquiry.

When I was young, maybe around 10 or 12, my grandmother threw a party on New Years' Day. School vacation schedules being what they were, I had to catch a flight home in the middle of that party. My grandmother decided to accompany my father and I to the airport, leaving family and friends behind at her home to carry on with the party. My aunt and her friends thought it would be a funny practical joke to "tag" furniture and other household items with their names, indicating what they might like when my grandmother died. I vividly remember how angry my grandmother was at this joke. She was appalled at the "poor judgement" (her words) these women showed and said she felt like they were just waiting for her to die so they could have her belongings. Further exacerbating the issue was that most of the women involved were not members of our immediate family and weren't in consideration to inherit anything from my grandmother. Though it would be another 20 years before my grandmother's death, this story stuck with me and I was always mindful of the ways I expressed appreciation for her belongings or asked about their origin. In their research on memory deAnda and Geist-Martin (2018) write about the ways autobiographical memories are useful to understanding familial relationships and pathways of communication.

Many years later, when I was in graduate school, a guest in my home told me, "You have too much nice stuff to be a graduate student." I respond by explaining that my grandmother's then-recent death left me with many of her belongings. I offered this explanation in part because I was proud to be the owner of such fine pieces, and I understood the cultural and social meaning behind them. They indicated that I was loved enough by my grandmother to be entrusted with her treasured valuables upon her death. These family artifacts tell other people that I am viewed as a responsible and valued member within my family. And they let people in my social circle know that I place an appropriate amount of importance on family and that I am able to understand the cultural significance placed on "family."

"Where is my grandmother's table?" For me, this question conjures several images. The speaker, my grandmother, her mother, the table itself. It is a small end table, round with intricate details, the outer ridge reminiscent of a piecrust. Because of this feature I have always called it "the pie table." The base sits atop three legs, each with their own detailed carvings. The table feet are traditional "ball and claw" style. The table originally belonged to my great-grandmother. It was passed to my grandmother upon her mother's death, and ultimately passed on to me after my grandmother died.

The question regarding the table's whereabouts seems harmless—a simple query into the location of an object. Nothing about this question is simple, however. The asker of the question, my first cousin once removed, has a vested interest in what happens to this table. My family culture is such that we value our inherited and antique artifacts and keep a close account of where the significant pieces end up. She, my first cousin once removed, would be my father's cousin. Her grandmother is my great-grandmother, the original owner of the table. The question, asked during a time of transition just after the death of my grandmother (her aunt), is many layers deep.

Curiosity is surely present but is not her only motivation for asking. She is also looking to protect my interests in the division of my grandmother's assets. My grandparents had two children, my father and my uncle. My grandmother outlived both her husband and my father, leaving her possessions to my uncle and I to divide equally. However, my uncle and I did not agree on what it would mean to be an equal division, leaving the two of us with heated discussions and angry words. Word of our inability to agree reached the larger branches of the family tree, prompting concern over the disagreement and lack of family harmony. The pie table was known to be one of my grandmother's prized possessions and there was a lot of curiosity from family members wondering who would end up with it in the division of things.

The story of how the table actually ended up in my possession is considerably longer and more drawn-out than is relevant to the overall story. I want to tell this story to the fullest and yet I also feel bound to maintain some sense of familial privacy (Petronio, 2002). Although the ethics of family communication during periods of grief, stress, and mourning are not the focus of this text, the pie table story is further complicated by the fact that at various points toward the end of her life my grandmother "promised" the table to both my uncle and I. My focus here, however, is to examine family artifacts as communicative of family history. My aim is to better understand the way that my grandmother's artifacts become representative of her life, her position in the family, and the cultural value ascribed to the artifacts by other family members. We all have our own family stories, many of which are linked to family artifacts. It is important to recognize these stories as markers of family identity and communication practices. Bochner, Ellis, and Tillman-Healy (1999), examine this when they state:

> We are born into a world of stories. Our births mark the beginning of a distinctive story in which each of us assumes a leading part. Our deaths end our unique stories, which live on in the minds and hearts of our survivors. Between birth and death, we rely on stories circulating through our culture to make sense of our everyday lives and guide our actions. Much of who we are and what we do originates in the tales passed down to us and the stories we take on as our own.

Traditionally speaking, items that are inherited are often domestic, and the domestic sphere is often associated with the feminine. With the exception of jewelry, clothes, and tools, most family artifacts not only come from the home, but are also objects associated with women's everyday use. Items such as furniture, china, glassware, silverware, linens, and cookware are often coveted items when a family member dies. Many times these objects come with their own story, one that chronicles how the item came into possession, or a story about a particular time the item was used. Sometimes the story is simply about how much it was loved by the deceased. The stories surrounding these objects follow the objects to their new homes, bringing with them the memory of the previous owner.

However, these stories (and objects) are often relegated to the private lives of families. Women's stories and voices have consistently been ignored and devalued in our culture, contributing to the overvaluation of all things masculine. Much like the domestic items passed along in families, the stories of women have maintained a space only in the private sphere, rarely in the public. By examining such stories through the meaning inscribed to familial artifacts, I believe a space will be created to better appreciate the lives of women, specifically their work within the domestic sphere.

In his text chronicling his own family story, Goodall (2005) introduces the term *narrative inheritance*. He states:

> I use this term to describe the afterlives of the sentences used to spell out the life stories of those who came before us. What we inherit narratively from our fore-bearers provides us with a framework for understanding our identity through theirs. It helps us see our life grammar and working logic as an extension of, or a rebellion against, the way we story how they lived and thought about things, and it allows us to explain to others where we come from and how we were raised in the continuing context of what it all means. We are fundamentally *homo narrans*—humans as storytellers—and a well-told story brings with it a sense of fulfillment and of completion.

Sometimes, however, the story is incomplete, and it is left to us to finish the unfinished family business. Often, it may be impossible to complete the story, as those with the answers have already come and gone. Ellis (2008) asks if we really do need to know the stories when it involves sharing secrets. This gives me pause, as I know that my grandmother was an intensely private person. And yet I am compelled to share some small part of her story with the world, some fraction of our connection to one another. Hocker (2010) writes about similar struggles and asks who this work is for, saying "I now see that it is hard for me to distinguish the line of separation: Is this work for me, as it helps me clarify my identity, or is (sic) for the ancestors whose narrative lines have broken?" (p. 865).

I have some questions about this pie table, my inherited artifact. Aside from its beauty, what is it that made it so special to my grandmother? There is a second table, similar in style and age, which also belonged to my great-grandmother. That table was passed down to my great-aunt (my grandmother's sister), then to her daughter, and ultimately to her daughter's children. While it is not an exact match to the one I have, it is pretty close in size, shape, wood stain, and craftsmanship. I sometimes wonder if they were purchased together. While there were two tables, there were four children (my grandmother and her three siblings), leaving me to wonder what artifacts the other two children received. Were they of equal value within the family? Was the dividing of family heirlooms as fraught with tension for them as it was for my uncle and I? And this one may seem odd, but I wonder if the size and portability of these two tables is one of the aspects that made them so special to their previous owners?

My grandmother was 11 years old when the Great Depression began in the United States. As the story goes, she and her three siblings, along with their parents, were home-less for a period of time after her father lost his job. During this time of difficulty, my great-grandmother entrusted her most valued possessions to her sister, one of the few peo-ple in our family who was able to keep her home. My grandmother and her immediate family did what they had to for survival, often relying on the kindness of friends and family to sustain themselves. Once the economy began to stabilize, the family was able to recover and begin to rebuild. When my great-grandmother was able to reestablish her household, she contacted her sister to reclaim her most treasured possessions.

Unexpectedly, her sister was unwilling to return many of these items and instead claimed that they rightfully belonged to her, offering a variety of reasons why she believed that to be true. My great-grandmother was able to retrieve a few items from her sister, but many of them were lost to her forever. The items her sister kept were eventually passed on to her only daughter (my grandmother's cousin) upon her death. That daughter never married or had children and in her old age relied upon her younger cousins (the granddaughters of my great-grandmother, or my father's cousins) for care, transportation, and household help. Because of the close relationship they shared, especially late in her life, these cousins were the ones to clean out her home upon her death. As there was no one left on that side of the family to inherit her belongings, many of them went to her cousins and their families. Ultimately this meant that my great-grandmother's belongings, stolen by her sister in the 1930s, are now back with the rightful descendants, her granddaughters.

These family stories are just two that are passed along throughout my extended family, and as I hope is clear, I know there are some key parts missing from each of them. There are gaps in memory and knowledge of all the people involved. Gone is the chance to ask some of those directly impacted, and what remains are the ideas and values these stories represent. Hearing the story of my grandmother's childhood experience during the Great Depression was incredibly illuminating to me. Although I knew that all my grandparents had survived the Great Depression, it was never something my paternal grandmother spoke of. Hearing about the struggle that she, her siblings, and parents went through helped me come to know and understand her better. It now made sense to me why she was constantly squirreling money away, "Just in case." Further, the relationship between her mother and her aunt, and the betrayal that came with it, allowed me to better understand why my grandmother didn't ever trust anyone completely, including those of us so closely connected to her. I am sure that witnessing her aunt steal her mother's most valued possessions had quite an impact on her, possibly leaving her to believe that no one was trustworthy, not even those with whom you share blood.

This newfound insight into the life of my grandmother would not have been available to me had my family not been discussing particular artifacts. It was told to me in a way that made it seem as if it was something that everyone knew, something that was discussed regularly. I was 32 years old when I first heard this story. My grandmother had just died so I never had an opportunity to ask her about these specific stories. McNay (2009) writes "absent memories become family secrets, known to some members of the family, not known to other members, and often, intuited by still others" (p. 1179). No matter how or when I came to the information, however, it completely altered my concept and understanding of my grandmother. Further, it allowed me to better understand her communication patterns, as well as how those patterns affected not only my own communication style but also my understanding of my "place" within the family structure. Poulos (2006) discusses a similar situation when he recounts the story of his uncle's death, and the impact it had on him as a young boy. Trujillo (2004) also discusses the ways his family communication patterns were altered by his grandmother's willingness to share pieces of her story, while keeping others secret. The differences between these stories, mine and the others, are vast. But in each story the researcher comes to terms with pieces of their own family puzzle. No matter what those pieces are, each of us is better able to place them into her or his own private puzzle, triumphant at being one step closer to solving the "narrative inheritance" mystery.

"Writing is not an innocent practice," says Denzin (1999, p. 568). As I share this case study with you, I am aware of my obligation to be as accurate and truthful as possible, while still protecting the cast of "characters" that own the stories I am sharing. Giorgio writes, "To write autoethnographically—about self in culture—is to reveal the hidden, denied, and the wished for. When we write we become vulnerable to others' readings of our words and lived experiences" (2017, p. 130). With that in mind, I would like to revisit my original question regarding the positionality of this artifact. Does the artifact tell the family story, or does it become the story? I would argue that it does neither, at least not in totality. While the table does tell *a* family story, I do not believe it tells *the* family story. Nor does it become the story. One is not able to obtain the story simply by looking at or touching the table. One must come to this family story through an understanding of both the people, the artifacts, and the inherited narratives involved. The story lies in how those things became entwined, how each became representative of the other. Having a better understanding of family narrative(s) and communication is critical to scholars of society and culture, as family is the portal through which members of society are introduced to that culture. Our family origins, family artifacts, and family narrative become the foundation on which we grow and function in the world.

DISCUSSION QUESTIONS

1. What family artifacts are you aware of in your own family? What are the stories that accompany the items?
2. When thinking about these artifacts does the artifact tell the family story, or does it become the story?
3. What is your role in these stories and how does it help you better understand your place within the family culture/structure?
4. Are the stories tied to these inherited artifacts more skewed to the masculine or feminine realm? Why do you think so?
5. How will you work to complete the story of your narrative inheritance?

REFERENCES

Bochner, A. P., Ellis, C., & Tillman-Healy, L. (1999). Relationships as stories. In S. Duck (Ed.), *Personal relationships: Theory, research and interventions* (pp. 307–324). New York, NY: John Wiley & Sons Ltd.

deAnda, C., & Geist-Martin, P. (2018). Memory as insight: Navigating the complexities of generational mother-daughter relationships. *Qualitative Inquiry, 24,* 403–412.

Denzin, N. (1999). Two-stepping in the '90s. *Qualitative Inquiry, 5,* 568–572.

Ellis, C. (2008). Do we need to know? *Qualitative Inquiry, 14,* 1314–1320.

Giorgio, G. A. (2017). Family feuds are forever: A writing story. *Qualitative Inquiry, 23,* 130–133.

Goodall, H. L., Jr. (2005). Narrative inheritance: A nuclear family with toxic secrets. *Qualitative Inquiry, 11,* 492–513.

Hocker, J. (2010). It's all come down to me: meaning making with family artifacts. *Qualitative Inquiry, 16,* 863–870.

McNay, M. (2009). Absent memory, family secrets, narrative inheritance. *Qualitative Inquiry, 15,* 1178–1188.

Petronio, S. (2002). *Boundaries of privacy: Dialectics of disclosure.* Albany, NY: State University of New York Press.

Poulos, C. N. (2006). The ties that bind us, the shadows that separate us: Life and death, shadow and (dream) story. *Qualitative Inquiry, 12,* 96–117.

Trujillo, N. (2004). *In search of Naunny's grave: Age, class, gender, and ethnicity in an American family.* Walnut Creek, CA: AltaMira Press.

CHAPTER 11

Mommin' Ain't Easy: Conforming to Societal Expectations on Facebook and in Real Life

Tennley A. Vik – *University of Nevada Reno*
Jocelyn M. DeGroot – *Southern Illinois University Edwardsville*

ABSTRACT

Goffman's dramaturgical theory focuses on how we perform in our daily lives, guiding our expectations and disciplining our actions. We utilize back stage areas (private spaces) and front stage areas (public spaces) in these performances. This case study explores how mothers engage in the difficult work of motherhood while portraying themselves as "the perfect mother." This performance includes completing the invisible labor of motherhood (contained within the back stage area) as well as recognizing social media as a new front stage area in which to perform motherhood.

CASE STUDY

Work–life balance is often discussed when talking about how we as humans exist within organizations; however, the focus is usually not gendered in nature. To avoid this focus means that we are not examining how women's lives have changed as more women have shifted from working in the home to working within organizations. When scholars consider the workload of domestic responsibilities, we are able to reflect on how work–life balance may be more difficult for women to achieve than men. Research from as early as the 80s points to an uneven distribution of household work and household responsibilities (Berk, 1985; Huber & Spitze, 1983). Not surprisingly, women engage in more household labor and domestic work than their male significant others. Although there is some evidence that the work may be shifting burdens of household labor to both parents, it appears that the mother still assumes the vast majority of household labor (Bittman & Wajcman, 2000). These domestic responsibilities are not limited, but include caring for children, cleaning homes, doing dishes, cooking, and doing laundry.

Goffman (1959) illuminates his theory, dramaturgy, in his book *The Presentation of Self in Everyday Life*, by defining five ways in which "life is like drama." These include: (1) actors (the people involved in the interaction), (2) scene (the situation/context of the interaction), (3) maintaining front stage (the performance that other people see), (4) maintaining back stage (the performance that other people do not see), and (5) script (the norms and expectations for the exchange). These five suppositions provide a foundation for us to use dramaturgy to explain everyday interactions (and performances). Other scholars have written extensively about how dramaturgy plays out in our everyday experiences. For example, Ellingson (2005) describes her observations of medical professionals and patients in a cancer clinic. Ellingson describes how medical providers (doctors, nurses, social workers, pharmacists etc.) use front stage spaces (such as exam rooms) to discuss private matters with the patient, but they use backstage spaces (such as hallways and nurses stations) to talk about the patient and different ways the other providers on the team can help reinforce messages or provide the patient with better care. In this way, we all experience dramaturgy. We are all actors existing in the world—scenes unfold as we move from space to space and interaction to interaction. We have private spaces (back stage) and public spaces (front stage), and we are expected to negotiate within the social expectations/norms of the situation and interaction (script). We learn over time how to navigate these interactions and what the social implications are for violating expectations and reinforcing expectations.

The following vignettes emphasize the invisible work of mothers as well as how motherhood is performed in online and face-to-face interactions. The focus is on Goffman's dramaturgical theory and understanding how performance guides our expectations and disciplines our actions (i.e., mothers are only able to show the positive things they do with their children and for their children, particularly online, creating a myth of what it actually means to exist as a mother).

DOING IT ALL, AND NOBODY NOTICES

"What did you do today?" asked Drew as he set down his briefcase and threw his coat across a chair.

"What *didn't* I do today?" thought Nessa. She ran through the day in her head: *I fed the kids breakfast, got Jake to school, went grocery shopping, threw in a load of laundry, put dinner in the crock pot, scheduled a time for pest control to come get rid of the moles in the backyard, finally got Parker down for a nap when the cable guy rang the doorbell and woke him, texted Gabby the babysitter so we could go out for dinner next week, ordered a birthday gift for Drew's mom, picked up Jake from school and took him to karate, and then straightened up the living room before sitting down to help Jake with homework.* Nessa glared at Drew's briefcase and coat. And now she was going to be responsible for hanging up Drew's coat and putting away his briefcase so the dog didn't chew on them. Her work was never done. "We were busy all day," she finally replied.

"I bet it's nice to hang out at home and spend time with the kids," Drew commented. It was an innocuous comment, but it always made Nessa silently seethe with anger.

Nessa stared at Drew. It *was* nice that she got to spend time with her children, but all of the additional, unseen labor required to run the house was overwhelming. Making doctors' appointments, remembering birthdays, signing permission slips, knowing that the shampoo is going to run out soon, swapping pants for shorts in the kids' dressers when it began to get chilly, and keeping track of everyone's schedules were all her responsibility. Yet, no one notices these tasks unless they fail to get accomplished in a timely fashion. Before Nessa could respond, Drew added, "Oh, also change of plans. I have to travel next week for work, so can we do our date night tomorrow?"

Nessa's mouth fell open. *Does he have any idea what it's like to find a babysitter on such short notice?* "I'll text Gabby to see if she's available."

Drew smiled. He figured it wouldn't be a problem.

"Maybe I'll also see if Gabby has a friend who cleans houses and picks up groceries, and schedules appointments…" muttered Nessa, as she went into the other room to grab her phone.

"What?" called Drew.

"Nothing."

THE INVISIBLE WORK OF MOTHERHOOD

In the narrative above, Nessa works tirelessly to present a flawless performance of mothering and domestic life for her family (DeGroot & Vik, 2018). Whether or not it is deliberate, Nessa is constantly working back stage to keep her family life running smoothly. Because this work is largely concealed, Drew does not recognize the effort it takes to successfully (and flawlessly) manage the domestic side of his life. It is only when the performance is flawed (e.g., when the toilet paper runs out, or when Drew's favorite tie is not drycleaned) that the other family members notice the backstage work. This kind of unseen, unpaid work is referred to as invisible labor (Daniels, 1987; Weidhaas, 2017).

Although many explanations are possible for the incongruent expectations of men and women concerning domestic labor, gender norms are performed by everyone, and these gender norms reinforce that mothers are primary caregivers and primarily responsible for household duties. However, their male counterparts are able to perform masculine gender norms by simply going to work (something which most women need to do as well to support their families financially). Jolly and colleagues (2014) explained, "Scholars have described gendered performance as an explanation [for this incongruity]: Men attempt to preserve some presentation of themselves as masculine, and because domestic labor is culturally defined as feminine, not doing it is masculine" (p. 351). In other words, domestic work is the expectation and responsibility of women, not men. This dominant perspective is reinforced by traditional gender norms, and rather than questioning these expectations, the shift of domestic labor and shared incomes puts women in a precarious place. Women are expected to perform all of the household duties as well as contribute to the shared household income, whereas their male counterparts are only expected to contribute to the shared income. This is especially compelling for future generations as women are now outearning their male counterparts in terms of education (Wang, 2017), and perhaps, in the future, in terms of wages.

In fact, many people consider the household tasks to simply be what mothers like to do as an expression of love for her family (Daniels, 1987). Daniels goes on to explain, "Planning, restocking, improvising, and adapting to family quirks and demands require effort that the housewives themselves do not recognize as work; they say they cannot understand why they become so tired or use so much time in making the effort" (p. 407). Drew demonstrated this assessment when he told Nessa that "it must be nice" to be home with the children, completely disregarding the additional labor it involves. Research has revealed the importance of spouses recognizing invisible labor for the health of the couple's relationship (Blair & Johnson, 1992; Hatfield, Rapson, & Aumer-Ryan, 2008). Equity and fairness in a romantic partnership have been linked to sexual satisfaction, marital happiness, and marital stability (Buunk & van Yperen, 1989; Byers & Wang, 2004; Schreurs & Buunk, 1996).

Invisible workload is a gendered experience which creates a disproportionate stress on mothers. It is not just the housework that mothers must complete, nor is it simply the mental labor that she assumes ("remember to buy shampoo," and "Sally has play practice on Friday"), but the fact that this labor is unseen unless it is not completed. In the narrative above, no one will notice that the cool weather is approaching until Monday morning, 15 minutes before the bus arrives, when none of the kids can find their pants. This labor is constant and is rarely recognized. As more mothers assume more work responsibilities, their hidden labor has not shifted to their partners or other members of the family. If mothers would like the support of those around them, they must continue to perform these responsibilities with "flawless perseverance" (DeGroot & Vik, 2018, p. 22) in front of other actors (including other mothers).

A NOT-SO-MAGICAL VACATION

> We had a great time at Thunder Pointe! We stayed at the incredible Beach Canyon Resort, swam in the pool, watched fireworks every night, and ate the most amazing food. Can't wait until the next family vacation!!
>
> —Allie's Facebook post

"How was your visit to Florida? I saw your pictures on Facebook. It looked like you had an amazing time!" Trish was excited to hear all about Allie's family trip to Florida. Allie and her husband, Todd, had planned a vacation with their five-year-old daughter, Vivi, and three-year-old twins, Cade and Cole. Based on Allie's Facebook pictures and status updates, the family had an awesome week at Thunder Pointe.

"Yeah. It was nice to spend time with family and see the kids get so excited. But…" Allie paused, "It was…" Allie trailed off, looking for the right word.

"What?" Trish recognized the change in Allie's demeanor. She wasn't being completely honest about something. "It was what?"

"Tiring. It was exhausting. I'm glad to be home, and I'm glad the kids are back in school and daycare," admitted Allie. "I need a break."

"Well it's difficult traveling with such young children," Trish offered as support. She had just driven six hours with her two young children to visit family for the holidays, so she knew how difficult it can be to take children anywhere.

Allie sighed, "It wasn't just the awful flight where Vivi kept kicking the seat in front of her and Cole spilled milk everywhere. The kids hardly slept in the hotel, and they were so loud. I was worried the whole time that they were disturbing other people on our floor."

Allie leaned in, "And Cade decided that last week would be a good time to perfect his velociraptor screeches at 5:30 a.m."

Trish grimaced and nodded sympathetically. She had the same experience over Christmas when her family stayed at a hotel instead of at her mother's house. It was hardly a vacation.

"And of course Todd slept through everything," Allie continued. "He was the only one who got any decent rest."

"Yep. Yep. Been there," murmured Trish.

"So I'm going on like five hours of sleep trying to manage the family away from home. Todd was absolutely no help with the kids at Thunder Pointe. And he was as grumpy as the kids! He whined about waiting in lines and the food and the money we were spending. Ugh!" Allie took a deep breath. She didn't mean to vent about her "awesome" vacation. "It was just really stressful. I don't want to go on another family vacation until Vivi is at least 15 and the boys are 12. I feel traumatized."

"Well at least you got cute pictures," Trish remarked, trying to salvage the conversation.

"I suppose you're right," agreed Allie. "Facebook thinks I had a magical time."

THE ONLINE PERFORMANCE OF MOTHERHOOD

Self-presentation behaviors are consistently monitored by people (Goffman, 1959). Mothers are no exception to this rule, and as they engage in self-presentation of motherhood, they aim to put on the best appearance for their audience(s), creating positive associations and attributions. Additionally, these performances often involve face-saving strategies, such as being polite, and making oneself look good to others. This is especially noticeable on social media such as Facebook (DeGroot & Vik, 2018).

In the narrative above, Allie made a post on Facebook about how wonderful her vacation to Thunder Pointe was, when actually, it was an exhausting, dreadful trip for her. Her Facebook post represents Allie's front stage, revealing only the type of vacation she wanted to portray to people. Allie's confession to her friend Trish illuminated her backstage (private) self. Here, she is able to honestly and openly describe the negative aspects of the trip without worrying about performing as a perfect mom with the perfect family on the perfect vacation.

Goffman (1959) suggests that we monitor our self-presentation, "accentuating certain facts and concealing others" (p. 65) as we engage in interactions with other people. It is important to note that dramatism is process. Our identities and the perceptions other people have of us are shaped by our interpersonal interactions. When our identities (and self-presentations) are believed by other actors, our identity is reinforced. But the inverse is true as well: when other actors do not believe our performance our identity can be questioned, or multiple perceptions of our identity will be created. It is important to understand that dramaturgy is a give-and-take process—as we reveal parts of ourselves, the parts that are welcome are reinforced by others, but the parts that are not welcome are not reinforced by others. Our social identities are co-constructed with other actors through this ongoing process.

In addition to the notion of the ongoing process of dramaturgy, this theory has evolved with a focus on the concept of face. It should be noted that face in this contact is not your actual anatomical face, but rather the positive sense of self you share with others. Goffman (1967) defines face as "the positive social value a person effectively claims for himself by the line others assume he [sic] has taken during a particular contact" (p. 5). In other words, face is the positive parts of ourselves that we present to others when we meet them in the world. In her Facebook post, Allie sought to present her "best mom face" to others. She did this by highlighting the positive portions of a less-than-perfect family vacation while leaving out the negative aspects.

Cupach and Metts (1994) stated, "When a person interacts with another, he or she tacitly presents a conception of who he or she is in that encounter, and seeks confirmation for that conception" (p. 3). That is, face is present in a person's interactions. Face threats occur when an individual's presentation of positive identity is challenged by another actor. Moore (2018) makes the argument that actors engage in facework to maintain a positive impression of who they are, or, as Moore states "to maintain a positive value." Typically, actors in a situation will engage in cooperative communication behaviors and reinforce the other' person's social identity in order to protect the other person's face. When someone's face is threatened (sometimes due to embarrassment or failure), others in the conversation help engage in face-saving because they also feel awkward or embarrassed for that person (Cupach & Metts, 1994). In her conversation with Trish, Allie admitted that the trip was exhausting. Trish first tried to help save Allie's face by agreeing that "travelling is hard," and attempting to temper the strong negative sentiments Allie was projecting. When Allie rebuffed Trish's attempt at face-saving, the discussion truly became a backstage conversation.

Goffman's theory of face has been recently extended into a theory called performative face theory. "Performative face theory adopts and extends [Goffman's theory of face] to take into account how power/knowledge informs negotiations of face, and how negotiations of face subsequently sediment power/knowledge" (Moore, 2018, p. 271). In other words, when we are looking at how we present/maintain/change our identities with others, power and knowledge are crucial factors to consider. This theory is especially pressing because it places emphasis on how we perform our identities and co-construct identity with others by maintaining positive face. It helps explain the pressure to present oneself as the perfect mom.

DISCUSSION QUESTIONS

1. Do we need to change how we talk about domestic labor and workload? Why or why not?
2. What can we do to recognize the struggles of mothers? How do we start to create different stories/narratives of mothers? Why is this important?
3. How can we create more space for narratives online? What would those stories look like? How can we start to talk about the stress that mothers experience online?
4. Describe front stage and backstage spaces. Why is this distinction important for mothers?
5. How do mothers maintain positive face for themselves and face-save for others? What would it look like for mothers to maintain face in other situations?

REFERENCES

Berk, S. F. (1985). *The gender factory: The apportionment of work in American households*. New York, NY: Plenum.

Bittman, M., & Wajcman, J. (2000). The rush hour: The character of leisure time and gender equality. *Special Forces, 79*, 165–189.

Blair, S. L., & Johnson, M. P. (1992). Wives' perceptions of the fairness of the division of household labor: The intersection of housework and ideology. *Journal of Marriage and the Family, 54*, 570–581.

Buunk, B. P., & van Yperen, N. W. (1989). Social comparison, equality, and relationship satisfaction: Gender differences over a ten-year period. *Social Justice Research, 3*, 157–180. doi:10.1007/BF01048064

Byers, E. S., & Wang, A. (2004). Understanding sexuality in close relationships from the social exchange perspective. In J. H. Harvey, A. Wenzel, & S. Sprecher (Eds.), *Handbook of sexuality in close relationships* (pp. 203–234). Mahway, NJ: Erlbaum.

Cupach, W. R., & Metts, S. (1994). *Facework*. Thousand Oaks, CA: Sage.

Daniels, A. K. (1987). Invisible work. *Social Problems, 34*(5), 403–415.

DeGroot, J. M., & Vik, T. A. (2018). *"Fake smile. Everything is under control.": Performing motherhood on Facebook*. Presented at the annual convention of the National Communication Association, Salt Lake City, UT.

Ellingson, L. L. (2005). *Communicating in the clinic: Negotiating front stage and back stage teamwork*. Cresskill, NJ: Hampton Press.

Goffman, E. (1959). *The presentation of self in everyday life*. New York, NY: Doubleday.

Goffman, E. (1967). *Interaction ritual: Essays on face-to-face behavior*. New York, NY: Pantheon Books.

Hatfield, E., Rapson, R., L., & Aumer-Ryan, K. (2008). Social justice in love relationships: Recent developments. *Social Justice Research, 21*, 413–431. doi:10.1007/s11211-008-0080-1

Huber, J., & Spitze, G. (1983). *Sex stratification: Children, housework, and jobs*. New York, NY: Academic Press.

Jolly, S., Griffith, K. A., DeCastro, R., Stewart, A., Ubel, P., & Jagsi, R. (2014). Gender differences in time spent on parenting and domestic responsibilities by high-achieving young physician-researchers. *Annals of Internal Medicine, 160*, 344–353.

Moore, J. (2018). From "I'm never having children" to motherhood: A critical analysis of silence and voice in negotiations of childbearing face. *Women's Studies in Communication, 41*(1), 1–21. doi:10.1080/07491409.2017.1421282

Schreurs, K. M. G., & Buunk, B. P. (1996). Closeness, autonomy, equity, and relationship satisfaction in lesbian couples. *Psychology of Women Quarterly, 20*, 577–592.

Wang, W. (2017, November 7). A record share of men are "marrying up" educationally. *Institute for Family Studies*. Retrieved from ifstudies.org

Weidhaas, A. D. (2017). Invisible labor and hidden work. In C. R. Scott & L. Lewis (Eds.), *The international encyclopedia of organizational communication* (pp. 1–10). Hoboken, NJ: John Wiley & Sons.

CHAPTER 12

When One Just Doesn't "Fit": Family Dynamics in the Context of Fat and Fitness

Phillip E. Wagner

ABSTRACT

This case study outlines family dynamics in the context of fitness and fatness. Set against the nonfictional backdrop of autoethnographic reflection, this case highlights the role and responsibilities families have to shape and guide discourses of weight, size, health, and wellness when it comes to children. Pitting lived experience against medical science, this case study examines aspects of social identity, stigma, sensemaking, social support, and family/health communication.

"Another great workout, Carol!" Jake shouted across the gym to his fitness instructor as he slipped his hand into Shai's sweaty palms. "You did a great job today!" he affirmed to his partner. Shai looked at him, wiping the sweat off her brow with that breathless knowing look she always gave—the one that said, "I totally hate that you dragged me to this workout but I'm also so glad you did."

Shai and Jake had been working out together for the last 10 years; it was the catalyst through which both of them found their identity. Jake had always been athletic—a football player in high school, experimenting with the weight-lifting fascination that seems to capture the hearts (and massive pecs) of men during college, and now an avid participant in group fitness. Shai had a different sort of relationship with fitness. Once 335 pounds, she knew all too well what it was like to be on the *other side* of fitness. At 21, she set out to establish a healthier lifestyle and, step by step, pound by pound, strategic choice by strategic choice, she found herself now in a love-hate relationship with fitness, much fitter (and lighter, not that she cared) than ever before.

Both Shai and Jake have a healthy relationship with fitness. It isn't a mechanism to lose weight, fulfill certain body ideals, or really for any other reason than to simply keep active and healthy—not just for themselves but for the two things they hold closest to their heart, their two daughters, Sage and Petra.

This family of four prides themselves on staying busy. Sage, the oldest, got involved with her school's runner's club in kindergarten and that early involvement spawned a love for athleticism. From junior cheerleading to basketball, Sage clearly fits the mold of her father, who was much the same way in his childhood. Petra, on the other hand was a lot like her mama. She preferred to be left alone, if only because she was so analytical, constantly reading and absorbing new information. Whereas Sage would prefer to be outside running around, Petra enjoyed letting her imagination run free—reading, drawing, and expressing herself more artistically. Instead of runner's club, it's art club for Petra. "They couldn't be more different," Jake and Shai regularly affirm to others; and indeed, their girls were both unique in their own ways—a true reflection of the "opposites attract" narrative that defined their parents' story.

In many ways, Shai and Jake prided themselves on their reproductive abilities to spawn two very unique and special children. It had helped create a smooth and uncomplicated dynamic in their household, a sort of *one like you and one like me* dichotomy. All had been well, and these differences helped make their family what it was—a truly loving and engaged, if not eye-rolling-ly stereotypical, prototype of the nuclear American family. All was well.

Until it wasn't. As both girls began to develop through adolescence, it was clear that their differences weren't just internal. Whether because of the drives of their interests or simple biological decisions dictated by the universe, Petra and Sage were quite different. Sage had a lot of her mother's features—the piercing eyes that showed great drive, the smile that lit up the room (even with those braces that she fought so hard), and that golden-brown hair that radiated in the sun. But at the end of the day, Sage was her daddy's daughter. She had his build, with her love for athleticism mapping directly onto her young body. She wasn't frail, but she often looked it because her metabolism had not yet caught up to her athletic drive. Petra had characteristics of her father, too. The dimple that she was just starting to notice had always caught her parents' eye, and her eyes, a bit more relaxed and friendly, left no doubt about who her daddy was. But through and through, inside and out, Petra was a spitting image of her mom.

***

Shai's life wasn't a tragedy, but it wasn't a fairy tale, either. Growing up with just her mom, and a dad who should have been paying child support but often didn't, Shai's childhood was…complicated. She moved 30 times before the age of 18 as her mom scrambled for work and tried to recover from a divorce she had never planned for. Food stamps were the means by which they received food, but with a few people living under her roof, they never went far, so it usually meant food with little to no nutritional value. Her weight reflected this and as she grew into adolescence, so did her size. Shai was, by many standards, "obese" as a child, and that label—or its less medicalized, more in-your-face substitutes—defined much of her existence.

"I remember what it's like to be called a fat pig in front of the whole class, Jake," Shai said with a tear streaming down her face. "I remember how it feels to get the stares when you sit down to eat your lunch and it doesn't matter what else you bring to the table, the other kids only see *that.*" Of course, *that* was size. As Petra had started to grow, it became clear that her body looked a bit different than her sister's. She was, indeed, a spitting reflection of her mom during adolescence—*pudgy*, some might say if they were being nice. But as Shai remembered from her childhood, kids were often anything but nice when it came to this.

The family as a whole ate fairly healthy, but that health involved "balance"—so a pizza on a Friday evening or a quick fast-food meal on a trip to Sage's weekend basketball tournament wasn't uncommon. Still, a preoccupation with weight simply didn't really fit within their parenting style. At their core, Shai and Jake didn't care about Petra's size. After all, it's a new season and we all know just a bit more about health and wellness; size doesn't really give us the best picture of health. But kids don't always see that, and unfortunately nor do grown adults. Even those who should know better.

***

"So, let's talk about Petra," said Dr. Conover, with a serious tone that might have been better reserved for a more serious diagnosis. Shai and Jake had been around Conover a long time. He delivered both of the girls as an OBGYN before moving to open his own practice as a general practitioner. Of course, it made sense that they'd stick with him through this move; after all, he had never been anything less than wonderful and their life was so busy—having a reliable doctor meant one less thing to think about. But the magic of that historical relationship started to fade when Shai took Petra and Sage to a yearly physical and to get their routine vaccines.

"Petra is in the 95th percentile for her weight," noted Dr. Conover. Shai looked over and locked eyes with her daughter. "*She's too young to know what this means, but I know she's listening*," Shai thought. "This really needs to be a wake-up call to you all. If she keeps going in this direction, she may wind up with health problems—childhood diabetes or other complications."

That was it. Just 30 seconds of comments that Shai graciously shook off as she and Dr. Conover wrapped up the visit. But as she drove home, she tried her best to hold in her tears behind her dark sunglasses. Just 30 seconds. Nothing horrific. But those words stoked the coals of a fire that had laid dormant for many years. She knew that things were going to be different from here on.

***

"I remember how it feels to get the stares when you sit down to eat your lunch and it doesn't matter what else you bring to the table; the other kids only see *that*." Jake listened intently. He cared deeply for his children, but this was a battle that he had never lived, only observed. When he met Shai, she was at the end of her weight loss journey; he marveled at her 170-pound weight loss, though truthfully, he had never cared much about her size. Because it had been such a large part of her life, he knew that Shai's "weight journey," as they called it, was a defining feature of who she was. It bore its mark on her body, which held pounds of extra *skin* where excess fat had once been and, more saliently, it impacted how she saw herself. Despite being victorious by many standards, Shai still saw herself as overweight and *less* than the rest of the world around her. They had agreed to do all they could to instill healthy behaviors in their kids so they wouldn't have to go through what Shai did. Yet, here they were, engaging with what Shai was convinced was just the first step of a life of torment, bullying, and body anxiety for Petra.

"Ok, but he's a doctor," Jake said out loud, knowing immediately that he was using two letters behind a man's name to invalidate 30-odd years of lived experience by the one he loved the most. "And I'm her mother, and I've been through it, Jake," Shai said, with a tinge of anger and disgust. "I remember going to the doctor and every time—every single time, Jake—whatever I had had to do with my weight. Trouble breathing? For most kids, that meant allergies but nope, for me, it was probably my weight. Not feeling well? My weight. Depressed as a teenager? Surely it wasn't that my dad left us high and dry or that I wasn't getting proper nutrition or that I was bullied incessantly, right? No, it was my weight. Common cold or flu? My weight. This is what it's like Jake. Once it's 'your weight' it is never NOT your weight."

Jake knew inside that he'd have to tread carefully. Truthfully, he didn't see anything "wrong" with Petra. Was she *stockier?* Sure. But ever the analytical one, Jake always measured his kids up to those around them at school, at the mall, at the playground. Petra was *just a normal kid.* She'd grow into her body or puberty would have a way of ironing things out, he assumed. Kids have so much else to worry about these days—why stress them out about this?

***

In the United States, obesity has often been cited as enemy numero uno. When asked about the top threat to American life and livelihood in 2006, the surgeon general at the time, Richard Carmona, noted that that enemy was *obesity.* He called it the "terror within." "Unless we do something about it, the magnitude of the dilemma will dwarf 9/11 or any other terrorist attempt" (Jackson, 2006). In many ways, obesity has been epidemicized and framed as a public health "crisis" of sorts, for a variety of reasons. Philosophically, framing obesity as a mechanism of terror helps "incite, reinforce, control, monitor, optimize, and organize the forces under it" (Foucault, 1978, p. 136; Rail, Holmes, & Murray, 2010). Practically, it's a lucrative business.

The health and wellness industry, which rests sizably upon issues of weight and body composition, is one of the world's fastest growing industries today. In fact, this behemoth is a multitrillion-dollar industry (Global Wellness Institute, 2017). From fad diets and magic pills, to the promise of six pack abs through some as-seen-on-TV equipment that could never scientifically be guaranteed to provide abdominal definition alone, there is quite an industry ready to capitalize on the growing panic surrounding weight.

Yet to be fair, the United States also rises to the top when it comes to obesity—and not in a good way. According to the Centers for Disease Control (CDC; Hales, Carroll, Fryar, & Ogden, 2017), 39.8% of the population is obese and obesity impacts just over 93 million US adults. Though there are many ready to profit from obesity, it is also an expensive industry. The CDC estimates that the annual medical cost of obesity was $147 billion in 2008, with the medical cost for obese individuals weighing in at $1,429 higher than those of "normal" weight (Hales et al., 2017).

The term "normal weight" should give anyone pause, particularly when used in such scientific framings. Despite living in a multidimensional world, the medical community has maintained a singular framework by which obesity is measured. Body mass index (BMI) is the metric by which humans are classified as "overweight" or not—and if you're not, you're often seen as *normal.* There have been many critiques over the years about the inaccuracies of making such definitive classifications on BMI alone, including the fact that it does not account for muscular composition, exaggerates the outcome based on height, and/or may lead to those who carry fat in more risky places than others to believe they are the picture of health because their BMI suggests they aren't overweight (Nordqvist, 2013; Nutall, 2015).

Even the mathematician (not physician) who invented this scale noted that it should not be used to make such definitive claims. Thus, using BMI to classify individuals as normal or not normal should give us pause.

It should also make us think about the sociological conditions that undergird many cases of obesity in the United States. This "condition" is far more likely to impact non-White individuals—particularly Hispanic and African American sections of the population. Further, those who are not college-educated, those from low- and working-class economic backgrounds, and rural Americans are far more likely to be obese. Thus, the language of "normal" weight versus the other perceived alternative (decidedly *not normal*) should be called into question, as it does not fully account for socioeconomic class, race, ethnicity, and other identity-related variables. If an intersectional view of health and wellness is to be totally achieved, it must move past a binary classification system that is, at its core, not scientifically, medically, or logically sound.

Still, those who are obese, overweight, or even on the perceived path to becoming one of those are often chided, labeled, and stigmatized in society, with the medical community supporting that stigmatization through such classification systems. The relationship between fat stigma and the medical community's framing of fatness cannot be understated. A significant volume of research demonstrates that physicians (including medical students) harbor internal fat stigma (Foster et al., 2003; Miller et al., 2013; Wear, Aultman, Varley, & Zarconi, 2006). Research also confirms examples like the one Shai remembered from childhood, wherein fat patients are prescribed a diagnosis that presents weight and/or size as the underlying reason such a problem exists (Kreuter, Scharff, Brennan, & Lukwago, 1997; Pause, 2014; Stafford, La Puma, & Schiedermayer, 1989).

The effect of this stigma may have consequences for many, but those consequences are particularly salient for children. Research has documented an alarming phenomenon: children as young as three hold negative attitudes towards other overweight children (Cramer & Steinwert, 1998; Holub, 2008). This holds true even if those young children are, themselves, overweight (Cramer & Steinwert, 1998). As Puhl and Latner (2007) note, "a stigmatized child possesses an attribute or characteristic that is linked to a devalued social identity and is ascribed stereotypes or other deviant labels that increase vulnerability to status loss, unfair treatment, prejudice, and discrimination (p. 558; see also Crocker, Major, & Steele, 1998; Goffman, 1963, Link & Phelan, 2001).

These are the effects that reflect Shai's experiences with weight and body image, and they are precisely the effects that Shai is now immensely concerned with when it comes to her daughter's overall well-being. These weren't just studies or data that live in papers somewhere—these were facts that, when brought to life can have profound effects on the life and livelihood of anyone, much less a child. Shai wondered what to do—confront Dr.

Conover? Find a new doctor? Take his advice? Begin talking with her daughter(s) about fat and the role it plays in women's lives, fair or not?

And more importantly, Shai wondered what this meant for her family. Would the dynamics now change? The *one like you and one like me* dichotomy had worked so well, but she hadn't accounted for the fact that that dichotomy might also bring along some of the struggles that both her and Jake had experienced. What are families to do in situations like these? Whose perspective wins—medical science or a mother's lived experience? And what of Jake? He seems apathetic at best. How could she, alone, help ensure that her daughter emerged from this situation without any of the damage that had left permanent scarring on her own identity? Shai felt like nothing had equipped her for this moment in parenthood; and yet, at the same time, she felt like her whole life had been in preparation for this.

DISCUSSION QUESTIONS

1. How should Shai approach the situation outlined above? Specifically, what communication practices should she use with (1) Jake, (2) Petra, and (3) Dr. Conover?
2. When individual or family experience defies other common cultural discourse (e.g., medical diagnoses), which perspective should be taken?
3. What type of social support can Shai and/or Jake offer to Petra to navigate this situation?
4. How should medical practitioners respond to families who have may have healthcare profiles that do not fit neatly within a standardized assessment or framework?
5. What can families do behind closed doors to ensure their children are prepared to encounter a world wherein they may be stigmatized and/or bullied?

REFERENCES

Cramer, P., & Steinwert, T. (1998). Thin is good, fat is bad: How early does it begin? *Journal of Applied Developmental Psychology, 19*, 429–451.

Crocker, J., Major, B., & Steele, C. (1998). Social stigma. In D. T. Gilbert, S. T. Fiske, & G. Lindzey (Eds.), *Handbook of social psychology* (4th ed., Vol. 2, pp. 504–553). Boston, MA: McGraw-Hill.

Foster, G. D., Wadden, T. A., Makris, A. P., Davidson, D., Sanderson, R. S., Allison, D. B., & Kessler, A. (2003). Primary care physicians' attitudes about obesity and its treatment. *Obesity Research, 11*(10), 1168–1177.

Foucault, M. (1978). *The history of sexuality.* New York, NY: Vintage.

Global Wellness Institute. (2017). Statistics and facts. Retrieved from https://globalwellnes-sinstitute.org/press-room/statistics-and-facts

Goffman, E. (1963). *Stigma: Notes on the management of spoiled identity.* Englewood Cliffs, NJ: Prentice Hall.

Hales, C. M., Carroll, M. D., Fryar, C. D., & Ogden, C. L. (2017). Prevalence of obesity among adults and youth: United States, 2015–2016. *CDC NCHS Data Brief, 288.* Retrieved from https://www.cdc.gov/nchs/data/databriefs/db288.pdf

Holub, S. C. (2008). Individual differences in the anti-fat attitudes of preschool children: The importance of perceived body size. *Body Image, 5*, 317–321.

Jackson, K. A. (2006). Surgeon General: Obesity "terror within." *Boston Globe* (March 1, 2006). Retrieved from: http:www.boston.com/yourlife/health/diseases/articles/2006/03/01/surgeon_general_obesity_terror_within/. Last visited December 2014).

Kreuter, M. W., Scharff, D. P., Brennan, L. K., & Lukwago, S. N. (1997). Physician recommendations for diet and physical activity: Which patients get advised to change? *Preventive Medicine, 26*(6), 825–833.

Link, B. G., & Phelan, J. C. (2001). Conceptualizing stigma. *Annual Review of Sociology, 27*, 363–385.

Miller, D. P., Spangler, J. G., Vitolins, M. Z., Davis, S. W., Ip, E. H., Marion, G. S., & Crandall, S. J. (2013). Are medical students aware of their anti-obesity bias? *Academic Medicine, 88*, 978–982.

Nordqvist, C. (2013). Why BMI is inaccurate and misleading. *Medical News Today.* Retrieved from https://www.medicalnewstoday.com/articles/265215.php

Nutall, F. Q. (2015). Body mass index: Obesity, BMI, and health: A critical review. *Nutrition Today, 50*, 117–128.

Pause, C. (2014). Die another day: The obstacles facing fat people in accessing quality health-care. *Narrative Inquiry in Bioethics, 4*, 135–141.

Puhl, R. M., & Latner, J. D. (2007). Stigma, obesity, and the health of the nation's children. *Psychological Bulletin, 133*, 557–580.

Rail, G., Holmes, D., & Murray, S. J. (2010). The politics of evidence on "domestic terrorists": Obesity discourses and their effects. *Social Theory & Health, 8*, 259-279.

Stafford, B. M., La Puma, J., & Schiedermayer, D. L. (1989). One face of beauty, one picture of health: The hidden aesthetic of medical practice. *Journal of Medicine and Philosophy, 14*(2), 213–230.

Wear, D., Aultman, J. M., Varley, J. D., & Zarconi, J. (2006). Making fun of patients: Medical students' perceptions and use of derogatory and cynical humor in clinical settings. *Academic Medicine, 81*, 454–462.

CHAPTER 13

I Get It from My Mamma: Doing Race, Doing Gender

Savaughn Williams – *Ball State University*
Katherine J. Denker – *Ball State University*

ABSTRACT

In this case, the authors use autoethnographic narratives to situate and understand how conversations about race occur in the family, specifically within the mother–daughter context. Through the frameworks of strong Black womanhood and feminist theory, Autumn, with her mother, grandmother, and other various family members, works to navigate her identity as a Black girl/woman. Using the literature as a guide to better understand her experiences over the span of her youth through young adulthood, Autumn unravels her past and gives an insight into the transformation of herself, and her racial and familial identity through the formative years of her life. Through Autumn's self-reflection, identity formation and management within family communication is highlighted in an African American family. This narrative also demonstrates how familial communication impacts the understanding of identity. Further, the use of autoethnography helps build out the self-reflection and understanding of identity. Discussion questions are provided to build conversations surrounding how families communicate about race and identity.

CASE STUDY

Autumn walks into the kitchen one day after coming home from school, bubbling with energy from show-and-tell in her third grade class. She sees her mother getting things ready for dinner, and breathes in and smells spaghetti, Autumn's favorite. Mommom, her maternal grandmother, is sitting at one of the bar seats by the counter. Autumn walks in, trying not to interrupt their conversation or listen to "grown-folk business". She finally decides to jump into the conversation.

Autumn: Hey Mom?

Mom: Yes, Autumn?

Autumn: At school today, Victoria brought in these super cool dolls, they're called "Groovy Girls" and you can dress them and stuff. They're so cool, do you think I could get one?

Mommom (interjects here, scoffing and rolling her eyes)*: You are always trying to be like them.* Even in third grade Autumn knew "them" to be the White girls in class.

Autumn: No, I don't, I just want to play with them. They are super cool, all my friends have one.

Mom: You don't even play with what you have now, are you going to play with them?

Autumn: Yes, I will, I promise I will.

Autumn leaves the kitchen full of excitement to get these dolls and show her friends at school.

Autumn got the dolls, but the joy was fleeting, as she was soon on to the next cool (White) thing.

Even during these moments, identity was not something that concerned Autumn; while she understood her skin color, she did not understand its significance. Conversations like these linger in Autumn's mind when she reflects on her own identity as a Black woman and how it has developed (Scott, 2017). As a child, she never thought "Why am I different from them?" or considered that her identity was impacted by society before she ever came to be in the world (Griffin, 2012). Autumn could not really fathom why it was so important that she understood that the differences came down to her skin color, hair, and even how she dressed as a little Black girl (Duke, 2000). In this case study we aim to shed light on conversations about race within the family. By using narratives of family conversations and weaving literature throughout to pull out the experiences further, we will introduce issues of identity, race, and intergenerational families.

***

Autumn is now ten and is woken up by her mother turning on the lights and telling her to get ready for school. She gets out of bed and looks over at her outfit for the day placed at the foot of her bed. She turns on MTV *Hits and Starts* getting ready. As Autumn puts on her clothes, she looks in the mirror on her dresser, liking the look of the black gauchos and the red, white, and blue T-shirt. Hearing her mother call her name signaling that it's time to leave, she walks to the front door, but her mother stops her.

Mom: What are you wearing?

Autumn: (looks down at her outfit she spent so much time getting together the previous night. Attempting to understand what is wrong, Autumn is both genuinely confused and hurt; she was excited to wear her new gauchos, but careful not to show it) *What's wrong?*

Mom: Why are you wearing that with that...You need to change, that doesn't look good.

Autumn: This is how you wear it mom (Autumn tries to get her mom to understand).

Mom: That's how your white friends dress, that's not how you dress.

After the conversation, Autumn left for school feeling sad and unsure about why her clothes upset her mother. At 10, she was yet to understand how apparel is tied to appearance in avoiding negative stereotypes surrounding little Black girls (Duke, 2000). Her mother was coaching her to "dress better" to both fit in and pass. Even in elementary school, Autumn's mother was shaping her identity in a way that would exemplify her mother's definition of Black womanhood (Scott, 2017).

***

In her elementary school environment, Autumn was surrounded by White culture (DiAngelo, 2016). Mom sits at the head of the kitchen table, looking through the mail and sighing in distress. Mommom is watching her with an understanding smile, dressed in her favorite pajamas and slippers with a long purple robe. Mom stands up and paces across the kitchen to turn around and lean on the counter, facing Mommom.

Mom: Autumn was crying today.

Mommom: Why? (she frowns, concerned as to why her granddaughter would be crying).

Mom: This boy at church made fun of her braids (she sighs remembering that Autumn did not really like them before, and now this happened). *She said he called her "ugly."*

Mommom: That's ridiculous? Was this boy White? (she is disgusted that anyone would use such words).

Mom: Yeah Mom.

Mommom: Well he doesn't know nothing about anything. She's beautiful, Black, and that's that.

Mom: I know mom, we tell her all the time. I think Autumn just thinks she's so much like them and doesn't realize she's different.

Mommom: Well she will, eventually (nodding her head and showing that it's inevitable). *It's because she's always around them White folk, at school and in gymnastics.*

Mom: (heaves a sigh and shakes her head in agreement).

Mommom: (turns her head and calls out) *Autumn, come on here!* (looks over at her daughter and smiles encouragingly)

Autumn: Yes, Mommom (Autumn is looking down, and speaks very quietly—the opposite of her boisterous grandmother).

Mommom: You know you are beautiful, and your hair is beautiful too.

Mom: Don't let anyone tell you otherwise, that boy is just ignorant.

Mommom: Next time you see him, you tell him that you are beautiful, and it doesn't matter because what he says he is wrong.

Mommom reaches in and gives Autumn a tight hug, smelling sweet of perfume and cigarettes. Mom walks over and gives Autumn a kiss on the cheek. Both instilling strength and beauty into Autumn's mind.

***

Eleven-year-old Autumn along with her teammates, all White girls, traveled to a gymnastics meet out of town. After the meet ended, Autumn rides in her friend's car to the mall, and rehashes the victories from the meet. Her mom has followed behind and meets them at the mall. Autumn enters the build-a-bear shop with her friends, excited to see how it all works. Before she walks in, Autumn's mom stops her.

Mom: Now when we get in here you know not to ask for anything.

She nods her head in understanding, thinking about the financial struggle to even be at that meet. Yet, Autumn is torn when she watches her friend throw a tantrum to get more clothes and another bear to add to her collection. Autumn turns to her mother, takes a deep breath and walks into trouble.

Autumn: Mom, could I pretty please get one? I'll play with it and take care of it, I promise.

Mom: No Autumn, you know we can't get that.

Any other time Autumn would know that Mom's response meant the end of the conversation, but she decides to push her luck and imitate her friend.

Autumn: (balls up her fists, eyes start to tear up) Mom please, please, please! Mom, please I promise I won't ask for anything else! Please mom!

Mom looks down at Autumn with a controlled face, narrowing her eyes, giving Autumn "the look". Yet, she caves in, letting Autumn choose a bear. Autumn is ecstatic. As they finish up at the mall, Autumn heads to her mom's car. She gets into the back seat and gets everything settled, including her new bear. Her mother waits until the door is closed and then turns around, looking Autumn squarely in the eye.

Mom: Don't you ever do that again! You are lucky those White people were standing there or you would've got your ass whooped. You don't ever act like that again, you understand? I can't believe you did that! It will not happen again I will tell you that!

As her mother turns around, Autumn sinks back into the seat as far as possible. She feels ashamed to have acted so badly and embarrassed her mother. Autumn starts to cry, aware of her mother's disappointment. Autumn's perception of strength is drawn from moments like these where her mother controlled her emotions and set her straight at the same time. Here Autumn is crucially taught what is appropriate for her a Black child and what is not, as well as what is appropriate for her Black mother (Davis, 2015).

***

As she went through high school, Autumn began to understand how being Black impacted her interpersonal relationships as well as her own identity. Growing up she recalled the occasional questions over her hair ("Did you cut it?" "How did you get it braided like that?") and skin ("Do you use sunscreen?"), but it was never something that Autumn dwelled on (Duke, 2000).

***

Autumn is walking up the stairs with the pride of a senior and cheer captain, excited to get out of class early and head to lunch with friends. As she walks to the door, she notices a girl she knows and stops to say hello.

Autumn: Hey Cara, what's up?

Cora: Hey Autumn, how's it going? (she speaks with a southern twang) Autumn struggles to hear Cora's response over the other students in the hall, who happen to be Black students.

Autumn: Everything is good! How did you do on that lit test?

Cora gets distracted by the other students around her locker, speaking loudly and walking about. As they leave Cora rolls her eyes in obvious annoyance.

Cora: (turning to face Autumn, with the annoyance on her face quickly changing to relief with a smile) *I'm glad we're friends—you're not like Black-Black, you're like White-Black, you're not ghetto like they are.*

Thinking through how her mother and grandmother would respond, Autumn ignores the string of explicit words running through her head. Remembering the reactions anger usually earns and knowing that Black has been categorized socially and physically as different, Autumn is stuck. She begins to straighten her face with a fake smile and slightly tilting her head responds.

Autumn: Uhh thanks? (giving an awkward laugh)

Autumn watches Cora leave and sits, lost in thought about Cora's comment. In the back of Autumn's mind she thinks about conversations with her mother and grandmother, and how her responses in moments like this have been built up through them (Beauboeuf-Lafontant, 2007).

***

Autumn is home from college for the holidays and she and her mom are shopping at the mall, the usual activity when she visits home. Her mom is dressed in jeans and a sweater with a jacket over it, carrying a Louis Vuitton purse. Her hair is curled, and her make-up is simple with a nude lipstick. Autumn is more casual, wearing leggings with a sweater, having had her hair done the other day so that it hangs straight. They wander through the women's clothing sections, picking up things here and there to try on, and showing each other what they found. Her mother looks over her shoulder, gives an exasperated sigh, and rolls her eyes in frustration.

Autumn: What's wrong?

Mom: That woman has been following us.

Autumn: Who? (looking around and seeing the sales associate nearby, knowing that this is not the first time this has occurred in this store)

Mom: Her (motioning over to a sales associate)

Autumn's mom is visibly upset that this woman is hovering over her daughter and herself as they shop through multiple sections in the store. Autumn is more blasé about it thinking that maybe it was a coincidence. As they continue to shop, Autumn also begins to notice that every time they move sections the women has followed them. Mom is now looking visibly frustrated with the White sales associate who looks to be in her mid-20s to 30s. Mom sharply turns around with her purse on her shoulder to approach the sales associate.

Mom: You don't need to follow us, we are not going to steal anything!

Sales associate: I-I wasn't umm following you…

Mom: Yeah you were. I shop in here frequently (voice slightly raising). *Do you think there is anything in here that I want that I can't buy?!*

Sales associate: I wasn't following you, ma'am.

Autumn stares at her mom and then looks over to the sales associate, noticing how she keeps denying this but looks shocked and embarrassed to be so blatantly called out on her profiling. Autumn is a little shocked but not surprised, since Mom usually doesn't take shit from anyone. While in the past this has embarrassed Autumn, she witnessed it so clearly this time that it seemed unfair to just keep quiet and keep getting followed.

Mom: (turning to Autumn after the sales associate walks away) *I don't understand! Do we look like we would steal something?*

Autumn: (she looks down and observes how they are both dressed and how their hair is done) *No, if anything, we look like we're going to spend money…She did follow us throughout the store though, so I get why you are upset.*

Mom: Please! Dillard's doesn't have anything that I want that I couldn't buy!

Mom swings her Louis bag over her shoulder and leaves Dillard's, with Autumn following behind her. They then go around the mall searching for their traditional matching Christmas pajamas.

***

Autumn reflects on this interaction and similar events. Her mom has been modeling this definition of strong Black womanhood. She begins to understand that tropes like the angry Black woman have silenced her past interactions and built feelings of shame surrounding sticking up for herself and other Black women (Griffin, 2012).

***

Autumn and her mom are going through papers in the laundry room; dressed in pajamas with scarves still on their heads, they begin sorting. Autumn is reading through some things and giving others to her mother, when she notices the name of her birth father on a form.

Autumn: What's this? (holding up some documents)

Mom: Those are the divorce papers from your father.

Autumn pauses. She rarely wants to discuss this man, but now she is curious.

Autumn: Oh… why did you get divorced? (While they had had short interactions around this, Autumn had never actually seen the documents, nor processed the events leading to that point).

Mom: Well, his family didn't think I was good enough for him (she pauses and nods her head at Autumn's shocked expression). *I remember leaving him when you were a baby. I had nothing and two children.*

Autumn's first thought was that it was strange that they thought her mom was not good enough since Papa is definitely a rollin' stone. Her next thought was trying to comprehend the strength that her mother would have needed to survive during this time.

Mom: You know, I was in a shelter for a while and eventually got to your uncle's and lived there for a while before I decided to enlist in the army. This is why I am always trying to get you to understand the importance of independence and having your own money. You have to be strong and take care of yourself first. Never depend on a man's money, make your own.

As Autumn listens, she continues to clean and organize with her mother. Afterwards, Autumn hugs her mom and leaves to go clean her room, while thinking more about the importance of independence, not only for necessities, but also for happiness (Boylorn, 2014; Scott, 2017).

***

Flash forward to Autumn's senior year in college when she is visiting home for the weekend. She and her mom are shifting through all the photo albums and come across Mommom's prom pictures. This picture is one of Autumn's favorites—her grandmother is dressed in a beautiful white dress fitted at the top with tiers down the waist that poof out. Mommom is standing next to a tall man, looking very statuesque herself with her hair swept up. Autumn looks up from the picture and shows it to her mom who smiles in response.

Mom: I miss Mom (she looks sad).

Autumn: Me too (Autumn looks down at the picture).

Mom: When we were kids, your Mommom raised us by herself ya know. She was a bit of a hot tamale (chuckles). *She didn't get any help from any of our dads and raised us a single mother.*

Autumn listens solemnly and proudly as she often does when her late grandmother is brought up.

Mom: (Mom picks up a picture of Mommom in a nurse uniform) *Did you know Mommom was once arrested?*

Autumn: What?! Why did she get arrested? (Her jaw slightly drops; she is shocked that this is the first time she is hearing this)

Mom: When we lived in Philly, she used to work at the hospital. All of the Black workers went on strike due to the discrimination that was happening with unequal pay for the Black workers. While she was protesting, she got arrested.

Autumn feels a swell of pride in her chest that her grandmother was such an amazing and strong woman. This creates a domino effect bringing to light other moments when Mommom displayed her strength to those around her (Bradford, Buck, & Meyers, 2001). Mommom was independent, raising a family of three, and standing up for her own rights as a Black woman. Autumn thought back to all the times that Mommom didn't take shit from anyone, no matter the situation, and all the times her mother has told her about Mommom's strength and grace, reinforcing matriarchal strength as well as reifying strong Black womanhood.

***

Autumn sits around the table smiling fondly at everyone meandering through the kitchen for breakfast. Her uncle John, brothers, and grandma Joan are all sitting at the kitchen table, having just finished eating. Autumn's dad is washing the dishes and her mom comes to sit down at the table. Autumn's mom and uncle begin to talk about their childhood.

Uncle John: Your great grandma Estelle, now she was a tough woman.

Mom: Oh yes (she gives a light chuckle and smiles at uncle John).

Uncle John: She and her husband were both illiterate. She used to cook food and sell plates to raise all seven of her children.

Autumn and her two brothers all smile at each other, admiring her hustle to provide for her family.

Mom: Yes, and remember how she used to walk through the neighborhood to sell it as well?

Uncle John: We'd go over there every Sunday and eat dinner; she used to make shrimp and grits that would drive you crazy.

Mom: Do you remember that time she had her money stolen by her cousin?

Uncle John: Yes, she went to her cousin's house with a barbed-wire wrapped bat, and told him she wanted her money back. She waited for him to come outside and hit him one good time with the bat, demanding her money. Your great-grandmother was kind of a gangster (he laughs).

Autumn and her brothers are shocked yet impressed by how badass this woman was. She displayed strength that one could only dream about.

Mom: She was a force to be reckoned with and you never wanted to be on her bad side.

Uncle John: Oh no, you did not. And that was your Mommom's mother, so just imagine (he smiles and shakes his head wryly). *We have had such a strong line of women in this family. They have built the paths for you all today to follow* (he motions to Autumn and her two brothers).

Mom: They are truly behind us and everything we do.

Uncle John: Our ancestors are always with us and carry us.

Autumn is amazed at this story and sits with a small smile, proud to have come from such strong and amazing women. She feels as though her identity is further solidified through the actions and stories of her great-grandmother.

***

Autumn is finally beginning to understand how the phrase, "I get it from my Mama" is enacted through these conversations (Davis, 2015). Through these various conversations between Autumn and her family, strong Black womanhood is reified (Davis, 2015). Autumn's mother plays an important role in how her identity has been shaped. Throughout the multiple dialogues, Autumn also experiences intergenerational identity framing. Autumn is now proud to say and understand that she is a "strong Black woman".

DISCUSSION QUESTIONS

1. **Interracial friendships:** Central to the conversations involving Autumn, her mother, and her Mommom is the concern about relationships across race. How do each of these individuals approach these relationships? How would you describe each one's views and what do you think influenced these views?

2. **Intergenerationality:** Looking back at the conversations that Autumn has with her mother and grandmother about family and history, how do you see generational norms and expectations communicated? How are these communicated in your family?

3. **Racial and individual identity:** As families are one of the first sites for socialization, Autumn is constantly being taught how she can and cannot behave as a Black woman. What messages of socialization stood out for you? What messages did Autumn pick up? Were there times in the narrative that she missed these messages? What messages did your parents share with you as part of your socialization?

4. **Racial and unconscious bias:** What instances of racial and unconscious bias were present in the story of Autumn's family? How did these shape their lives? How did Autumn's family prepare her for these interactions? What messages of race have been shared in your family?

REFERENCES/SUGGESTED READINGS

Beauboeuf-Lafontant, T. (2007). "You have to show strength:" An exploration of gender, race, and depression. *Gender & Society, 21*, 28–51. doi:10.1177/0891243206294108

Boylorn, R. M. (2014). My daddy is slick, brown, and cool like ice water. In J. Wyatt & T. E. Adams (Eds.), *On (writing) families: Autoethnographies of presence and absence, love and loss* (pp. 85–93). Rotterdam, Netherlands: Sense Publishers.

Bradford, L., Buck, J. L., & Meyers, R. A. (2001). Cultural and parental communicative influences on the career success of White and Black women. *Women's Studies in Communication, 24*, 194–217. doi:10.1080/07491409.2001.10162434

Davis, S. M. (2015). The "strong Black woman collective": A developing theoretical framework for understanding collective communication practices of Black women. *Women's Studies in Communication, 38*, 20–35. doi:10.1080/07491409.2014.953714

DiAngelo, R. (2016). *What does it mean to be White? Developing White racial literacy* (revised edition). New York, NY: Peter Lang.

Duke, L. (2000). Black in a blonde world: Race and girls' interpretations of the feminine ideal in teen magazines. *Journalism & Mass Communication Quarterly, 77*, 367–392. doi:10.1177/107769900007700210

Griffin, R. A. (2012). I am an angry Black woman: Black feminist autoethnography, voice, and resistance. *Women's Studies in Communication, 35*, 138–157. doi:10.1080/07409.2012.724524

Guerrero, L. K., Andersen, P. A., & Afifi, W. A. (2018). *Close encounters: Communication in relationships* (5th ed.). Los Angeles, CA: Sage.

Scott, K. D. (2017). *The language of strong Black womanhood: Myths, models, messages, and a new mandate for self-care.* Lanham, MD: Lexington Books.

Steele, C. M. (2011). *Whistling Vivaldi: How stereotypes affect us and what we can do*. New York, NY: Norton.

Turner, L. H., & West, R. (2006). *Perspective on family communication* (3rd ed.). Boston, MA: McGraw Hill.

TEACHING MATERIALS

We hope that this case be applied to interpersonal, family, gender, and intercultural communication classes by having students examine the relationships between Autumn, her mother, and her grandmother. We envision students analyzing the evolving conversations that Autumn has over the years with family members as both her racial identity and self-identity develop. Additionally, discussions about family communication and intercultural communication as situated in historic time periods would be of interest to students in the communication classroom.

TERMINOLOGY

Identity: "the person that we think we are and the self we communicate to others" (Guerrero, Andersen, & Afifi, 2018, p. 441)

Intergenerationality: "establishing a legacy that affects the development of individual family members and the patterns of adjustment found in subsequent family generations" (Turner & West, 2006, p. G-7)

Strong Black womanhood: a conceptualization of Black women that functions as a source of strength and community building, as well as a reclamation/reification of patriarchal racist notions that enforces Black women's strength in a way that silences any deviant experiences and normalizes their labor, both real and emotional

Unconscious bias: social stereotypes that individuals have of other identity and social groups outside of their conscious awareness, however often able to influence behavior in ways that are unjust; also known as implicit bias (Steele, 2011)

Part III

NEGOTIATION OF BOUNDARIES WITHIN THE FAMILY

CHAPTER 14

In-Law Communication and Privacy Management: Rules, Boundaries, and Turbulence

Jocelyn M. DeGroot – *Southern Illinois University*
Valerie J. Young – *Hanover College*

ABSTRACT

When people get married or are in long-term relationships, involuntary relationships with in-laws are often created. In this case study, we exclusively focus on the relationships between daughters-in-law (DIL) and their mothers-in-law (MIL). This is a complex relationship to navigate, as the DIL may feel equal pressure to maintain in-law relationships while establishing boundaries and managing privacy within her own nuclear family. This case study offers vignettes that focus on communication privacy management within three distinct DIL/MIL relationships, illustrating aspects of privacy rules, boundary turbulence, topic avoidance, person avoidance, and coordinated boundaries.

CASE STUDY

Relationships with in-laws can be complex, as they are predominantly nonvoluntary relationships that are maintained for the sake of the extended family (Hess, 2000). In particular, the relationship between the daughter-in-law (DIL) and her mother-in-law (MIL) is complex, as the DIL often feels tension to maintain in-law relationships while establishing boundaries and managing privacy within her own nuclear family (DeGroot & Young, 2016). These privacy-based issues are evident in the various vignettes presented in this case study that focus on in-law relationships. Each scenario highlights a different aspect of the roles that communication privacy management play in these family relationships.

Communication privacy management (CPM) theory is highlighted in this case study, as aspects of privacy rules, boundaries, and turbulence (Petronio, 1991, 2002; Petronio & Reierson, 2009) are emphasized throughout the presented interactions between the DIL, MIL, and DIL's partner. CPM explains how people coordinate and control the communication of private information based on privacy rules or by creating and coordinating privacy boundaries (Petronio, 1991). The vignettes in the case study portray privacy rules and resulting boundary turbulence, person-based boundaries, and coordinated boundaries in addition to other components of CPM.

MIL as the (Privacy) Invader

"How was Carter's parent–teacher conference? Is he still struggling in math?" asked Linda as she burst through the door.

"It was fine," replied Julia through gritted teeth, trying not to let her annoyance at the intrusion show on her face. Linda is Julia's mother-in-law. Julia married Linda's son, Michael, 10 years ago, and they have a six-year-old son named Carter. Linda frequently stops over at their house without warning. Linda continued moving through Julia's home in a whirlwind of questions for Julia and hugs for Carter.

By the time Michael arrived home from his shift at the hospital, Linda had already left to go pick up groceries before she returned to her house. Michael greeted Julie and Carter before heading upstairs to change. Julia followed Michael up to their bedroom. As Michael was getting changed from his work clothes, Julia announced, "Your mother was here today."

Michael froze and sighed. His mom had become a source of contention between him and Julia. "Oh yeah? What did she have to say?"

"The usual. She wanted to know how badly I was screwing up as a parent, and then we played 20 questions about how much we were planning on spending for Carter's birthday gifts next month, and were we going on vacation, and 'are those decisions financially sensible'—I swear she thinks she is our accountant." Julia's eyes were flashing with anger.

Michael grimaced slightly, "Hun, you know that's not true. She just likes to take an interest in Carter and our family."

"I thought you said you were going to talk to her about her overbearing interrogations."

"I did," Michael replied. "Kind of. I told her that she needed to be nicer when asking you questions."

Julia glared at Michael. "And you need to stop telling her things too! She also asked when we were going to give Carter a brother or sister because 'my clock is a-ticking,' and that you said we might start trying next month," Julia hissed. "That. Is. Private."

Michael nodded. He told his mom this information because she asked about it, and he didn't want to be rude. But he could see that Julia was not on board with being so open with Linda.

"And how did she know Carter is having trouble with math? And that we had to save up if we wanted to go on vacation next summer?" Julia demanded, already knowing the answer.

"I told her," Michael sheepishly replied.

Julia scowled, "We talked about this! Some topics are private! Stop telling your mother everything that you and I discuss." Then she stomped downstairs to make dinner. This conversation was over.

Privacy Violations and Boundary Turbulence

The first narrative focuses on the in-law family relationship between Julia (DIL), Linda (MIL), and Michael (Julia's husband). Linda expects to know everything about Julia and Michael's relationship and family, especially as it pertains to Julia and Michael's six-year-old son, Carter. Julia consistently attempts to maintain harmony with her MIL for the benefit of the family, but she is bothered by Linda's intrusive questions about her marriage to Michael. Linda asks about the couple's finances, health issues, and parenting. Julia feels that Michael sometimes divulges too much information to his mother, which causes friction in their own marriage. Julia prefers to keep some topics private (e.g., finances and family planning) and wants Michael to also uphold these privacy boundaries.

In nonvoluntary relationships, individuals in Julia's situation may feel a tension between maintaining a satisfying relationship with an in-law and maintaining interpersonal space and privacy (Petronio & Reierson, 2009). Julia prefers to keep more information private than her spouse, Michael, and the narrative displays the *boundary turbulence* that Linda and Michael encounter as a result of Michael sharing private information with his mother. Julia's attempts to specify the type of information or topics that she wants to stay private is an example of a *privacy rule* that she has specified, although Michael's responses do not indicate that he follows the same privacy rules as his partner.

Julia and Michael are *authorized co-owners* of the information (Petronio, 2013) related to their nuclear family, such as their son and their decisions regarding family planning. Julia reminded Michael that they had talked about what he could and could not tell his mom, indicating that they have set *explicit privacy rules* regarding what should and should not be shared with others. These rules are direct and clearly stated so all co-owners know what is expected of them in terms of disclosures (Petronio, 1991, 2002). In this respect, Julia is trying to control the flow of information by establishing a boundary, so her private information does not reach Linda. By telling his mother information co-owned by Julia and him, Michael made a *boundary rule mistake*, which is a common cause of boundary turbulence (Petronio, 1991). This privacy violation has the propensity to disrupt Julia and Michael's relationship, as it can "compromise a sense of trust" (Petronio & Reierson, 2009, p. 376). It is likely that privacy recalibration occurred, as Julia and Michael adjusted their privacy rules to "restore" their privacy management (Steuber & McLaren, 2015).

MIL as the Constant Gossiper

After grabbing her coffee from the counter, Tara sat down at a nearby table with her friend Kiora. "So, what is Mama Joyce up to this week?" asked Tara, referring to Kiora's insufferable mother-in-law.

Kiora rolled her eyes. "Into everyone's business and exaggerating their stories each time she gossips with a new person. As usual."

"Oh yeah? What's this week's story?"

"I don't even pay attention anymore. Someone from church group bought a pie from Kroger and tried to pass it off as 'home-made,' and one of Davis' high school classmates might be cheating on his wife because Joyce thought she saw his car at a house on 15th Street when he actually lives across town." Kiora paused before continuing, "She tries to get me fired up about these 'major transgressions,' but I'm so exhausted by her nonstop talking that I just can't pay attention anymore."

Tara laughed, "But why does she care about this—and more importantly, why do people keep telling her things?!"

"I don't know! I certainly don't tell her anything. I don't even like to be around her."

"Does she still like to tell everyone about your parents' divorce?" asked Tara.

"Ugh. YES! That was finalized three years ago, and she likes to insert it into any conversation she can." Kiora's parents had been legally separated since she was in elementary school, but they finally divorced a few years ago because her mother wanted to get remarried. Kiora recollected, "I told Joyce about the divorce and my mother's remarriage just so she was up-to-date on the basics of my life. She took that story and ran with it. She told anyone who would listen. And, of course, it was embellished each time."

Tara shook her head and took a drink of her coffee.

Kiora continued cynically, "By the time the story got back to me, my mother had dated five people simultaneously and cheated on my dad." Kiora rolled her eyes and sarcastically added, "If in fact, he is my real dad."

Tara stared. She had heard this story before, but it shocked her each time. How could someone be so ill-mannered?

"And that was the last time I told Mama Joyce anything personal about my life," declared Kiora.

"So what on earth do you two talk about?" Tara inquired. "I can't picture sitting with my mother-in-law and just making mind-numbing small talk."

Kiora raised her eyebrows, "I try not to ever talk with her when it's just the two of us. Davis knows to never leave me alone with her."

"Really?" Tara was amazed. She had a challenging relationship with her mother-in-law too, but her issues were quite mild compared to Kiora's problems. Tara couldn't imagine how difficult it must be for Kiora and Davis to navigate social situations with Joyce.

"Mmhmm. That's one of our rules. After the divorce story and what she broadcast about my mother, Davis and I decided that would be best for our family. And actually, I try not to be around Joyce at all. It's just easier to not talk to her than to try steering her away from her irrational gossip and toward a conversation about the weather. Or her beloved flower garden."

Tara took another sip of coffee and smiled teasingly, "It'd be a shame if anything ever happened to that flower garden."

Person-Based Avoidance

In this second case, Kiora (DIL) does not like to share any information with her MIL, Joyce. In the past, Joyce has told other family members private information that Kiora divulged to her. Joyce has also used some of Kiora's disclosures against her in arguments or when trying to make Kiora look foolish in front of other family members. As a result, Kiora avoids being around Joyce at all costs. When she does find herself in unavoidable physical proximity to Joyce, Kiora only talks about "safe" topics, such as the weather or Joyce's flower garden.

When Kiora shared private information with her MIL, although it was not her intention, the information became *co-owned*, which means that Joyce thought it was okay to share the information with others (Petronio, 2002). As Kiora learned that Joyce was sharing her information with others, she decided to engage in avoidance. *Topic avoidance* (Afifi & Guerrero, 2000) is a strategic decision not to talk about certain topics, and Kiora's reason for avoidance are twofold: she thinks her MIL is going to share personal information with others, and she believes her MIL to be dishonest and untrustworthy. When a privacy breach occurs, trust is damaged, and individuals often increase the strength of privacy boundaries (Petronio, 2002) or exclude that person from future disclosures (Petronio & Durham, 2008). Self-protection, relationship protection, and social inappropriateness are just a few possible motives for topic avoidance in relationships, as one party aims to protect themselves from judgment or criticism (DeGroot & Young, 2016; Guerrero & Afifi, 1995a, 1995b).

Kiora is using avoidance to protect herself (Caughlin & Afifi, 2004), and maintain distance in her relationship (Dainton & Gross, 2008). In the narrative, Kiora acknowledges that she uses topic avoidance by only talking about certain topics, but she is also avoiding all communication with her MIL which is associated with lower quality relationship perceptions (Mikucki-Enyart, 2018).

DIL as the Sidestepper

"I'm meeting your mom for lunch in 10 minutes," Stassi told Blake, as she grabbed a light jacket from the closet. Stassi and Blake have been together for over 15 years but never married. Stassi considers Blake's mother, Elaine, to be her mother-in-law.

"Uh…hun? Remember not to tell her about…the thing," Blake reminded Stassi. Blake was recently laid off from his job at the local packaging plant due to significant downsizing and corporate restructuring. He knew the layoff was coming, but it was distressing, nonetheless. Although he already had a job interview lined up next week, he was sensitive about his current unemployed status.

"I remember," sighed Stassi. "But you're going to have to tell her sometime. You know she'll find out from someone."

Blake agreed, "I know. But I don't want to do it today."

"Alright," said Stassi. "I'll see you later," she called as she shut the door.

When Stassi got to the restaurant, Elaine was already seated and drinking an iced tea. Stassi took a deep breath. It was going to be difficult not talking about Blake's unemployment. Stassi and Elaine meet for lunch once a month just to talk. Elaine is a retired emergency room nurse and always has interesting stories to tell. Stassi's friends frequently complain about their mothers-in-law, but she rarely joins in that conversation. She genuinely likes Elaine's company and hasn't encountered the challenging situations her girlfriends describe.

"Stassi!" greeted Elaine. "Good to see you. I ordered you an iced tea as well."

"Great, thank you," replied Stassi, as she sat down. "How has your week been?"

Elaine and Stassi chatted about Stassi's job and Elaine's failed attempts at training her dogs not to bark at the squirrels. After a few minutes, the discussion turned to Blake.

"How is Blake's job? I heard their profits were down and they might have to restructure," inquired Elaine.

Stassi almost choked on her salad. How does Elaine always find things out? "Same old, same old," Stassi managed to respond. She wondered if Elaine could tell that she was dodging the question.

Elaine tilted her head to the side and furrowed her eyebrows. She knew something was amiss. She started another question. "Is Blake concerned about—"

"Oh my goodness, did you see the second part of the *Housewives* reunion?" Stassi quickly interjected. Elaine loves to watch *The Real Housewives of New York*. She refers to it as her "one guilty pleasure."

"Yes! Those women really went after Bethenny, didn't they?!" exclaimed Elaine. Stassi breathed a sigh of relief. The remainder of the lunch conversation turned to rehashing the latest *Housewives* episodes, and Stassi was finally able to relax a bit.

Coordinating Privacy Boundaries

The final vignette describes a situation in which Stassi (DIL) and her partner, Blake, discuss Blake's recent layoff. Blake asks Stassi not to say anything about his unemployment to anyone. When Blake's mother, Elaine, and Stassi have lunch together, Elaine asks Stassi about Blake's job, among other topics. Stassi does not want to tell Elaine anything about Blake because he asked her not to do so. Stassi changes the subject and tries to engage Elaine in a conversation about the latest season of the *Real Housewives of New York*.

In-law relationships are considered a triad, and the *linchpin* (Duck, Foley, & Kirkpatrick, 2006) describes the person (Stassi) who connects the two individuals to one another. In this scenario, Blake has drawn distinct *privacy rules* about the *co-owners* (he and his partner, Stassi) of the information and created a thick, *impermeable boundary* around his job loss so that Stassi knows to keep that information private from Elaine, an *outsider* (Afifi & Guerrero, 1998). Stassi and Blake have communicated openly about the boundary rules, coordinating boundary preferences for who should disclose the information to Elaine. Limiting information with Blake's mother is a form of *preemptive privacy control* (Petronio & Reierson, 2009). Blake and Stassi serve as co-owners of the information about Blake's unemployment and have discussed *explicit privacy rules* to follow regarding that topic. Blake's rule is that he tells his mother on his own terms; Stassi's rule is that she is not the one to tell Elaine that information.

Because Stassi typically has a friendly, honest relationship with Elaine, she likely experiences a *dialectic tension* (Petronio, 2002; Petronio & Reierson, 2009) as she adheres to her previously determined privacy rules to control the flow of private information. She seeks to uphold the privacy rules created with Blake by concealing information about his unemployment. At the same time, Stassi feels pressure to reveal this information to Elaine as a means to maintain the relationship with her. Stassi is also concerned about Elaine's perception of her if Elaine finds out about Blake's situation from a different source.

DISCUSSION QUESTIONS

1. How does topic avoidance take on different roles (and relational outcomes) in each of these three scenarios? In which scenarios might topic avoidance serve to maintain the status quo of the relationship? To create distance? To create closeness?
2. How does a privacy violation affect the relationship between the two co-owners? What are some potential outcomes if privacy rules are not followed? What actions are likely taken after a violation?
3. What is the role of the linchpin in boundary management, coordination, and privacy rules in these scenarios?

REFERENCES

Afifi, W. A., & Guerrero, L. K. (1998). Some things are better left unsaid II: Topic avoidance in friendships. *Communication Quarterly, 46*(3), 231–249.

Afifi, W. A., & Guerrero, L. K. (2000). Motivations underlying topic avoidance in close relationships. In S. Petronio (Ed.), *Balancing the secrets of private disclosures* (pp. 165–179). Mahwah, NJ: Lawrence Erlbaum Associates.

Caughlin, J. P., & Afifi, T. D. (2004). When is topic avoidance unsatisfying? Examining moderators of the association between avoidance and dissatisfaction. *Human Communication Research, 30*, 479–513.

Dainton, M., & Gross, J. (2008). The use of negative behaviors to maintain relationships. *Communication Research Reports, 25*(3), 179–191. doi:10.1080/08824090802237600

DeGroot, J. M., & Young, V. J. (2016). *"I'd rather not give her ammunition": Avoidance strategies in relationships with mothers-in-law.* Presented at the annual convention of the National Communication Association, Philadelphia, PA.

Duck, S., Foley, M. K., & Kirkpatrick, D. C. (2006). Relating difficulty in a triangular world. In D. C. Kirkpatrick, S. Duck, & M. K. Foley (Eds.), *Relating difficulty: The process of constructing and managing difficult interaction* (pp. 225–232). Mahwah, NJ: Lawrence Erlbaum Associates.

Guerrero, L. K., & Afifi, W. A. (1995a). Some things are better left unsaid: Topic avoidance in family relationships. *Communication Quarterly, 43*, 276–296. doi:10.1080/01463379509369977

Guerrero, L. K., & Afifi, W. A. (1995b). What parents don't know: Taboo topics and topic avoidance in parent-child relationships. In T. J. Socha & G. Stamp (Eds.), *Parents, children, and communication: Frontiers of theory and research* (pp. 219–245). Hillsdale, NJ: Erlbaum.

Hess, J. A. (2000). Maintaining nonvoluntary relationships with disliked partners: An investigation into the use of distancing behaviors. *Human Communication Research, 26*, 458–488. doi:10.1111/j.1468-2958.2000.tb00765.x

Mikucki-Enyart, S. L. (2018). In-laws' perceptions of topic avoidance, goal inferences, and relational outcomes. *Journal of Family Communication.* Advance online publication. doi:10.1080/15267431.2018.1492411

Petronio, S. (1991). Communication boundary management: A theoretical model of managing disclosure of private information between marital couples. *Communication Theory, 1*, 311–335. doi:10.1111/j.1468-2885.1991.tb00023.x

Petronio, S. (2002). *Boundaries of privacy: Dialectics of disclosure.* Albany, NY: SUNY Press.

Petronio, S. (2013). Brief status report on communication privacy management theory. *Journal of Family Communication, 13*, 6–14. doi:10.1080/15267431.2013.743426

Petronio, S., & Durham, W. T. (2008). Communication privacy management theory. In L. A. Baxter & D. O. Braithwaite (Eds.), *Engaging theories in interpersonal communication: Multiple perspectives* (pp. 335–347). Thousand Oaks, CA: Sage.

Petronio, S., & Reierson, J. (2009). Regulating the privacy of confidentiality: Grasping the complexities through communication privacy management theory. In T. Afifi & W. A. Afifi (Eds.), *Uncertainty, information management, and disclosure decisions: Theories and applications* (pp. 365–383). New York, NY: Routledge.

Steuber, K. R., & McLaren, R. M. (2015). Privacy recalibration in personal relationships: Rule usage before and after an incident of privacy turbulence. *Communication Quarterly, 63*(3), 345–364. doi:10.1080/01463373.2015.1039717

CHAPTER 15

The Big Bang: Adding a New Generation to a Family

Tim Dun – *Brock University*

ABSTRACT

Emma's family grew last year when she and her husband Ted had their first child, Flora. Like with any couple's first child, Flora created new relationships (parent–child and grandparent–grandchild). The arrival of a new generation also forms a major turning point for existing relationships, such as between new parents and their parents, the grandparents. By taking a look at several new parent–grandparent relationships, this case uncovers some of the many smaller events that lead up to and follow childbirth. Although the process is unique in each family relationship, the unfolding events form common patterns. This case illustrates four particular patterns or trajectories: peak, valley, growth, and steady. In addition to exploring relational change, the case has a second theme: Issues of autonomy and connection, which affect all family relationships, come to the forefront in intergenerational ties between new parents and grandparents.

Emma. Looking back, Emma remembered how happily she worked with her mom to plan the baby shower for her first child, Flora. Since their regular lives didn't allow them to spend so much time together, planning the baby shower was special, an unusual opportunity. Emma's mom, Winsome, had an eight-year-old grandson, but no granddaughters, which seemed to add to her excitement. Emma had been looking forward to becoming a mother, and Winsome had been both happy for her daughter and glad to have her first granddaughter on the way. As they bought pink balloons and other decorations for the baby shower, prepared games, and so on, Emma and her mom talked a lot, mostly about little things. While planning the shower for her friends and family was just part of the build-up to childbirth, it was a small turning point in the relationship that brought mother and daughter closer to each other.

It's Tim here. All of the stories in this chapter come from new parents and grandparents that I met during my research (Dun, 2010; Dun, & Sangster, 2013; Dun, & Sears, 2017). Where possible, I include direct quotations from what people said to me, but I did change names to protect their privacy. I also edited details to make this one combined case. That is, the real Emma, Winsome, and Ted did not know each other.

Even though Emma and her husband Ted had waited to become parents (they were both in their thirties now), Emma always knew that she would be a mom someday. Throughout her pregnancy, motherhood became more and more real, as Emma looked forward to finally becoming a mother. She hoped her labor and delivery would be like her older sister Diane's. Diane had both her husband and mom with her for labor and delivery, so their first child's arrival was greeted by different generations of the family all together. Of course, Emma had also worried about the possibility of complications during her pregnancy, and she took care to avoid alcohol or anything that could have hurt Flora, but for the most part Emma was full of happy expectations for Flora's birth.

Unfortunately, Emma's mom fell and broke her collarbone the day before Flora's birth, which dashed all of Emma's hopes of having mom with her for labor and delivery. It had been beyond disappointing. With her mom already in the hospital receiving treatment her injury, things were far from what Emma expected. Instead of coming to see her and being there to help, Emma's mom was elsewhere in the hospital, recovering from the painful fall that broke her collarbone. When Emma came home from the hospital with Flora, Emma continued to miss her mom, who was also at home recuperating. Luckily, she had her husband Ted, but he was unable to take much time off work, so Emma had felt somewhat isolated with her newborn daughter.

During that first week at home alone with Flora, Emma had a couple of low moments when she would list all the new moms she knew who'd had their mothers present for their first child's birth. The list included friends, coworkers, neighbors—just about everyone Emma knew. And the list kept growing. Emma's coworker Julie, who recently returned from

CASING THE FAMILY: Theoretical and Applied Approaches to Understanding Family Communication

maternity leave, told everyone at work how much she loved having her mom there during childbirth. One day last week, Julie told the story to the office, explaining how she hadn't even wanted her mother at the delivery.

> I remember my sister telling me, she was you know—I didn't think I wanted my mom in there—and I can remember my sister saying, "You just wait till you're in there." You know, "When you're in pain the only thing you're gonna want is your mom…" And that's exactly how it was. You know, because it was, you're in so much pain and you do what, you revert back to childhood almost where you just want your mom…I can remember I was like, I don't know, five or six centimeters dilated, and we were waiting for the anesthesiologist. Waiting, waiting, waiting. Nobody was coming; my mom was out in the hall, you know, just raising hell.

Hearing the story last week during a coffee break reminded Emma of the disappointment she felt last year. Reflecting back after a year, Emma knew that now she was as close as ever with her mom. Despite feeling separated from her mom during Flora's birth, Emma and Winsome had persevered through the valley and emerged happy again.

Tim here. Emma's trajectory from a daughter–mom relationship to become mom and grandmother was less common than what Julie and Diane experienced. Not many new parents that participated in my research described a valley (Dun & Sangster, 2013). Instead, the most common trajectory was peak, where the new parents were most satisfied during or just after delivery. I included Emma as the main voice in this chapter, because she gives us a valuable perspective to make sense of the more common trajectory for new parents and grandparents, a peak at childbirth. Emma was on track to and was hoping for the special closeness with her mom. It was the gap between what did happen and the peak trajectory like Diane's delivery that made childbirth disappointing for Emma and created a low point in her relationship with her mom. That is, Emma had been told to expect something special like other new mothers and fathers.

While her husband and her dad played out back with Flora, Emma marveled at how Flora had brought the two men together. Flora gave Ted and her dad something in common, and they'd become close to one another thanks to shared involvement with Flora.

Ted. As a tax accountant, Ted felt that his professional background had made a bit of a barrier between himself and Harry, who had worked his whole life as a truck driver, first as long-haul and later for a local beverage distributor. So, when he married Emma, Ted and Harry started with little in common and had short, stunted conversations, awkward conversations. They didn't share any interests in sports, politics, or much of anything else. However, each milestone for little Flora allowed them to build on a shared bond with her. While Harry had been away much of the time when Emma was a baby, he now had more time and was happily involved with his granddaughter. For example, Harry and Ted had really connected a few weeks ago at Flora's first birthday party, where they talked about Flora's sudden ability to walk and get herself into trouble so quickly. She loved chasing the wary cat around the house and removing pots and pans from the cupboard. After the party, Ted and Emma chatted about how pleased they were that Flora and Harry were bonding so well. Ted told Emma, "It definitely increases my sense of, 'yeah, this is working the way I thought it would.'"

Emma smiled wistfully, thought back to the birth last year, and said, "Well, you know some things did not go as I had expected, but it is working well now." Emma paused briefly and her smile grew as her thoughts returned to how Flora was bringing the two men in her life closer. That wasn't something she'd expected either.

Tim here. Notice that the same turning point—Flora's birth—was part of two completely different relationship trajectories. Childbirth was part of Harry and Ted's increasingly satisfying bond and the same event led Emma to describe a valley, or dipped trajectory in her relationship with her mother. Events like this turning point take on meaning in the context of relationships, with their past ups and downs and expectations for a shared future.

As she finished her goodbyes to her parents in the driveway, Emma's neighbor Jerry appeared to return a casserole dish. (Emma had baked a lasagna for Denise and Jerry after their son's birth.) With all the changes in her family on her mind, Emma said, "I bet things are really different in your family now that you've become a father." Jerry said yes emphatically but paused a moment before adding he was glad for his own mom, "because that's absolutely solid—our relationship hasn't changed." Compared to all of the differences in her own family, Jerry's response surprised Emma a little bit, and her face showed it.

"Hasn't changed?" she asked.

"No," he said. "My mom and I have had the most awesome relationship all of our life—and becoming a father hasn't changed that."

Mentally reviewing the many changes in her own family, Emma found that sort of 'steady as she goes' hard to grasp. Emma always loved her mom, but that love could be painful, as it was when they were unable to spend time together with Flora when she was a newborn. Still, she couldn't argue with how Jerry felt, and she knew that Jerry and his mother shared a close bond. Instead of following up, Emma asked about Alex and Denise (the new baby and Jerry's wife).

Winsome. Emma's mom and dad, the new grandparents, began the drive home silently, both reflecting upon the time with their daughter, granddaughter, and son-in-law. While Harry had a slight scowl, Winsome enjoyed herself planning the next gift she should get for them. Winsome enjoyed buying them presents, especially when she found something that they might have trouble affording for themselves. She paid the tab for Emma's baby shower and knew that her daughter truly appreciated it. On the other hand, Winsome would have been surprised to know how disappointing the childbirth was for Emma. Although both mother and daughter felt that it was a dip in their relationship, Winsome felt that such ups and downs were part of any relationship, especially a lifelong one. That is, Winsome took challenges in her stride.

When Harry broke the silence, it was clear that he wasn't taking things in stride. Or maybe, he was talking himself into accepting his daughter's decisions about co-sleeping. Thus, Winsome and Harry began to chat about Flora and their family on the way home. Well, really it was more Harry talking—sharing his concerns about Flora sharing Emma and Ted's bed at night.

"I hope they move her into that crib soon," Harry began. "You remember the posters down at the Y a few years ago, don't you? They said that sleeping with your child can be deadly."

Winsome nodded, remembering the large posters warning new parents to put infants in their crib, but she suspected the campaign may have overstated the dangers of co-sleeping. She also knew that Harry didn't really need her to answer. Harry continued while Winsome listened to his worries. It was a generational difference; Winsome and Harry had not slept with either of their daughters.

At the end of the 15-minute drive home, Harry arrived at the conclusion she expected: Flora was in very good hands; we trust Emma. What he said was, "It's important to respect their decisions; they're the parents." This statement summarized their philosophy as grandparents, a simple approach that allowed them to voice concerns but to let go and avoid interfering with the new family. Harry had brought up co-sleeping months ago, and now he was going to let them continue to make their own decisions without feeling interference.

Winsome remembered how years ago Harry's mother had been so directive and opinionated about her grandchildren (Emma and her sister Diane). Winsome and Harry agreed that their roles and their approach to grandparenting would not be that of the advisor-in-chief. She told her husband, "We'll be happier; they'll be happier."

Sometimes she worried that since Harry had been less active as a parent, he might want to speak up more with Ted and Emma's decisions. Even though he had some friends who took a much more active role as grandparents, she felt the extra space in her family actually allowed her to be closer to Emma. That is, Winsome felt that if she became too directive, her help might be seen as butting in and could imply that Emma was not a good mother.

Tim: There are very few moments in the life of a family as fundamental as a couple's first child. There are so many changes. They both become parents while the immediate family changes from just one relationship to three relationships. Of course, the relationship between the parents experiences many substantial changes, but other family ties are also impacted, as the stories in the chapter show. Because a new generation has so many consequences, I think of it as the 'big bang' for families.

DISCUSSION QUESTIONS

1. What are all the different ways that autonomy and connection appear in the family relationships discussed in this chapter?
2. A turning point is an event that changes a relationship, either bringing people closer or hurting their relationship in some way. Turning points in this case study include childbirth, planning a baby shower, a birthday party, and giving advice. What are some major turning points in your relationship with a parent?
3. What would a trajectory of your relationship with a parent look like? If you graphed all of the ups and downs—turning points that affected the closeness of your connection to your father or mother—would it be pretty flat like Emma's neighbour Jerry or have more bumps along the way, like the way Winsome sees her relationship with Emma?
4. Besides having a new child in a family, what are other ways that one relationship can affect other relationships?

REFERENCES

Dun, T. (2010). Turning points in parent-grandparent relationships during the start of a new generation. Journal of Family Communication, 10, 194–210. doi:10.1080/15267431.2010.489218

Dun, T., & Sangster, L. (2013). Family trajectories: Intergenerational relationships during the birth of a new generation. Qualitative Communication Research, 2, 255–280. doi:10.1525/qcr.2013.2.3.255

Dun, T., & Sears, C. (2017). Relational trajectories from parent and child to grandparent and parent. Journal of Family Communication, 17, 185–201. doi:10.1080/15267431.2017.1281281

'Help, My Teen Is Sexting!': A Case Study of Seeking Mediated Social Support for Parents Who Caught Their Teen Sexting

Elizabeth M. Jenkins – *Ohio University*

ABSTRACT

In this case study, a parent discovers sext messages on her teenager's cell phone. The parent (Julie) must consider how to approach this difficult conversation with her son (talking to her son about the dangers of sexting). After considering several potential avenues for reasons why her son is sexting, including several concerning self-blame, Julie turns to an online social media thread for parents of teens for online social support from other parents who are strangers to Julie personally, but seem to be connected through similar experiences that they have encountered with their own teenagers. This anonymous and mediated communication allows Julie to feel support that she often does not experience as a single parent. Therefore, this case study will help students consider and analyze aspects of parent–child communication about difficult topics. Specifically, students will better understand how mediated social support through online forums can serve as a communicatively based social support system for parents of teenagers.

CASE STUDY

Teenagers are the largest population who use digital technologies (Mesch & Frenkel, 2011). The effects these technologies have on teenagers and the wider implications of those technologies on families warrant research attention (Mesch & Frenkel, 2011). Galvin (2013) argues that family communication scholarship needs to study how parents and teens navigate the sometimes difficult aspects of the internet, including identity development (Campbell & Park, 2014, p. 32), cyberbullying (Nguyen & Mark, 2014), and navigating privacy concerns (Boyd, 2014).

The majority of sexting research involving teens and young adults has provided evidence for the dangerous consequences of this behavior. For example, sexting research with teenage samples has largely framed sexting as a bad or negative behavior for reasons such as the relationship of sexting to risky sexual behaviors (Klettke, Hallford, & Mellor, 2014), the fear of having sext messages forwarded (Renfrow & Rollo, 2014), the actual forwarding of sext messages (Drouin, Vogel, Surbey, & Stills, 2013), the possibility of coercive sexting (Drouin, Ross, & Tobin, 2015; Drouin & Tobin, 2014), revenge porn (Stroud, 2014), and the legal ramifications involved in teen sexting (Strohmaier, Murphy, & DeMatteo, 2014; Wastler, 2010). In a specific example, teens who sext are also more likely participate in other risky sexual behaviors, such as not using a condom during sex (Klettke et al., 2014). Furthermore, young adults do not only fear that their sext messages are getting forwarded (Renfrow & Rollo, 2014), but a fair amount of sext messages are actually forwarded without consent (Drouin et al., 2013). Moreover, many young adults are consenting to sexting when they do not want to sext. This unwanted but consensual sexting has been related to partner violence, trauma symptoms (Drouin et al., 2015), and negative mental health symptoms, such as depression and anxiety (Drouin & Tobin, 2014). These findings are rather alarming considering the possible legal ramifications of teens who are in possession of sext pictures or videos of other minors.

However, Jenkins and Stamp (2018) demonstrated that the general public disagrees about the level of inherent danger involved in sexting. These negative aspects of sexting are not explicitly putting all teens at risk, rather these technologies "create a new site where risky behaviors are made visible and troubled youth engage in new types of problematic activities" (Boyd, 2014, p. 113). Therefore, sexting via technology creates a new platform of risky behavior for teenagers who are probably already participating in other risky behaviors. Thus, there is a possible argument that not all teens and young adults who participate in sexting will do so in a negative way. That being said, it is probably not the technology that is causing these issues, rather it may be that at-risk teens will be likely to behave badly regardless of whatever technology exists. There is a chance that parents could mitigate this issue of detrimental teenage technology use.

Parents often hope to help and protect their children to the best of their abilities (Boyd, 2014). While no parent wants their child to be harmed, "internet use…presents a challenge to family boundaries as it increases unsupervised exposure of adolescents to a wide variety of content" (Mesch & Frenkel, 2011, p. 290). Parents have an opportunity to discuss the potential harm in a way that is nonthreatening to teens and that invites further dialogue. These "hard conversations" or "difficult dialogues" often shape teens' long-term memories and life narratives (Holman & Koenig Kellas, 2018; Rubinsky & Cooke-Jackson, 2017). When parents put their own pride, fears, and awkwardness aside, they can often establish a culture of shared information, private discussions, and strengthened trust between themselves and their teenage children (Boyd, 2014). By doing so, these teens feel as if they are supported. This reciprocal and open discussion between teens and parents is often related to long-term outcomes well into adulthood (Schrodt, Ledbetter, & Ohrt, 2007). The alternative option of not discussing these difficult topics can lead to negative mental health outcomes (Babin & Palazzolo, 2012). These conversations are incredibly difficult to initiate and sustain, but the familial, interpersonal, and intrapersonal payoff is immense.

***

In the first half of the narrative below, Julie starts to process what it means to find sext pictures from teenage girls on her son's phone. As you read this narrative, attempt to consider Julie's feelings. Specifically:

1. Name specific and implied emotions that Julie is expressing. Why do you think these emotions are being expressed in these ways?
2. Predict what Julie is going to do about the situation with her son.
3. Try to put yourself in Julie's shoes. As a parent, how would you feel? How would you react and why?

***

Julie just did the one thing she swore she never would do, and immediately regretted her decision. Despite having a son who follows most rules, does well in school, and doesn't act out, Julie has been concerned about how much time he has been spending alone and away from the family. Julie has had an internal debate about how to determine if her son is in pain or suffering in some way, or if he is just being a typical 16-year-old.

Julie had been especially concerned about him recently because she and her husband have recently separated. After 21 years of marriage, they decided to take some time apart in order to determine if continuing their marriage was worth it, or if they should consider divorce. Julie worried about the outcome of this split on her son. Would he be okay? Would he shake this off and keep going? Would it impact his own relationships? Would he treat his partners differently because his own parents struggled to make their relationship work?

Last night, Julie decided that several weeks of excessive sneaking with his phone into the bathroom, away from the living room, or into his bedroom equated to suspicious phone use. She snuck into her son's room while he was showering later that evening to check his phone.

Sure enough, there were several pictures of girls' boobs on his phone. Julie knew these girls and knew they were friends with her son. Julie was absolutely mortified. She wanted to immediately delete them, but knew her son would be highly suspicious. As she quickly scrolled, Julie thought to herself: "Well, at least he didn't talk any of these girls into doing this." Then she immediately hated herself for condoning the behavior at all. "These are kids!" she silently screamed at herself. "They don't know what they've done. I have to tell their parents. No, no, no. That would get my son in hot water and also risk his trust in me. What do I do about this now?"

***

"Adolescence is a period of life replete with conflicts between parents and children" (Mesch & Frenkel, 2011, p. 294). At this time of tumultuous conflict within the family, it is vitally important for parents to know what the potential dangers are for their teenagers in terms of sexting. Parent's knowledge and awareness of their teen's sexting behaviors is important for the argument that scholars should be examining sexting from a family communication lens.

For example, a study conducted by Ahern, Kemppainen, and Thacker (2016) showed that in terms of the overarching category of teenage risk behaviors, parents generally have only minor understandings of the potential risk activities for teenagers. Specifically related to teen sexting behaviors, most parents are aware that sexting is potentially problematic (Ahern et al., 2016). Parents also generally understand the implications of mediated solicitation (e.g., someone asking a teenager to sext) and the forwarding of sexually explicit images (Nguyen & Mark, 2014). Thus, parents seem to know about sexting, about sexting being problematic, and about the asking of and sharing of sext messages between teens.

However, only a little over a third of the parents in the study had previously talked to their teens about sexting (Ahern et al., 2016). If parents could discuss this (and other) difficult, stigmatized, and otherwise "dark" topics with their teens who are or most likely will be exposed to them, then the positive behavioral outcomes may outweigh the uncomfortable feelings associated with having these discussions. A culture of parent–teenager communication based on open dialogue (even about hard things) and explicit communication could be created and could influence the teenager, the parent, and the long-term relationship between the two. Thus, a shifting shape of family dynamics stands in the balance between having a hard conversation or not.

***

At 2 a.m., Julie is still lying awake thinking about on the images on her son's phone in the next room. She contemplates trying to sneak in again and stealing his cell. "I can convince him he lost it. Yeah, that might work." She wondered if every parent in the world worried like she did. "I'm doing parenting all wrong. I don't know what's wrong with me. I can't even keep my marriage together, how am I supposed to keep my son safe?" Julie also considered that her son was one of the good ones. "As bad as this is, at least my son isn't sending any messages like that of his own privates…oh crap, what if I just missed them or he deleted them?"

As the minutes and hours passed, Julie's restlessness compelled her to take action. She logged onto Facebook to see if there might be someone online she could talk to about her situation. After a few minutes of searches and a few failed attempts, Julie found a private Facebook group called "Parents of Teens in the Internet Era." Julie requested to join and within two minutes had been added by an administrator to the group, located in a different time zone overseas. "Hmm, that was quick," she thought. "Let's see…"

Over the next half hour, Julie learned a lot by merely looking at other's posts and the comments below them. She could see that some parents were voicing full concerns about problematic phone, internet, and even gaming issues. Other parents seemed to contribute "good news" type posts where they sought affirmation for a tough conversation with their teen about internet use or talked to a school administrator about issues their teen was having with cyberbullying. Some parents just posted messages such as: "I just want to say, I'm doing my best, but I am drowning as a parent." These posts, in particular, seemed to receive substantial responses from the over 5,000 members in this forum. The comments and reactions were so comforting. "Keep it up, friend. You're doing great, I promise it will get easier."

Julie took a breath and realized how supported she felt just hearing that other parents were struggling like she was. She felt relief knowing that others were also showing kindness rather than judgment. All along she just felt ashamed that her son was doing something so unlike himself. She was incredibly concerned that her failing marriage was to blame for his behavior.

After another few minutes of scrolling, Julie decided she wanted to post her concerns about the sext messages on her son's phone:

Julie: Hi parents of teenagers. I am a very new member, but I need help with my teen-age son. He is sexting. I saw his texts on his phone. These girls are sending him pics of their boobs and I am mortified. He doesn't know I snuck into his room and looked through his phone, but now that I have, I don't know what to do. I have to do something. I can't un-see these pictures. I am overwhelmed thinking about how to best protect him and how to help the other teens sending these messages. How do I tell him this behavior is not okay, but still come off as a supportive parent? I don't want to lose my good kid over something like this.

Julie hit send and two seconds later she saw the bubbles indicating that commenting had started. Within an hour, several parents from all over the globe were chiming in on the issue. Julie went from feeling alone, isolated, and as if she was dealing with a unique situation to feeling comforted by the kind support she was receiving. There were certainly some terrible comments by a couple of parents, but Julie was amazed how other members often patrolled and moderated those negative messages. It was as if Julie did not even have to expend the energy to redirect negativity.

Julie finally set her phone down at 5:28 a.m. Her alarm to get up to start her day and to help her son start his day was set for 5:45 a.m. She might not have slept, but Julie felt refreshed and rejuvenated despite the lack of sleep. A couple of comments from the night stood out to Julie and she contemplated them more fully as she lay there for her last 15 or so minutes of rest.

Max: "Julie, thanks for being vulnerable and sharing. I recently found out my 15-year-old daughter was sending sext messages to her partner and it terrified me. I felt alone because even though I assumed other parents were dealing with this, I didn't want to talk to anyone I actually knew for fear of judgment. I ended up sitting my daughter down and having a really hard conversation about sex and how sexting is different in some ways. I talked about how this is a new way to be "sexy" but that she might not be thinking fully about what could happen to her. I pulled up some news stories about how teens have been charged as pedophiles for sending sext messages and how others have been kicked out of school. I didn't want to scare her, but I did want to talk to her about what could happen. I don't think it went perfectly, but it was a start. Good luck. Isn't parenting fun?"

Jasmine: "Oh, Julie. Yeah. Every day I wonder if I am parenting correctly or if I have just officially messed up my four kids (ages 9, 11, 12, 17). I am doing this all on my own because my wife died two years ago. I don't even know when to find the time to check their phones and social media. I am lost and just trying to make their lives the best they can while saving some of my sanity. I have seen all these same news stories about teen sexting as Max. And honestly, it makes me sick. How dare we condemn teens for something that I might do if I could find someone who would actually want a 46-year-old widow with four kids as a partner? But I also know this is the world we find ourselves currently. So, I take the same approach as Max: talk, talk, and talk until I am blue in the face. I talk to my kids about everything I can, including sexting. I often think I did it all wrong, but hey, at least they know I care enough to open my mouth. I will say that it seems like overall we have a family that shares a lot of intimate details with each other. If I can just keep that going for the next 15 or more years, I guess I'm winning, right?!"

These two posts in particular captured so much of what Julie had been experiencing: feeling sorrow about the idea of your child growing up in a world where it just is the standard now, feeling ashamed because you know you are somewhat hypocritical about their technology use, and genuinely feeling fearful for both the implications of teen sexting and the implications of not talking about it.

Julie decided at 5:44 that she would do it—she would have the hard talk with her son about sexting and all that goes with this behavior. She would try hard not to condemn him, but rather try to have an open space that invites him to express his concerns and also his arguments for sexting. Julie truly believed this was a make-or-break moment for her and her son. She could run and hide, or she could do all she could to be there for him through openly discussing topics that are hard. In the back of her mind she thought, "If I don't create a two-way cycle of discussing sexting, how am I going to create it for discussing drugs, the potential for his father and my divorce, or any types of identity concerns?" Julie took a deep breath as her alarm went off. Julie smiled to herself as she put her feet on the floor and said: "I've got this. Well, at least I've got a plan; we'll see where it goes from there."

***

Computer-mediated communication (CMC) is both good and bad. In fact, DeAndrea, Tong, and Walther (2011) argued:

Whatever social good or social ill that individuals or groups may be inclined to bring to a situation, the Internet, or the affordances it offers, allows people to accentuate these proclivities (p. 96).

In other words, the technology itself is not inherently dark or light, but rather that the people who communicate through these technologies come to use them for both good and bad purposes.

In sum, this case study took the perspective of describing what happens prior to a parent deciding to talk to his or her teenager about a difficult (i.e., dark) topic. The dark topic focused on Julie, the parent, deciding how to handle the dilemma of finding sext messages on her son's phone. During Julie's pre-communication preparation, she reached out for social support online. Through an already established (and fictional) online social support group for parents, Julie could seek help and advice from parents whom she did not know personally. Mediated communication across social media support groups helped a mother normalize her experience and build her confidence in having a difficult conversation with her son about the dangerous use of his phone. Therefore, this case study demonstrated how CMC can be approached as both dark and light sides of family communication.

DISCUSSION QUESTIONS

1. When should family members strategically use technology to communicate? When should family members specifically choose to communicate face-to-face?
2. What unintended (both good and bad) consequences might come from family members' use of computer-mediated communication?
3. What forms of privacy management are involved in this story?
4. How could Julie engage with her son through more straightforward, explicit conversations about her son's behaviors? What positive and/or negative outcomes could stem from difficult conversations?
5. How did mediated social support help Julie in this situation? Why might this have been the case? Hypothetically, what aspects of the mediated social support could have helped Julie more?

REFERENCES

Ahern, N. R., Kemppainen, J., Thacker, P. (2016). Awareness and knowledge of child and adolescent risky behaviors: A parent's perspective. *Journal of Child and Adolescent Psychiatric Nursing, 29*, 6–14.

Babin, E. A., & Palazzolo, K. E. (2012). The relationships between parent communication patterns and sons' and daughters' intimate partner violence involvement: Perspectives from parents and young adult children. *Journal of Family Communication, 12*, 4–21.

Boyd, D. (2014). *It's complicated: The social lives of networked teens.* New Haven, MA: Yale University Press.

Campbell, S. W., & Park, Y. J. (2014). Predictors of mobile sexting among teens: Toward a new explanatory framework. *Mobile Media & Communication, 2*, 20–39.

DeAndrea, D. C., Tong, S. T., & Walther, J. B. (2011). Dark sides of computer-mediated communication. In W.R. Cupach & B. H. Spitzberg (Eds.), *The dark side of close relationships II* (pp. 96–118). New York, NY: Routledge.

Drouin, M., Ross, J., Tobin, E. (2015). Sexting: A new, digital vehicle for intimate partner aggression? *Computers in Human Behavior, 50*, 197–204.

Drouin, M., & Tobin, E. (2014). Unwanted but consensual sexting among young adults: Relations with attachment and sexual motivations. *Computers in Human Behavior, 31*, 412–418.

Drouin, M., Vogel, K. N., Surbey, A., & Stills, J. R. (2013). Let's talk about sexting, baby: Computer-mediated sexual behaviors among young adults. *Computers in Human Behavior, 29*, A25–A30.

Galvin, K.M. (2013). The family of the future: What do we face? In A.L. Vangelisti (Ed.). *The Routledge Handbook of Family Communication (2nd Ed.), 531-545.* New York: Routledge.

Holman, A., & Koenig Kellas, J. (2018). "Say something instead of nothing": Adolescents' perceptions of memorable conversations about sex-related topics with their parents. *Communication Monographs, 85*, 357–379.

Jenkins, E. M., & Stamp, G. H. (2018). Sexting in the public domain: Competing discourse in online news article comments in the US and the UK involving teenage sexting. *Journal of Children and Media, 12*, 1–17.

Klettke, B., Hallford, D. J., & Mellor, D. J. (2014). Sexting prevalence and correlates: A systematic literature review. *Clinical Psychology Review, 34*, 44–53.

Mesch, G. S., & Frenkel, M. (2011). Family imbalance and adjustment to information and communication technologies. In K. B. Wright & L. M. Webb (Eds.), *Computer-mediated communication in personal relationships* (pp. 285–301). New York, NY: Peter Lang.

Nguyen, T. T., Mark, L. K. (2014). Cyberbullying, sexting, and online sharing: A comparison of parent and school faculty perspectives. *International Journal of Cyber Behavior, Psychology, and Learning, 14*, 76–86.

Renfrow, D. G., & Rollo, E. A. (2014). Sexting on campus: Minimizing perceived risks and neutralizing behaviors. *Deviant Behavior, 35*, 903–920.

Rubinsky, V. & Cooke-Jackson, A. (2017). "Tell me something other than to use a condom and sex is scary": Memorable messages women and gender minorities wish for and recall about sexual health. *Women's Studies in Communication, 40*, 379-400. Doi: 10.1080//07491409.2017.1368761.

Schrodt, P. Ledbetter, A.M., & Ohrt, J.K. (2007). Parental confirmation and affection as mediators of family communication patterns and children's mental well-being. *Journal of Family Communication, 7*, 23-46.

Strohmaier, H., Murphy, M., DeMatteo, D. (2014). Youth sexting: Prevalence rates, driving motivations, and the deterrent effect of legal consequences. *Sexuality Research and Social Policy, 11*, 245–255.

Stroud, S. R. (2014). The dark side of the online self: A pragmatist critique of the growing plague of revenge porn. *Journal of Mass Media Ethics, 29*, 168–183.

Wastler, S. (2010). The harm in "sexting"? Analyzing the constitutionality of child pornography statutes that prohibit the voluntary production, possession, and dissemination of sexually explicit images by teenagers. *Harvard Journal of Law and Gender, 33*, 687–702.

CHAPTER 17

0 to 30 to 60 to 90: Four Generations

Michael W. Kramer – *University of Oklahoma*

ABSTRACT

Dennis was pleased that over 40 children, grandchildren, and great-grandchildren attend the 65th wedding anniversary celebration he and his wife organized for his parents. The joy of the moment was somewhat overshadowed by all the other issues facing him. Many of those issues involved deciding between two desirable choices (what scholars call dialectical tensions). He recently had to tell his parents it was time to quit driving. He wanted to spend time with his grandchildren in part to help his children with childcare which closed one week each summer, but that also meant making sure a sibling was in town to watch his parents while they traveled. It also seemed like it might be time to move his parents into assisted living to get help managing his father's dementia. Trying to manage all of these issues was challenging as he continued to work and try to maintain work-life balance.

CASE STUDY

For the moment, Dennis felt satisfied. Over 40 people from four generations of Andersons were gathered together celebrating his parents' 65th wedding anniversary. Their four children and their spouses, along with most of the 14 grandchildren and their spouses, and most of the 12 great grandchildren had come from as far away as Portland, Minneapolis, and Miami to be there for the special day. He listened as one of his sisters finished her tribute to Robert and Janice.

"And so, Mom and Dad, we are truly blessed that you have been together all these years. Your love for each other and every person in this room, and those who couldn't make it, has given us all the kind of love and support we needed to succeed in life. Here's to the coming years we still have together. We love you."

His parents glowed throughout the speeches, or at least Janice's eyes did. Robert's eyes did at times, too, but at other times, he had the vacant look that Dennis saw far too often lately. A lot had changed in the last six years.

Six years ago, when his parents first moved near him and his wife, Martha, to be close to family if they needed help, they pretty much took care of themselves doing their own shopping and doctors' appointments, attending church, and the bi-monthly seniors' group social. Dennis enjoyed the weekly walks with his dad where they discussed family, life, and careers, and he and Martha enjoyed eating out with them after church every Sunday. Some weeks the four of them played cards or went to theater or music performances together. He had never felt closer to his parents. He also felt like they really did not depend on Martha and him for much. They mostly provided some social activities and a feeling of security. That was all they seemed to need.

That had changed lately as Robert's dementia became increasingly problematic and Janice's physical abilities continued to decline. But after all, they were over 90 years old and it was to be expected. Simple things, like playing cards, were too confusing to Robert now. As a result, he stopped driving a few years ago. Janice had taken over that responsibility for the first time in their marriage, but now her eyesight had become quite narrow with little peripheral vision. Dennis had dreaded the conversation he needed to have with her, but it actually went rather well after the last visit to the eye doctor.

"Mom, what do you think about continuing to drive?" Dennis asked her.

"Dennis, I always have told you that if you think it is time for me to stop driving, you should tell me. Is it time?" she replied with a certain sadness in her voice.

"I'm worry about you getting into an accident. You don't seem to see the other drivers like you used to. Do you understand my concern?"

"Yes. So you think I should stop driving?" After he nodded, she added, "That will mean a lot more trouble for you. You'll have to take us everywhere."

"It won't be a big change. Martha has been doing most of your shopping for a while. One of us already goes with you to doctor appointments because you want us to be there to ask questions and remember what the doctor said."

"I suppose that's true."

"So, it's decided then?"

Janice nodded reluctantly and looked rather distant as if she realized what she was giving up. Dennis didn't say anything more. He was grateful it had been so easy. He recalled his friend Gary telling him about how he practically had to wrestle the keys away from his father after a heated argument about the same issue. His mom made it easy on him. After the conversation, he took care of selling the car, cancelling insurance, and so forth, but he felt down as the new owner drove the car away.

Since the last speeches were done, the family began to mill around. His son, Marcus, with grandson in tow, came up. "Nice job, Dad. It was really nice you planned all this."

"Be sure to thank your mom. She did most of the work. She found the venue and caterer and everything. I just confirmed the decisions she made."

"I'm sure you did more than that, but I'll be sure to thank her, too."

"Mostly, I'm glad you made it. It meant a lot to your grandparents that you came. And to us."

"We wouldn't have missed it for the world. Um, sorry to bring this up, but have you decided about next month? We're trying to finalize our plans."

Dennis knew this was going to be another difficult decision. Marcus and his wife, Cheryl, were hoping that he and Martha would be able to come for a few days to help cover when the daycare was closed for summer vacation. Because they lived nine hours away, it would mean that they would be too far away to be "on call" for Mom and Dad. His brother, Jerry and his wife, Janet offered to fill in. They had done that before, staying in Dennis's house while he and Martha were on vacation. It seemed like a big request.

Before Dennis could answer Marcus, Jerry walked up and joined the conversation.

"Are you talking about next month?" Jerry asked.

"Yes, Marcus just asked about that," replied Dennis.

"We are more than happy to do this. We're both retired and so it really is not a big deal for us to be here while you go."

"But you already did that once this year. It seems like a lot to ask. And we're going to Portland to see our granddaughter in August. We can't expect you to plan your life around our travels," Dennis protested.

Jerry responded, "You've been watching Mom and Dad for several years. It's the least we can do. What are the dates again?"

Marcus answered, "July 2 through the 6th. Daycare is always closed the week of the 4th."

Jerry seemed surprised. "Oh, I thought it was the last week of June. We have our time-share scheduled for that week. I'm not sure if we can. . .maybe we can reschedule."

"You shouldn't have to do that. Mom and Dad should be okay for a few days or maybe Carol and Steve can come."

"I'll check with them," Jerry said as he walked off to talk to their sister and his husband.

"It's okay Dad if you can't come. We can make other plans. I just thought you might enjoy spending time with your grandson."

"We'd like to, but we worry about what if something happens to Mom and Dad while we are gone, like that time."

"I remember," Marcus interrupted. "You were in New Orleans when Grandpa had that false alarm he thought was a heart attack. They managed without you."

"Yes, but that was three years ago. With Dad's dementia, I don't think they could manage anymore."

"Dad, you don't have to come. We can manage. We just thought..."

"I know. But maybe something will work out."

Right then Carol approached. "I hear from Jerry that you need someone to be here for Mom and Dad the week of July 4th. We can come for most of the week. We need to leave Friday. When will you get back?"

"We hadn't decided."

"Dad, you don't have to stay Friday. We can manage."

Carol offered, "If we leave Friday morning and you come back Friday evening, they'll only be alone a few hours. That should work."

"Yeah, that might work," Dennis replied. He was relieved actually. He wanted to help his son and be with his grandson but felt like someone needed to be in town for his parents. A plan was taking shape. He added, "Now we just need to figure out what to do we're gone the last week of July."

Carol quickly replied, "I think Jerry said they could take care of that. And if not, we can always come back. You know how much we love to come to see Mom and Dad." Then she quickly added, "And you and Martha, of course."

That brought up another thing that Dennis really did not want to address at this time. His brother and two sisters made frequent visits to see his parents, not just when they were away. He was always glad to see them, but they didn't seem to realize the stress it actually put on his parents. His parents were used to being alone most of the time. When his siblings came, they wanted to make the most of their visits and so they would go see Mom and Dad after breakfast, stay through lunch, leave briefly for what had become the daily afternoon naps Robert and Janice took, and then return before taking them out to dinner and then visiting afterwards until they went to bed. Dennis understood that they wanted to squeeze extra minutes with them because it might be the last time they saw them, but he also saw how exhausted his parents were after one of their visits. They were not used to that much activity in one day, let alone for four or five days in a row. It had been relatively easy to get them to stay at his house instead of with his parents a couple years ago because of Robert's dementia, but convincing them to spend less time with his parents was much more challenging. He dropped hints occasionally, but they didn't get it.

It also put a lot of stress on him. Although he had cut back on his medical practice now that he was 60 years old and nearing retirement, he still kept a rather full schedule and had occasional emergencies to deal with. His siblings and their spouses were all retired now and didn't seem to realize how much their visits disrupted his routine. He was glad the house was big enough that they could always stay there, but it was a bit draining to have them always there in the morning and evenings. During their visits, he missed having a quiet cup of coffee alone after his early morning jog. Someone was always up by the time he finished wanting to talk to him. And he missed being home alone with Martha for the evening. Instead of relaxing dinners alone, they usually ate at local restaurants so that Martha didn't have to cook for them, but then instead of catching up on some work emails and maybe watching a little TV before an early bedtime, there were long talks about his parents and work and current issues. Sometimes these talks were tense since they didn't agree on everything and they often went on quite late. Dennis often felt tired while they visited and hated to admit it, but he was sometimes relieved when they left so he could get back to his normal routine.

Rather than address either of those concerns, Dennis simply responded with, "It looks like everything is coming together. Thank you all for helping." Then the topic changed to the day's events and Dennis eventually went over to talk to his daughter, Cindy, who was with Martha and their six-month-old granddaughter, Lisa.

Cindy quickly complemented the celebration. "You two did a great job planning this. It was wonderful to see everyone. I don't remember the last time I saw some of my cousins. And now so many of them have children."

Martha interjected, "Speaking of children, or I should say grandchildren, Cindy just invited me out to watch Lisa during the second week of August, when *her* daycare is closed for their summer break. I know it's just two weeks after our visit, but it will be great to spend more time with them. We see them so infrequently. And Ryan is going to use frequent flier miles so I can fly for free. Isn't that nice?"

"I didn't expect that, but I imagine that will be fine," Dennis responded.

"Dad, thanks for letting Mom do this. It's so nice to have help especially if Ryan is traveling that week."

"No problem," Dennis replied, but he didn't really think that. For one thing, it was pretty inconvenient for him when she was away. Since Martha quit working full-time and eventually working at all, they had divided up the domestic duties pretty unevenly. She still did the vacuuming and he still did the dusting, but now, she did nearly all the cooking and shopping, unlike when they were both working. He tried to do the kitchen clean up as often as possible, but it didn't work out as often as he wished it would. So when she took these grandchildren trips by herself, he had to manage his meals himself. Sometimes she generously planned lots of frozen leftovers that gave him easy evening meals. Sometimes he went out to eat with his "single friends" and so it really wasn't that bad. He particularly liked eating with Bob, a retired hospital administrator, whose wife was in a memory care unit going on three years. They compared notes about Bob's wife and Dennis's dad. But as much as he enjoyed having dinner with Bob or others, he preferred dinner with Martha. He knew it was good for her to do the grandmother thing, but it didn't mean he liked it.

Another inconvenient part of Martha's travels was that when she was away, his parents would call him at work for various "emergencies." They normally called Martha to add something to the shopping list or to remind her that they were counting on her being present during a doctor's appointment. When they knew she was out of town, they would call him instead. They did not seem to recognize that it interrupted his work for them to call during the day. He would remind them that he was working and they would apologize, but that did not seem to stop them from finishing the request or from calling again the next time they thought of something. One time they did call because Mom fell. Dennis was thankful that they called that time and told his dad to call 911. Then with his flexible work schedule, he was able to take off from work immediately and meet them at the hospital. Fortunately, it had turned out to be nothing serious—that time. However, most of the time when they called him at work, it could have waited until the evening when he was home. He appreciated it that Martha was a buffer for those calls when she was home.

In addition, while yes, it was nice that Ryan's frequent travels for work earned enough miles that Martha could visit them for free, he also knew that Cindy wished Ryan traveled less. It had been an inconvenience before they became parents and they had even delayed having children until she was 30, but now with Lisa, it was more of an issue and not just inconvenient. His travels simply made life difficult for Cindy since she returned to work after her twelve weeks of family medical leave ran out. Each day he was gone now, she had to get Lisa ready for daycare on her own while getting herself ready and then drop her off a few minutes after it opened, rush to work, put in full day, pump breast milk during her breaks throughout the day, hope she could leave work on time to pick up Lisa just before the penalty for late pickup would kick in, and then still have to feed and care for Lisa once they were home. Only after Lisa was asleep for the night could Cindy have a moment for herself. When Ryan was in town, he was a terrific help and father. He helped get Lisa ready and he could either drop Lisa off or pick her up or sometimes both. He usually cooked and cleaned up afterwards so that Cindy just had to play with Lisa in the evening. So when he was in town, life was good for Cindy, but when he traveled, it was different. Dennis wanted to say something, but Ryan's job was beyond his control and so he did not.

Dennis could only imagine what it was like for Cindy to try to be an ideal employer and a super mom with Ryan's help, let alone when he was out of town. When their kids were young, they could afford for Martha to stay home until the kids were older and then she took a low paying job at a daycare center so that she was with them until they started school. She had sacrificed the career that she thought she would have by doing that, but she never seemed to regret it, at least as far as Dennis could tell. They probably should have had longer talks about it. Dennis could only recall brief conversations. He thought they went something like this.

"Are you sure you want to do this, work at a daycare center to be near the kids?"

"I love our kids. It's been great being with them while they are little, but I need some adult conversation during the day."

"But we could put them in daycare without you and you could go back to your work at the bank. The bank would take you back in a flash."

"I want to be with the kids and I want adult conversation. Working at their daycare gives me both. And besides, they grow up so fast."

Dennis recalled that their conversations about taking care of his parents also seemed to be quite short.

"I'm sorry that you are ending up doing most of the running around for my parents. It really shouldn't be your responsibility. They're my parents."

"It's fine. I'm happy to do it. You're still working. I have the time. I figure this is my 'retirement job,' taking care of your parents. I didn't get to take care of my parents because they both died suddenly. I love your parents and am glad I can do this for them."

"You're sure?"

"Yes, I'm sure. I want to do whatever I can to help them for as long as I can. We don't know how long they have."

"Thank you so much. I love you."

Dennis reflected on both of those brief conversations. His children had grown up quickly. Now both his children were raising their own children. He was a grandfather and his parents needed assistance. Martha was doing the bulk of the caring for both his parents and his grandchildren. Dennis wished it was different, but he wasn't ready to retire yet and that is probably what it would take to change the way things were.

Then there was one more conversation that needed to occur soon. His parents had managed to live in their own house while hiring people to take care of the yard and clean the house and Martha helping out more often lately. But it was getting to be too much for Janice to take care of Robert. His brother and sisters were beginning to ask when, not if, it was time to move them into assisted living or maybe move his dad into a memory care unit.

His conversations with Bob only heightened his awareness of the issues. He remembered how Bob initially felt guilty for putting his wife in a facility. Dennis had reminded him, "You couldn't take care of her at your house and you really are taking care of her by hiring people who can." Dennis would certainly feel the same guilt when he moved his parents into assisted living. He wondered what it would take to convince him that he was doing what was best he for them. And he knew what the future likely held. Bob's wife's dementia was more advanced than Robert's to the point that when she spoke, which was rare, it was often impossible to understand the words, let alone the meaning. Dennis always complimented Bob for his twice weekly visits despite the fact that his wife rarely remembered he came and sometimes did not seem to know if Bob was her husband or son or a stranger. Dennis hoped he could make the same commitment to visit his father. He worried about the strain it would put on his marriage if it was after he retired.

Dennis tried to put all of that out of his mind for the moment. Instead he tried to focus on the day. Over 40 people were celebrating his parents' 65 wedding anniversary. He needed to relish in that. He would face the other challenges as they arrived. Worrying about what might happen was not going to do him or anyone else any good.

QUESTIONS:

1. Relational dialectics examines the tension between two desirable but incompatible goals and the strategies individuals use to manage those tensions (Baxter & Montgomery, 1996). What are some of the dialectical tensions evident in the case for Dennis and for others? What strategies do they seem to be using to manage them? Are the strategies effective?

2. Consider how different members of the Andersons define their roles. Consider the roles the individuals have in their work, immediate family, and extended families. How are societal expectations influencing their roles (Drago, 2007)? Discuss the merits of defining roles in different ways.

3. With increasing life expectancies, multigenerational families are more common but often they are not located in nearby communities. Discuss how multigenerational families complicate work-life balance. How do the geographical locations (all same community versus spread across multiple states) of multigenerational families affect work-life balance and family communication?

4. Some individuals like to separate work and other life activities (segmenters) while others do not mind if they overlap (integrators) (Ashforth, Kreiner, & Fugate, 2000). What are the merits for each approach for someone in Dennis's situation?

5. Dennis and Martha are one unit within the Anderson multi-generational extended family. Consider the Anderson family from a systems theory perspective (Kast & Rosenzweig, 1972).. What characteristics of systems theory are evident in the case?

6. Dennis recalls making major decisions in short conversations and avoids a number of difficult conversation. How does this compare to how some families communicate with each other across time and generations?

REFERENCES

Ashforth, B. E., Kreiner, G. E., & Fugate, M. (2000). All in a day's work: Boundaries and micro role transitions *Academy of Management Review, 25*, 472-491. doi:10.5465/amr.2000.3363315

Baxter, L. A., & Montgomery, B. M. (1996). *Relating: Dialogues and dialectics*. New York: Guilford Press.

Drago, R. W. (2007). *Striking a balance: Work, family, life*. Boston, MA: Dollars & Sense.

Kast, F. E., & Rosenzweig, J. E. (1972). General systems theory: Applications for organization and management. *Academy of Management Journal, 15*, 447-465.

CHAPTER 18

Recalibrating Privacy Rules in the Eldercare Family

Kristina A. Wenzel Egan – *Eckerd College*

ABSTRACT

Family members are often a critical source of care for individuals encountering age-related health and ability issues. This case study sheds light on the eldercare family by exploring the privacy challenges families face while caring for an older family member. The Williams, a fictional family created on a composite of the author's experiences interviewing eldercare families, are challenged by decisions to discuss their aging mother's finances, abilities, and health information, among other topics. Questions are posed, including what reasons eldercare families may avoid discussing health information and what face concerns may prevent families from talking openly about declining abilities to live alone and drive.

CASE STUDY

Eldercare families, or families with at least one older family member requiring informal care, is a family type that is increasingly common in the United States. Adults over the age of 85 are predicted to be the fastest-growing segment of the population, with estimates projected to more than triple from 5.9 million in 2000 to 18.2 million in 2030. Many of these individuals are expected to spend years dependent on others for care, with one estimate suggesting that about one third of older people require informal family care for at least two years (Kemper, Komisar, & Alecxih, 2005).

Family caregivers spend an average of 20.4 hours per week providing care (National Alliance for Caregiving, 2009) and perform a variety of activities. These caregiving activities include assisting older parents with illness-related care, care management, and day-to-day activities. Illness-related activities include performing minor at-home medical procedures, managing symptoms, and administering treatments. Care management activities include monitoring health issues, managing healthcare information, navigating the healthcare system, and making health decisions (Coupland & Coupland, 2001; Schumacher, Stewart, Archbold, Dodd, & Dibble, 2000). Day-to-day activities include helping individuals perform both activities of daily living (ADLs), which include walking, getting dressed, incontinence management, bathing, and feeding, and instrumental activities of daily living (IADLs), which include transportation, meal preparation, and managing finances (Covinsky et al., 2003).

Many adult children negotiate their parents' care with adult siblings and in-laws (Amaro, 2017), and while some adult children find genuine support in their adult siblings, others encounter inequities, disagreements, and jealousy. Findings from Halliwell, Wenzel Egan, and Howard's (2017) study on negotiating the care of older parents with adult siblings indicate that families who narrate their family as a "team" appear to fare better. For instance, one sibling manages their parents' finances, one sibling provides instrumental day-to-day care, and another sibling manages their parents' healthcare. While this appears to be an ideal arrangement, disagreements about care management are common among adult children (Lashewicz & Keating, 2009). Growing evidence suggests that the eldercare family encounters frequent disruptions to the family system, especially the privacy management system (Plander, 2013; Wenzel Egan & Hesse, 2018).

Petronio (2002) argued that aging adults' personal privacy boundaries must shift to allow for the assistance from informal family caregivers and boundary turbulence results when boundary coordination fails. Supporting Petronio's claim, evidence from Wenzel Egan and Hesse's (2018) study found that eldercare disrupts family privacy rules, in particular privacy linkage rules, permeability rules, and co-ownership status rules. Linkage privacy rules regulate the individuals who can or cannot know the private information. Permeability rules regulate how much information individuals can reveal, and co-ownership status rules establish who can control the information and how much power they have to control the information. In the proceeding case study, the privacy rules regulating Margaret Williams' personal private information are questioned, broken, and recalibrated as the family becomes increasingly responsible for controlling her private information.

The Williams' family matriarch, Margaret, is 84 years of age and has lived alone for two years in a small house located in the rural area she raised her three children—Angela, Dave and Leah.[1] Recently, she has felt a bit overwhelmed tending to the necessary upkeep of her house and has encountered a string of health issues. Margaret survived two husbands, whom she cared for until their deaths. Since her second husband died, she became more involved with her local garden club and the women's club at her church, though she has stopped going to evening events because it is hard for her to see while driving at night.

Out of Margaret's adult children, Leah is the only child who still lives close. Leah and her husband have three middle- and elementary-school-aged children. Her husband works full-time at the local university and is often required at work events on the weekends. Leah has a part-time tutoring job, which she enjoys because it gives her the flexibility to coordinate all the practice schedules, health appointments, and meal preparation that her family of five requires. Recently, however, a lot of her free time has been spent caring for her mother. Leah and her siblings text frequently about their kids and jobs, and recently, they text and talk a lot about their mom. Leah gives Angela and Dave updates about their mother's latest health issues and consults them on decisions that need to be made about their mother's care.

Angela, the oldest of the Williams' children, lives a few states away and visits home as frequently as she can. She has become worried that her sister is becoming burned out by all the caregiving responsibilities. Leah revealed to Angela that her marriage is under a lot of stress and that they have been arguing a lot about finances. Angela thinks that caring for their mother has become a bit much for Leah. Angela wishes she lived closer, but she has been unable to find work in their hometown. Angela has been bugging Leah about moving their mom to an assisted living facility closer to town, but Leah thinks her mom is still able to live independently albeit with a lot of her assistance. Their brother Dave lives close to their mother's vacation home just a few hours away and visits his mom nearly every other weekend. He has been taking her grocery shopping every trip and completes the seasonal yardwork and house repairs that are needed. Dave and Angela argue a lot. Since Leah feels close to both of her siblings, she tends to assume a peace-keeper role and appreciates that they visit separately and contribute in their own unique ways.

Fall

While her daughter works at her tutoring job, Margaret babysits Leah's three children around twice a week at her daughter's house, which is about a 25-minute drive into town. On a recent visit, she fell in one of her grandson's bedrooms. Margaret did not want her

---

1. The Williams' family is a fictional family created as a composite of the author's experiences interviewing eldercare families.

daughter to know that she had begun to fall more frequently. She felt that it was best not to concern her children with such a minor issue, especially since she could always find a way to stand up. As her grandsons rushed to her side to help her, she started laughing partly because the dogs were licking her face and partly because she wanted to lighten the situation as to not concern the boys. She explained,

> I couldn't get up. He said, "I'll help you up [Grandma]." I said, "Joey, you cannot help me up." So I say, "What time is it?" It was about 3:30. "Alright, I gotta be up by 4:00, [your mother] is going to be here." I backed, sat on my little behind, and backed all the way down a corner and another corner and to the basement steps, and if I can get to the steps I can get up. I was just about there and Eric says, "She's here!" He says, "I'll have her come in the back way, so that will give you time" [But] she came in the front way. Back right where we were at. And by the time she got there we were all laughing. She says, "What's so funny?" "Oh, it was just a funny joke?" "You can't tell me what it was?" (Wenzel & Poynter, 2014[2])

Leah's son Joey had his grandma standing by the time Leah was near enough to help. Leah gathered enough information to assess that her mother fell, but did not want to embarrass her mother by asking too many questions. The whole family continued on with their evening dinner like nothing happened. Before leaving, Grandma whispered to Joey, "Let's keep that little mishap to ourselves, huh?"

As the week continued on, Leah became increasingly more worried about her mother. She called her a bit more than usual, but never explicitly expressed her concerns. Leah felt strongly that she did not want her mother to know that she was worried about whether she was becoming less able to live in the rural house on her own, like her sister Angela has been saying repeatedly over the past year. So to ease her uncertainty, Leah drove over to her mother's house one evening without calling ahead. She parked on the street and walked up to the house trying to be quiet so that her mother did not know that she was there. As she peeked in through a window, she found her mother walking to her dining room table. Her mother sat down and broke off part of what was on her dinner plate and slipped it to her dog. Leah felt guilty that she snuck around her house, but she was comforted knowing that her mother was doing okay and walked to the front door to say hello.

Winter

Ever since her late husband passed, Leah attends her mother's health appointments. The first time she joined her mother, there was a snowstorm and Margaret nearly cancelled the

---

2. All of the quotations are from in-depth interviews with family caregivers or care recipients who were participants in research studies conducted by the author.

appointment when Leah proposed she drive her instead. Once they arrived at the appointment, her mother invited her to join her in the exam room. Her mom was very open about her health issues with Leah. In fact, Leah knew that her mom told her more about her health issues than she told Leah's siblings, Angela and Dave. Leah thought it might have been because she never pushed her mom to do anything she did not want to do. Margaret was appreciative that her daughter joined her at her appointments because Leah asked intelligent questions and took notes that they could discuss later. The physicians also welcomed her daughter, but they seemed to make a point to talk directly to Margaret instead of Leah, which Margaret appreciated. Margaret, commenting on her child's involvement in her health issues noted:

> When I go to the doctors, she always takes me . . . 'cause I have my heart specialist and I've got an orthopedic in there. But she takes me, and she [long pause] now you—maybe you'll think it's terrible [laughter], she goes in with me and she doesn't care if they have to take my clothes off. She wants to know! Then what does she do? When she goes home she calls my son and tells him what she finds out and then he calls my doctor and they all get—[laughter] See? I'm protected all around (Wenzel & Poynter, 2014).

After the appointment at the health clinic, Leah dropped off her mom at her house in the country. Unfortunately, as Margaret was stepping out of the car she slipped and fell on the ice in her driveway. Since Leah was in a rush to get to work for a tutoring appointment, she suggested to her mom that they call her sister Angela, who is a nurse, but her mother refused. Leah explained:

> And she refused to call my sister [who's] a nurse because she was afraid she would yell at her and tell her she needed to move into assisted living. And, so, I told her I was gonna call [my sister]. And she said, "No. Don't—just don't call her." And, so yeah, she's not as open with my sister that's a nurse anymore. I think [my mom's] afraid she'll end up in the hospital or something, and she doesn't want that (Wenzel Egan & Hesse, 2018).

With the help of a neighbor down the road, they moved Margaret into the house and Leah visited her late that evening to check up on her. Leah agreed that her mother needed more help around the house, but she worried that her mother would stop being so open with her if she expressed this opinion. She thought, "I'm not gonna ruin my relationship with my mom because of it" (Wenzel Egan & Hesse, 2018). Leah knows that she has stopped sharing some private information with her sister, and she wondered whether making decisions that went against her mother's preferences was worth threatening their close relationship.

Spring

After a series of minor accidents, all of the Williams' siblings began talking and texting about whether it was still safe for their mother to drive. Angela was adamant that they needed to take her keys away, but Dave and Leah were hesitant. Leah hoped that their mother's occupational therapist would make the decision, but it turned out that none of their mother's medical professionals took any initiative to demand that Margaret stop driving. On a weekend visit, Dave explained that he rode in his mom's golf cart while she drove. He explained:

> I was told that the occupational therapist would make that decision. But they all backed off. And I realized that she was gonna have to make that decision and, you know, we just weren't gonna push her too far along. And...I made her...I drove in the golf cart with her, not when she really wanted to do it, in any event. She kinda did all right. She was decisive. But she, you know, she hit a couple of corners on a turn and...she wasn't real consistent looking behind her when she backed up. And that was concern. But that was, you know, slower and less dangerous than a car goin' 35 [mph].

Once he was alone in the car headed back home, he called Leah to talk about his interaction with their mom. He told Leah that he thought he might have persuaded their mother to stop driving, but that he worried that Leah would be under even more stress if she were also responsible for all their mother's transportation needs. They talked a bit more without any resolution, and Leah avoided talking to Angela for the next few days because she worried that her sister was right—that they needed to talk to their mom about selling her house and moving closer to town.

Angela and her three children relocated to another state around 10 years ago for her husband's promotion. She and her sister texted and spoke often about everything going on in their lives, but lately they spoke mostly about their mom and her ailing health. Angela enjoyed going home to help her sister Leah out with the day-to-day care of their mom. She explained:

> So, that's kind of how I got involved. Because every time I would go back for a visit, it seemed like all I did was try to set up doctors' appointments, clean their house, do some cooking for her, and...and try to, you know, kinda see about where she was. So, that's when I thought, okay, we need a bit more help into the house. And that didn't go over well. (Wenzel Egan & Hesse, 2018)

Angela suggested strongly that her mom either hire in-home care or move to an assisted living facility. Her mother Margaret adamantly refused, noting that Leah thought that she was doing just fine. Angela noticed that her sister Leah was gaining weight and was easy to anger over the past year as she had become a lot more involved in their mother's caregiving. Angela was afraid that Leah was burned out. Angela explained:

> There were times that I came in and you know, came in hard on my mom because I was trying to be protective of Leah. There's a blessing to have other people also, you know, taking a share of it. But it's hard, too, to see your sister in pain, and, you know, especially in that case, when you felt like she was doing more than her fair share. And, you know, if circumstance could have changed, we wanted it to be even. But the circumstances were the way they were, you know. (Unpublished transcript).

Summer

Following a few health scares, Leah became very involved with her mother's day-to-day life. She visited her mother's house nearly every day to ensure that she was doing okay and had a proper dinner to eat. Leah would become very emotionally upset when her mother would tell her, "You know what? I'm getting older, I'm not going to be here forever." Leah responds, "Oh mother! You're not ready to die" (Wenzel & Poynter, 2014). When Leah was asked whether she has discussed her mother's end-of-life preferences, she explained:

> When I go to leave, there's been quite a few nights where I just lay my head on the steering wheel and cry because…yeah, we had talked about that. Unfortunately, we need to go back and readdress that. My brother may know more about that than I do (Wenzel, 2014).

Margaret, on the other hand, knows that her daughter Leah is postponing the inevitable. She appreciates that her son Dave asked about what preferences she has for her funeral and her burial arrangements. For now, Leah is concerned about her mother's ability to manage her finances. She oversaw an envelope on her mother's desk that looked like a late-notice for a cable bill, but she decided to not say anything to her mom about it because she did not want to embarrass her. She wondered whether she should tell her older siblings, but decided to keep it to herself until she saw another one. No need to worry them, especially since they both worked demanding jobs and were caring for young children. Then, when Leah, Leah's husband, and their three children moved into Margaret's house for six weeks while they renovated their house, Leah noticed another late-notice and decided she should discuss whether her mother was becoming a bit overwhelmed with paying her budget. She explained:

> And that happened because she went online, she looked at her account. She did not have enough money to pay for some of her bills. And, so, I went back through her checking account. You know, I asked her, "Is it okay if I do this?"

I always, always ask her, "Is it okay if I do this?" And to which she'll say, "Well, of course. You know I don't care if you do it." But I just have to ask her that. (Unpublished transcript)

Leah explained to her mom, "If you continue to spend this amount, in this way, this is how much time you'll have until you'll have gone through all of your annuities and all of your accounts." Leah's mom was surprised because she did not realize she was spending money that fast. Leah explained that it was at this point when she talked about her mom's budget. Leah is now listed on all of her mother Margaret's financial accounts and even pays all her bills for her.

Dave lives near their mother's vacation home. Since his mom has stopped visiting the vacation home, he has assumed full responsibility for maintaining the home and was added as a beneficiary on the deed. He recently spoke to his sisters about whether they should sell it to save for their mother's future care expenses. Dave reported that his sisters told him, "Don't tell mom if you sell it." He knows it is only right to let his mother know but wants to wait until the time is right. He explained:

So, yeah, we do hold onto certain things. You know, so she doesn't have to think about and worry about 'em. There's no reason to let her know about all this when she's just tryin' to get through the day.

Dave and his sisters know that the selling the vacation home would disappoint their mom, especially since she thought her children would want to continue using the home for family vacations.

Fall

Margaret was ambulanced to the hospital after she fell and broke her hip. She spent a week in the hospital, and her medical team required that she move to a rehabilitation center while she recovered. With the help of the hospital's social worker, the Williams' siblings scrambled to search for a rehabilitation center that had space for their mother. They found a center, though it was not ideal and spent the next few months searching for a more comfortable long-term care facility.

DISCUSSION QUESTIONS

1. What topics were sensitive for the Williams to discuss? What prevented the family members from discussing these topics?
2. Which scenarios may have led to boundary turbulence?
3. Was it unethical for Leah to spy on her mother? What conditions, if any, may call for violating an older family member's privacy?
4. What are some of the reasons aging adults may avoid discussing health information with their families? What are some reasons adult children may avoid discussing their parents' health information?
5. What risks do older parents face when they reveal that they are struggling with activities of daily living (e.g., walking, getting dressed, feeding) or instrumental activities of daily living (e.g., meal preparation, managing finances, transportation)?
6. What face-concerns may prevent families from talking openly about aging family members' declining abilities to live alone, drive, and care for themselves?

REFERENCES

Amaro, L. M. (2017). Dyadic effects of gratitude on burden, conflict, and contribution in the family caregiver and sibling relationship. *Journal of Applied Communication Research, 45*(1), 61–78. doi:10.1080/00909882.2016.1248464

Coupland, J., & Coupland, N. (2001). Roles, responsibilities, and alignments: Multiparty talk in geriatric care. In M. L. Hummert & J. F. Nussbaum (Eds.) *Aging communication, and health: Linking research and practice for successful aging* (pp. 121–156). Mahwah, NJ: Lawrence Erlbaum Associates.

Covinsky, K. E., Palmer, R. M., Fortinsky, R. H., Counsell, S. R., Stewart, A. L., Kresevic, D., . . . Landefeld, C. S. (2003). Loss of independence in activities of daily living in older adults hospitalized with medical illness: Increased vulnerability with age. *Journal of the American Geriatrics Society, 51*, 451–458. doi:10.1046/j.1532-5415.2003.51152.x

Halliwell, D., Wenzel Egan, K. A., & Howard, E. (2017). Flying in a V formation: Themes of (in)equity, reality, and togetherness in adult siblings' narrative explanations of shared parental caregiving. *Journal of Applied Communication Research, 45*, 256–273. doi:10.1080/09909882.2017.1320574

Kemper, P., Komisar, H. L., & Alecxih, L. (2005). Long-term care over an uncertain future: What can future retirees expect? *Inquiry, 42*, 335–350. doi:10.5034/inquiryjrnl_42.4.335

Lashewicz, B., & Keating, N. (2009). Tensions among siblings in parent care. *European Journal of Ageing, 6*, 127–135. doi:10.1007/s10433-009-0109-9

National Alliance for Caregiving and AARP. (2009). Caregiving in the U.S. 2009. Washington, DC.

Petronio, S. (2002). *Boundaries of privacy: Dialectics of disclosure.* New York, NY: SUNY Press.

Plander, K. L. (2013). Checking accounts: Communication privacy management in familial financial caregiving. *Journal of Family Communication, 13*, 17–31. doi:10.1080/15267431.2012.742090

Schumacher, K. L., Stewart, B. J., Archbold, P. G., Dodd, M. J., & Dibble, S. L. (2000). Family caregiving skill: Development of the concept. *Research in Nursing & Health, 23*, 191–203. Retrieved from http://www.ncbi.nlm.nih.gov/pubmed/10871534

Wenzel Egan, K. A., & Hesse, C. R. (2018). "Tell me so that I can help you": Private information and privacy coordination issues in the context of eldercare. *Journal of Family Communication, 18*, 217–232. doi:10.1080/15267431.2018.1466784

Wenzel, K. A. (2014). *"Tell me so that I can help you": A turning point analysis of privacy in the development of parental caregiving relationships* (Unpublished doctoral dissertation). University of Missouri, Columbia, MO.

Wenzel, K. A., & Poynter, D. (2014). "I'm mother! I can take care of myself!": A contrapuntal analysis of older parents' relational talk with their adult children. *Southern Communication Journal, 79*, 147–170. doi:10.1080/1041794X.2014.881540

Part IV

DARK SIDE OF FAMILY

CHAPTER 19

Family Communication and Political Identities: A Negative Case Analysis of Parental Partisan Socialization

Jayne Goode – *Governors State University*

ABSTRACT

This chapter argues for a new line of political communication research within the family focusing on political differences between marital partners. Partisan and ideological separation of spouses can cause tension and argumentation in the household and this influences the socialization of the child. Through negative case analysis, this chapter explores three cases where parents were of differing political parties and, in their own words, participants reflect on the conditions of familial communication in the household and their personal attachments to American political parties.

CASE STUDY

Let's imagine for a minute the young girl whose parents are recently divorced. Her mother and her mother's family identify strongly with the Republican party. Her father and her father's family, likewise, are strong Democrats. Each side of her family blamed the other for the divorce, perhaps, not the least, for characteristics, beliefs and behaviors which caused the dissolution of the marriage. What was her socialization experience in the home prior to the separation? What does her socialization experience look like from this point forward? Now, she spends a little more than half of her time hearing why people need to work harder. She also hears why organization and efficiency are central to being a good girl. She spends a little less than half of her time hearing that being a part of the family, contributing to the community, and helping those in need is a blessing. How might these potentially contradictory and competing messages in childhood regarding the relationship between the self and community, the nature of being, and morality influence her development?

The vast majority of political socialization research focuses on familial transmission of partisanship and political behaviors. However, little of this research explores the actual communication within the family and how these belief structures are transmitted. Further, socialization research has assumed a dual-parent household of similar political affiliations and value orientations. Such instances present the need for negative case analysis. A negative case analysis allows researchers to interrogate assumptions of theoretical frameworks taken for granted. This methodological approach challenges researchers to question the connections between concepts (Lindlof & Taylor, 2002). What occurs when the parents are of differing ideological and political dispositions? Problematizing the "inheritance" of political ideology and identity formation is necessary to articulate more clearly the socialization processes, specifically familial political communication. This piece problematizes the expectations of familial socialization processes by examining the lived experience of individuals in politically heterogeneous families and families in which familial political communication can be negative and polarizing—in other words, those families who experience political difference. This chapter explores the partisan socialization process of three individuals who grew up in multiparty homes—one parent of one party and one parent of another—with a high degree of political difference.

Problematizing Partisan Identity

Once activated, psychological membership in parties is most predictive of future electoral behavior (Converse, 1969). When partisanship progresses intergenerationally, the political environment experiences a relative climate of equilibrium (Carmines & Stimson, 1989; Converse, 1969). Thus, the more people we have adopting party affiliations and, in turn, voting, the more we ensure our democracy reflects the interests and will of the people. However, skepticism over politics and participation continues to plague our society (Delli Caprini & Keeter, 1996; Dudley & Gitelson, 2002; Rahn & Hirshorn, 1999). Researching the roots of this disaffection towards participation in American democracy may prove useful.

The first step, perhaps, is rethinking partisanship as more than a check-box or something we do every two or four years. Turner (1999) argues that "the self is a varying, reflexive representation of the perceiver which is inherently fluid and flexible because it is a comparative, relational judgement" (p. 29). One's self-defined identity is influenced by a multitude of factors, including knowledge, context, expectations, etc. Political parties, as identity objects, are social groups and declared membership has several implications for both the individual and their environment (Green, Palmquist, & Schickler, 2004; Sapiro, 2004). Because no one is born with a marker of party membership, partisanship is a voluntary, subjective self-concept (Green, Palmquist, & Schickler, 2004; Iyengar, Sood, & Lelkes, 2012; Iyengar & Westwood, 2015; Warner & Villamil, 2017). How one chooses to identify should have influence on one's self-perception, such that a positive social identity will lead to positive distinctiveness, compared to membership within other groups (Turner, Hogg, Oakes, Reicher, & Wetherell, 1987). For party membership to take hold, one must perceive that claiming the identity of a party leads to some positive distinctiveness versus another party or no party.

Political Socialization

Socialization research has assumed a dual-parent household (and, similarly, a heteronormative one). What occurs when the parents are of differing ideological and political dispositions? What occurs when the child is an occupant of two households? Hyman (1959) argued that socialization is an intricate process that continually shapes political behavior. Children are socialized by parents, peers, and institutions (Hyman, 1959; Prewitt, Eulau, & Zisk, 1966). Children are perceived to be similar to their parents in party identification and attitudes toward civic engagement (Achen, 2002). Some research has argued that one parent may be more influential than the other (Acock & Bengston, 1980). The past decade has again seen a call to return to the study of political socialization (McLeod & Shah, 2009). Specific focus on the development of partisanship is critical, and the demise of American political activity might be because of dispositions towards politics developed in childhood and adolescence. Thus, researches have returned to the study of socialization to understand and, in some cases, find ways to intervene in the decline of American political and civic life.

Parental Political Socialization

Early research was also plagued by debates regarding the psychological development of children, some arguing that children are not complex, rational thinkers and therefore could not process partisanship (Sapiro, 2004). Merelman (1973) contends that political thought must be reasoned, and children could not be political if they were not rational thinkers. For some, party affiliation was nothing more than an "inherited disposition" (Erikson, Mackuen, & Stimson, 2002, p. 126). However, policy and ideological distinctions between Republicans and Democrats can develop during this time and parents can contextualize this differentiation with familial circumstances, the desired outcome being partisan affiliation. Beck (1974) argues partisanship is the most important political orientation of socialization.

As with all large fields of study, there are several areas of contention within the literature. Scholarship has substantiated claims that there is a stronger correlation between parent–child partisanship than specific political or social issue agreement (Niemi, Ross, & Alexander, 1978); additionally, research suggests that party identification develops earlier than policy awareness (Fiorina, 1993; Jennings & Niemi, 1968). Some research has focused on the communication style within the family. Parenting styles influence the interactions between parents and children (Meadowcroft, 1986), and in turn, influence the socialization process (Chaffee, 1973). Murray (2012) interviewed parent–child dyads and found that the largest correlations between parent and child ideology was with mothers that exhibited authoritarian parenting styles. Parental attitudes and behavior remain among the most widely accepted political influences on children. However, little is known about how these attitudes are communicated and less about how these attitudes are translating into a working political schema for children.

Familial Communication in the Multiparty Home

How do multiparty homes develop? Most individuals tend to choose partners that resemble themselves in a variety of ways. Couples tend to be more similar in political attitudes than even personality (Alford, Hatemi, Hibbing, Maritin, Eaves, 2011). Alford et al. (2011) describes two similar theories regarding mate selection. In assertive mating, individuals often choose to be around those who share similar sociopolitical orientations. Another theory, social homogamy, holds the similarity is due to the availability of potential partners. You are more likely to find someone to marry close to where you live and within your social circles. Thus, you will tend to be similar because you already share similar social influences or economic conditions. It is likely that a person living in a middle-class area meeting a potential mate who also lives in the same area would share similar economic situations.

CASING THE FAMILY: Theoretical and Applied Approaches to Understanding Family Communication

However, a modest amount of research has begun to investigate differences between men and women in heterosexual partnerships. Women tend to more sympathetic to the Democratic Party than men (Kaufmann & Petrocik, 1999) and tend to be more concerned with social issues (Howell & Day, 2000); these differences in political party preferences may become more substantial in more conservative time periods (Box-Steffensmeier, De Boef, & Lin, 2004) such as the one we are living in now.

What does the familial communication look like when parents are of different political and ideological orientations? The following looks at three cases of individuals and their experience of multiparty familial environments. Julia explains her experience of coming home on a break from school.

> I'm going to go back to just two weeks ago. I was sitting there, we're watching, uhh, *Meet the Press*, they've got, uhh, Condoleezza Rice was on there. My mom's just talking about it, she makes like these bold statements—George Bush is a criminal. It's just like, oh gosh, here we go again and so then my parents go on their little tangent about it and my mom, of course, brings other cultures into it and how he would lie in Brazil, I don't know, the Nazi came here and we had our peace protests on the other side of town. They did the same thing in Southern Brazil when George Bush visited; they had a peaceful protest on the other side of town. So, that came up. Just discussing that, of course. My dad is all for George Bush, my mom felt like she was being attacked. I got up and left the room and was like, great, I'm glad I came home.

Julia describes an uncomfortable environment where her parents perceive the other to be hostile and attacking. She also alludes to the fact that this might be a typical type of exchange when she says, "Here we go again." Her dislike for this type of exchange is evident in her remark, "Great. I'm glad I came home."

Julia appears to withdraw from conversations with her parents—mom who is a Democrat and dad who is a Republican. "It depends on who I'm speaking with or what I'm watching. The first thing I think about is who's talking, how credible is this individual. When my mom talks about politics I try not to listen because she's not credible, she's so narrow-minded. But my dad, he influences me. I try not to let that happen because he is so conservative that it makes me sick too." For Julia, being consistent in belief structure means one is narrow-minded. And having "too" much of a particular belief structure is also negative. This framework for belief structures is highly troubling, where consistency and adherence reflects faults.

MaryAnn recalls her interactions with her parents as less transactional and more confrontational. This is within the scope of her parents' conflictual perspectives. She states,

> Yeah, it was mainly things that they, they would, you know, it was like a one-sided informative discussion. I remember talking to my mom about... I

was kind of regurgitating something about a Republican. I just I tried to have a conversation with my dad and said what they said and they kind of attacked me. He said I guess you just believe that because that's what your mom said. I don't have anything against the Republicans but that's just myself. I thought, yeah, I was probably right.

In this episode, her father is attributing her perspective to her mother. He dismisses her opinion and loses an opportunity to discuss his belief systems and possibly influence his daughter's understanding of what it means to be a Republican. In this sense, he cements her perspective of "I thought, yeah, I was probably right."

Divorced now, MaryAnn's parents have entered new marriages with partners of the same party. Her father and stepmother are Republicans and her mother and stepfather are Democrats. She continues to express frustration at the lack of conversation around politics. The two families continue to act like competing entities. She states, "So like, to me they were just like here's this person that doesn't know any better, so let me explain we're right and they're wrong or the other half would say the same thing. This is right; they're wrong."

One might imagine that in cases where parents express no animus toward the other parent during political discussions or as a member of another party in general, there might be greater opportunity to have open dialogue regarding differences. Damien describes his familial communication around politics as more jovial around issues of disagreement. He states,

And I think, uh, there's also a lot of joking and kidding in our family by a grandpa, a Republican, and an uncle was like that. There's a lot of kidding and banter…and that kind of stuff. It's always talked about and always kidded about, but that's just lots of food and loud, lots of talking. No one gets upset at each other, but they get into what they've read or what they've heard. They said, 'I voted for Clinton. I voted for Bush. Ha! I canceled you out.'

Damien describes his parents' communication very differently than MaryAnn and Julia. In this case, he describes vivid, but amicable discussion around issues and beliefs and an openness to difference.

Partisanship

As mentioned earlier, the best predictor of participation is party membership.

How do individuals who grew up in multiparty homes describe their current belief systems? How do they articulate how this experience might influence their identity? It is worth investigating how individuals describe their attitudes and opinions regarding political participation upon reflecting on their lived experiences?

In each of these three cases, the individuals described themselves as independents.

It is not surprising that Julia and MaryAnn also expressed distaste for partisanship, partisan dialogue, and a lack of political self-efficacy. Contrary to partisan behavior, these participants expressed an aversion to discussing politics and a particular distaste for partisan rancor. MaryAnn comments, "I think sort of the stress of those kind of discussions made me want to like stay out of it."

Julia is slightly more extreme in her distaste for political parties. She states, "I think political parties are only necessary to get a bad administration out of the office, but as soon as that administration is gone so should the parties." She goes on to emphasize that she does not even acknowledge the label of independent. "My views,...I don't believe in political parties at all and I don't call myself an independent or a moderate. So that's why I'm always, not trying to label people." Julia refuses to place herself with the discourse of partisanship by denying she is even independent, a label which would be used for someone without a party affiliation.

For two of the three cases, tensions between contested viewpoints appear to have led to a negative perspective of politics. Previous research has found that when individuals are exposed to more diversity in their social network, it may lead to ambivalence (Huckfeldt, Mendez, & Osborn, 2004). For the third case, one might be apt to perceive Damien's experience as less subversive to democracy. Damien's declaration of independence appears slightly more positive than MaryAnn and Julie. He states,

> I think I picked up that sense of "as long as you are informed, then it's OK."
> I didn't grow up...I met people in high school, some of my friends were, like,
> their dad is conservative and so they're conservative and liberals are evil and
> vice versa, but I didn't have that, which probably influences, but then again, we
> all think we're right, but well, see I didn't have that so I'm unbiased, but that's
> probably not the case.

> What I got from them was be informed and always vote and that neither
> side could be horrible or evil because here they are joking about it. As much as I
> like to think I'm not like other people as far as influence, I think that's what I got
> from them and why I'm very comfortable being independent.

Damien appears to reject the logic that members of opposite parties are somehow lesser. However, Damien also appears to judge others who follow their parents' political philosophies. In other words, he dismisses familial identity and party membership as sharing a natural link. The sense that he must "be informed" could also be seen as troubling. Without party membership, there are no shortcuts on at least some of the issues. His lack of membership might create more burdens as he tries to gain information and he also might feel a lesser urgency to vote.

This negative case analysis of multiparty parental socialization provides a look at three individuals as they recall parental communication in the home and attempt to negotiate their political identities. Political difference in the home can create discord, particularly among strong partisans and may lead to negative and hostile communication among family members. This case presents an argument for the systematic study of political difference in the home. What role does political difference play in the dissolution of marriage? Further, in each of the three cases, participants seemed unwilling to declare party membership. Does political difference play a role in the growing number of independent voters, or the number of voters (and nonvoters) claiming to be independents?

Given the importance of familial communication to the development of political thoughts, attitudes, and behaviors, more research is necessary to understand how our everyday communication behaviors may be influencing the stability of our democracy.

Application of This Case Study

Parental attitudes and behavior remain among the most widely accepted political influences on youth. However, little is known about how these attitudes are communicated and less about how these attitudes are translating into a working political schema for youth. Acquisition of the partisan identity, even if removed from specific political and social issue discussion or comprehension, must be communicatively constructed. Membership, or the desire to be a member, must be seen as a positive identity. With these ideas in mind, consider the following questions.

REFLECTION QUESTIONS

1. How did your parents talk about politics when you were younger? What was their communication like?
2. Was discussion of politics a common topic in your home? Can you recall an instance? Were you able to participate?
3. How do you think discussion of politics in your home helped form your perspective on politics and party membership?
4. Do you have a partisan affiliation? When do you disclose your partisanship and with whom? Why?
5. How does your family handle conflict and/or issues of disagreement?
6. What topics have come up as taboo topics in your household? What makes a topic a taboo topic? Does it always start from a disagreement?

REFERENCES

Achen, C. H. (2002). Parental socialization and rational party identification. *Political Behavior, 24*(2), 151–170.

Acock, A. C., & Bengtson, V. L. (1980). Socialization and attribution processes: Actual versus perceived similarity among parents and youth. *Journal of Marriage & Family, 42*, 501–516.

Alford, J. R., Hatemi, P. K., Hibbing, J. R., Martine, N. G., & Eaves, L. J. (2011). The politics of mate choice. *The Journal of Politics, 73*(2), 362–379. doi:10.1017/S0022381611000016

Beck, A. (1974). A socialization theory of partisan realignment. In R. G. Niemi (Ed.), *The politics of future citizens: New dimensions in socialization* (pp. 199–219). San Francisco, CA: Jossey-Bass.

Box-Steffensmeier, J. M., De Boef, S., & Lin, T. (2004). The dynamics of the partisan gender gap. *The American Political Science Review, 98*(3), 515–528. doi:10.1017/s0003055404001315

Campbell, A., Converse, P. E., Miller, W. E., & Stokes, D. E. (1960). *The American voter*. Chicago, IL: University of Chicago Press.

Campbell, D. E. (2002). The young and the realigning: A test of the socialization theory of realignment. *Public Opinion Quarterly, 66*, 209–234. doi:10.1086/339849

Carmines, E. G., & Stimson, J. A. (1989). *Issue evolution: Race and the transformation of American politics*. New Jersey, NJ: Princeton University Press.

Converse, P. E. (1969). Of time and partisan stability. *Comparative Political Studies, 2*, 139–171.

Creswell, J. W. (1997). *Qualitative inquiry and research design: Choosing among five traditions*. Thousand Oaks, CA: Sage.

Dalton, R. J., & Weldon, S. (2007). Partisanship and party system institutionalization. *Party Politics, 13*(2), 179–196. doi:10.1177/1354068807073856

Delli Caprini, M. X., & Keeter, S. (1996) *What Americans know about politics and why it matters*. New Haven, CT: Yale University Press.

Dudley, R. L., & Gitelson, A. R. (2002). Political literacy, civic education, and civic engagement: A return to political socialization? *Applied Developmental Science, 6*(4), 175–182. doi:10.1207/s1532480xads0604_3

Erikson, R. S., Mackuen, M. B., & Stimson, J. A. (2002). *The macro polity*. New York, NY: Cambridge University Press.

Fiorina, M. P. (1993). Explorations of a political theory of party identification. In R. G. Niemi & H. F. Weisberg (Eds.), *Classics in voting behavior* (pp. 247–262). Washington, DC: CQ Press.

Glaser, B. G., & Strauss, A. L. (1967). *The discovery of grounded theory: Strategies for qualitative research*. Chicago, IL: Aldine.

Glesne, C. (2006). *Becoming a qualitative researcher: An introduction* (3rd ed.). Boston, MA: Pearson Education, Inc.

Green, D. P., Palmquist, B., & Schickler, E. (2004). *Partisan hearts and minds: Political parties and the social identity of voters*. New Haven, CT: Yale University Press.

Howell, S. E., & Day, C. L. (2000). Complexities of the gender gap. *Journal of Politics, 62*(3), 858–874. doi:10.1111/0022-3816.00036

Huckfeldt, R., Mendez, J. M., & Osborn, T. (2004). Disagreement, ambivalence, and engagement: The political consequences of heterogeneous networks. *Political Psychology, 25*, 65–95. doi:10.1111/j.1467-9221.2004.00357.x

Hyman, H. H. (1959). *Political socialization: A study in the psychology of political behavior*. New York, NY: The Free Press.

Iyengar, S., Sood, G., & Lelkes, Y. (2012). Affect, not ideology: A social identity perspective on polarization. *Public Opinion Quarterly, 76*, 405–431. doi:10.1093/poq/nfs038

Iyengar, S., & Westwood, S. J. (2015). Fear and loathing across party lines: New evidence of group polarization. *American Journal of Political Science, 59*, 690–707. doi:10.1111/ajps.12152

Kaufmann, K. M., & Petrocik, J. R. (1999). The changing politics of American men: Understanding the sources of the gender gap. *American Journal of Political Science, 43*(3), 864–887. doi:10.2307/2991838

Lazarsfeld, P. L., Berelson, B., & Gaudet, H. (1948). *The people's choice*. New York, NY: Columbia University Press.

Lindlof, T. R., & Taylor, B. C. (2002). *Qualitative communication research methods* (2nd ed.). Thousand Oaks, CA: Sage.

Meadowcroft, J. M. (1986). Family communication patterns and political development: The child's role. *Communication Research, 13*(4), 603–624.

Niemi, R. G., Ross, R. D., & Alexander, J. (1978). The similarity of political values of parents and college-age youths. *Public Opinion Quarterly, 42*, 503–520.

Prewitt, K., Eulau, H., & Zisk, B. H. (1966). Political socialization and political roles. *Public Opinion Quarterly, 30*(4), 569–582.

Rahn, W. M., & Hirshorn, R. M. (1999). Political advertising and public mood: A study of children's political orientations. *Political Communication, 16*(4), 387–407.

Rubin, M., & Hewstone, M. (2004). Social identity, system justification, and social dominance: Commentary on Reicher, Jost et al., and Sidanius et al. *Political Psychology, 25*(6), 823–844. doi:10.1111/j.1467-9221.2004.00400.x

Sapiro, V. (2004). Not your parents' political socialization: Introduction for a new generation. *Annual Review of Political Science, 7*(1), 1–23. doi:10.1146/annurev.polisci.7.012003.104840

Strauss, A. (1987). *Qualitative analysis for social scientists*. Cambridge, England: Cambridge University Press.

Strauss, A., & Corbin, J. (1998). *Basics of qualitative research: Techniques and procedures for developing grounded theory* (2nd ed.). Thousand Oaks, CA: Sage.

Turner, J. (1999). Some current issues in research on social identity and self-categorization theories. In N. Ellemers, R. Spears, & B. Doosje (Eds.), *Social identity context, commitment, content* (pp. 6–34). Malden, MA: Blackwell.

Turner, J. C., Hogg, M. A., Oakes, P. J., Reicher, S. D., & Wetherell, M. S. (1987). *Rediscovering the social group: A self-categorization theory*. Oxford, England: Basil Blackwell.

Warner, B. R., & Villamil, A. (2017). A test of imagined contact as a means to improve cross-partisan feelings and reduce attribution of malevolence and acceptance of political violence. *Communication Monographs, 84*, 1–19. doi:10.1080/03637751.2017.1336779

CHAPTER 20

"It Was Shocking to See Her Make It, Eat It, and Love It!": How a Mobile App Can Transform Family Food and Health Conversations in Low-income Homes

Deborah Neffa-Creech – *USC Annenberg*
Joanna Glovinsky – *Fruitstitute*
Susan H. Evans – *USC Annenberg*
Peter Clarke – *USC Annenberg*

ABSTRACT

Family discussions of food and nutrition are uncommon in low-income homes but can be important for stimulating healthy lifestyle changes. We explored the potential of an evidence-based mobile phone app—filled with vegetable-based recipes and healthy food tips—in stimulating these conversations. In this chapter, we share the stories of three families who made unusually heavy use of the app, called VeggieBook, and successfully transformed their food and health dynamics. In these homes, the app was used in social contexts, particularly with children who were encouraged to share their opinions about foods and their cooking skills in the kitchen. VeggieBook also helped bring families to the dinner table, where they discussed family matters, as well as issues about food and health. The app provoked communication and helped jumpstart low-income families' journeys to better health.

CASE STUDY

Forty-year-old Soledad considers herself a confident, creative cook and is proud of the meals she prepares for her husband and three sons, ages 9 to 13. She began cooking when she got married and has since leaned on her Peruvian heritage for inspiration, using traditional recipes for meat-based dishes that her family enjoys. Her meals, however, steer clear of vegetables. This makes Soledad feel slightly guilt-ridden because she and her husband have high cholesterol and weight concerns.

She feels intimidated by the vegetables she receives from her local food pantry—vegetables she does not know how to prepare—and has fallen into a cooking rut. Although she enjoys fixing meals, her family members do not share kitchen responsibilities and seldom eat dinner together. They also rarely discuss matters related to food or health. As Soledad puts it, they lack "la unión familiar," a sense of family bonding. Nonetheless, Soledad cooks for her family every day and prides herself on serving them homemade meals, even if they often eat apart.

Soledad's story is one that resonates with many women nationwide who frequent food pantries and cook at home. They are interested in adopting healthier eating habits, but they have limited knowledge about how to cook with fresh produce (Clarke & Evans, 2016). They default to using the unhealthier recipes that they know, and they grow discouraged by their families' lack of interest in pursuing the healthiest lifestyle that they can afford.

Soledad felt discouraged searching for vegetable-based recipes on her own, but she gladly accepted the opportunity to learn more as part of a program offered at her local food pantry. University of Southern California (USC) researchers recruited female household cooks for a study that allowed the women to use a mobile app with vegetable-based recipes and healthy food tips. The study was part of a randomized controlled trial that tested the app's effects on household eating (Clarke, Evans, & Neffa-Creech, 2018).[1]

Women like Soledad who signed up for the program were given a Samsung Galaxy phone loaded with the app, called VeggieBook,[2] and were trained to use the app, alongside their 9 to14-year-old children (see Figure 1 for screenshots from the app; Clarke, Evans, & Hovy, 2011; Evans & Clarke, 2019; Evans, Clarke, & Koprowski, 2010). Women could use VeggieBook on their own and with their families.

---

1. The study was funded by the Agriculture and Food Research Initiative, Childhood Obesity Prevention: Integrated Research, Education, and Extension to Prevent Childhood Obesity. Grant/Award #: 2012-68001-19592.
2. VeggieBook is available in English and Spanish and has: customized and personalized profiles and content; content sharing capability via email, social media, or printed materials; 260 field-tested recipes and other food ideas that use familiar, affordable ingredients; and 83 no-cost tips to improve family meals and food shopping. To learn more about the app, visit https://www.youtube.com/watch?v=BBmlMQ2QuEw

Figure 1 – *Sample recipes (left) and healthy living tip (right) from the app, available in English and Spanish.*
Courtesy of Deborah Neffa-Creech, Joanna Glovinsky, Susan H. Evans, Peter Clarke.

VeggieBook was designed with help from food pantry clients who, during focus groups and other interviews, voiced the need for having a visually appealing, simple app for cooking. The content, graphic design, and navigation, which were pre-tested, allow family members of all ages and education levels to become engaged.

Women and their families can access the app through dual pathways that allow them to build individual profiles and customize their selection of recipes for 10 vegetables commonly offered at food pantries (e.g., broccoli, onions, carrots, and potatoes). Users can choose recipes that meet their individual needs (e.g., child-friendly, recipes with meat or chicken, or for just one or two persons) and that align with their taste preferences (i.e., Latino, Asian, or Soul Food flavors). All recipes require few ingredients and kitchen appliances that families likely already own.

In this chapter, we share the stories of three families who made unusually heavy use of VeggieBook. These cases are "positive deviants," instances where an individual or a group finds solutions despite having poor odds or access to similar resources as their peers (Singhal & Durá, 2017). The three families were picked from a group of 12 that stood out as positive deviants from a larger pool of 122 participating households.

CHAPTER 20: "It Was Shocking to See Her Make It, Eat It, and Love It!"

201

In Soledad's home, as well as in other homes, children became instrumental in channeling their family's use of the app, which often sparked changes in food decisions. Generally, children's technology literacy levels were higher than their parents', enabling them to teach their mothers additional ways to navigate the app. This enhanced children's self-efficacy since they could lead the way using the technology. This newly gained confidence, in addition to curiosities about food, drew children towards the app to learn about nutrition and meal preparation tasks, which previously were reserved for the adults at home.

Soledad and 11-year-old Alex often used VeggieBook together to find recipes and tips for healthful living. Their joint interactions with the app planted the seed for what would become positive changes in food and health conversations for the family. As their interactions became more prevalent, Alex became a valued, eager contributor of food decisions in the home. Soledad explained: "When I would say, 'Alex, let's look at the app,' he wanted to do everything. He wanted to choose all the recipes, go through all the information, and tell me which ones to cook. He took full control." VeggieBook did not include multiuser interactive features that can enhance parent–child exchanges when co-using technologies (Hiniker, Lee, Kientz, & Radesky, 2018). However, the app's family-centered focus on food and dual pathways, which allowed for customization of content, were apparently enough to stimulate parent–child engagement in many families.

Alex's involvement choosing the day's meals made Soledad more likely to buy new vegetables and try recipes using non-Latino flavors and ingredients. It also motivated her to ask her other children for their food preferences. When it came to cooking, however, Soledad did not encourage her sons to help, mainly out of fear that they were too young to manage a stove or use knives. She allowed her 13-year-old to help with basic food preparations, such as making lemonade and vegetable salads. "Even though they're boys, it's good that they know what happens in the kitchen, or at least have an idea of how these things are done and what they require."

Other mothers in the program held similar gendered expectations of their children's involvement with food. Although Soledad had no daughters, 60-year-old Patricia chose her 12-year-old daughter, Isabel, to participate in VeggieBook with her instead of her 13-year-old son, Matt. As a co-user of the app with her mother, Isabel became a large part of the food decision-making process at home and an instigator of her family's adoption of new vegetables.

Patricia and Isabel often chose recipes together, which made Isabel curious about foods and eager to learn new cooking skills. Patricia explained in an interview: "I let [Isabel] clean and cut the veggies and showed her the amount of seasoning to use. She really enjoyed being a part of preparing the meal. The app has brought her into the kitchen to learn how to cook. She asks me questions about how I cook: 'Why add that?' and 'How is it going to taste?' She's like a child growing up with a new toy. … One of the reasons that she is liking this food is that she is helping to make the dishes. It was shocking to see her make it, eat it, and love it!"

In another account of her daughter's involvement in the kitchen, Patricia described how Isabel singlehandedly got the family to eat carrots, a vegetable they seldom enjoyed. "I asked, 'What would you like to have for dinner?' and she said, 'Let's look at VeggieBook so I can tell you better.' She picked out carrots. She had to peel a couple of bags of carrots and then said she was tired but was not going to stop. She put them in a dish with sliced apples and some butter and then in the oven. That was really the first time she ate carrots. Combining apples and carrots was new to the family. Everyone tried it and loved it, and nobody really liked carrots before." Inspired by the app, Isabel became creative and confident in the kitchen, which inspired the family to incorporate her vegetable-based dishes into their diets.

In Jimena's home, her daughter Evelyn became her partner-in-crime in the kitchen. Forty-year-old Jimena and 13-year-old Evelyn often used the app together to make meal decisions. Evelyn was quick to enter the kitchen, where she shared her voice, made contributions, and gained confidence. Jimena explained during an interview: "She started using the app and started helping me cook and saying to everyone, 'Look! I chose this, and I did that and that.' She started doing things with me, and then her sisters started doing it, too. . . . She's more confident, more like she's knowing. She feels very big."

Evelyn proudly shared her vegetable creations with her four sisters (six to 20 years old), who noticed her achievements and became motivated to contribute, too. This made Jimena happy since she believes that cooking is a woman's responsibility. "Learning how to cook is important. I told my daughters, 'You know what? You have to learn because you're big enough, and when you get married, you need to know how to cook.' I had no way to get them into the kitchen before. VeggieBook was a good way to get them started."

As time passed, Jimena began to think of Evelyn as a true partner in meal decision-making and in cooking, both learning and adapting vegetable recipes together. "I would choose a recipe, and I would say to Evelyn, 'Look, I'm trying to do this one. What do you think about it? Do you want another one? What do you want me to put in it? The recipe calls for these things but if you want, we can change them with other stuff...' I would choose the recipe, and if she didn't like it, she would choose another one for us to do. That's the way we did it mostly."

When introduced to the VeggieBook app, children took initiative to use it, to share their preferences for nutritious meals, and to cook. This often inspired families to try new vegetables and recipes that pushed them outside of their comfort zones; conversations about food in the home become routine.

For families who were not used to eating meals together, the increased sociability around food also led them to share more time together at the dinner table. Soledad admitted that meals together were not something she prioritized before VeggieBook. She read about the

CHAPTER 20: "It Was Shocking to See Her Make It, Eat It, and Love It!"

203

importance of family mealtime on the app, which gave her the courage to try it. Mealtime soon after became a valued, staple activity in her home. "It was an amazing moment when we all sat down to eat dinner together as a family. It's one of the best times of the day, I think. It's very important. I learned that I can make this happen, that I can make this daily experience a happy and special time for everyone."

Patricia's family also began eating dinner together, a monumental change in her home. Before VeggieBook, Patricia would often try to get her family together for dinner to no avail. Her husband, who often worked late, would not be in the mood to eat, and her son and daughter would be distracted in their bedrooms or watching television. Eating apart was difficult for Patricia to accept because she was raised eating meals as a family. "I'm the youngest of 12 children, and my single mom would sit us all around a big table and eat together. That's how I want it to be."

Although family meals were something mothers often wanted, it was not something they bothered asking their families to do until they saw the "Secret to Better Dinners" tip in the app. In fact, this is what motivated Patricia and her daughter, Isabel, to get the rest of the family to the table. Patricia explained: "Using VeggieBook tips, we did the dinner planner—all the TVs and computers are off, everyone is at the table, and it's really something! I have always wanted for my family to share the good and the bad. There's always something to talk about at the table."

Once families made it to the table, conversation was plentiful. For Soledad, it allowed her to receive feedback on her vegetable-based recipes and to ask for suggestions for the next day's meal. Her sons always had an opinion about the foods they wanted to eat, something that Soledad previously had never noticed or asked about. "I realized it is important to have the participation of everyone, because food is something everyone should participate in."

For Patricia, mealtimes allowed her husband to have more conversations with the children about their daily activities and to become more involved as a parent. "Before, the kids would ask me, 'Why doesn't Dad come to the park or shopping or to school events with us?' Now, the kids ask him to participate, and he's starting to! Now, we put on the calendar times for Mom and Isabel, Mom and Matt, Dad and Isabel, and Dad and Matt, and the entire family."

Mealtimes offered opportunities for families to discuss food, health, and other topics in ways that cut through generational and gender boundaries. Such socialization, often facilitated by the app, sparked motivations for mothers and children to cook nutritious meals for family feedback and enjoyment. It also motivated women to share recipes with other family members and close friends, either electronically or in print.

In most cases, mothers were eager to spend time learning about and preparing vegetable-based dishes, prompted by an outgrowth of concerns about personal and family health.

These concerns also motivated changes in family eating, likely galvanized by the app. Jimena, for instance, admitted that, before VeggieBook, she seldom cooked with vegetables and sometimes allowed them to rot in her kitchen. Her go-to meals were mainly Mexican dishes that were "greasy" and "unhealthy." Over the years, the lack of vegetables in her diet led to a diagnosis of high cholesterol. Taking care of her health and setting a positive example for her family were key motivators for her using the app. "I don't want my family to get sick either, so I wanted to change," she explained. "I wanted to bring vegetables into our home and to cook healthy foods. When VeggieBook came, I was like, 'That is just what I need.'"

By bringing her daughters into the kitchen and sharing mealtime work with them, Jimena was able to redirect her time and energy to becoming healthier. In particular, she spent her time on VeggieBook and in the kitchen learning to cook an array of vegetables, many of which she previously found daunting. The app also propelled Jimena to sharpen her parenting skills by educating her daughters on the importance of health and meal preparation in the home.

Throughout the program, Soledad witnessed her husband lose weight, and she attributed it to the vegetable-based meals she prepared daily. This positive change also motivated her husband to become more involved with VeggieBook. For instance, he would help Soledad cook vegetables and get the children involved in mealtime chores such as setting the table and washing the dishes. Soledad said that his "vámonos todos," or "let's all do it," attitude made her feel supported and was critical to making the app a part of daily family interactions.

Mothers also saw the value of using VeggieBook to keep their children healthy, often encouraging them to use the app's nutrition tips and information to make healthier food choices. Some women specifically targeted their older, teenage children, knowing that they were concerned with their body image and/or athletic performance at school. These youth applied what they learned on the app to lose a few pounds or to become better athletes.

Soledad, for one, noticed her children become more conscious of the calories and fats that they consumed. "I know they saw the healthy living tips on VeggieBook about reading the ingredients list on the package, and now they all take more care about what they choose to eat," she explained. "I realized that for the kids to eat well, for them to be healthy, depends on me."

CONCLUSION

Over the course of only a few months, the mothers in these stories witnessed their families become more unified, social, and engaged in matters of food and health. This seemed to revitalize the home food environment and to relieve mothers from perceived pressures of making decisions about meals on their own. Although mothers retained their titles as main cooks, they gladly shared food tasks with others, something that the VeggieBook app facilitated.

Success stories such as these are encouraging, yet surprising, given the number of barriers that families often had to overcome: (1) limited financial and food resources, (2) mothers' limited experiences using food and nutrition apps, and (3) a socially fragmented family that did not value spending time together. As positive deviants, the three narratives in this chapter provide insights into behaviors and contexts that allowed families in low-income homes to achieve better food practices and related family communication with help from a mobile app.

In these homes, the app was used in social contexts, with children—particularly daughters—encouraged to be part of the meal preparation process, to voice their opinions about food, and even to take the lead in cooking. Some mothers also used the app to corral their families to the dinner table, where the family engaged in meaningful conversations and valued feedback about new recipes and healthier foods. Lastly, personal and family health concerns motivated app use, with recipes and healthful living tips from VeggieBook helpful in guiding families on how to cook vegetable-based meals in tasteful ways. These dishes, and tips for how to involve family in food-related tasks at home, led to perceived improvements in health.

DISCUSSION QUESTIONS

1. In what ways might these findings about positive deviants in lower income homes be applied when promoting the app to users from a wider range of socioeconomic backgrounds?
2. How might family food dynamics be different in homes where men, instead of women, are the main household cooks and, potentially, promoters of the app?
3. As they age, children become more involved with peer culture. How might this change the child's likelihood to use the VeggieBook app, alone or with a parent?
4. VeggieBook allows an adult cook and a child to enter the app and to select and save their own recipes and other food ideas. How important are dual pathways like this for health apps to inspire parent–child collaboration?

REFERENCES

Clarke, P., & Evans, S. H. (2016). How do cooks actually cook vegetables? A field experiment with low-income households. *Health Promotion Practice, 17*(1), 80–87. doi:10.1177/1524839915597898

Clarke, P., Evans, S. H., & Hovy, E. H. (2011). Indigenous message tailoring increases consumption of fresh vegetables by clients of community pantries. *Health Communication, 26*(6), 571–582. doi:10.1080/10410236.2011.558337

Clarke, P., Evans, S. H., & Neffa-Creech, D. (2018). Mobile app increases vegetable-based preparations by low-income household cooks: A randomized controlled trial. *Public Health Nutrition*, 1–12. doi:10.1017/S1368980018003117

Evans, S. H., & Clarke, P. (2019). Resolving design issues in developing a nutrition app: A case study using formative research. *Evaluation and Program Planning, 72*, 97–105. doi:10.1016/j.evalprogplan.2018.10.010

Evans, S. H., Clarke, P., & Koprowski, C. (2010). Information design to promote better nutrition among pantry clients: Four methods of formative evaluation. *Public Health Nutrition, 13*(3), 430–437. doi:10.1017/S1368980009990851

Hiniker, A., Lee, B., Kientz, J. A., & Radesky, J. S. (2018, April). Let's play!: Digital and analog play between preschoolers and parents. In *Proceedings of the 2018 CHI conference on human factors in computing systems* (p. 659). ACM.

Singhal, A., & Durá, L. (2017). Positive deviance: A non-normative approach to health and risk messaging. In *The Oxford research encyclopedia of communication: Communication theory, health and risk communication*.

CHAPTER 21

Don't Mention the Office: Workplace Bullying Spillover at Home

Sarah E. Riforgiate – *University of Wisconsin, Milwaukee*
Lynn Turner – *Marquette University*

ABSTRACT

Nearly half (47%) of surveyed American employees report experiencing at least one negative act *weekly* in their work career (Lutgen-Sandvik, Tracy, & Alberts, 2007). Ongoing negative communication exchanges can target a particular employee over time and result in workplace bullying. Unfortunately, more than a quarter of workers in the United States experience workplace bullying and over a third indicate they are aware bullying is occurring (Desrayaud, Dickson, & Webb, in press). Workplace bullying creates serious negative consequences for the organization and the employee, but also extends to family members as the employee struggles to cope with work difficulties. Family members are thought to be potential resources in dealing with workplace bullying (Tye-Williams, in press), yet negative workplace experiences take a toll on family relationships (Lutgen-Sandvik, 2018). This case study chronicles the issues for family relationships when Adam is targeted and bullied by his supervisor at work. Exchanges between family members highlight work–life boundary theories regarding boundary strength and permeability, including how work-to-home spillover can negatively influence family relationships. Further, social support and communication privacy management theories can be used to explain how family members attempt to help Adam while also protecting his secret. The deleterious influences of bullying, including withdrawal, rumination, and negative interaction patterns, are demonstrated through discussions among Adam and his wife, children, and in-laws.

CASE STUDY

Adam turned the car off and let out a deep sigh. As he sat in the car listening to the thick raindrops splash on the roof, he rested his head on the steering wheel. Tears cascaded down his cheeks and turned into soft sobs. It was better to do this alone in the car than subject his family to the pain he felt. It was too hard to explain to them all the small things that added up to his pain. A year ago, he was a valued employee at Pond and Northfield Enterprises, and received a promotion to the division headed by Helen Smith. But for the last 11 months, his boss Helen had squashed the hopes he had of being successful. She berated him in front of his colleagues; her watchful stare kept track of his every moment in the workplace; she stopped by his desk the moment he left for the washroom, commenting aloud to anyone who was in earshot, "Is he gone again? Does he ever work?" He knew she was taking notes about him in meetings because she would turn to others and whisper just loudly enough so he could make out his name and realize they were all staring his direction. She was evil, but everyone assured him that he was reading too much into her behaviors.

"Am I losing my mind?" Adam questioned the empty car. Maybe it *was* all in his head. He reached for the box of Kleenex and pulled the last one out to blow his nose. He could not linger too long or his wife, Judy, would worry.

Gathering his belongings, he thought of their last family trip to the lake. He had caught a fish and the children had squealed with glee. He focused on this happy memory to sustain him. As he opened the front door he faked a cheerful voice yelling, "Hello, I'm home!" Meredith, his five-year-old daughter, and Jacob, his seven-year-old son, came racing toward him hugging his knees and waist so hard he almost toppled over. Judy was in the kitchen and something smelled wonderfully of garlic and tomatoes. He was safe. It was going to be all right.

Judy's voice wafted over the giggles of the children asking, "How was your day honey?"

"Oh, fine."

Judy probed, "Did your presentation go well? I bet they loved your ideas."

"Ahm . . . well . . . ah . . . it was all right. Ahm . . . but they decided to go another direction."

"Really, that seems odd. You were so excited about your ideas and all the research backed them up. What are they going to do instead?"

Adam's face felt warm and he bit his lip. He was relieved Judy was in the other room and couldn't see his embarrassment. He tried to sound casual, "Oh, ah... they are going to keep the current campaign." He breathed in deeply, "Helen thought that was for the best."

Judy rounded the corner and knew something was amiss. She paused. "Well, I certainly thought it was a great idea and I loved your practice presentation. It's their loss."

Judy wanted to be supportive. She knew Adam was having a hard time at work, but he rarely wanted to talk about it. He tossed and turned at night and she often woke up to find he had gone to watch TV downstairs at two or three in the morning. He also wasn't eating much and would tell her "It's nothing" when she asked about what was wrong. She felt shut out and was concerned things were getting worse. What if it wasn't work? Was it something she had done? She pushed those thoughts aside and began serving dinner.

The kids filled the dinner conversation with stories from school and excitement over the school end-of-the-year program on Friday. Meredith's class was singing several songs and Jacob's class had planned on performing some magic tricks.

"So what is the secret to make the magic work?" Judy winked with a sparkle in her eye.

"Come on Mom! It's magic! There is not any secret, we are just AWESOME!" Jacob laughed. "You will love the show though! You are both going to be there, right?"

"Absolutely!" Adam confirmed. "We wouldn't miss it if our eyebrows were on fire!"

Things seemed normal and easy at dinner. Adam wished he could bottle that feeling. All he wanted to do was support his family and keep them safe. "It's just a job," he thought, "I need to keep my head down and things will be better tomorrow." He had been saying this for 11 months now, though, ever since Helen vowed to "mentor" him; he shivered.

Once the kids were in bed and the house was quiet, Judy sat by Adam and held his hand. They sat quietly for a while, just being together. She was worried. Why wouldn't he tell her what was going on? Lately he had been so distant; was he just overwhelmed at work or was he unhappy in their marriage? She decided she should at least try to talk about it. "Adam, are you just tired because of work? What happened today with the presentation really? Is everything all right? You worked for months on that."

"Honey, I really don't want to talk about it. Helen is just Helen. She's difficult to work for and doesn't know what she wants." Adam was exhausted and the last thing he wanted to do was talk about work or get into an argument.

"Well, I guess you will have chance to shine by figuring out how to make the old plan work." Judy was trying to be positive. "I mean, it isn't the end of the world. I know you can make the most of things and come out ahead."

"I suppose." Adam sighed. In his head he was thinking, "That is, if I still have a job." He dreaded going in to the office, yet he needed the income and insurance for his family. He thought about looking for another position, but he knew Helen wouldn't give him a good reference. With her tight control and watchful eye on him, he had no chance to even talk with other employers, much less go to interviews. The last time he was sick, Helen called him, demanded he go see a doctor, and required him to bring a note in to work. It was ludicrous! He wouldn't have been surprised to hear that she had called the doctor to make sure he really visited. She was a crazy control freak.

Adam squeezed Judy's hand and said, "I am really tired, I'm going to go to bed." It was the easiest way to end the conversation.

"I know it was a big day. Hopefully you can get a good night's sleep." Judy kissed him gently and wished him good night. She was left sitting alone on the couch. In the quietness of the house, she wondered how she could help him. He wouldn't let her in. She didn't want to worry her parents or the children. It was hard feeling like she couldn't talk through this with anyone—not even her husband.

The next day, Adam went in to work early. He couldn't sleep, so he kissed Judy and the kids as they slept and left at 5:40 a.m. At least the office was quiet then and he could think. He worked through emails and started feeling better. He had some new ideas to float by Mike, one of his coworkers. Maybe if the two of them were on the same page, Helen would be more amiable to making some changes.

When Mike got in, Adam showed him five years of marketing data and pitched his new idea. Mike loved it! When they stopped by to explain it to Helen, she responded with a big smile, saying "YES! This is fantastic teamwork and a great idea! Let's do it!"

Adam was taken off guard and even managed a tentative smile. Maybe things would be alright. He decided to work through lunch to build on the momentum. The rest of the office cleared out for "taco Tuesdays" at a nearby restaurant.

As he scrutinized the numbers one more time, Helen came by and sat on the edge of his desk, blocking the path to the door. She picked up a red sharpie marker and started randomly drawing large X marks through his projections, all the work he had spent days compiling.

"What are you doing?" Adam was alarmed.

"What are YOU doing???!!!" Helen accused. "I know that you are trying to make me look bad. How DARE you bring Mike into this and double-team me. Your idea is shit and you are shit and if you EVER make me look bad again..." She leaned down from her perch on his desk and her face was so close to his that he could feel her warm breath as her face grew a darker pink. She continued to lean in as he tried to make space between them until he had nowhere to go. Her eyes narrowed, locked on his eyes, and didn't blink, "...you'll be fired and I will make sure you never get work in this industry again. Don't think I can't do it, Adam! I own you."

A bead of sweat dripped down the side of Adam's forehead and he almost stopped breathing. She did have a lot of power and knew all the influential people in his field. The office was empty; no one was there to witness her threats. As his heart and mind raced he asked himself how this could be happening. He pleaded with Helen, saying "I'm sorry. It was my fault. I won't let it happen again." He felt paralyzed and trapped, afraid that any movement would make things worse.

Helen's face was tense, her brows furrowed, and her stone-grey eyes stared deep into his soul, and all he could see was pure hatred. It seemed like time had stopped and he was frozen. There was movement outside. People were coming back from lunch. Helen leaned even closer and whispered, "I hope we understand each other." Then leaning back, Helen loudly commented in a lighthearted voice for others to overhear, "Adam, you shouldn't have to work through lunch time. I am not a taskmaster; you can reprint those reports and give them to me tomorrow."

Adam quickly gathered the papers that were now scattered across his desk and on the floor so no one would see all the red markings. He quickly went to the washroom to calm down and wash his face. Even if he told people what had happened, would they believe him? It was crazy. He had no witnesses, so it was her word against his. He was quiet the rest of the day and left before the office cleared out so there was no chance of being alone with Helen. When he got home he went right to bed, saying he didn't feel well and avoiding any discussion.

"Why isn't daddy having dinner with us?" Jacob asked.

Judy quickly covered, "He isn't feeling well tonight. A bit of a tummy bug probably."

"But I wanted to tell him about what I learned today and tell him a new joke," Meredith objected. She pouted slightly.

"Can you save it for tomorrow?" Judy asked and then quickly reminded, "We want him to be healthy to go to your performance on Friday."

"Yeah, Meredith! I want to show him my magic trick surprise!" Jacob reminded. "Besides, we don't want his eyebrows to catch fire!" he giggled, thinking about his dad's expression the night before.

Adam stayed home sick the next day. Judy was helping with costumes and the dress rehearsal at the school all day, so Adam was alone. He didn't open his email. His cell phone rang every hour and then at 2 p.m. the home phone started ringing. He didn't answer. He lay in bed, staring at the ceiling in a daze, listening to the phone ring over and over and over.

On Thursday Adam stayed at home again. Judy said she would cancel helping at the food bank to stay home with him, but Adam insisted she go. Judy was worried about him. He wouldn't tell her anything and he looked terrible. He wouldn't eat, was pale, and disoriented. He refused to go to the doctor.

As he lay completely still on the bed, Adam watched the lighting change through the window from the soft morning glow to the bright early-afternoon blaze. If he were completely still, could he just disappear? At 11:30 a.m. the phone rang four times before the answering machine picked up.

"Ah... Adam. It's Mike. Ahm, Judy called in and said you were sick. She sounded worried. I hope you are all right. Ah... well... I don't want to rush your recovery, but if there is any way you can get in to the office, ahm... you should come in. Helen is really preoccupied with your sickness and seems to think you are faking it. I know that isn't the case... I mean, you always work harder than the rest of us, coming in early and working late. But, ah, she has her assistant calling all the golf courses and is insisting you are just goofing off. If you feel up to it, give me a call at work or at home. I hope you feel better. I thought you would want to know."

Adam continued lying there until he heard the garage door. Judy and the kids must be home. He mustered every ounce of energy to roll on his side and gradually get out of bed to go to the bathroom. Then he held the railing carefully as he took one step at a time to go downstairs. He ate dinner with his family but didn't say anything. They carried on a conversation and he felt like a ghost eavesdropping. He knew he had to go in to work tomorrow or Helen would find a way to fire him. There was no way but forward, as painful as that was.

When Adam went upstairs again he heard the TV turn on followed by Meredith and Jacob's laughter. He owed it to them to go to work—to take care of them, feed them, make sure there was a roof over their heads, and ensure they had health insurance.

Judy entered the dark bedroom and sat next to his prone body on the bed. "Honey, are you all right? Did something happen at work? I heard the message from Mike on the answering machine and he sounded really worried." She waited quietly and grasped his hand.

Adam felt the warmth of her hand and wondered how much he should share. Would she believe him? It was so crazy. He didn't want to sound paranoid about Helen keeping tabs on him. He needed to keep this job until he found another one. They needed the money.

Adam let out a deep sigh and they sat in silence for a good four minutes. Then he decided to confide in her, "I will tell you what happened, but you can't tell ANYONE. I mean it Judy. No one would believe it anyway."

When Judy agreed, Adam recounted all the small things that had been happening in the last 11 months: Helen lurking outside the washroom to get him to sign urgent documents while complaining he was never at his desk; negative performance reviews suggesting he never took initiative and was lazy; Helen telling him project parameters and then changing them 15 minutes before he presented; Helen moving his desk closer to her office so she could see him at all times. Then he finally described the interaction when Helen threatened that she could make it so he never worked again.

The details came out in a jumble and Judy just listened and tried to piece the timeline together. She was horrified that he had been shouldering so much without telling her for almost a year. How could this possibly be happening? It didn't make any sense. Why would Helen do this? Adam had been promoted to Helen's division because he consistently won awards for his work. He had been told he was on a fast track to management.

"Have you talked with Human Resources about this? Or what about Helen's boss?" Judy had no idea where to start, but she knew this wasn't right and something needed to be done.

Adam forcefully sat up and said "NO! No one can know about this. They wouldn't believe me anyway and it would just make things worse with Helen. The last thing I need is for her to think I am going behind her back. She will crush me, Judy." Adam started to sob uncontrollably.

Judy was stunned. She held him while he cried and felt completely helpless. How could she not have known? She knew sometimes when he came home that he had had a rough day at work. He had mentioned Helen was really involved in his projects, but she thought that was a sign that Helen was mentoring him and was interested in his future. When he had complained that Helen didn't like his ideas, she had started to think that maybe Adam wasn't reading the audience right. It never dawned on her that he had been harassed all this time.

When Adam calmed down Judy held the sides of his face tenderly and said, "You can't go back there, Adam. I know you can find another position. Just email her a resignation and I can pick up your things tomorrow." Deep down Judy was furious that Adam had been subjected to ongoing abuse for so long and deeply saddened that he didn't tell her about it.

"Judy, I can't quit. It isn't just about the money, although that is a real issue. If I quit she would win. Besides, I would not have any references, and she basically promised she'd use her connections to poison others against me. She knows everyone in the industry."

Judy thought about this; she didn't want him to go back, but she was afraid he was right. Helen did seem to know everyone. She always was name-dropping and flitting about talking to everyone at company events. She *could* do a lot of damage to Adam if he quit.

"Alright Adam, but you need to make sure you are not in the office alone with her again. This weekend, I can help you work on your resume and go through job postings. We need to get you out of there."

Adam agreed with her, switching jobs might be his only escape. It felt better to share this all with Judy, but he didn't want her to worry. He was concerned about changing his patterns—not going in early or staying late. He was productive when no one else was in the office, but he didn't want to be alone with Helen either.

The next morning, Meredith and Jacob reminded Adam it was the "big day." "Dad, don't forget to come home early for our performance!"

Adam hugged them saying, "I will be there! I don't want any singed eyebrows!"

When he arrived at the office, he worked in his car, reading through documents. He wanted to wait until he saw Mike arrive so they could walk in the office together. He inhaled quickly when he noticed a shadow; Helen was peering into his window and looking in at him. She tapped on the window and yelled through the glass "What are you doing in there instead of in the office? Are you trying to hide something?"

Adam's heart pounded and his palms started sweating. He was sure his face was flushed. He looked up at her with a panic-stricken expression. She laughed and walked into the office.

Could he leave and never come back? Mike's car pulled up next to his and Mike gave him a friendly wave. Adam felt like he could go in now.

"Hey Adam, are you feeling better? You look flushed. Are you all right?" Mike asked.

"Ah, yeah, I am fine. I must have caught something the kids brought home from school." Adam quickly lied.

Mike smiled kindly. "Well, I hope you get over it soon. I was worried about you."

They walked in together and Adam felt slightly safer that Mike was with him. Adam sat down at his computer and saw he had 487 emails. He sighed and opened the first one which read:

> *Adam—now that you are back from your "sick" days, you should be refreshed and ready to work. I noticed how tan you looked through the car window. You must have rested on a sunny golf course to recover from your illness. We are behind on your proposed project and I need to make sure we get on schedule. Every day I want you to submit an email of who you talked with and what you are working on in 15-minute increments. This will help me coach you on how to improve your use of time to get back on track.*
>
> *Helen*

Adam read it again. Was she really asking him to report every little thing he did? Could he ignore it and say he missed the email? He didn't have time for this! It would probably take him a half hour just to make the list of his activities in 15-minute increments to send to her. This was not a good use of his time and he had two days of work to catch up on. Adam dug into his emails, opening all of them except the ones from Helen. Since over 100 of them were from her, he was making good progress.

At noon Helen stopped by his desk right as people were leaving for lunch. He started to get up when she loudly said, "Wait, you are not seriously leaving for lunch after coming in late and taking two days off golfing?" She blocked his path out.

"Helen, I was sick. I need to visit the doctor today." Adam looked at Mike for help.

"Yeah, Adam did tell me that." Mike covered and waited for Adam.

Helen stood at the window and watched them. Adam was afraid to say anything further to Mike in case it got back to Helen.

Adam drove to the urgent care clinic just in case Helen followed him. It seemed paranoid, but he wouldn't put it past her. He figured he could sit in his car and work, but then decided he better go in. Entering, he heard the receptionist say, "I am sorry, I can't tell you who has appointments at the clinic." Then after a pause, "No, patients' records are confidential, I cannot tell you if a particular person is a patient here or not."

When the call ended, the employee looked at him and handed him some forms to fill out. Had he imagined that call? Would Helen really call urgent care? How would she know where he went? He glanced out the window and saw her car pull out of the parking lot. His hands shook as he filled out the forms. What was he going to tell the doctor?

Meanwhile, Judy had gone to her parents' home and was helping them with some yard work. As they worked, her mom started asking about Adam. "How is he doing, dear?"

Judy smiled and lied as best she could. "Oh, he's great. I wish he didn't work so hard, but I know he's in high demand for this project he's planning."

Her mom looked at her carefully and noted, "It's just that the last few times we saw him he seemed a little on edge. Did we say something wrong?"

Judy assured her that Adam had a lot going on at work and then added, "You didn't do anything wrong, Mom; he adores you and Dad."

Her parents gently probed about Adam's project and his work most of the morning. Judy wanted to ask for their advice. She needed their help, but she had promised not to say anything. She felt the heavy burden of Adam's secret, and wanted to be open about things. She didn't like having to be evasive and could really use their support.

After a full day of yard work, Judy returned home and was scrambling to get the children fed and in costume for the school program. Where was Adam?

"Is dad meeting us at the school?" Melanie asked.

Judy quickly sent a text message to Adam. "Where are you?" She covered for him. "He must be running late. I'm sure he will meet us there."

Jacob chimed in, "He'd better!"

When Judy got the children settled backstage with their teachers, she met her parents in the seating area. "Where's Adam?" her dad asked.

Judy was getting worried. She kept looking toward the door as the show started. Was he all right? How can she explain this to her parents and the children? At intermission she called him, but he didn't answer.

Five minutes before the grand finale, Adam slipped into the back of the theater. Judy noticed him at the back and was happy he'd arrived, but worried that something more was wrong. When the performance ended, her mom approached Adam saying, "We missed you tonight!"

Adam looked pale. "I'm sorry. A project at work ran late and I couldn't leave."

"They work you too hard," Judy's dad insisted, "What project is so important on a Friday night? You almost missed the whole performance."

Judy deflected the comments by inviting everyone to the house for ice cream. How could she explain, and still protect her promise to Adam? Was Adam going to be all right? Were they going to be all right? She pushed her concerns aside and faked a warm smile as they all told Meredith and Jacob what a great show it was.

This case is based on a compilation of workplace bullying experiences from interviews and research to provide a realistic representation. Unfortunately, experiences like this are all too common with nearly half (47%) of surveyed American employees report experiencing at least one negative act weekly in their work career (Lutgen-Sandvik, Tracy, & Alberts, 2007). More than a quarter of workers in the United States experience workplace bullying and over a third indicate they are aware bullying is occurring (Desrayaud, Dickson, & Webb, in press).

DISCUSSION QUESTIONS

1. What communication behaviors in this case could be considered bullying? How do you tell the difference between communication to keep employees on track and communication that is considered bullying?
2. While Adam is the target of workplace bulling, who else in this story is influenced by the destructive communication of bullying and how are they influenced?
3. Considering boundaries between home and work, describe how permeable are work-to-home and home-to-work boundaries? What events precipitate boundary blurring and which area (home or work) is most heavily influenced?
4. Adam asks Judy not to disclose information about his work experiences. How is this request helpful and hurtful to them individually and as a couple? How does managing privacy influence other relationships in the story? How does the communication privacy management theory (Petronio, 2002) explain what goes on in the story?
5. Family members are thought to be potential resources in dealing with workplace bullying (Tye-Williams, in press), yet negative workplace experiences also take a toll on family relationships (Lutgen-Sandvik, 2018). How does Adam's family support or not support him and why?
6. Nearly half (47%) of surveyed American employees report experiencing at least one negative act *weekly* in their work career (Lutgen-Sandvik, Tracy, & Alberts, 2007). Further, more than a quarter of workers in the United State experience workplace bullying and over a third indicate they are aware bullying is occurring (Desrayaud, Dickson, & Webb, in press). How can you identify workplace bullying if you or someone you know is experiencing this destructive communication?
7. What factors stifle communication when bullying occurs? What constructive communication strategies can be used to reduce the negative effects of bullying?

REFERENCES

Desrayaud, N., Dickson, F. C., & Webb, L. M. (in press). The theory of bullying conflict cultures. In R. West & C. S. Beck (Eds.), *The Routledge handbook of communication and bullying*. New York, NY: Routledge.

Lutgen-Sandvik, P. (2018). Vicarious and secondary victimization in adult bullying and mobbing: Coworkers, target-partners, children, and friends. In M. K. Duffy & D. Yamada (Eds.), *Workplace bullying and mobbing in the United States* (pp. 171–200). Santa Barbara, CA: ABC-CLIO.

Lutgen-Sandvik, P., Tracy, S. J., & Alberts, J. K. (2007). Burned by bullying in the American workplace: Prevalence, perception, degree and impact. *Journal of Management Studies, 44*(6), 837–862. doi:10.1111/j.1467-6486.2007.00715.x

Petronio, S. (2002). *Boundaries of privacy: Dialectics*. Albany, NY: SUNY Press.

Tye-Williams, S. (in press). Disciplining the office: The past, present, and future of communication research on bullying. In R. West & C. S. Beck (Eds.), *The Routledge handbook of communication and bullying*. New York, NY: Routledge.

CHAPTER 22

"I Won't Be Home for Christmas": Accomplishing and Maintaining Family Estrangement

Kristina Scharp – *University of Washington*

ABSTRACT

Despite both scholarly and laypeople's beliefs that family relationships are nonvoluntary (Baxter et al., 2009; Hess, 2000), Conti (2015) contends that family estrangement could be as common as divorce in some segments of society. Family estrangement occurs when at least one family member voluntarily and intentionally distances him/herself from another family member because of an ongoing negative relationship (Scharp & Dorrance Hall, 2017). Similar to other contexts (e.g., divorce, family member marginalization, military deployment, or even going away to college), family estrangement is a process (Scharp & Dorrance Hall, 2019). Unlike some dissolution processes, estrangement does not have a binary outcome (i.e., together or not), but rather should be thought of as a continuum; meaning people can be more or less estranged (Scharp, Thomas, & Paxman, 2015). The following case study focuses on a woman named Sophie and her best friend Riley, who are at different points along this estrangement continuum.

TRIGGER WARNING: This case study describes severe child abuse and cases of intimate partner violence. Although all names have been replaced with pseudonyms, the majority of events are based on real people's lives and experiences.

THE HOLIDAYS APPROACH

Snow began falling early this year; it was only October but Sophie knew what snow meant . . . the holidays. Although many of her friends and coworkers at the art gallery could not wait for the holiday season, Sophie dreaded every Christmas tree, Hanukkah menorah, and Kwanzaa kinara that would soon be in sight. It's not that Sophie was the Grinch; rather, Sophie knew that the holiday season inevitably brought well-intentioned questions from everyone about her plans. She also knew that she couldn't continue to keep her family's history a secret from her best friend Riley any longer.

Sophie hadn't known Riley for very long, even though it felt like they had been friends for their whole lives. Really, their friendship only started a year ago. Even though Sophie knew that Riley did not have the best relationship with her parents, it wasn't anything close to what Sophie experienced growing up with her twin brother Bryan and her older sister Lily. She was determined, though, that this was the year she would be brave enough to tell someone the truth about her holiday plans; maybe this year she wouldn't have to spend them alone.

SOPHIE AND RILEY

Riley: Hey Soph, what's going on?

Sophie: Oh nothing, just thinking about whether I am going to take any time off from work this year around the holidays.

Riley: You mean, you are considering working through the holidays again? I bet your family really misses you. You should go home, at least for a little while.

Sophie: Um … I … Well, I won't be home for Christmas. In fact, I never go home. I always just spend it here. I spend it here alone.

Riley: You spend Christmas ALONE!? Why? I feel like you never talk about your family; are they still … alive?

Sophie: My mom passed away last year. We were really close. I actually still feel close to my siblings. They are still alive … so is my father. He and I don't have a very good relationship, to put it mildly. I don't know where he is and I sure hope he doesn't know where I am.

Riley: I can tell this is really hard for you. Do you want to talk about it?

Sophie: Not really, but I promised myself I would try and tell you what happened …

SOPHIE'S STORY

I guess the easiest way to explain it is that my parents got divorced when I was two and there was a 15-year-long custody battle. My mom kept on trying to win us, but we essentially lived with my dad until I was 17. We were actually removed from his house by the department of child services. From the time I was removed, I haven't ever spoken to him since.

I don't really know where to start because it really kind of all comes back to the relationship he had with my mother. They married pretty young and he began to slowly cut her off from her friends and family. After he isolated her, they had my sister and then four years later me and my twin brother Bryan. By the time we were born, he had started to sexually abuse my sister Lily and possibly my mom as well. I mean, it's something she doesn't talk about and Lily never talked about it either. He was emotionally abusive and physically abusive to everyone. And, uh, my mother decided that she needed to divorce him and take us with her. So, she went into hiding for, I want to say a year, to start the divorce proceedings. But when it came time for my mom to gain custody, she didn't have a good lawyer and my father had a really expensive, very skilled one. She lost any rights to us because they painted her to be a neglectful drug addict. So, my sister, brother, and I went to live with my father.

Most of my childhood was horrible but the funny thing was, I did not know how horrible at the time. I thought it was normal. I just remember trying to be as invisible as possible. My sister still lived with us then. I think she deflected a lot of the abuse away from us. She really had it the worst. When Lily was there it was easier, but eventually she was old enough and moved out of the house. She was able to go to college which was really great for her. But it wasn't for me. It was like I lost the only person who was looking out for me.

When I became a teenager, right after my sister left home, I became very boyish and kind of shunned any femininity because I kind of viewed that as a bulls-eye in my house. But it still seemed like no matter what we did, we were beaten. He would sit me and my brother down in the TV room and then he'd take us one by one into his bedroom and just spank us and we would be sitting there, and we would be listening to our sibling being beaten. It was the hardest part. And I didn't really understand religion at the time, but I always felt guilty that I had done something and that's why I was living there, and all of these bad things kept on happening.

And then finally, I just kind of lost it during my junior year and had a mild breakdown. I didn't have anyone to talk to, mostly because I had just stopped talking. But I remember trying one last time. I went to a teacher and I said "I can't bathe at home." I was so paranoid that that he was recording me or could see me through the keyhole. I showered in my bathing suit for two years before I just stopped showering all together. And my teacher was surprised, but she took me seriously. And I felt like someone believed me, so I told my soccer teammate's mom that I had seen my father taking pictures of her daughter at one of the games. And I think she was finally the person who reported my dad to the DCS. I mean, the department of child services. I don't know who it was exactly, but I think it was her. And from that point on, lots of things started to happen. A strong-looking woman from DCS came to our house and we showed her how we were living. We showed her how cold it was in the house because my dad refused to turn on the heat even in the winter. There were also dead bugs everywhere and so much mold. It was really dangerous for my brother because he had asthma. We told her … we told her what he was doing to us. Then, she told us to put everything we had into garbage bags because she was going to take us away. We couldn't believe it but we did what she said. She confronted my father and told him there was nothing he could do to stop her. He was never used to anyone standing up to him and telling him no. He didn't know what to do, so, he let us go.

SOPHIE AND RILEY

Riley: What the hell Sophie! I can't believe that happened to you. I am SO sorry. I just, I just can't believe a parent would treat their child that way. I mean, I believe you, but aren't parents supposed to protect their children?

Sophie: Uh, yeah. I mean, that's part of why it's so hard to talk about. There's a lot of pressure even if no one says it. There's that message that to be a parent is to love. There's that message that there is forgiveness for all things and that all relationships can be healed. So, it's hard to believe that that's not necessarily true.

Riley: So, what happened after DCS took you away? What about your twin? I mean, you don't have to tell me anymore if you don't want to …

Sophie: No, it's okay. I want to tell you the whole story.

SOPHIE'S STORY CONTINUES

So, after DCS took us, we had to wait a week in the foster care system before there was another court hearing. Finally, my mom was awarded custody, but they also instituted visitation for my father. But there was no way I was ever going back. It was like: I'm 17, and if they want me to go over there, they can put me in handcuffs because there was no way I was going back there. And he never fought it—he never wanted us, he just wanted to control my mom, he wanted to control us and control my mom. I guess he did call sometimes though. It didn't matter because I wasn't going back even though my brother—I guess he felt guilty—would go and visit.

Then at school, I talked to my French teacher. I was taking French at the time and I was asked to choose some stupid French name. But I thought, maybe I want to change my name.

So, I asked if I could change my name and I changed it to what it is today, and she said, "Well, it's not really a French name." I said, "This is really important to me," and she let me do it. And then when I turned 18, my mom knew I wanted to change my name and she gave me $114 dollars, took me to the courthouse, and I changed my name and I took her last name. And that was awesome. And uh, I had the idea of getting a tattoo just to symbolize all we've been through; so, we talked about it and designed it and consulted with some tattoo artists. When I turned 18, right after my brother and I turned 18, we went to a tattoo parlor and all got our tattoos and uh, we were really proud of them. All four of us got them, even my sister.

I remember at some point during high school his father passed away. So like, my grandfather. And, his father was a sweet man, he loved us, he was never abusive; he was just a sweet old man. And, for some reason I remember being in the back yard and getting the news and then immediately saying that I couldn't go, that I didn't want to go. So, my brother and my sister went. I didn't want to see him because I knew that he would be there.

Then, I went to college on a soccer scholarship. It was the easiest way to get some physical distance. And it was great, but I also had this thing in my mind that I was still close enough to where my father lived for him to come and see my games or show up somehow. And I was always terrified that he would somehow find out where I was and find me. And he wouldn't even have to do anything; he would just have to be there and I wouldn't know what to do, but I was always terrified that he would find me. I am still so anxious that one day he will find me, even though I have blocked him on social media. I remember, sometime after college, my name and picture were in the newspaper because I was helping kids do a photography workshop and I realized he might see it and come find me. I mean, every time the door jingles to alert me that someone is coming into my shop I wonder if it could be him. My sister has a business with her picture and information online and that's how he found her. It can be really scary sometimes.

SOPHIE AND RILEY

Riley: I can't even imagine!!! I mean, and here I was thinking that I had it bad!
Sophie: I mean, for the most part it's alright, but it's still complicated about Christmas.
Riley: What do you mean? It sounds like you are close with your siblings.
Sophie: Well, things have gotten weird with Lily and Bryan.

FAMILY SYSTEMS

So, after my father found my sister, I guess she felt guilty or something. Maybe it has to do with the kind of abuse she sustained. Maybe she was feeling pressure from her friends or coworkers. I don't know exactly. I don't think she understands it either. I think she's just curious and says that she's just curious and just wants to know where he is and what he's doing. So, over the past couple of years they have had some regular contact. Not so much with my brother. He, uh, he actually got his named changed too. And this was a big deal because he was named the same as my dad. So, he got both his names changed and took my mom's last name just like I did. I don't know what my father thought about that. My father occasionally asks about us and I told Lily that I don't understand why she is in contact with him. I have told her outright, "I don't want you to tell him where I am, and I don't want you to tell him anything about me. Don't tell him where I am; don't tell him what I'm doing." But, here's the thing. She started inviting him over for the holidays. And Bryan, he feels like he needs to go back; He has something called the 24-hour rule, though, where he won't spend more than 24 hours around my father. I just, I just can't go back and see him. Even if my siblings can, I can't. So, that's why I never go home.

SOPHIE AND RILEY

Riley: Wow. That totally makes sense now.

Sophie: Really? You don't think I'm a bad person for not wanting to see my family?

Riley: No way! Are you kidding me! I'm just so glad you're safe. That must have been a nightmare. Maybe you want to come to my house for the holidays this year?

Sophie: Are you sure? You mean, your family wouldn't mind?

Riley: No, they won't mind … uh, they don't really care about anything. Maybe I should warn you …

Sophie: Warn me?

Riley: So, before you agree to come with me, let me tell you a little bit about my family.

RILEY'S STORY

Now, don't get me wrong; I didn't have the same childhood that you did. It's more like they didn't pay any attention to me at all. My dad was ALWAYS working. I mean, he traveled a lot, I get it. He's the reason why I don't have student loans. Sometimes I think though, I would have traded the student loans for just one time my dad chose me over work. I never had parents who showed up to my dance recitals. I am not sure they even went to back-to-school night when I was a kid. My mom was around, kind of … she suffers from a pretty severe mental health disorder. Sometimes she needs to go away for treatment. My grandma would come and watch us; sometimes for weeks or months at a time. I used to think parents were the people who would tuck their kids in at night and take care of them when they were sick. I realize now that not every kid gets that; even if that's how TV shows and movies portray families.

Is it bad that I feel bitter? I mean, if I am being perfectly honest, I don't love my parents. Um, like who doesn't love their parents? Who doesn't love their mom? Like prisoners, rapists, they love their mother probably. They probably got a prisoner tattoo saying, "I heart mom," but I don't. Does it say something bad about you that you can't love your parents? Um, but I've gotten over that recently. There are just some things in life you can't control. You can't control how other people treat you. I mean, I can't make them love me. So, I guess even though I have a place to go, it's not really what other people have.

So, when I go home for the holidays, I don't really stay all that long. It's kind of an expectation that I show up. I don't even know what to do when we are together. Because of how I grew up, it's like I just feel like I am with strangers—acquaintances masquerading as family. I feel more comfortable not being together and trying to think about them fondly. How messed up is that? The only way I feel close to them is if we are far away!

SOPHIE AND RILEY

Sophie: I don't think you are messed up at all! Even though what happened to you is different than what happened to me, the outcome is the same. Don't let people tell you there is something wrong with you. Or at least, that's what I am trying to work on. We both just needed some distance from our families. We are quite the pair!

Riley: I know, right.

Sophie: So, why would you even go to your parents' house if you don't have a relationship with them?

Riley: I guess, because I didn't want to be alone. And there is the message in the world that blood is thicker than water and we can't choose our family.

Sophie: We don't have to be alone. We have each other. I mean, why does family have to be people who are related by blood and law. Why can't family be the people who do the things that families should, like take care of one another, spend the holidays together … Why can't family be the people we talk to everyday and the people who love us? Who says we can't be family?

Riley: I know! You're the sister I never had. I mean honestly, who made the rule that we can't choose our family?

Sophie: I feel the same way. From now on … sisters.

Riley: Maybe it will be a merry Christmas this year after all.

DISCUSSION QUESTIONS

Discourse Dependence

Discourse-dependent families require more communication to construct their identity both within the family and to explain their family to people outside of it (Galvin, 2014). Although research on discourse-dependent families has typically focused on how communication constructs alternative family types, recent research also suggests that communication can deconstruct a family (and their family identity).

1. Galvin (2014) argues that internal boundary management practices (e.g., naming, discussing, narrating, and ritualizing) help families make sense of who they are to each other. For families with a degree of estrangement, this might be very complicated because it requires so much coordination. What internal boundary management practices emerge in Sophie and Riley's stories?

2. Not only do family members need to manage their identity inside the family but they also must talk about their families to people outside of it. Galvin (2014) argues that external boundary management practices (e.g., labeling, explaining, legitimizing, and defending) accomplish the family's presentation to nonmembers. What external boundary management practices emerge in Sophie and Riley's stories?

Relational Dialectics Theory

Relational dialectics theory (RDT; Baxter, 2011) is the third most cited theory in the study of family communication (Braithwaite, Suter, & Floyd, 2018). Recently rearticulated as a critical/dialogic theory, scholars who frame their work in RDT 2.0 often focus on discourse-dependent families that face stigma for deviating from traditional definitions of family.

1. RDT emphasizes the ways people talk based on and in anticipation of evaluation from general members of a shared culture. In their research on estrangement, Scharp and Thomas (2016, 2018) identified that an ideology surrounded family permanence that emphasized biological ties, shared history, and obligation. How did Sophie and Riley reflect this cultural ideology in their talk?

2. RDT is a theory of meaning-making that emphasizes competition between dueling cultural ideologies, or what we call discourses. One way to identify the interplay of competing discourses is by looking for diachronic separation. This means that although one discourse is articulated at one time, the speaker later

(over time) gives voice to an alternative. Can you identify any examples of diachronic separation?

3. To identify discursive competition, RDT scholars also look for something called synchronic interplay. This means that competing ideologies battle at the same time instead of over a course of time. Synchronic interplay is identified through three discourse markers—negating, countering, and entertaining. Discourse markers flag efforts to resist dominant ideologies that silence alternative experiences. Negating refers to instances when one discourse refutes another outright. Countering occurs when one discourse is acknowledged, only to be overruled by another. Entertaining occurs when one discourse acknowledges the presence of an alternative ideology. Can you identify any of these discursive markers of resistance in the case study?

4. Finally, dialogic transformation refers to instances when competing discourses coalesce to form new meanings. In other words, can you identify the example of when Riley blends the discourses of closeness and distance?

General Estrangement Questions

1. Scharp (2019) argues that family deconstruction is not inherently the same as family construction. Not only is accomplishing distance difficult but maintaining distance can be equally, if not more, difficult. What were some behaviors Sophie and Riley enacted to both accomplish and maintain distance with their families?

2. Even if estrangement can be a healthy solution to an unhealthy environment, it often can be stressful and rife with uncertainty (Scharp & McLaren, 2018). Specifically, Scharp (2016) found that adult children who sought distance from their parents often felt unsupported and had a variety of reasons why they did not talk about their estrangement. How can social network members support people going through the estrangement process, especially if the person does not want to discuss their problem?

REFERENCES

Baxter, L. A. (2011). *Voicing relationships*. Thousand Oaks, CA: Sage.

Baxter, L. A., Henauw, C., Huisman, D., Livesay, C., Norwood, K., Su, H., … Young, B. (2009). Lay conceptions of "family": A replication and extension. *Journal of Family Communication, 9*, 170–189. doi:10.1080/15267430902963342

Braithwaite, D. O., Suter, E. A., & Floyd, K. (2018). The landscape of meta-theory and theory in family communication research. In. D. O. Braithwaite, E. A. Suter, & K. Floyd (Eds.), *Engaging theories in family communication* (pp. 1–16). New York, NY: Routledge.

Conti, R. P. (2015). Family estrangement: Establishing a prevalence rate. *Journal of Psychology and Behavioral Science, 3*, 28–35. doi:10.15640/jpbs.v3n2a4

Galvin, K. M. (2014). Blood, law, and discourse: Constructing and managing family identity. In L. A. Baxter (Ed.), *Remaking families communicatively* (pp. 17–32). New York, NY: Peter Lang.

Hess, J. (2000). Maintaining nonvoluntary relationships with disliked partners: An investigation into the use of distancing behaviors. *Human Communication Research, 26*, 458–488. doi:10.1111/j.1468-2958.2000.tb00765.x

Scharp, K. M. (2016). Parent-child estrangement: Conditions for disclosure and perceived social network member reactions. *Family Relations, 65*, 688–700. doi:10.1111/fare.12219

Scharp, K. M. (2019). "You're not welcome here:" A grounded theory of family distancing. *Communication Research*. doi:10.1177/0093650217715542

Scharp, K. M., & Dorrance Hall, E. (2017). Family marginalization, alienation, and estrangement: A review of and call for research that questions the nonvoluntary status of family relationships. *Annals of the International Communication Association, 41*, 28–45. doi:10.1080/23808985.2017.1285680

Scharp, K. M., & Dorrance Hall, E. (2019). Reconsidering family closeness: A review and call for research on family distancing. *Journal of Family Communication*. doi:10.1080/15267431.2018.1544563

Scharp, K. M., & McLaren, R. M. (2018). Uncertainty issues and management in adult children's stories of their estrangement with their parents. *Journal of Social and Personal Relationships, 35*, 811–830. doi:10.1177/0265407517699097

Scharp, K. M., & Thomas, L. J. (2016). Family "bonds": Making meaning of parent-child relationships in estrangement narratives. *Journal of Family Communication, 16*, 32–50. doi:10.1080/15267431.2015.1111215

Scharp, K. M., & Thomas, L. J. (2018). Making meaning of the parent-child relationship: A dialogic analysis of parent-initiated estrangement narratives. *Journal of Family Communication*. doi:10.1080/15267431.2018.1484747

Scharp, K. M., Thomas, L. J., & Paxman, C. G. (2015). "It was the straw that broke the camel's back": Exploring the distancing processes communicatively constructed in parent-child estrangement backstories. *Journal of Family Communication, 15*, 330–348. doi:10.1080/15267431.2015.1076422

CHAPTER 23

When is It Right Time to Talk about It?: Individual and Parental Concerns about Disclosing a Mental Illness

Shawn Starcher – *Kent State University*

ABSTRACT

Societal-based stigmas dictate that individuals should avoid talking about a mental illness because they often fear that others will label, judge, or reject them. Do those same rules apply when sharing depression-related struggles with a spouse or a child? Parents have to consider the risks and benefits of sharing with both when talking about depression. At what point should individuals have discussions about depression in the family environment? Most research will identify that depression typically begins to manifest in early adolescence, but are children mature enough at that point to handle that type of disclosure? Do children have a right to know since they may experience similar issues due to their genetic link with their parent? If parents do decide to disclose, how much information should they share and what kind of expectations should the parents impose on children for the management of that sensitive information? Using a communication privacy management (Petronio, 2002, 2013) theoretical perspective, this case study will explore the different dynamics that a parent must consider when managing his or her depression-related private information with children.

CASE STUDY

Difficult Childhood

Xavier was forced to make many tough decisions at an early age. He had little help from his parents who often struggled with their own personal issues. Due to his family life, Xavier had to be more mature at an earlier age than many of his peers. He would typically have to do his own laundry and find his own way to and from school. There were many nights when he would have to scrounge dinner from whatever he could find in the cupboards. Xavier also struggled with his emotions and would often cry himself to sleep because he was worried and anxious about doing well in school and all of his responsibilities for the next day.

Xavier loved his parents, but he was always concerned about how they felt about him. He rarely talked with his parents and the conversations that they did have together were brief. This may have been due to his parents' relationship with each other, but there may have been other factors as well. His parents divorced before Xavier was able to walk and the living arrangements were a bit complicated. Xavier would stay with his mother Monday through Friday and then go visit his father on the weekends. This made it tough for Xavier when making friends because many of his classmates would make plans for the weekend and Xavier could never be included because he would have no way to get there. It was hard for him to make friends at his father's house as well because he was only there on Saturday and Sunday. This caused Xavier to feel like an outsider in both living situations and often left him alone with no close friends.

Xavier's parents did not offer any assistance or guidance as friends either. His father Chad was a functioning alcoholic who always seemed to keep his distance from everyone else, including Xavier. Chad had a tough upbringing himself and Xavier would later determine that he probably drank every day to help him deal with his own issues as a child. Valerie, Xavier's mother, was an occasional drug user who had also had a difficult childhood. If that weren't enough to deal with, Xavier also noticed that his parents' behaviors were often erratic. Xavier wanted to talk with them about some of the things happening in his life, but he did not know how. Each of his parents seemed to have their own lives and Xavier was somehow caught in the middle. This became increasingly more difficult on Xavier as he got older, as he often struggled with his emotions, including sadness, anger, and anxiety. Since he had no close friendships and he wasn't close with his parents, Xavier never really had an outlet to share his struggles. This pattern would continue for much of Xavier's childhood and adolescence.

The Struggles Continue

After high school, Xavier gets an apartment with his high school sweetheart Laura. Xavier and Laura were both going to college at the time, but they couldn't afford for both to attend classes when they moved in together. The couple eventually decide that it's best for Laura to continue with her education and Xavier decides to get a full-time job to pay the bills. Things are going well at first, but Xavier becomes increasingly more frustrated when he can't find a good job. As things get more difficult, Xavier finds it harder and harder to control his emotions. He is often irritable, anxious, and has severe mood swings. Getting sleep is becoming more and more difficult. All of the same emotions that Xavier felt as an adolescent are getting progressively more difficult to maintain. Xavier tends to keep these emotions bottled up around Laura and he never really talks about his feelings with her. Xavier doesn't want to add to any of Laura's stress due to her college studies by telling her about his problems and he doesn't feel like he should tell her anyway. He has always dealt with these problems on his own and he feels that he can get through this as well.

After a few years, Xavier and Laura decide to get married and start a family of their own. Although there were complications from infertility, they are finally lucky enough to have a baby girl and they name her Rey. Xavier is proud to be a father and hopes to be a better father for Rey than Chad was for him. After a short period of time, Xavier quickly realizes how hard it is to keep his emotions in check and be a parent at the same time. Based on his own upbringing, Xavier has become accustomed to having his own time where he can get away and be by himself when he starts to become too irritable, sad, or anxious. This becomes a bit harder when he's alone with Rey and she becomes upset or is crying. He's not getting much sleep and he always feels like he's one step away from exploding due to his emotions. Rey means everything to him, but there are some times when Xavier has to walk away from his daughter out of fear for what he might do if he were unable to contain his anger. Xavier would never hurt his daughter, but he understands that his emotions can sometimes get the best of him. He wouldn't dare tell Laura about his inner struggles as he would worry what she may think of him.

To make matters worse, Xavier finds himself bouncing around from job to job while looking for the ideal career during Rey's younger years. He finally lands a job that seems interesting and it comes with an increase in pay. The job is an entry-level position at a government agency performing IT work. Xavier doesn't have much experience in the IT field, but the hiring supervisor tells him that they will teach him everything that he will need to know in order to succeed. The first few months are exciting for Xavier and he thinks that he may have found his calling. Unfortunately, those feelings don't last. Xavier's workload begins to mount and he now has to occasionally work different shifts. This adds to Xavier's issues of feeling overwhelmed. He feels like he can't keep up and is often depressed and anxious about what is happening in his personal and professional lives. Xavier does his best to keep his emotions under wraps, but as the pressure mounts he slips and blows up when he can't fix a computer. His supervisor happens to see his behavior and it forces them to have an awkward conversation about his emotions. Xavier is ordered to seek anger management classes in order to keep his position and he also spends some time doing a little self-reflection.

The Diagnosis

Xavier begins to realize that his sadness, anger, irritability, and anxiety may be a bigger issue than he can deal with on his own. Instead of confiding in Laura about his problems, he makes a doctor's appointment without her knowledge. He decides to speak with his family physician Dr. Vardell. When seeing Dr. Vardell, Xavier describes his mood swings and his sadness, anger, and irritability. He also talks about how anxious he is at times. Dr. Vardell looks over the chart and tells him that he's struggling with depression and anxiety. He explains that there are many ways to treat his issues, including medication and therapy. Xavier isn't sure how to take the news and he isn't sure that he agrees with the doctor. He starts to think about what he knows about people with some type of mental illness, and he starts to get a little scared.

As Xavier exits the doctor's office and makes his way back home, he begins to think about all of the television shows and movies that include people with mental illness and he wonders if people will see him in the same way. He begins doing his own research online and nearly all of the symptoms that he is experiencing are linked to depression and anxiety. He starts to retrace different time periods of his life and realizes that he has had these feelings all of his life at some point. Xavier always thought that every person had similar experiences as a child with their emotions, but he now understands that his thinking might have been wrong. He begins to worry about opening up to Laura and telling her about his diagnosis, but he's not sure how. Xavier is worried that she might look at him differently. In addition, he never heard his parents talk about anything like this so he wonders if he should even share this information with her.

Xavier reluctantly decides to tell Laura about his diagnosis. Although he is now willing to talk to her about it, he is only going to tell her a little bit at a time to test her reactions at first. Xavier feels unprepared and ill-equipped to have this type of conversation. He is relieved to find out that Laura is supportive and wants to do everything she can to support him. She is happy that he opened up with her and he is excited that he doesn't have to go through this journey alone anymore.

Thinking Ahead

After feeling the relief of telling Laura about his diagnosis of depression and anxiety, Xavier begins to attend therapy sessions and is placed on medication. After a few months, Xavier seems to have a good grasp on his depression and anxiety, but he still struggles occasionally. Laura helps him a great deal in being supportive and often provides Xavier with space when he needs it. She has done her own research on depression and anxiety to make sure she provides as much assistance as she can when Xavier runs into an issue. In addition, she and Xavier have decided that they will not be sharing his diagnosis with anyone else unless they talk about it first and come to an agreement to share his private information with others. Xavier is still worried that people may negatively judge him because of his depression and anxiety. In fact, Xavier is so worried that others may look at him differently that he parks in the rear parking lot of his therapist's office for his appointments to make sure that no one sees his car and realizes that he is seeing a therapist.

Before one of those therapy sessions, Xavier is a bit early for his appointment and decides to sit in his car for a bit. He notices children playing on a school playground just across the street. As he is watching the children, Xavier takes note of one child who looks sad and is off by himself on the swings. He thinks back to his own childhood and realizes that he was that child once. He begins to think about how he has experienced depression and anxiety his entire life, but no one ever noticed. Looking back, he begins to think about how his life might have been different if his parents had paid more attention to his behaviors. He vows to himself that he will be different from his parents. It is at that moment that Xavier realizes that Rey may inherit his depression and anxiety. He had never really thought about it before that day and he wasn't sure how to process the thought right now. Although Rey is only now entering middle school, he realizes that he will have to tell her at some point about his struggles and he also has to pay close attention to her behaviors for any signs of depression and anxiety.

Over the next several years, Xavier thinks about the conversation that he will have with Rey about his mental illness. There are days when the mere thought of having the conversation with Rey gives him anxiety. So many thoughts and questions run through his head. "Will she look at me differently? Will she be afraid of me? Will she think less of me? I don't want to ruin my relationship with Rey. Maybe I won't tell her. What if I'm having a bad day and she thinks it's her fault? I don't want that. What if she asks Laura about it? I don't want her to have to lie to Rey to keep my private information safe. What if I don't tell her and Rey finds out anyway? Will she resent me for not telling her? Will she think that she should not tell anyone else if she is struggling with depression and anxiety? Do I want her to go through that like I did? What kind of example am I setting if I don't tell her about my struggles? I want her to be open with me about everything. How can she do that if I'm not willing to be open with her?" All of these thoughts swirl in Xavier's mind as he wrestles with his decision.

The Doctor's Appointment

It's early in the morning and as Xavier begins to climb out of bed, he can hear Rey coughing in her bedroom down the hall. He heads down to check on her and to make sure she's getting up and ready for school. Rey is in eighth grade now and Xavier usually takes her to school before he heads off to work. She continues to cough as he enters her room. Xavier feels Rey's forehead with the back of his hand. She seems to be running a fever and her face is flush. Xavier tells her to stay in bed and heads back to talk with Laura. Laura is the one who typically handles all of the doctor appointments, but she has a big presentation due today and can't be late for work. Xavier decides to take the day off work and take Rey to the doctor to get checked out. The flu is making its way around the middle school and he is afraid that Rey may have finally picked it up. He calls the doctor's office to set up an appointment. Luckily, the doctor has a cancellation and she can be seen right away.

Xavier and Rey enter the doctor's office and there are a lot of people already waiting in the lobby. Xavier has to fill out some paperwork before they head to find some seats and wait for Rey's name to be called. After a short wait, Xavier and Rey are called back to a small room where they meet a nurse who begins to ask Rey how she's feeling. Rey tells the doctor that she's really hot and that her stomach and head are hurting. The nurse begins to take Rey's temperature and other vital information. The nurse then looks at Xavier and begins to ask him questions about any medical procedures or issues that Rey may have had as a child. The tone begins to change when she looks at Xavier and begins to ask questions about family history. They are almost done when the nurse asks the following, "Is there any history of mental illness in the family?" Xavier is taken aback. He was not expecting that question. He doesn't know how to answer the question. He looks at Rey and then back at the nurse. He has not spoken to Rey about his struggles with depression and anxiety and he doesn't want this to be the place where that conversation takes place. After a brief pause, he lies and says that there is no history of family mental illness.

As the nurse leaves and the doctor comes in, Xavier's mind is elsewhere. He is still thinking about the nurse's question in his mind over and over. He's considering all of those questions he had in his mind from when Rey was younger; "Will she look at me differently if I tell her about my depression and anxiety? Will she be afraid of me? Will she think less of me?" He wonders if it may finally be the time to share with her. He's brought back to the present when the doctor begins talking about the diagnosis. Rey does have the flu and is going to have to miss school for a few days. The doctor offers up a prescription and advises that she should drink lots of fluids. They both thank the doctor and head out to the car to go back home. As they enter the car and get buckled in, Xavier takes a deep breath. Rey looks at Xavier and asks him if everything is ok. Xavier reflects back to his childhood and thinks about how important it may have been for him if his parents were available to talk to him about important matters. He looks at Rey and says, "There is something that I want to talk to you about."

DISCUSSION QUESTIONS

1. According to Petronio (2002, 2013), one assumption of communication privacy management theory is that individuals decide for themselves what is private based on what makes them feel vulnerable. In this case, what was the private information that made Xavier feel vulnerable? How does Xavier's privacy boundary change regarding his issues with his struggles about depression and anxiety change throughout the case? While Xavier may identify his struggles with depression and anxiety as highly sensitive and private information, what sorts of topics might you or others you know identify as highly private?

2. Communication privacy management theory (Petronio, 2002, 2013) identifies specific criteria for determining the appropriateness of a disclosure, including criteria for culture, gender, motivation, context, and benefit/risk ratio. In this case, which of these criteria were most impactful for Xavier when making the determination to disclose with Laura? Likewise, which of these criteria were most impactful for Xavier when making the determination to disclose with Rey? Think about your own private disclosures that you've had regarding your private information—which of these criteria were most important for you? Provide an example that you are comfortable sharing with others.

3. Petronio (2002) states that as families develop and mature over time, they tend to adopt typical responses and access rules regarding interactions, including when it is appropriate to reveal or conceal private information. These privacy rules tend to become the unique privacy orientation of the family that members use to guide how they share private information with family members and those outside of the family unit. How do you think the family privacy orientation of Xavier's childhood family influenced his privacy management behaviors with his current family directly after his diagnosis of depression and anxiety? What do you think influenced Xavier's privacy behaviors with his current family that may have been different from his family when growing up? What was the privacy orientation of your family with other family members when growing up? How did those privacy behaviors differ with how you managed private information with those outside of the family unit?

4. Goffman (1963) identifies that stigma is a broad concept that combines the concept of labeling, stereotyping, separation ("us" from "them"), status loss, and discrimination, within the context of power differences. In what ways may have Xavier experienced the influence of feeling stigmatized? Where do you think we get our perceptions of stigmas? Have you ever felt stigmatized? If you are comfortable, share an example of when you may have felt stigmatized about something.

REFERENCES

Goffman, E. (1963). *Stigma: Notes on the management of spoiled identity*. Englewood Cliffs, NJ: Prentice-Hall.

Petronio, S. (2002). *Boundaries of privacy: Dialectics of disclosure*. Albany, NY: State University of New York Press.

Petronio, S. (2013). Brief status report on communication privacy management theory. *Journal of Family Communication, 13*, 6–14. doi:10.1080/15267431.2013.743426

Part V

SUBSTANCE ABUSE

Using CPM to Understand (Im)Permeable Boundaries: Stories of Adult Children of Alcoholics

Kerry Byrnes-Loinette – *Collin College*
Maria Brann – *IUPUI*

ABSTRACT

The present case study examines how adult children of alcoholics (ACOAs) communicate about living and growing up in an alcoholic home. A decidedly complex communication issue for families, this case utilizes communication privacy management theory (CPM; Petronio, 2002) to understand the experiences of ACOAs. To expose readers to the complex nature of families managing addiction and to elucidate CPM's constructs of privacy boundaries, rules, and co-ownership, a composite case of a teenager who witnesses parental behaviors of an alcoholic father and must make sense of the familial experience and how to communicate about it within and outside the home is presented. After briefly presenting the prevalence of alcoholic homes and describing key constructs of CPM, the case begins with an illustration of how ACOAs learn about family privacy rules associated with disclosing about their alcoholic parent. Largely kept to family members who live in the alcoholic home, ACOAs alter their impermeable boundaries with those outside the family. Described as "standby stories," ACOAs share either (a) stories that are powerfully negative or (b) more tame, light-hearted, even humorous stories about their alcoholic father to develop hemophilic relationships.

CASE STUDY

I came home for Christmas break, and my family went to see a play. My dad was already drunk before we left. He passed out during the performance and then woke up and couldn't move. I had to help him up, and it was at the point when he fell towards the bathroom that I knew the drinking had consumed him; he hadn't eaten all day, just drank (Lindsey, age 9[1]).

PREVALENCE OF ALCOHOLIC HOMES

Historically, defining alcoholism, also known as alcohol dependence, has proven to be difficult. If normal drinking behaviors mean drinking less than what is required to produce psychological, medical, or social problems, alcoholism is repeatedly exceeding those limits (Manzardo, Goodwin, Campbell, Penick, & Gabrielli, 2008). One definition that is widely adopted is from Keller's (1958) work which argued that "alcoholism is a behavioral disorder manifested by repeated drinking of alcoholic beverages in excess of the dietary and social uses of the community and to an extent that interferes with the drinker's health or his [sic] social or economic functioning" (p. 2). It is estimated that 16 million adults in the United States, or about one in every 12 adults, with a majority of these people being men, are alcoholics (National Institute on Alcohol Abuse and Alcoholism [NIAAA], 2007). Additionally, an estimated 53% of American adults reported that one or more of their relatives has a drinking problem (Alcoholics Info, n. d.), and an estimated 28 million children, or roughly one in seven, live in an alcoholic home (Grant, 2000).

Alcoholism's effects can be felt among the entire family. Described as a transactional system that affects one another (Hecht, 1973), alcoholism has the ability to affect all aspects of life within the family (Berlin, Davis, & Orenstein, 1988). Steinglass (1980) further contended that the family unit may be particularly situated to investigate how daily patterns of interaction are informed and influenced by the use of alcohol. He indicated that patterns of behavior in the family would become "flavored by the style and consequences of alcohol use" (p. 213). Thus, the family members' behaviors are influenced by the presence of alcoholism in the home. The family environment is disrupted (Rangarajan, 2006; Rangarajan & Kelly, 2006) and behaviors and communication practices are altered. Although experiences with alcoholism are somewhat common, individuals living with alcoholic family members often do not discuss the alcoholism, leaving family members with undisclosed experiences and unclear patterns of communicative behaviors.

---

1. The case presented is a composite of the narratives of 20 men and women who recalled growing up with an alcoholic father or stepfather. Messages are actual statements made during interviews. The names used are pseudonyms.

Answering a call issued by Grant (2000) that indicated more research is needed to examine how children of alcoholics (COAs) cope and manage their exposure to alcoholismbecause this disease affects not only the person with the disease but also those with whom the person comes into contact—the present case examines how COAs share information with others. The act of sharing information with others is best conceptualized by self-disclosure literature. To self-disclose, an individual verbally shares information about oneself to another person (Derlega & Chaikin, 1977). Although the health benefits associated with revealing information and sharing secrets with others is plentiful (see, e.g., Pennebaker, Zech, & Rimé, 2001), individuals still choose to remain silent and conceal secrets from others close to them (Afifi, Olson, & Armstrong, 2005; Afifi & Steuber, 2009). These individuals may perceive concealing private information to be beneficial if they anticipate negative consequences once the information is shared with others. Information may be selectively shared because of fear of negative evaluation (Black & Miles, 2002), rejection from others (Cline & McKenzie, 2000), or self-protection (Afifi & Guerrero, 2000). However, when disclosive attempts are made, individuals experience increased physical health (Greenberg & Stone, 1992), self-esteem (Afifi & Caughlin, 2006), and insights about information (Kelly, Klusas, von Weiss, & Kenny, 2001).

Thus, it appears that individuals need to weigh the costs and benefits of disclosing private information with others as it can have both positive and negative effects.

For families dealing with alcohol addiction, the need to manage information is arguably increased. Disclosing information about the alcoholic can be especially difficult because of the social stigma attached to alcoholism (Brady, Tolliver, & Verduin, 2007). The purpose of this case is to expose readers to the complex nature of families managing addiction and to elucidate CPM's constructs of privacy boundaries, rules, and co-ownership, We present a composite case[1] of a teenager, Lindsey, who witnesses parental behaviors of an alcoholic father and must make sense of the familial experience and how to communicate about it within and outside the home.

COMMUNICATION PRIVACY MANAGEMENT THEORY

Individuals living in the same home as an alcoholic keep information about alcoholism private. Petronio (2002) argued, "information is considered private when individuals perceive it as belonging to them" (p. 381). Thus, private information is something that individuals share with others at their own discretion, and until shared, it belongs to the individual. Adult COAs, arguably, feel as though their parent's addiction is private information that they must manage. Socially, addiction is stigmatized and viewed negatively. Additionally, it seems unlikely that COAs would freely discuss their parent's alcoholism, possibly because of uncertainty of what another person may do with that information or because of family rules established surrounding experiences with alcoholism. Rather, this information would be deemed private or as information only members of the family own because of the cultural stigma associated with alcoholism. How to manage this private information, individually and once shared, can be explained by communication privacy management theory (CPM; Petronio, 1991, 2000, 2002). CPM provides a useful framework to understand the processes that occur when one is deciding whether to share information. CPM is a rule-based theory that focuses on the revealing and concealing processes an individual uses to share private information. To understand the ways people make decisions about what to do with private information, it is necessary to consider private information as a commodity that can be owned by people, shared with others, and negotiated for use.

TO SHARE OR NOT TO SHARE

Lindsey grew up in a traditional home with her mom, dad, and brother. Her dad always had a beer with dinner, but that was just his usual drink at night, and it never seemed abnormal. Looking back after that night at the play, Lindsey started to see her dad and his behaviors in a new light. As she reflected on her life, she realized that deep down, she knew her dad was an alcoholic, but it just wasn't something the family talked about. Everyone in her family knew, but no one said anything, which was how she learned what the boundaries were for discussing what it was really like at her house. Now that she was talking with her two close friends who also have alcoholic fathers, it almost felt like a betrayal and a relief at the same time to share this information. Still, she knew that by sharing her story, she would now co-own this experience, and she could set her own rules and begin to negotiate what new boundaries could be put around this information.

Alexis: Lindsey, I'm so sorry to hear about what is going on with your dad. Why didn't you ever tell us before?

Lindsey: I don't know. My mom never talked about it so I just grew up not talking about the situation a lot. I just mimicked her behavior. In fact, our entire immediate family never really talked about what was going on and how it impacted anyone in our family. It was almost like if we don't talk about it, it's not a problem; when in all honesty, there was a problem. When we do talk about it, it makes my brother and mom upset so we just ignore the topic. Even the extended family doesn't talk about it. Now that I think about it, not many people in the family know about the specific instances that came out of his drinking. It was made pretty clear in the immediate family that we didn't share a lot of that.

Reagan: Yeah, we never really talked about it in my family either. What made you want to talk about it now?

Lindsey: It's a big part of who I am. Sometimes, if it comes up in any way whatsoever, I just say it. Like if it pops into my head "should I tell or not tell," I always tell. I mean, I

CASING THE FAMILY: Theoretical and Applied Approaches to Understanding Family Communication

don't shout it from the rooftops, but you are my two closest friends so I want to be open with you. I guess the closer you get to me, the more you know. When I heard you say something, Alexis, about your dad, I knew we were experiencing the same thing, and I wanted you to know that you are not alone. That's why I shared, Reagan, to let you know that you are not alone. I hope that in sharing it helps other people.

Alexis: I'm really glad you trusted us with this information Lindsey. What can we do for you?

Lindsey: I don't really know yet. Well, I guess one thing is please don't tell anyone about my dad. I'm not sure I'm ready for other people who I'm not that close with or who don't have a dad like mine to know what I've been going through. Yeah, if they have a dad like mine, it just makes things easier. I almost feel an immediate bond with them and it is comforting to know that so many other people have been through situations where they felt like they couldn't rely on a parent. Plus, I want to protect him some. That's why if I do talk about his drinking, I always try to stick up for him and tell people that he was always highly functioning and he wasn't physically abusive.

Reagan: I understand. I don't ask others to keep information private, but I feel like they would do that, kind of an unwritten rule. I think I just usually allude to the fact that I don't talk about it much. If I am talking to them about it, it is usually for a reason. But, one time my sister told one of her friends about our dad, and then she went and blabbed it to everybody. I was so embarrassed, and now she and my sister aren't friends anymore. Some people just don't know how to keep a secret.

Alexis: Yeah, you have to be careful what you tell people. I don't have to explicitly ask either; it's in the stories I share. Like for me, I have two types of stories that I tell people. Not shocking is funny stories, standard, cursory info—that is, he drank a lot—but I also share shocking stories. Those include information about him forgetting to pick me up at school, the occasional punched wall during an argument with my mom, the real serious dysfunction. I call these my standby stories, my go-to stories. These are the stories that I'm ready to share with other people. I guess I share the shocking stories more. I remember when my dad was drinking at work. He called my mom to tell her that he couldn't drive home, and he had to stay in his office. My dad's brother's wife came over and took care of my mom, and my dad felt real bad so he came home anyway. I watched him walk in and play pinball with the hallway as he walked back to the bedroom, meaning he'd hit the left side of the hallway and bounce to the right and so forth. Another story that I share with people is from when I was leaving for New York city to move to college. My dad was angry about something, probably about the fact that he was sad I was leaving, but he couldn't deal with the emotion so he just went for angry. We stopped at Walmart about five minutes from home, to pick something up, and my mom was like you're drunk, and made him let her drive. It was this exciting life-defining moment, and he sort of ruined it for me.

Lindsey: Yeah, I guess you sort of share war stories with other people who are in your situation to let them know they aren't alone.

Reagan: Yeah, I'm in a play and one time, I was out with some cast members, and I offhandedly mentioned that my dad was in recovery, and my director immediately sort of, locked in on what I said and asked some questions and ended up sharing that his dad had died at 50 from alcoholism, and never got into recovery.

Lindsey: Wow, that's crazy. I don't even want to think about that happening to my dad.

COMMUNICATION PRIVACY MANAGEMENT ANALYSIS

Boundary Structures

Boundary structures are composed of four components: ownership, control, levels of control, and permeability. When an individual perceives information to be something he/she possesses, an individual is experiencing ownership. Private information is thought to belong to the individual and as a result is controlled by that person; the process of revealing, concealing, and managing information is done by those with ownership. Petronio (2002) indicated that people want to control the flow of the information. The flow of information is managed in two types of boundaries: personal and collective boundaries. These are levels of control. Personal boundaries include any information that is known only by the self, while collective boundaries include information that has been shared with others or information that others have shared. Thus, once information is shared, it no longer belongs solely to the individual. Instead, it is now co-owned.

Collectively owned information is managed by all those with knowledge of the information (Petronio, 2002). At any given time, individuals are managing personal boundaries for information that only they know and collective boundaries for information in which they are part of an ownership team. Once information is known, a metaphorical boundary is created around the information. This boundary surrounds the information and safeguards it from others. These boundaries are managed on varying levels of permeability. That is, the metaphorical boundary surrounding some private information may be relatively porous and information is more freely able to proceed through the boundary (i.e., disclosed). However, other information is highly safeguarded by an impermeable boundary through which limited, if any, information is revealed to others.

Learning Boundaries

For Lindsey, a general sense of observation was utilized to learn what information to keep a personal versus a collective boundary around. As a result of these observations, the alcoholic father's behaviors and the effect the behaviors had on family members was initially not discussed. A secretive climate was created and reified as normal. This type of secretive climate helped to deny the presence of a drinking problem. Scholars (Ackerman, 1986; Black, 1985) have indicated that this secretive climate is quite common because most family members do not want to discuss the problem; instead, they use silence as a way to suggest the problem does not exist.

COAs describe their confidants as keepers of information, but discussing issues of control and actively negotiating what can be done with the information does not seem to occur. Reagan and Alexis indicated that these types of conversations did not occur because they "didn't really put rules on what can be done." Rather, COAs tell their confidants one of their "standby" stories and after sharing, do not actively negotiate ownership responsibilities. Thus, it appears that COAs view ownership as something that is relatively implied, that their confidants will just know to keep the information within the dyad.

Rule Management Processes

In CPM, the boundary structures undergird rule management processes. As individuals develop rules through which to manage the flow of information, the aforementioned boundary structures are used as a foundation. They promote the creation of privacy rules that are then used to provide access to information. The rule management process contains three distinct components: privacy rule foundations, boundary coordination operations, and boundary turbulence.

Privacy rule foundations: The first management process outlined by CPM is privacy rule foundations. Rule foundations include two features: development and attributes (Petronio, 2002). Access rules to private information are developed along several criteria including culture, sex and/or gender, motivations, context, and the risk-benefit ratio. These criteria inform and shape the types of boundaries and disclosure processes an individual uses. Embedded in Lindsey's story is a discussion of motivations and context as key components of privacy rule development. She described factors that motivated her to develop privacy rules, which included (a) communicating with others who have a similar experience and (b) sharing information with those individuals with whom the COA has an emotionally close relationship. Lindsey gives voice to the importance of sharing her story with other COAs. As a COA herself, she was hopeful that in sharing her story she could help someone and make them feel less alone. Additionally, Lindsey shared her story with her two closest friends. She conveys a sense of connection in sharing her stories with them. Her boundary is permeable with individuals she perceives will safeguard her information.

Boundary coordination operations. The second rule management process Petronio (2000, 2002) outlines is boundary coordination operations. In this management process, individuals make decisions about what they choose to reveal and conceal. When individuals change individual boundaries into collective boundaries (i.e., they disclose private information to others), a carefully coordinated system of boundary linkages, ownership, and permeability are utilized. First, individual boundaries are managed in such a way that linkages with others can be made that change an individual boundary into a collective boundary. Lindsey created linkages when she shared her story with her friends and when she shared the details of her family to those with similar situations. Second, boundaries are regulated in such a way that access or protection is allowed to certain types of information. This boundary permeability is an important part of the process as it determines what information others are exposed to. The standby stories that are shared are an attempt at controlling the permeability, making careful decisions about what to share and when to share it. Third, boundary ownership is negotiated such that decisions pertaining to who is responsible for the information are made by those who now have access to the information. For Lindsey's friends, these discussions were implicit; friends and confidants seemingly knew, without being asked, to keep information private. However, Lindsey explicitly asked her friends not to share the information with others. As a result, ownership extended between only Lindsey and her confidants.

WHY SHARE THE DYSFUNCTION

In determining why Lindsey would share dysfunctional information that could cause negative evaluation by others, research indicates that sharing private information has contributed to individuals' increased sense of understanding of their experiences (Bochner, Ellis, & Tillmann-Healy, 1997), and disclosers have also experienced positive benefits to their well-being (Pennebaker, Kiecolt-Glaser, & Glaser, 1988). The non-shocking stories that were described as cursory information were likely easier for COAs to process and as a result did not need to be shared with others to gain a better understanding of the event. Additionally, because the COAs were sharing stories with those who were emotionally close or had similar experiences, it is likely that these targets could help the COA process their experiences as they likely had extensive knowledge of the COA or had similar experiences. Although these stories are dramatic and traumatic in nature, the COAs admitted that these experiences were only a few of the events they witnessed growing up. Instead of sharing all their experiences, they used these "standby" stories. Telling of these similar experiences provides a sense of shared experience and can benefit both COAs and the recipients. Based on research by Yalisove (2004), Lindsey was using experiential expertise because she used her own experience to help other COAs develop an understanding of the occurrences in their own homes. Using this technique can be beneficial as individuals can use empathy to serve as role models for other COAs.

In sum, CPM provides a useful framework for understanding self-disclosure decisions and the revelation of private information. For Lindsey, she learned about what she could share with family outsiders from her mother and sibling. As she grew up, she started sharing her family's secret with others who were in a similar situation or she deemed emotionally close. As a result, her confidants became keepers of her information and knew to not share her stories with anyone else.

DISCUSSION QUESTIONS

1. How does this family secret function as a commodity controlled by family members?
2. As family outsiders, are Reagan and Alexis' reactions appropriate? How else might outsiders respond?
3. What other family secrets or topics could operate in the same way as Lindsey's situation?
4. How could the management of this family secret be improved?
5. As a family member, how could Lindsey and/or her family's communication about alcoholism be enhanced?

REFERENCES

Ackerman, R. J. (1986). Alcoholism and the family. In R. J. Ackerman (Ed.), *Growing in the shadow: Children of alcoholics.* Pompano Beach, FL: Health Communications.

Afifi, T. D., & Guerrero, L. K. (2000). Motivations underlying topic avoidance in close relationships. In S. Petronio (Ed.), *Balancing the secrets of private disclosures* (pp. 168–180). Mahwah, NJ: Erlbaum.

Afifi, T. D, Olson, L. N., & Armstrong, C. (2005). The chilling effect and family secrets: Examining the role of self protection, other protection, and communication efficacy. *Human Communication Research, 31,* 564–598. doi:1093/hcr/31.4.564

Afifi, T. D., & Steuber, K. (2009). The revelation risk model (RRM): Factors that predict the revelation of secrets and the strategies used to reveal them. *Communication Monographs, 76,* 144–176. doi:10.1080/03637750902828412

Afifi, W. A., & Caughlin, J. P. (2006). A close look at revealing secrets and some consequences that follow. *Communication Research, 33,* 467–488. doi:10.1177/0093650206293250

Alcoholics Info. (n.d.). Retrieved from http://www.alcoholics-info.com/

Berlin, R., Davis, R. B., & Orenstein, A. (1988). Adaptive and reactive distancing among adolescents from alcoholic families. *Adolescence, 23,* 577–584.

Black, B. P., & Miles, M. S. (2002). Calculating the risks and benefits of disclosure in African American women who have HIV. *Journal of Obstetric, Gynecologic, & Neonatal Nursing, 31,* 688–697. doi:10.1177/0884217502239211

Black, C. (1985). The family law in alcoholic homes-don't talk. In M. Miller (Ed.), *Changing legacies: Growing up in an alcoholic home* (pp. 39–42). Pompano Beach, FL: Health Communications.

Bochner, A. P., Ellis, C., & Tillmann-Healy, L. M. (1997). Relationships as stories. In S. W. Duck (Ed.), *Handbook of personal relationships: Theory, research, and interventions* (2nd ed., pp. 107–124). Chichester, England: John Wiley & Sons.

Brady, K. T., Tolliver, B. K., & Verduin, M. L. (2007). Alcohol use and anxiety: Diagnostic and management issues. *Treatment in Psychiatry, 164,* 217–221. doi:10.1176/appi.ajp.164.2.217

Cline, R. J., & McKenzie, N. J. (2000). Dilemmas of disclosure in the age of HIV/AIDS: Balancing privacy and protection in the health care context. In S. Petronio (Ed.), *Balancing the secrets of private disclosures* (pp. 165–180). Mahwah, NJ: Erlbaum.

Derlega, V. J., & Chaikin, A. L. (1977). Privacy and self-disclosure in social relationships. *Journal of Social Issues, 33,* 102–115.

Grant, B. F. (2000). Estimates of US children exposed to alcohol abuse and dependence in the family. *American Journal of Public Health, 90,* 112–115.

Greenberg, M. A., & Stone, A. A. (1992). Emotional disclosure about traumas and its relation to health: Effects of previous disclosure and trauma severity. *Journal of Personality and Social Psychology, 63*, 75–84. doi:10.1037/0022-3514.63.1.75

Hecht, M. (1973). Children of alcoholics are children at risk. *The American Journal of Nursing, 73*, 1764–1767. doi:10.2307/3422939

Keller, M. (1958). Alcoholism: Nature and extent of the problem. *Annals of the American Academy of Political and Social Science, 315*, 1–11. doi:10.1177/000271625831500102

Kelly, A. E., Klusas, J. A., von Weiss, R. T., & Kenny, C. (2001). What is it about revealing secrets that is beneficial? *Personality and Social Psychology Bulletin, 27*, 651–665. doi:10.1177/0146167201276002

Manzardo, A. M., Goodwin, D. W., Campbell, J. I., Penick, E. C., & Gabrielli, W. F., Jr. (2008). *The facts: Alcoholism* (4th ed.). New York, NY: Oxford University Press.

National Institute on Alcohol Abuse and Alcoholism. (2007). *FAQs for the general public.* Retrieved from http://www.niaaa.nih.gov/FAQs/General-English/

Pennebaker, J. W., Kiecolt-Glaser, J. K., & Glaser, R. (1988). Disclosure of traumas and immune function: Health implications for psychotherapy. *Journal of Consulting and Clinical Psychology, 55*, 1243–1254.

Pennebaker, J. W., Zech, E., & Rimé, B. (2001). Disclosing and sharing emotion: Psychological, social, and health consequences. In M. S. Stroebe, W. Stroebe, R. O. Hansson, & H. Schut (Eds.), *Handbook of bereavement research: Consequences, coping, and care* (pp. 517–539). Washington, DC: American Psychological Association.

Petronio, S. (1991). Communication boundary management: A theoretical model of managing disclosure of private information between martial partners. *Communication Theory, 1*, 311–335.doi:10.1111/j.1468-2885.1991.tb00023.x

Petronio, S. (2000). The boundaries of privacy: Praxis of everyday life. In S. Petronio (Ed.), *Balancing the secrets of private disclosures* (pp. 37–49). Mahwah, NJ: Erlbaum.

Petronio, S. (2002). *Boundaries of privacy: Dialectics of disclosure.* New York, NY: State University of New York Press.

Rangarajan, S. (2006, May). *Lonely in a crowd: The social and emotional consequences of growing up with parental alcoholism.* Paper presented at the meeting of the International Communication Association, Dresden, Germany.

Rangarajan, S., & Kelly, L. (2006). Family communication patterns, family environment, and the impact of parental alcoholism on offspring self-esteem. *Journal of Social and Personal Relationships, 23*, 655–671. doi:10.1177/0265407506065990

Steinglass, P. (1980). A life history model of the alcoholic family. *Family Process, 19*, 211–226. doi:10.1111/j.1545-5300.1980.00211.x

Yalisove, D. L. (2004). *Introduction to alcohol research: Implications for treatment, prevention, and policy.* New York: Pearson.

CHAPTER 25

"Don't Talk, Don't Feel, Don't Trust" and Family Systems Theory

DeAnne Priddis – *Middle Tennessee State University*

ABSTRACT

Alcoholism does not just affect the alcoholic, but every member of the family. This case study addresses the impact a mother's alcohol use disorder has on the rest of the family system. The children and husband follow the alcoholic family rule of "don't talk, don't tell, don't trust" with other family members, friends, school, and employer. This silence may be caused by the perceived stigma associated with alcoholism. Furthermore, stigma may cause family members to not receive the social support needed or desired to live with and love an alcoholic. When family members receive social support from a support organization such as Al-Anon or a counselor, they often learn that others also experience worry for a person with alcohol use disorder, and then they may begin to accept the situation and learn coping and management skills for self. At this time, family members will need to define their "new normal" relationship with the alcoholic.

CASE STUDY

Alex and Alyssa Olson live with their mom and dad in a small apartment. Their mom, Anna Olson, is a second-generation alcoholic who lost her father to alcoholism four years ago. Alcoholism is a serious problem in the United States with approximately 53% of men and women reporting one or more close relatives with a drinking problem (Family Alcoholism). Alcoholism does not just affect the alcoholic, but all members of the family system. Children and spouses of alcoholics suffer from more emotional and physical problems overall. In addition, children of alcoholics are four times more likely to become alcoholics themselves than other children (American Academy of Child & Adolescent Psychiatry, 2011; Barry & Fleming, 1990).

Anna's husband, Kevin, is an over-the-road (OTR) truck driver who leaves for several days at a time. Kevin is concerned about the stability of his family while he is on the road. Although his parents live nearby, he is hesitant to get them involved in their current problems with Anna's alcoholism. Anna's mom, Elise, is often more willing to help Kevin with the kids, because she seems more understanding of the role of alcoholism in the family.

Anna has a family system around her that is impacted by the alcoholism. Anna has the role of mother, wife, daughter-in-law, and daughter within her family system. Each family member is impacted by her alcoholism when Kevin is working. Although the kids are living with Anna, Elise often makes daily check-ins while Kevin is at work to make sure the kids go to school, there is food in the refrigerator, the kids have clean clothes, and that Anna is taking care of the list of extra activities and chores that Kevin has left for her. If Anna is sober, it is more likely that the list has been completed and the seven-year-old twins have what they need. The family system is operating around Anna, as a functioning member of the family system in her dry condition, when she is abstinent, or not drinking (Liepman, Silvia, & Nirenberg, 1989).

However, if Anna has been drinking or intoxicated, she is in a wet condition (Liepman et al., 1989). Elise may find evidence of a wet condition because the children had walked to school, or Alex and Alyssa stayed home because of the inability to find clean clothes to wear to school. This wet condition also may cause Elise to step into a new role as the caregiver for the twins and Anna by bringing over groceries, taking care of the children, or attending events that usually Anna would attend (e.g., parent–teacher conferences).

The family rule of "don't talk, don't feel, don't trust" occurs in many families of alcoholics. The family secret of Anna's alcoholism may be kept from others within the family, or outside of the family circle. Alex and Alyssa may be afraid to tell Elise that Anna has been drinking, because their grandmother will either get upset with them or force them to stay at her house, which is far away from their friends and school. If they tell friends or their teachers, then they will be viewed as "different" from the other children, or their mom will be viewed as a "bad mom." The teacher may also tell their dad, or worse yet, someone that can take them away from home. This would make their mom very angry, and would also cause her to drink more.

The second part of the family rule is "don't feel." Alex and Alyssa may be afraid to feel the emotion that is associated with Anna's alcoholism. Anna may show up embarrassingly drunk to pick them up at school, or forget to pick them up from school altogether. These hurt feelings should not be felt, as the family is currently busy focusing on helping Anna or dealing with her anger. The family is not addressing the impact of the alcoholism on the children.

Lastly, Anna often pleads that she will not forget to pick them up again, because she feels terrible later. The children will often experience the "don't trust" when promises made by Anna have been broken in the past, and for repeat intoxicated behaviors. Not only will the children of alcoholics not trust the alcoholic, but they lack trust of their own perception in other relationships (Arbetter, 1990). These three parts of "don't tell, don't feel, don't trust" are rules for families affected by alcohol (Black, Family Rules).

The "don't tell, don't feel, don't trust" rule may cause alcoholic families to avoid outside relationships in fear that something is wrong with their family. The fear is often supported by stigma about alcoholism in society. Stigma can occur either inside or outside of the family. Kevin takes a risk by discussing Anna's alcoholism with his parents. Last time he was forced to ask them for help when he was out of town, they declined and told him to get professional help for his problems. Kevin now avoids communication with his parents when Anna is drinking. He will let their calls go to voicemail, and avoid calling them. He prefers the typical conversations with his parents to include only the positive things that are happening within his family, as in something funny Alyssa has done or a grade Alex received in school.

Stigma also impacts Kevin outside of the family. He feels unable to discuss Anna's drinking with friends or family members outside of Elise, because Kevin fears he will then be forced to quit his job to stay home with Anna and the twins. Kevin needs his job to fulfill his role of provider, as he supports his family with the only family income available. The risk of turning down work at his trucking firm can cause him to be overlooked for future work requests. Kevin does not know what alternatives are available for him and feels trapped in his current job and his role as provider for Anna and the twins.

Alex experiences stigma outside the family. He does not want to get together with friends after school because he does not know if his mom will be sober or drunk. He may avoid the conversation because his mom cannot pick him up from their house and because of his mom's condition at their home. Alex may cope with the problem by ending the friendship rather than take the risk of a friend finding out the real reason why he cannot get together. The stigma associated with the alcoholism prevents family members discussing the impact of the alcoholism, and will reduce the level of social support that is sought by the family members close to Anna.

Kevin feels lost and alone in dealing with the alcoholism in his family. Kevin searches the internet on his phone to find ways he could help from almost 200 miles away, and found the Al-Anon organization for people worried about a person with a drinking problem (Al-Anon). He attended his first meeting in the city he was spending the night in. Although Kevin was very nervous about what he would find at the meeting, he found the meeting was filled with people just like him. He was assured that the reason for his action was to help Anna, the twins, and himself though this difficult family matter.

The meeting sparked Kevin's interest in the family roles in an alcoholic family. Kevin learned that there are six roles that family members can take in an alcoholic family: the hero, enabler, mascot, scapegoat, lost child, and the alcoholic (Arbetter, 1990; Fischer & Wampler, 1994; MARR Inc.).

The first role in the family is the hero. The hero is the family member that will attempt to take care of self, siblings, parents, and household chores. The goal of the hero is to prevent the alcoholic from getting upset with things left undone or family members making it more difficult on the alcoholic. The hero will also attempt to make life feel more "normal" for the younger siblings, alcoholic, and other family members (Fischer & Wampler, 1994). The hero will often be an overachiever who will then turn into a workaholic. No matter how much the hero does, the hero cannot control the alcoholic to stop drinking (Arbetter, 1990).

The enabler will also help the alcoholic. Enablers often put the needs of the alcoholic before their own. The enabler may attempt to help the alcoholic by buying alcohol, paying for tickets, or borrowing money. The enabler may also assist the alcoholic from the consequences of her own behavior as an attempt to protect the alcoholic (MARR Inc). For example, the enabler may quickly bail the alcoholic out of jail, before family members and employers realize the severity of the drinking problem.

The third role family members may take within the family is the mascot. The mascot often uses humor as an escape from the real truth. If the mascot can get people to laugh, then they will appear happy and distracted from the truth (Fischer & Wampler, 1994). The mascot is often the youngest child in the family, and will take the role of the cutie, the class clown, or the charmer. Even as an adult the mascot will attempt to use charm to avoid responsibility (Arbetter, 1990). The mascot is a positive alternative to the reality of alcoholism in the family.

While the mascot will find a positive distraction, the scapegoat will often find a negative distraction to the alcoholism. The scapegoat will cause trouble as an attempt to become the new family problem that requires attention. For example, a scapegoat may start a fight at school, shoplift, or also abuse alcohol as an attempt to increase their role in the family system and decrease the role of the alcoholic. As scapegoats become adults, they may continue to be troublemakers, or may also struggle with addiction (Arbetter, 1990; Fischer & Wampler, 1994). In addition, scapegoats will often avoid conflict as adults (Artbetter, 1990).

The last family role is the lost child. This person is often forgotten in the family because the person is quiet, withdrawn, and independent from the family. The lost child may become a heavy reader that hides behind reading a book as an attempt to pretend to not know what problems are taking place. This child is often overlooked in school, and at home (Arbetter, 1990; Fischer & Wampler, 1994). The lost child may also find ways to be away from home when most problems occur. For example, the lost child may find a job at a banquet hall on weekends when the alcoholic is most likely to abuse alcohol.

After evaluating all of the roles the family members take in his family, Kevin identified himself as the enabler. Kevin has provided the money for Anna to drink and protects her from the consequences of her addiction. He also found that the worse the addiction became, the more responsibilities Kevin took on for the family and home (Peled & Sacks, 2008). He also identified that he asked Elise to take over the enabler role when Anna is drinking. In wet conditions, Elise will take care of Anna's responsibilities when she is unable to maintain employment, or take care of her twins and/or the household because of her drinking.

Kevin also evaluated the family roles for the twins. He identified Alex as the hero and Alyssa as the mascot. Alex is the hero because he focuses on getting good grades in his classes, when he attends school. Alex also will attempt to protect Alyssa from harm from Anna, either physically or psychologically. Alex will often take the caregiver role when an adult was not present.

Alyssa was identified as the mascot. Alyssa will attempt to redirect Kevin's attention from the problems when he does get home from a few days at work. Alyssa will tell jokes as a way of lightening the mood and redirect Kevin. She has several joke books from school from which she will practice jokes on Kevin and Elise. Alyssa will often find other ways to immediately grab their attention upon entering the house, with an obstacle course or scavenger hunt that she says must be done right away.

When Kevin returned home after his trip, he was hopeful from his recent visit to an Al-Anon meeting and the research he found, and he was looking forward to sharing it with Elise. When he arrived home, he found Anna passed out on the couch, Alex surrounded by mounds of laundry and reading the directions on the laundry detergent box, and Alyssa building a tower out of her collection of books. Kevin immediately greets both kids, tells Alyssa he will be there in a minute, and walks over to help Alex with the laundry, as he wonders how the last four days have been for the twins.

Kevin notices how Anna is sleeping on the sofa. He assumes Alex has taken the role of caregiver for Anna (Brynes, 2010). Not only is Anna covered with blankets, but the coffee table is against the sofa as an attempt to prevent her from falling on the floor or waking. There are also two abandoned bowls of partially eaten dry cereal on the opposite side of the coffee table. The role reversal between Alex and Anna and calmness in the air made it appear that this is something that often happens when Kevin is over the road.

Kevin's new knowledge helps him understand the impact responsibility can have on children of alcoholics (COA) as adults (ACOAs). ACOAs may experience disenfranchised grief of missing their childhood by taking care of their alcoholic parent. Furthermore, they may have the inability to trust others based on the lack of trust in the family relationship with the alcoholic (Black, n.d.). Kevin understands the importance of positive relationships between the children and others. Both trust and control are lacking in their relationship with their mother, and he can make sure they experience them in other relationships. He can have the healthy trusting relationship with the twins by sticking to his word with them. He can also seek situations that allow the twins a healthy amount of control, as in letting them plan what they do together the following day (Emshoff & Valentine, 2006).

Kevin then attempts to wake Anna and walk her to bed. Anna spends their walk to the bedroom expressing her apologies for drinking, and promising she will never drink again. Kevin agrees to avoid a fight, but remembers many times before when she said she would not drink again but still did. He then hears a large crash from the living room, followed by Alyssa's scream and Alex's shush, and then the collection of books being cleaned up. Kevin loses track of the rest of the evening and his interest in helping Anna. He feels a small satisfaction knowing he is not the only one suffering from a family system controlled by alcoholism.

Kevin questions if things would have been better if he came home to a sober wife. He first realizes that the chances of finding her sober were very rare. He wonders if a career change that brings him home each night might help the situation. He realizes that his life will not be as it once was, because Anna will not likely quit abusing alcohol. Even if she did, the rest of the family will not be able to trust Anna for a very long time.

Kevin snaps back to the moment by his cell phone ringing in the kitchen. The caller is Alyssa's teacher reporting problems in class earlier in the day. Kevin realizes he must take some immediate action. He contacts the Employee Assistance Program (EAP) with his employer, and finds out that he and his immediate family members can attend five free counselor appointments per person per event. When asked by the EAP representative about the cause of the appointments, Kevin quickly bluffs that the reason is the loss of a family member.

He feels the counseling sessions are ineffective, until the third session when he learns he is experiencing grief. This grief is called "disenfranchised grief" because his grief is for loss of someone that has not actually died. Kevin is not getting the social support he needs from others, because they do not acknowledge his grief (Doka, 2016, pp. 188–190). The rest of the session consists of defining what he is grieving. He started with grieving his relationship with his wife, his family, and the way she was before her father's death. Furthermore, he is losing control of what is happening within his family, and with his life. He feels like he is spending every waking moment either dealing with the latest conflict from the alcoholism, or worrying about what is happening at home when he is away. He misses the trust and respect he once had for his wife, and the great mother she was for their children. Although this was an important step for Kevin, it is a difficult reality.

During the fourth session, Kevin realizes that he did not think that Alex was suffering from the alcoholism. He felt Alex was resilient to the impact of the alcoholism because he does not appear sad or anxious. He continues to bring home good grades and seems happy with his sister. After the coaching of the counselor, Kevin calls the EAP representative and tells him that Alex is also suffering from the loss of a family member. Alex eagerly attends his first counselor appointment.

Kevin realized that the counselor's exercise on disenfranchised grief was very similar to the reason he told the EAP representation—the loss of a family member. This connection made Kevin see the significance of grieving his relationship with his wife. Kevin was not sure if she would quit drinking. If she did quit, he wonders if he and the kids would be able to trust her. Alex and Alyssa may not even remember what "normal" was in their relationship with their mother before the alcoholism. Furthermore, their definition of "normal" had to be redefined for the "new normal," which was the life after what they have all been through the last four years.

DISCUSSION QUESTIONS

1. How does the family rule of "don't talk, don't feel, don't trust" impact each family member discussed in this case study? How does this family rule change with Anna's dry and wet conditions?

2. Was Kevin's assessment of his family role (enabler) accurate? Briefly describe each of the six family roles. Which of the six family roles would also describe Kevin's role in the family? Why?

3. What are some reasons not mentioned in the case study that prevent families of alcoholics from talking to others about the alcoholism?

4. What type of disenfranchised grief do you feel that other family members feel in this case study? Create a separate list for Elise, Alex, and Alyssa.

REFERENCES

Al-Anon. Retrieved from https://al-anon.org

American Academy of Child & Adolescent Psychiatry. (2011, December). Children of alcoholics. *Facts for Families, 17*. Retrieved from http://www.aacap.org

Arbetter, S. R. (1990). Children of alcoholics don't talk, don't trust, don't feel. *Current Health, 16*(6), 14.

Barry, K. L., & Fleming, M. F. (1990). Family cohesion, expressiveness, and conflict in alcoholic families. *British Journal of Addiction, 85*, 81–87. doi:10.1111/j.1360-0443.1990.tb00626.x

Black, C. (n.d.). *Family rules: Don't talk, don't feel. don't trust.* Retrieved from https://elunanetwork.org/resources/family-rules-dont-talk-dont-trust-dont-feel-dr-claudia-black/

Brynes, K. (2010). *Adult children of alcoholics' perception of communicative exchanges with family members and outsiders* (Doctoral dissertation). Retrieved from PsycINFO.

Doka, K. J. (2016). *Grief is a journey: Finding your path through loss.* New York, NY: Atria Books.

Emshoff, J., & Valentine, L. (2006, November). Supporting adolescent children of alcoholics. *The Prevention Researcher, 13*(4), 18–20.

Family alcoholism. Retrieved from http://www.alcoholism-statistics.com/family-statistics/

Family rules: Don't talk, don't feel, don't trust. Retrieved from https://www.promises.com/articles/family-and-parenting/family-rules/

Fischer, J. L., & Wampler, R. S. (1994). Abusive drinking in your adults: Personality type and family role as moderators of family-of-origin influences. *Journal of Marriage and Family, 56*(2), 469–479. doi:10.2307/353113

Liepman, M. R., Silvia, L. Y., & Nirenberg, T. D. (1989). The use of family behavior loop mapping for substance abuse. *Family relations, 38*(3), 282–287. doi:10.2307/585053

MARR Inc. *Roles in the addicted family system.* Retrieved from https://www.marrinc.org/roles-in-the-addicted-family-system/

Peled, E., & Sacks, I. (2008). The self-perception of women who live with an alcoholic partner: Dialoging with deviance, strength, and self-fulfillment. *Family Relations, 57*, 390–403. doi:10.1111/j.1741-3729.2008.00508.x

CHAPTER 26

Substance Abuse Within the Family: Coping Through Family Communication

Sydney O'Shay-Wallace – *Merrill Palmer Skillman Institute for Child and Family Development*

ABSTRACT

This case study is based on data collected from in-depth interviews with people who have a substance-dependent family member. It tells the story of how one family deals with the onset and cycle of addiction as well as the recovery process of one member's substance use disorder. Readers will examine how communication is central to a family's coping processes when experiencing a crisis. Discussion questions draw on Maguire's (2012) communication-based coping model.

CASE STUDY

Substance abuse is a prevalent issue in the United States. In 2014, 21.5 million people aged 12 and older in the U.S. had a substance use disorder (SUD) within the past year (Center for Behavioral Health Statistics and Quality, 2015). SUDs are identified when prolonged abuse of alcohol and/or drugs significantly impact a person's life in ways that negatively contribute to their health and their ability to perform their responsibilities at work, school, or home (Substance Abuse and Mental Health Services Association, 2016). The pervasiveness of substance abuse becomes increasingly evident when considering the friends and families that are impacted by a loved one's substance abuse. In 2017, 46% of U.S. adults reported having a family member or confidant with a current or past drug addiction (Gramlich, 2017), suggesting that a large portion of U.S. families deal with substance use issues.

When a family member becomes substance-dependent, immediate family members are likely to experience some level of unpredictable stress. Family members with a close relative who abuses substances have described struggling with stress related to uncertainty, worry, and the deterioration of relationships, among other stressors (Orford, Velleman, Copello, Templeton, & Ibanga, 2010). Though interventions surrounding substance abuse often focus on helping the person with the substance use issue recover from their addiction, recent interventions are turning towards helping families cope with the challenges of having a substance-dependent family member (see Gethin, Trimingham, Chang, Farrell, & Ross, 2016; Kelly, Fallah-Sohy, Cristello, & Bergman, 2017). This case offers a glimpse into how families experience unpredictable stress stemming from substance abuse and how they communicatively cope with that stress. Though the names of participants have been changed to protect their identities, this case is grounded in stories shared by immediate family members of an immediate relative with an SUD across 15 in-depth interviews. These interviews were conducted by the author in the spring of 2017 as part of a research study tasked with understanding how families communicated about substance abuse within the family. This case study reflects the ways in which communication is at the center of family coping processes.

PART 1: THE ONSET OF ADDICTION

Angela classifies herself as a helicopter parent. She was the parent–teacher association president, field trip chaperone, and sideline cheerleader for her daughter, Nora, as she played sports. Angela describes Nora as a lovely child. She was kind, considered popular by her peers, a member of the honor society, involved in cheerleading, and ranked number two in the country for volleyball. However, Angela and her husband, Jason, started to notice changes in their daughter during the summer she transitioned from her junior year to her senior year of high school. Angela was their only child, so they assumed they were experiencing the hellish teenage years they had heard so much about from their friends. Nora had become rebellious, dishonest, apathetic toward school and her friends, and even her hygiene had declined. Angela and Jason were concerned, but hoped it would pass. Over time Nora stopped hanging around with her friends altogether, refused to play volleyball, consistently wore dirty clothes, and appeared disheveled.

One day Angela received a call from Nora's grandma, whose home Nora had slept at the night before: "We can't wake Nora up. We can't wake her up! There's a needle on the bed. Papa can't wake her up! The ambulance is on the way." The entire family rushed to the hospital, not knowing whether Nora was alive or dead. Through the course of her treatment Nora's secret was revealed: she had become addicted to heroin and had overdosed at Grandma's house. Nora was 18 years old at this point in time and was attempting to leave the hospital without seeking treatment for her addiction. Her parents were shocked and didn't know what to do. Nora ended up staying in the hospital for a few days before returning home. Without having any guidance on how they should move forward, Nora and her family were left to figure out how to deal with her addiction on their own.

Angela: What do we do?

Jason: I have no idea. I honestly don't even know where to start.

Angela: You would think they would have told us what we should do when we were at the hospital instead of just sending us on our merry way. I just feel so helpless and unprepared to deal with something like this.

Jason: Nora says she wants to go live with her friend downstate.

Angela: A geographic change might be a good idea. It could get her away from the people here that she's doing drugs with.

Jason: Okay, let's try it.

PART 2: THE CYCLE OF ADDICTION

In the beginning, Nora seemed to be doing well. She had settled into her new apartment, kept a job, and was maintaining her sobriety. However, about three weeks after the move, Angela received a phone call in the middle of the night and learned that Nora had relapsed. Nora was calling to ask for help. Angela and Jason drove down, picked Nora up, and took her to a drug treatment facility the next day. On their drive home from dropping Nora off at rehab, Angela and Jason contemplated their new life circumstances:

Jason: Is this what our lives are going to be like now? Constantly worrying and wondering if Nora is okay? Scared to answer the phone because it might be 'the call', the one where we find out our only child is dead.

Angela: I know. I'm scared to even look at my phone, but I'm even more scared when we go days at a time without hearing from her. At least we know she is in a safe place right now.

Jason: Yeah, maybe some formal treatment is what she needs to help her stay clean for good. I just hope it works.

Nora successfully completed the treatment program and transitioned into a halfway house where she would still receive the support and structure she needed to maintain her sobriety. While living in the halfway house, Nora continued to follow the treatment program and fulfill her responsibilities at the house all while staying sober. However, the stress of worrying how long Nora's sobriety would last continued to wear on Angela and Jason. After too many restless nights and one long day at work, Angela opened up to Jason:

Angela: I'm done. I can't do this anymore. I can't keep worrying about whether Nora is going to end up dead or in jail, so I'm just not going to!

Jason: What do you mean?

Angela: As of today, I'm not going to worry about the things I can't control. I can't control whether Nora relapses any more than I can control whether she gets into a car accident, so I'm not going to. It's just too much. I'm taking my life back.

Jason: I mean, she's clearly not sitting around thinking about us. Why should we always be worried about her? These past few months have been really difficult, and since we haven't really told anyone else, it's also been pretty isolating. My coworkers and friends have been asking me what's wrong, because they can tell something is up. I keep making things up, but it's exhausting. I just need a break from it all.

Angela: That's it. Let's go. You and I, right now. We're going down to Old Joe's for dinner and a drink and we're not going to talk or think about Nora at all for the rest of the night!

Jason: Do you really think we can do that?

Angela: We're gonna try!

Nora remained in this halfway house for nine months. Over this time, Angela and Jason tried to balance supporting her and maintaining their health and relationships. Eventually, Nora felt she was ready to move out on her own, and her parents agreed. Together, the family moved Nora into her own apartment. Nora continued to attend Narcotics Anonymous (NA) meetings to support her sobriety and she got a job to help pay her bills, though her parents helped support her financially as well. Over the course of about five months Nora successfully maintained her sobriety. She checked in with her parents daily or every other day, and was becoming more of herself—the fun, outgoing, strong-willed girl she had always been, until she fell back in with her old crowd and relapsed. Two weeks went by and Nora wouldn't talk to her parents or tell them where she was.

Jason: I just got a text from Nora! It says, "I'm okay."

Angela: Well, we know what that means.

Jason: Yeah, "I didn't die today."

Angela: This has been a long couple of weeks. At least we know she's alive.

Two days later Nora called and asked her parents to help get her back into a drug treatment program. Once again, Angela and Jason drove to pick Nora up and took her to a drug treatment facility. While Nora was in this treatment center, family members were welcomed to join a recovery meeting, and Angela and Jason attended. Several other families attended alongside their loved ones who were also recovering from substance abuse. Chairs were set up in a circle so everyone could see and talk to one another face-to-face. A staff member of the rehabilitation center, Kyle, facilitated the meeting.

Kyle: So, who here feels guilty about what they've done?

Nora's hand shot up without a bit of hesitation, along with the hands of others in the group. Angela and Jason looked at each other, and Angela started to cry. They began to whisper to each other:

Angela: She loves us. She just wants us to be proud of her. She's not proud of herself.

Jason: I hadn't even thought about how we were making her feel. I don't want her to feel like we're judging her. She seems so ashamed.

Angela: We can't guilt her into stopping this.

Jason: We need to talk to her.

After the meeting ends Angela, Jason, and Nora stand out of their chairs. Angela starts crying again.

Angela: You know we love you, right? We don't want you to feel like we're judging you. We know you're not doing this on purpose. We get that you don't want to be this way.

Nora: I know. I just can't help but feel that way sometimes.

They all exchange hugs and goodbyes and families are escorted to leave the treatment facility.

Jason: Nora seemed really relieved to hear you say that.

Angela: I hope so. I just want her to be happy and healthy.

Weeks went by and Nora completed the treatment program and moved back into a halfway house. The cycle of addiction weighs heavy on families, but the longer a person maintains their sobriety, the risk of relapsing begins to decrease. Nora has now been in recovery for over three years.

PART 3: RECOVERY

Throughout the course of Nora's addiction, her family became comfortable talking with her and each other about substance abuse. They try not to make Nora's addiction the focus of their lives, but realize that it is a part of their family's story. Since recovery from an SUD is ongoing, like with other chronic illnesses, conversations about substance abuse continue to emerge in their family's daily lives. One day Angela and Nora were out to dinner, and the conversation happened to turn toward substance abuse:

Angela: Honey, there are some drugs called fentanyl and carfentanyl being mixed with heroin these days that could kill you instantly if you take them without knowing. You know, this is like, even worse than heroin. I need you to be extra careful—

Nora: You know what's messed up, mom? When you tell me about fentanyl, my first thought is hmm—I wonder what that's like? Isn't that crazy?

Angela: Yeah, that's crazy... It's conversations like these that help me understand how heroin really has changed how you think.

Another conversation about substance abuse emerged between Nora and her mother while filling out paperwork during a visit with an oral surgeon where Nora was planning to have her wisdom teeth taken out:

Angela: There's a spot here on the paperwork for drug use—what should we put?

Nora: Umm... Is 'all' an appropriate answer? [both begin to laugh]

Angela: I'm not sure, but we can try it!

Nora: Yeah... we should probably talk to the doctor about what they usually give for pain after the surgery just to be safe.

Angela: Good call, we can ask about some alternatives if they usually prescribe opiates.

As time goes on and Nora becomes even more stable in her recovery, her family is becoming more comfortable in this next phase of their life and they talk very positively about her future. They focus on her accomplishments and goals, such as her desire to graduate from college. Angela has even become an active advocate in their community for families experiencing substance use issues. Some of the family conversations have now turned to how and if they should inform the extended family of Nora's substance abuse.

Angela: How do you tell a 95-year-old grandma that their beautiful, perfect granddaughter is a heroin addict?

Jason: I don't know, but you're going to be on the news tonight telling the whole town, so we have to call and tell her just in case she sees it.

Angela: Alright, let's just get this over with. If we could survive these past four years, we can survive this phone call.

DISCUSSION QUESTIONS

1. How might communication have served as a source and/or symptom of stress during this family crisis?
2. In what way(s) did communication aid meaning-making during this family crisis?
3. Describe how communication was utilized as a coping resource.
4. Describe how communication was utilized as a coping strategy.
5. Based on this family's communication, how would you rate their ability to adapt during this family crisis on a scare of 1 to 10 (1 as adapting poorly and 10 as adapting well). Describe how this can be determined based on a family's communication.

REFERENCES

Center for Behavioral Health Statistics and Quality. (2015). *Behavioral health trends in the United States: Results from the 2014 National Survey on Drug Use and Health* (HHS Publication No. SMA 15-4927, NSDUH Series H-50). Retrieved from http://www.samhsa.gov/data/

Gethin, A., Trimingham, T., Chang, T., Farrell, M., & Ross, J. (2016). Coping with problematic drug use in the family: An evaluation of the stepping stones program. *Drug and Alcohol Review, 35*(4), 470–476. doi:10.1111/dar.12327

Gramlich, J. (2017). *Nearly half of Americans have a family member or close friend who's been addicted to drugs.* Retrieved from http://www.pewresearch.org/fact-tank/2017/10/26/nearly-half-of-americans-have-a-family-member-or-close-friend-whos-been-addicted-to-drugs/

Kelly, J. F., Fallah-Sohy, N., Cristello, J., & Bergman, B. (2017). Coping with the enduring unpredictability of opioid addiction: An investigation of a novel family-focused peer-support organization. *Journal of Substance Abuse Treatment, 77*, 193–200. doi:10.1016/j.jsat.2017.02.010

Maguire, K. C. (2012). *Stress and coping in families.* Cambridge, England: Polity Press.

Orford, J., Velleman, R., Copello, A., Templeton, L., & Ibanga, A. (2010). The experiences of affected family members: A summary of two decades of qualitative research. *Drugs: Education, Prevention, and Policy, 17*(S1), 44–62. doi:10.3109/09687637.2010.514192

Substance Abuse and Mental Health Services Association. (2016). *Mental and substance use disorders.* Retrieved from http://www.samhsa.gov/disorders

CHAPTER 27

Family Matters: An Autoethnographic Narrative of Addicted Selves and Addicted Others with/in the Family

Liahnna Stanley – *University of South Florida*

ABSTRACT

This chapter explores the negotiation of family relationships in the context of addiction, based on my experiences living with and through family addiction. I use autoethnography to recall the ways in which a sister, her sister, and the family experienced addiction in the home. Within these narrative fragments I consider how addiction consumes the family and family consumes the addiction. Guided by family systems theory, I examine our family as an emotional unit and ground my analysis in the interdependent functions of addiction. In seeking a clearer understanding of the complexities of one family member's story of enduring addiction, I reflect on my own struggles to gain a fuller sense of how these difficulties complicate recovery. Lastly, I make a case for a relational conceptualization of addicted selves, addicted others, and addicted families that brings into fore the participatory, co-constructive interactions of substance misuse and addiction. I end the chapter by providing questions for discussion.

CASE STUDY

Story is both the great revealer and concealer. There is the story of what gets said, and the story of what remains unsaid. There is the story that covers up story.

—Christina Baldwin (2005, p. 17)

I'm not an addict, but I loved one. And that was an addiction in and of itself.

In this chapter I use autoethnography to examine family addiction from a relational communication perspective. Through personal narrative, I invite readers to consider the ways in which a sister, her sister, and the family endure and survive addiction and dis-ease in the home. Motivated by family systems theory, I track the ways in which practices of addiction with/in the family are constitutive of realities, experiences, and ways of relating. Overall, these accounts aim to demonstrate a relational approach to addiction, addicted selves/others, and addicted families. In the conclusion of this case study, I offer questions for further consideration. I have obtained my family's consent to write this chapter and use pseudonyms to protect their privacy.

Confessions of an Addict

Dear Ari,

I worried about you. *Where are you? What are you doing? Who are you with? How are you going to get home? Are you going to come home? Are you safe? Are you alive?* You know, I could always tell when you were high. The biggest giveaway was your eyes. Once big and brown and full of light, they became dark and dodgy orbs that could never quite keep a focused gaze. The familiarity I had once found in them was far removed, and I felt uneasy whenever our eyes met. As your habit became more severe, this feeling became less frequent. Likewise, as drugs became a bigger part of your life, everything else became less important, including me.

I resented you. I resented you for having to hide my money and possessions in fear that you would steal from me. I resented you for trying to help me find my money and possessions when I knew that you stole them. I resented you for lying about trying to get sober. I blamed you for Mom and Dad's fights and having to find a job at 15 because our family went broke paying for your bonds and attorney fees. But I still missed you. I missed how close we were when we were younger. Don't you remember exploring the woods behind our house in Alabama, setting out on pretend adventures as legendary pathfinders in search of a rare forest berry that held the cure to the world's most infectious and fatal disease? What happened to my adventure partner, my distinguished botanist, my best friend, my older sister—the person who was?

You became a thief in my eyes. For nearly 10 years, every angle of our family life was consumed with your welfare—the moment the spotlight began to shine on someone else, you would steal it right back. Mom and Dad became mere shells of parents whose insides were entirely replaced with fear and shame. I obsessed over our dysfunctional family and so my anger festered into constant suspicion and vigilance. When you weren't home, I would snoop through your computer. I would read through your keystroke logs that Mom and Dad programmed, reporting information back to them. I would go into your room and look for drugs, pill bottles, straws, needles, and spoons, and figure a way to get rid of them. One time I found your buprenorphine prescription. I didn't know what it was. When I googled the drug and found out it was an opioid, I got upset because you'd previously told us you were trying to get sober. I stole the entire bottle. I flushed all but one, because I wanted to see what it felt like to be high. I wanted to know why you liked it so much.

I didn't take them sublingually like the prescription asked. No, I was afraid of the taste. Instead, I snorted the tiny round white pill. In just a few minutes, I spun into a rage of nausea and vomiting. Curled up on the cold, bathroom tile, I did some more research and found out that it was your treatment medication. I also found out that you get really sick when you take Suboxone when you're not an addict.

It's the guilt that hurts me most of all. I want to apologize. I am sorry for stealing from you. I am sorry I misinterpreted knowledge of substance misuse and addiction as understanding. I am sorry for thinking that you could easily stop and that you chose to be an addict. I am sorry for begging for you to say you're sorry before you were ready. I am sorry for not recognizing your pain and hurt or supporting you during your recovery. I am sorry I took your addiction and made it my own.

Sincerely,

Your little sister, Liahnna

A Family Affair

I try to fight it. I don't know what time it is, but I'm certain it's late and I've got school in the morning. I just want to sleep. I reach out and try to seize the remnants of the dream lingering in my mind, hoping I can soothe myself back into slumber. I project a visual slideshow of the last impressions of my dream: I was running through a green, lush forest. It was dark. Sheltered by the dense trees and their spreading canopy, I kept to a beaten path to avoid the thick and twisted roots. I felt like I was going in circles, but I still kept running. Twigs snapped beneath my feet as I squished them into the mushy, damp forest floor. Seedlings and dead leaves nestled between my bare toes. And then, without warning, the air filled with a choking mist that swirled and sprawled before me. I ran faster. I ran faster until my feet began sinking into the ground. And soon enough, the depressed ferns and grasses were swallowing up my feet.

It is Tuesday, 3:21 a.m. I am 16 years old. My efforts were unsuccessful and so the forest canopy reverts to my unattractive popcorn ceiling. Screams and cries break through my thin bedroom walls like a sledgehammer, crushing any opportunities for sleep. I listen. I listen generously. It is like channel surfing and happening across your all-time favorite television drama. You know exactly where you are in the series, noting what each character is thinking and their next course of action. You've seen it a million times, but you still can't get enough. When you resume, it feels as if you've never stopped watching.

Indeed, I cannot resist my curiosity. I decide to get out of bed. I open my door and walk out of my room. For a brief moment, I stand against the wall that marks the end of our living room. As if right on cue, my little sister, Remi, who sleeps across the hall, opens her door. Her eyes are big, blue, and red. She's been crying. Still unnoticed by my family, I motion for her to go back into her room. I know she won't listen, but I hate for her to see us—our family—like this. I remember when I was her age, when every cabinet slam and curse word yelled by my arguing parents shook my world to its core. This, though… this is much worse.

"What the hell do you think you're doing, Ariel? How on earth do you think you're going to keep this up? You're acting like a goddamn degenerate, NOT the daughter I raised," yells Mom. "Do you have ANY CLUE what this is doing to your family? I can't sleep without having nightmares that the police are at my door, or you've run off somewhere, or I found you dead." She pauses to catch her breath. "You know what, you don't. You don't have any idea what this is like. And even if you did, you wouldn't give a damn." Ariel, or Ari, my older sister, sits at the kitchen bar. Her fists are tightly balled and stuffed in the pockets of her hoodie. She doesn't say a word. "See, nothing," Mom throws her hands up. "Steve, why don't you say something?? See if she'll talk to you because whatever the hell I'm doing sure isn't phasing her."

"Talk to your mother; stop sitting there like a little brat," Dad declares. "It's disrespectful, you actin' like this."

Ariel groans, "I need a cigarette." She grabs a pack of Marlboro Reds from her purse and starts her way to the patio. I've tried cigarettes before, but they make me feel gross. Especially the harsh ones, like Marlboro Reds. I don't know how she does it.

"No fucking way," Mom screams. "You're not just gonna walk away from this. You're not allowed." Mom notices my little sister and I huddled by the couch. "Look, you woke up Liahnna and Remi. Another sleepless night before school, right girls? All thanks to your great big sister." Finally, someone acknowledges me. I wish it didn't involve me being dragged into this, though.

"I didn't wake her up. *I'm* not the one screaming," Ari sneers. "Anyways, *sorry* guys, for being a shitty sister and disrupting the sweet peace of this already dysfunctional family *yet again*." She continues to the patio, viciously packing her cigarettes into the heel of her palm. I've never understood why people do that.

Frustrated with her arrogance, Dad follows her. "You know what, yeah, how about you go take a smoke? Cool off for a bit?" His face turns red. "How 'bout you smoke the entire damn pack? Think you can do that? Think that's 'cool' enough for you?"

"I've done worse," Ari scoffs.

"Then let's see it. I want you to smoke until you puke."

"Steve…" Mom starts. Even she is concerned with this sick form of punishment.

"No, honey, I'm serious. She's too high to give a shit anyway."

"Fine by me. And you know what, Dad, you're right. I'm so stoned and I don't fucking care about anyone or anything and everything is my fault. Give me lung cancer and let me die so the family can rid the disgusting vermin that is me: your shitty, disappointing daughter."

As they left for the patio, Mom came over and caressed Remi and me. A soft, brief moment soon to be interrupted by a play-by-play of how the night unfolded. Her explanation was unsolicited yet expected. My parents—Mom in particular—shared every detail of my sister's addiction with me, while Remi suffered the collateral damage of both experiencing the ever-igniting, explosive family outbursts and not understanding how to make sense of and manage what was happening. It can be argued that no one in the family could make sense of Ari's addiction, but that was especially true of Remi, a sweet, innocent 10-year-old girl.

I eventually turn my attention to the patio. Through the glass windows, I watch my dad and sister sit together. I watch Ari light her first cigarette, taking deep, bold inhales. Then, she lit another, and another. I stopped counting, but she chain-smoked a good dent into her fresh pack. Ari adjusts her chair and for a brief moment, my eyes meet hers. They are still, cold, and unnervingly careless. Lips pursed and arms crossed, I can tell she is infuriated. But I can also tell she is sad. I can tell because I know her. I love her. No matter the drugs, I don't think she wants to do this to us. I wish I could help her, but I just don't know how.

"I swear, this is destroying us. It feels like I'm getting stabbed in the chest. Sometimes I wish she would just do it. Kill me. Or else I'll do it myself and do her a favor since she hates me so much," says Mom. "I'm gonna go see what's going on outside, what they're talking about. Y'all go back to bed, I'm sorry about this."

Remi sobs unceasingly, burying her head into my chest. I held her, rubbing her back as her tears merge with mine, melting into my night sweatshirt. The pain comes in waves, minutes of sobbing punctuated by short pauses for recovering breaths. Then came another howl of misery, like a wave washing in and crashing her sandcastles flat. In a desperate battle against the grief, she asked if she could sleep with me tonight. My lips quiver as I try to speak, but my throat weighs too heavy. I bring her closer, as if to say "of course, there is no need to ask."

Together we retreat into my bedroom. I shove the mountain of textbooks on the side of my bed onto the floor to make room. She snuggles under the covers and looks at me with her luminous, yet swollen, blue eyes. "Why does she hate us?" Remi asks.

I don't know what to say. I don't have an answer, really. How do I respond? How do I construct her fallen sandcastles that she's so carefully built and rebuilt over the years? Where can I find a shovel and pail that will rebuild her image of our family? "Ari doesn't hate us, she loves us," I pause. "She's just very sick right now because of her addiction."

"No, Lili," Remi utters. "Not Ari. I mean Mom. She wants to die. Why does she hate us?"

My walls, the walls that hold me up and let me be strong, collapse. It feels as if the oxygen has been sucked out of the room. I said nothing. I couldn't. But if I could go back to that moment, I would tell my little sister: "Mom doesn't hate us. She loves us. She's just very sick right now because of Ari's addiction."

SYSTEMS THEORY AND FAMILY ADDICTION

Systems theory is a theory about relationships. In other words, systems theory emphasizes that individuals should be understood not as separate entities, but components functioning together in relation to the whole (Polkinghorne, 1983). Accordingly, family systems theory (FST) acknowledges the various ways in which individual family members interact to develop and maintain a larger family system (White & Klein, 2002). A systems view of families is extensive and diverse. Family communication scholars have applied FST to examine interactions in marital and family systems (Olson, 2000), eating disorders and mother–daughter communication (Prescott & Le Poire, 2002), anorexia in the family (Minuchin, 1974), and practitioner perspectives on open adoption relationships and the influence on families (Colaner & Scharp, 2016).

FST takes a systemic approach when examining family interaction. Beyond illustrating the interconnectedness of family members and communicative patterns, FST is not without critique and limitations. For example, Yerby (1995) discusses problematic assumptions of FST that undermine constructionist and dialectical perspectives. Arguing against a reductive, static family model, Yerby advocates for one that is continually evolving to privilege localized meaning-making in the presence of dilemmas and contradictions in family processes and relationships. Indeed, it is fundamental to examine the problematic family patterns inherent in family addiction as interrelated dynamic tensions rather than as the wrongdoings of one person, if we are to reconsider traditional, individualistic frameworks of addiction. Hence, I take an approach to FST that acknowledges the interplay of both the power of family members working together as well as the individual complexities that occur within the individual components of the system. Further, in line with an interpretive, narrative framework in which this case study is interested, I ground FST in a relational orientation to focus on communication as a process of constituting selves and relationships

(Baxter, 2004). Given the complexity and ever-changing networks of family addiction, attending to a fluid systems view of family addiction allows for a greater illumination of the significant communicative interactions that sustain addicted relationships with/in the family.

AUTOETHNOGRAPHY AND NARRATIVE INTERVENTION

Autoethnography is an approach to research and writing that seeks to describe, explore, and analyze lived experience in order to bring into relation the personal and cultural, the micro and macro, and the private and public (Ellis & Bochner, 2000). Autoethnographic work offers important, nuanced, and highly contextualized insights about how we (relational partners) constitute our social worlds and realities. It follows that, as a research method, autoethnography unfolds as both a process and product (Ellis, Adams, & Bochner, 2011). Of particular interest for autoethnographers is reflexivity, which enables storytellers and researchers alike to bend back the lens toward the self to position the personal in conversation with broader cultural, social, and political systems and influences (Berry & Adams, 2016; Ellis, Adams, & Bochner, 2011). In addition to providing testimony to a broader social audience (Frank, 1995), conveying autoethnographic narratives allows storytellers to "break silence by addressing understudied, hidden, and/or sensitive topics" (Jones, Adams, & Ellis, 2016, p. 35) such as family addiction.

Autoethnography privileges a researcher's subjectivity, reflexivity, and personal voice, and thus subverts traditional approaches to scholarship and ways of knowing that neglect the complexity and tenuous nature of everyday life (Jones, Adams, & Ellis, 2016). In turn, autoethnography appears to be a viable method for addressing my concerns of sibling and family relationships in the context of addiction. By sharing personal accounts and theorizing about one's lived experiences, Adams and Manning (2015) argue that communication researchers "can use autoethnography to ask unique questions about family life, questions not necessarily possible with other research methods" (p. 351). To my mind, this perspective fosters a more intimate connection between my personal experiences and myself as a researcher. This intimate connection—or better, this intimate *relationship*—is vital for a present and mindful showing and telling of stories, particularly within the lived hardships of addiction with/in the family. Keeping to this ethos, autoethnography is used as a means to study other contexts of family addiction and coping: accounts of negotiating the relational tensions in a father–son relationship (Berry, 2012), a daughter's performances of healing in living through her mother's addiction (Stern, 2015), family cancer survivorship (Anderson & Geist-Martin, 2003), as well as competing perspectives of stigmatization toward chronic noncancer pain patients who rely on prescription opioids (Wilbers, 2015).

Beyond just a method, autoethnography becomes the genre in which we are able to reflect, contemplate, and engage with these tensions in order to mine the healing and transformative processes of communication and ways of relating. In this way, autoethnography contributes not only from a scholarly perspective, but also to one's own personal recovery. bell hooks speaks of a similar sentiment in her chapter on writing autobiography. hooks concludes:

> The longing to tell one's story and the process of telling is symbolically a gesture of longing to recover the past in such a way that one experiences both a sense of reunion and a sense of release. It was the longing for release that compelled the writing but concurrently it was the joy of reunion that enabled me to see that the act of writing one's autobiography is a way to find again that aspect of self and experience that may no longer be an actual part of one's life but is a living memory shaping and informing the present. (hooks, 1989, p. 158)

Through the process of storytelling, I too have become aware of my own complex relationship with addiction. I am reminded of my feelings of frustration, resentment, and regret. Similarly to how I invite my readers to consider my storied experiences of family addiction, the telling of my story extends an invitation for myself, too, to revisit these moments. While I am remembering and remembering these experiences, I am also asked to take the position of a listener and reader of my own narrative. These stories, then, reveal as hypothetical spaces in which I can meet again with these emotions as they (re)emerge, often in brush with feelings of love, resilience, and compassion. As hooks writes, the actual "doing" of narratives—the writing, living, and reliving—can be a form of therapy in and of itself. My story locates myself as well as my readers in a shaped world where, together, we can rouse to give meaning to our reflections on the sharing of our stories. What remains clear here is what we can take and (un)learn from this reflexive journey to work toward a more communicatively enhanced understanding of addiction in the context of family and family in the context of addiction. Of equal importance is attending to the particularity and contingency that run throughout these stories, like intertwining currents in a stream.

RELATIONAL ADDICTION

The present study utilizes family systems theory to explore one family member's story of living through family addiction. I do not list out my sister's crimes, because they are not unique. Lying, stealing, and manipulating are not new stories and can be considered ways in which people living with addiction are simply trying to survive. Examining the social and relational aspects of addiction urges us to consider addiction as an inherently communicative process that shapes and informs the way we create and negotiate meanings, identity, and relationships. Such a framework pervades traditional approaches to addiction that frame substance misuse and relational problems as individual and linear. Entrenched in these approaches are cultural narratives that mobilize reductionist and decontextualized ideologies that neglect the dynamic experience of addiction and reinforce individualistic thinking (Tootle, Ziegler, & Singer, 2015). Here, my aim is to reject a positivistic fixation with causality (the causes of addiction) and individuality and advocate for a more productive communicative approach that posits addiction as constitutive of realities and experiences. My intentions are not to replace a one-sided individual conceptualization of addiction with an equally one-sided social one, but rather to suggest the theoretical and practical significance of a communicative or relational investigation of addiction. Thus, examining the lived and storied experience of addiction emerges as one way to provide insight into what a relational conceptualization of addiction might entail. In particular, looking at addiction with/in the family illustrates the "in-betweenness" in which a relational and reflexive approach to communication is interested.

These accounts invite readers to consider the ways in which a sister, her sister, and our family survive addiction and dis-ease. These accounts are not meant to take on others' points of view, but rather encourage a theoretical move to conceptualize addiction as a profoundly embodied social and relational process that involves tensions, contradictions, and competing discourses. The focus remains on the participatory, or co-constructive, character of substance misuse and addiction and how communicative practices of family addiction operate relationally (Hughes, 2007) and collectively in family systems. This knowledge framework takes a significant step away from biopharmacological notions of addiction, as well as how we might generally understand addiction outside the context of stories and lived experience. Additionally, these stories may be considered against the backdrop of a wider cultural narrative, that is, the current "opioid epidemic" in the U.S. (Centers for Disease Control and Prevention [CDC], 2018). Such a reading can be helpful for using the personal to understand the cultural (Ellis & Bochner, 2000) while also meeting again with feelings of anger, frustration, and hopelessness (for storytellers and readers alike).

Several perspectives are offered in this chapter, including family conflict, violence, sibling tensions, coping mechanisms, and resistance. Baxter's (2004) relational dialectics theory (RDT) explains that these multiple, competing discourses are cultural and relational; that is, these experiences show and represent powerful cultural ideals regarding addiction and family which compete with feelings and memories of love and care. In an exhaustive reading and re-reading of my personal experiences, I realize my own anger and the complicated process of healing that developed from enduring addiction with/in the family. Coming to this realization clarifies how family members are implicated in family addiction, as well as helping understand the ways in which family members may manage and make sense of addiction. Family addiction is hardly experienced in isolation and involves unhealthy, compulsive, and dangerous behaviors and communicative processes. Therefore, in these accounts, we can also consider the ways in which we internalize relational struggles and how addiction necessitates a collective, relational experience, where the boundaries between relational partners are often blurred and confused (Berry, 2012).

CONCLUSION

This chapter is about family addiction. But it is also about how we make sense of *being* in a family fused together in addiction. Loving someone who is addicted to drugs is arguably inescapable. It can feel like being a user yourself, only instead of consuming pills and powders, your entire way of life becomes dependent on twisted feelings of anger and resentment that bubble over into misunderstanding and (self) condemnation. Still, I am grateful that the "ending" of my story is one that is hopeful, washing away all but a slight bittersweet aftertaste. At the time of writing this, my sister has been in recovery for several years.

We live our lives by the stories available to us (Goodall, 2000). For this reason, I hope this story will inspire others to engage with storytelling in families (Koenig-Kellas, 2005) and for family addiction in particular. Lastly, I hope this story will inspire others to revisit and revise the feelings of loss, absence, and disappointment that feed our anger and resentment.

DISCUSSION QUESTIONS

In reading this case study, I invite my readers to consider the following questions: What can we learn from examining storied addiction through the lens of family systems theory? What might a relational conceptualization of addiction entail or look like in theory and practice? In what other ways can we constructively and creatively attend to the care and treatment of addicted selves and others in the context of family addiction?

REFERENCES

Adams, T. E., & Manning, J. (2015). Autoethnography and family research. *Journal of Family Theory and Review, 7*(4), 350–366.

Baldwin, C. (2005). *Storycatcher: Making sense of our lives through the power and practice of story*. Novato, CA: New World Library.

Baxter, L. A. (2004). A tale of two voices: Relational dialectics theory. *Journal of Family Communication, 4*(3&4), 181–192.

Berry, K. (2012). Reconciling the relational echoes of addiction: Holding on. *Qualitative Inquiry, 18*(2), 134–143.

Berry, K., & Adams, T. E. (2016). Family bullies. *Journal of Family Communication, 16*(1), 51–63.

Centers for Disease Control and Prevention. (2018, December 19). *Opioid Overdose: Understanding the Epidemic*. Retrieved from Centers for Disease Control and Prevention: https://www.cdc.gov/drugoverdose/epidemic/index.html

Colaner, C. W., & Scharp, K. M. (2016). Maintaining open adoption relationships: Practitioner insights on adoptive parents' regulation of adoption kinship networks. *Communication Studies, 67*(3), 359–378.

Ellis, C., Adams, T. E., & Bochner, A. P. (2011). Autoethnography: An overview. *Forum: Qualitative Social Research, 12*(1).

Ellis, C., & Bochner, A. P. (2000). Autoethnography, personal narrative, reflexivity: Researcher as subject. In N. K. Denzin & Y. S. Lincoln (Eds.), *The handbook of qualitative research* (pp. 733–768). Thousand Oaks, CA: Sage.

Frank, A. W. (1995). *The wounded storyteller: Body, illness, and ethics*. Chicago, IL: University of Chicago Press.

Goodall, H. L. (2000). *Writing the new ethnography*. Cumnor Hill, Oxford: Rowman and Littlefield Publishers.

hooks, b. (1989). *Talking back: Thinking feminist, thinking black*. Boston, MA: South End Press.

Hughes, K. (2007). Migrating identities: The relational constitution of drug use and addiction. *Sociology of Health and Illness, 29*(5), 673–691.

Jones, S. H., Adams, T. E., & Ellis, C. (2016). Introduction: Coming to know autoethnography as more than a method. In S. H. Jones, T. E. Adams, & C. Ellis (Eds.), *Handbook of autoethnography* (pp. 17–47). New York, NY: Routledge.

Koenig-Kellas, J. (2005). Family ties: Communicating identity through jointly told family stories. *Communication Monographs, 72*(4), 365–389.

Minuchin, S. (1974). *Families and family therapy*. Cambridge, MA: Harvard University Press.

Olson, D. H. (2000). Circumplex model of marital and family systems. *The Association for Family Therapy and Systemic Practice, 22*, 144–167.

Polkinghorne, D. E. (1983). *Methodology for the human sciences: Systems of inquiry.* Albany, NY: State University of New York.

Prescott, M. E., & Le Poire, B. A. (2002). Eating disorders and mother-daughter communication: A test of inconsistent nurturing as control theory. *Journal of Family Communication, 2*(2), 59–78.

Stern, D. M. (2015). Engaging autoethnography: Feminist voice and narrative intervention. *Women and Language, 38*(1), 83–102.

Tootle, W., Ziegler, J., & Singer, M. (2015). Individuals are continents; or, why it's time to retire the island approach to addiction. *Substance Use & Misuse*, online. 1-7. Doi: 10.3109/10826084.1007684

White, J. M., & Klein, D. M. (2002). *Family theories* (2nd ed.). Thousand Oaks, CA: Sage.

Wilbers, L. E. (2015). She has a pain problem, not a pill problem: Chronic pain management, stigma, and the family—an autoethnography. *Humanity and Society, 39*(1), 86–111.

Yerby, J. (1995). Family systems theory reconsidered: Integrating social construction theory and dialectical process. *Communication Theory, 5*(4), 339–365.

CHAPTER 28

Relationship Wreckage and Recovery in an Alcoholic Family

Brendan Young – *Western Illinois University-Quad Cities*

ABSTRACT

The Browns seemed to be a typical family. Thomas and Lily met in college and later fell in love. They married, had two children, and were financially secure. The Browns, however, had a secret: Thomas could not control his drinking. Ultimately Thomas's problem became public. This case study illustrates how family members respond differently to alcohol use disorder and to recovery.

CASE STUDY

In 2017, according to the Center for Behavioral Health Statistics and Quality (2018), among adults in the United States, 26.4% had binged on alcohol in the previous month and 6.7% reported heavy alcohol use (i.e., binging for five or more days in that time). Further, the prevalence of 12-month alcohol use disorder (AUD) has been increasing dramatically, rising to 49.4% from 8.5% in 2001–2002 to 12.7% in 2012–2013 (Grant et al., 2017). The impact of problematic alcohol use stretches beyond the drinker. An estimated 10.5% of all children live with a parent who, in the previous 12 months, had an alcohol use disorder (Center for Behavioral Health Statistics and Quality, 2012). In short, problematic alcohol use is a problem for many people—for the alcoholic but also for the family of the alcoholic—and it is a growing problem. The following case exemplifies the role of communication in alcoholism and recovery.

THEY MEET

"That one's HOT!" Lily Norris, unsteady on her feet, laughed and pointed with her beer at a tall young man several feet away. She had not realized how loud she had said it, but she was too buzzed to care when Thomas Brown turned his head toward her and smiled, before resuming his conversation with his fraternity brothers. Lily's girlfriends hustled her across the crowded parking lot of tailgating students and alumni, toward the nearest stadium entrance. The football game would be starting within the hour and they wanted a good spot in the student section.

Lily was a college sophomore and Thomas was a junior. Although they did not technically "meet" at that first encounter, they became aware of each other then and would make eye contact when they passed each other on the rolling campus of the large state school they attended. They finally spoke to each other early the following semester at a fraternity mixer, but Thomas was in a relationship and Lily was focused on her studies and not looking for romance. They liked each other well enough to call themselves friends, but that was all.

Upon graduation, Thomas moved to the largest city in the state to see what job his business degree would gain him. He had lost track of Lily, when they ran into each other at a wedding a couple of years later. Mutual college friends were marrying. Lily had just completed her first year of law school. Thomas had not seriously dated anyone since his extended breakup with the college girlfriend the previous year and Lily was more open to dating now that she had secured a spot in a good law school. They looked good together and each relied on the other as their "plus-one" date for social functions.

Within a year, and without being intentional about it, Thomas and Lily realized they were a couple and moved in together. Thomas advanced in his career as a consultant and Lily established herself with the public defender's office, her first step toward her ambition: a more lucrative career as a litigator in private practice. They loved each other, but perhaps as important, they were comfortable together. Nearly all of their friends were paired up and starting families, so by the time they reached their late twenties, people frequently asked when they would marry.

THEY MARRY

Although both were career-focused, they both also liked children and spoke in general terms of having a family someday. Aware of her biological clock, and aware that having children would not be easier after she started private practice, it was Lily who finally broached the topic of marriage. Thomas was persuaded and they set a date. Neither had enough time to plan the event, so they overspent on a destination wedding at a resort in Napa Valley.

They were well-liked and both were respected in their careers, so they had an impressive turnout at their wedding. The only stain on an otherwise perfect occasion was Thomas's bachelor party. Two of his old fraternity brothers returned a drunk Thomas to their bridal suite at 3 a.m., who was sick the rest of the night and terribly hungover the next day—their wedding day. Thomas later explained that his friends repeatedly ordered flights of local wines before switching to harder alcohol. He minimized the episode and did not apologize. He saw no need to do so, given that it was a bachelor party, and he knew his boss (who had left the party around 11 p.m.) would see it that way too. Lily was mostly irritated, because they had much to do before, during, and after the ceremony and she needed Thomas's help. Although her mother said nothing, Lily could tell she was concerned. But Lily's mother had a brief, and bad, first marriage to an alcoholic, so Lily thought she was too sensitive about other people's drinking. Back home the next week, Lily was reminded of her mother's disapproving look as she reviewed the photos, trying to select the few in which Thomas looked semi-healthy and sober.

The small Brown family was happy and busy for the next few months, when Lily discovered she was expecting a child. She gave birth to a healthy baby girl, Julia, and during her maternity leave she began reviewing online listings for homes in the suburbs. They had talked about wanting a yard and a dog and their apartment in town would allow for neither. Thomas was too busy at his job to look at houses, so after Lily returned to work and established a regular (if busy) schedule, she hired a realtor to arrange visits to homes for sale within their budget.

Thomas arrived home one evening with a bottle of champagne, looking happier and more excited than she had seen him since Julia's birth. "I got a promotion! We're moving!" he shouted. John made a good salary and worked at least 10 hours every day, so Lily assumed he was good at his job. She hugged him and told him how proud she was, as he popped the cork and filled two glasses.

"That's great!" said Lily. "I've already looked at three houses and one of them might be perfect for us."

Thomas cocked his head. "How could you have looked at houses? I haven't told you where we're moving to."

It was Lily's turn to look surprised. "I told you I've been looking at houses with yards."

"Did you? Well it doesn't matter. We're leaving town. I've been offered the Chicago office."

Lily's surprise was turning to irritation. She set down her glass. "Chicago office? You never told me you were even considering relocating."

"I think I did. Or at least you knew I wanted to go higher than I could go in this city." Thomas offered a consolation, "Anyway, you've been wanting to leave the public defender and Chicago has some of the best law firms in the world. It will be a great move for both of us."

Lily felt confused, overwhelmed, and emotional. "Maybe, but dammit Thomas, you should have told me this was a possibility. I've been house-hunting here." Her voice was rising.

Thomas's tone met hers: "Don't play dumb. This is the opportunity I've been working for since we've been together. And maybe you should have told me you were looking at houses. After all, I do live here." He said the last sentence louder than he'd meant to.

Julia began crying. As Lily turned to leave the room, she said nothing. Tears were forming in her own eyes. Although she and Thomas did not speak the rest of the night, they both knew it had been their first big fight. Lily feared the foundation of her marriage might have shifted, but she dismissed the thought.

THEY DRIFT APART

After Thomas overcame his initial disappointment that his good news did not elicit the response he expected from his wife, he focused his attention on succeeding in his new position in Chicago. He would be in charge of a team of elite business consultants who would travel as needed to consult for global corporate clients. It was exciting work. Lily, however, was in a double-bind. If she refused to move and confronted Thomas about making unilateral decisions that affected them all, she would feel like she was being ungrateful and unsupportive. On the other hand, if she said nothing and moved to Chicago, she would abandon her plans for a home and a career in a town where she had spent years cultivating social and career connections. She spent several days saying nothing and weighing her options until the momentum of silence and the possibility that a new and fabulous career could open for her in Chicago led her to start packing.

Similar double-binds became more common in the coming years as a pattern emerged. Thomas would act—or fail to act—and Lily would feel wounded. She would react either by retaliating or remaining silent, but she never felt satisfied with either choice. This interaction pattern was not obvious to her, at least at first. She was too busy with the move and settling in. Although Thomas was earning a better salary, Lily would not have a job at first, and they would be unable to afford the house they wanted in Chicago's expensive suburbs. The money she had saved for a down payment instead was used to purchase a mid-sized condominium near the red line, to ease Thomas's commute to work.

Over Thomas's reservations, Lily did buy a dog. As Thomas established himself in his new office, she busied herself with dog training, setting up their new home, and taking care of Julia. After a few months, she began working her college and law school connections to set up job interviews. She was ready to get back to the courtroom. At her third interview, she felt ill. She attributed her queasiness to nerves, but soon discovered it was morning sickness. She was less excited about her second pregnancy, although their new son, Michael, brought them both a great deal of joy on his arrival.

Thomas and Lily never formally decided she would remain a stay-at-home mother. In truth, they never really discussed the future. Thomas might have encouraged Lily's career ambitions if they had, but she felt keenly the inertia of taking care of the home, the children, the dog, and the various social and volunteer obligations she was committed to. She tried not to think of her abbreviated legal career, but she could not avoid the questions of her contemporaries who asked when she would resume working. "Someday soon," she replied. Eventually, they stopped asking.

For his part, Thomas felt he was a good provider, a good father. After his initial burst of enthusiasm over his Chicago relocation, he realized how much extra work the promotion brought. Despite his career and financial success, as he approached 40, he became more exhausted, more stressed out, and more often absent from home, sometimes for weeks. The travel was exciting at first, but lately even the trips to Europe and Asia were tedious and he missed his children. And he missed Lily, but they talked exclusively about perfunctory things on the phone, and no longer had their previous meaningful and intimate conversations, even during their family vacations.

Thomas had always enjoyed drinking, and he switched from beer in his twenties to cocktails in his thirties. Drinking marked the end of a long day and helped him to destress. By his late thirties, he felt he needed stronger drinks to quickly shift him from his 110% intensity at work to sleep mode. Lily noticed and it bothered her. At first, she criticized his drinking, urging him to cut down or quit altogether, but these comments just made him defensive or led him to retreat to the office. She switched tactics and played the martyr, pointing out how hard she worked to make a home for their family and implying that his absence, inattention, and drunkenness ruined it for everyone. Over time, she opted for silence, and the distance she imposed in self-defense was interpreted by Thomas as a lack of interest in him or their relationship.

Thomas started drinking earlier in the afternoon, even when he worked until 8 p.m. Coworkers noticed, but it did not bother them as long as Thomas continued his good work. They also said nothing. Moving between these realms of silence, Thomas felt increasingly isolated from everyone, even his children, who seemed to thrive whether or not he was there. Drinking was a comfort, as well as a sleep aid, so he drank more.

THEY FALL APART

Thomas's ambition was to move into an upper management position which would, he thought, allow him to work less because those in upper management did little actual consulting and instead elicited contracts and coordinated the consulting teams' efforts from their home base. When a vice president retired after a long career, Thomas felt he was in line for the position and was bitterly disappointed when management instead hired someone from outside the firm. He complained bitterly. "It's because I'm so good at my job," he slurred. "They know our production would go down if I moved up."

Lily considered her response for a moment, then plunged ahead. She was tired of hearing his complaints, and if their conversation ended in sullen silence or a fight, she wanted to get it over with. "Maybe," she said softly.

"What's THAT supposed to mean?" Thomas knew what it meant, but he was daring her to say it. He wanted to fight somebody. Anybody.

"Maybe if you…took better care of yourself you would have been considered for the position." He stared at her malevolently before drinking down the rest of his vodka rocks and leveling a stare at her. She pressed on: "Maybe they don't want to promote a drunk to help run the company."

He exploded, "Don't get high-and-mighty with me! You were drunk the first time I laid eyes on you!"

This was true, Lily acknowledged, but also irrelevant. "You should take a good look in the mirror. You are 40 years old. You act like a child. Grow up and maybe you'll get what you want." He slammed the door as he left, waking the children and scaring the dog. She did not know where he went. She realized absently that she did not really care.

Lily had grown skilled at shielding the children from the worst of their father's drinking, but it required constant vigilance. His work schedule made this easier, as he often was not home. When he was on trips, she would arrange for him to phone earlier in the evening, when he was less likely to be sloppy. The children had learned to gauge his intoxication level by his voice, just as she had learned. And if he called late, she would let it go to voicemail, preferring to deal with his subsequent anger than expose his maudlin monologues to children who found them embarrassing. When he was home, or when they went on vacations, Julia and Michael watched him as closely as their mother did, although they learned to do so without drawing attention. Following their mother's lead, they never invited friends over when Thomas might come home.

The tense equilibrium might have sustained if Thomas's drinking had not spiraled out of control. Lily could not determine whether his tolerance shifted or he was drinking more, but by the time Julia was 12, silence and secrecy were harder to maintain. Thomas showed up, late and drunk, to his daughter's dance recital. From backstage Julia heard him loudly slurring, "Where do I sit?" during the performance of the beginner's class. She heard him stumble as he tried to locate a vacant folding chair. Julia's classmates giggled, but did not know who he was. She did not tell them. During and after her own performance, he hooted and called her name like he was at a basketball game. She was mortified and ran off stage as soon as she could.

At home, Julia poured all the alcohol in the house down the drain and would not talk to her father for a week. When Thomas sobered up, Lily told him what he had done and how he embarrassed himself, his daughter, and the whole family. He minimized her concern, saying she and Julia were being too sensitive and emotional. Lily—ever the lawyer—deployed the evidence. She had filmed him and she made him watch it. He wept. He apologized. He promised to make it up to Julia and to all of them. His shame led him to contemplate suicide, but he pulled himself together and resolved to stop drinking. He was drunk again within two days, although he made a greater, if ultimately unsuccessful, effort to hide it.

From that point, Julia, like her mother before her, threw herself into her studies. The chaos of her home life led her to focus her efforts on manufacturing perfection in all the other realms of her life, including dancing and school. Lily worried her daughter might be developing an eating disorder. Michael, always a quiet child, seemed to take everything in stride. Or that was what Lily thought until she was tidying his room and found a bag of marijuana stuffed in one of his socks. Michael was only 12 years old.

Despite the best efforts of the entire family to control Thomas's drinking, nothing worked. They may have continued on this path had Thomas not gone too far one night. He had spent Sunday afternoon—sober—with his family, in an attempt to improve their relationships. He caught a Sunday night flight to Los Angeles so he could meet early Monday morning with long-time clients. He started drinking at O'Hare and continued drinking steadily during the five-hour flight. He had just turned his rental car onto West Century

Boulevard when he sideswiped a convertible. The police arrived and he was charged with multiple offenses, including driving under the influence. He missed his meeting on Monday morning because he was still in jail.

THEY START RECOVERING

Thomas's arrest and its aftermath were nightmarish for everyone. Thomas, in the worst shape of his life physically and emotionally, was the least capable among them to process what was happening. News of his arrest spread fast among his coworkers and through his and Lily's social networks and extended families. Thomas was in a good deal of legal trouble, was in danger of losing his job, and still had a drinking problem. Ironically, though, as Thomas hit rock bottom he simultaneously felt a strange elation because he no longer had to lie about his drinking or try to hide it: everybody he cared about knew. Yet when he considered the humiliation he had brought to the people he loved most, he contemplated suicide. He saw no future and could not bear the present. But his attorney recommended he enter an inpatient treatment program in the hope that the judge might view this action favorably. His boss agreed to let the firm pay for treatment, a gesture which gratified Thomas. Thomas agreed to go, if only to buy some time until he figured out a way forward—or a way out.

The first couple of days in treatment required a supervised detox, which was excruciating. The subsequent week he rapidly alternated between suicidal depression, as he considered what he had done to his family and firm, and elation, as he realized he was one of many who suffers from addiction. The realization that he was not uniquely afflicted was a revelation. Over the course of treatment, Thomas became as close to his fellow patients as he had been to his fraternity brothers in college. By the end of the second week, his family was allowed to visit. It was an awkward visit, but their relationships had been strained for years, so it was no more awkward than usual.

Upon release from inpatient treatment, Thomas continued with intensive outpatient treatment for several weeks before gradually stepping down to ongoing cognitive behavioral therapy supplemented with 12-step group participation at least twice a week. Thomas did not love all aspects of recovery, and he frequently stumbled, lashing out inappropriately or indulging in self-pity. Recovery required a great deal of his time and energy and he resented the legal system which seemed to have no interest in meeting him halfway by removing some of the hurdles he was facing. He was attempting to do the right thing, and he had unrealistic expectations that others—including his firm and his family—would applaud his good intentions and sincere efforts. He was disappointed when they did not.

Thomas had a long talk with his boss about his career. Since Thomas had been such an asset to the firm for so long, his boss offered him his old position after he cleared up his legal problems and demonstrated he could remain sober. Thomas was surprised and flattered, but turned down the offer. He perceived—correctly—that the stress of his job contributed to his cycle of addiction. He asked instead if he could move into a lower-level position as a workaday consultant for mid-size clients in the Chicagoland area. His boss agreed.

True to form, Lily supported this decision, but resented it because Thomas made the decision without consulting her. It meant a significant reduction in their income at a time when they had multiple unbudgeted expenses. She should, at least, have been told before-hand. Like Thomas, Lily had unrealistic expectations. She thought the sobriety and the new position would keep him home most nights, but she found that between his therapy and his meeting attendance he missed many family meals. Lily was smart enough to realize, however, that she might also have resented him hovering around the house every night. Over many years, she and the children had developed their own routine and their own way of interacting with, and without, their father. As much as she embraced his efforts to be a better husband and father, part of her also perceived yet another example of Thomas act-ing without warning, leaving the family yet again scrambling to accommodate him.

Like Thomas, Lily would occasionally lash out. When she did, she surprised herself with the bitterness in her voice. She was alternately fearful and resentful that Thomas seemed to be improving while she felt even angrier than she had felt while he was drinking. Previously, she could at least blame the alcohol for his neglect. The children pulled away from their angry mother and continued to feel awkward around a father they no longer recognized. Lily did not know whether to attribute their distance to the shifting family dy-namic or to the teenage years they had both entered. On bad days, she blamed Thomas. Then she felt guilty. When he suggested she try therapy or attend an Al-Anon, she again lashed out: "I'm not the one with a problem!" As he continued to improve, however, she wondered, "Am I the one with a problem?"

DISCUSSION QUESTIONS

1. The disease model of the early 20th century attempted to reduce stigma by redefining alcoholism as a health problem rather than a moral failing. Later, family systems theory (Bowen, 1974) and family systems therapy (O'Farrell & Clements, 2012) expanded the focus, claiming the alcohol problem was not an individual problem but a family problem. What are the advantages of framing Thomas's drinking as a family problem rather than a personal problem? Can you think of reasons family members might resist this broader focus?

2. Punctuation is one of the axioms of systems theory (Watzlawick, Beavin, & Jackson, 1967) and explains how labeling one behavior as a "cause" and another behavior an "effect" is ultimately arbitrary. The demand-withdraw pattern of conflict is typical (Caughlin & Scott, 2010; Schrodt, Witt, & Shimkowski, 2014). In the Brown family, who was demanding and who was withdrawing? Do you see other patterns? In general, are people more likely to see their own behavior as cause or consequence of another's behavior?

3. Systems theory also proposes that family systems are goal-oriented (von Bertalanffy, 1968). One Brown family goal was keeping Thomas's drinking a secret from outsiders. Using communication privacy management theory (Petronio, 2010) describe the (co)owners of the information, the boundaries, the permeability of the boundaries, and the boundary coordination strategies. Can you identify other family goals during Thomas's drinking or during his attempt at recovery?

4. Systems are self-regulating, meaning they have self-correcting (communication) mechanisms to restore equilibrium. How does system self-regulation explain Lily's negative communication while Thomas is trying to recover? Does your explanation confirm or contradict the explanation offered by inconsistent nurturing as control theory (Duggan, Dailey, & Le Poire, 2008; Le Poire, 1995)?

5. Models of health behavior change tend to focus on behavior choices of individuals. Do the transtheoretical model (Prochaska & DiClemente, 1984), the theory of planned behavior (Ajzen, 1991), and the extended parallel process model (Witte, 1992) offer effective behavior change strategies for individuals with compulsive behaviors like substance use disorders? Can these models be adapted for use with alcoholic family systems? Why or why not?

REFERENCES

Ajzen, I. (1991). The theory of planned behavior. *Organizational Behavior and Human Decision Processes, 50*, 179–211.

Bowen, M. (1974). Alcoholism as viewed through family systems theory and family psychotherapy. *Annals of the New York Academy of Sciences, 233*(1), 115–122. doi:10.1111/j.1749-6632.1974.tb40288.x

Caughlin, J. P., & Scott, A. M. (2010). Toward a communication theory of the demand/withdraw pattern of interaction in interpersonal relationships. In S. W. Smith & S. R. Wilson (Eds.), *New directions in interpersonal communication research* (pp. 180–200). Thousand Oaks, CA: Sage.

Center for Behavioral Health Statistics and Quality. (2012). *Data spotlight: More than 7 million children live with a parent with alcohol problems*. Rockville, MD: Substance Abuse and Mental Health Services Administration.

Center for Behavioral Health Statistics and Quality. (2018). *2017 national survey on drug use and health: Detailed tables*. Rockville, MD: Substance Abuse and Mental Health Services Administration.

Duggan, A. P., Dailey, R. M., & Le Poire, B. A. (2008). Reinforcement and punishment of substance abuse during ongoing interactions: A conversational test of inconsistent nurturing as control theory. *Journal of Health Communication, 13*(5), 417–433. doi:10.1080/10810730802198722

Grant, B. F., Chou, S. P., Saha, T. D., Pickering, R. P., Kerridge, B. T., Ruan, W. J., ... Fan, A. (2017). Prevalence of 12-month alcohol use, high-risk drinking, and DSM-iv alcohol use disorder in the United States, 2001–2002 to 2012–2013: Results from the national epidemiologic survey on alcohol and related conditions. *JAMA Psychiatry, 74*(9), 911–923. doi:10.1001/jamapsychiatry.2017.2161

Le Poire, B. A. (1995). Inconsistent nurturing as control theory: Implications for communication-based research and treatment programs. *Journal of Applied Communication Research, 23*(1), 60–74. doi:10.1080/00909889509365414

O'Farrell, T. J., & Clements, K. (2012). Review of outcome research on marital and family therapy in treatment for alcoholism. *Journal of Marital and Family Therapy, 38*(1), 122–144. doi:10.1111/j.1752-0606.2011.00242.x

Petronio, S. (2010). Communication privacy management theory: What do we know about family privacy regulation? *Journal of Family Theory & Review, 2*(3), 175–196. doi:10.1111/j.1756-2589.2010.00052.x

Prochaska, J. O., & DiClemente, C. C. (1984). *The transtheoretical approach: Crossing the traditional boundaries of therapy*. Malabar, FL: Krieger.

Schrodt, P., Witt, P. L., & Shimkowski, J. R. (2014). A meta-analytical review of the demand/withdraw pattern of interaction and its associations with individual, relational, and communicative outcomes. *Communication Monographs, 81*(1), 28–58. doi:10.1080/03637751.2013.813632

von Bertalanffy, L. (1968). *General systems theory: Foundations, development, applications*. New York, NY: Braziller.

Watzlawick, P., Beavin, J., & Jackson, D. D. (1967). *Pragmatics of human communication*. New York, NY: W. W. Norton & Company.

Witte, K. (1992). Putting the fear back into fear appeals: The extended parallel process model. *Communication Monographs, 59*, 329–349.

Part VI

HEALTH AND THE FAMILY

Finding Strength in Methodology: Confronting Trauma and Embracing Love for a Sibling with Severe Disabilities

Sean Fourney – *University of Southern Mississippi*

ABSTRACT

The following is a layered account of loving and leaving a sibling with severe mental disabilities. While traditional research ethics separate the researcher from the subject to ensure impartiality, autoethnographies treat the researcher as the subject and embrace personal narratives as worthy scholarship. I take readers through a nonlinear timeline of past and present experiences of trauma, stigma, and joy in being a big brother to someone who needs constant supervision and protection from himself. Although my experiences are not the norm, this story is woven with research from disability and stigma scholars that illuminate my world to let me know that I am not alone in this journey. In the spirit of reflexivity, I discuss my anxiety about not only opening up about my relationship with my brother but also my reluctance to use a criticized methodology like autoethnography.

CASE STUDY

It is the late summer of 2015, and I am in Brooklyn, New York, lying in bed with a girl that I met a month or so ago at a friend's wedding. We are watching *Catfish*. This isn't the eponymous TV show, however, which I have seen a few times. This is the movie that started it all, a true "love story" where individuals track down potential romantic interests whom they have never physically met but with whom they share an extensive online relationship. She tells me it's really good and that I have to watch it, so I reluctantly agree. She is a friend of a friend, and our relationship was more like a fling—in my mind at least—because in less than a month I will be moving over 1,100 miles away to pursue a doctorate degree in communication studies. I would rather spend time with friends and family than watch a movie that appears to have no new surprises. I didn't know it at the time, but I wish I was right about the no new surprises.

As the story unwinds, it is the story I knew was coming: man stumbles upon a beautiful girl through the world wide web, man seeks to contact the girl, girl never seems to be where she says she is, and man physically tries to track down the girl. What is all too familiar to me, though, is the revelation of the girl's "real" life. In the closing scenes, the filmmakers peer inside the home they thought housed a beautiful young artist to find something completely different, something hidden too often from mainstream society: a middle-aged woman who cares for two severely mentally disabled stepsons, one of whom hits his head with his own hands while being confined to a chair-like, self-safety device. I immediately get physically hot despite being next to an air conditioner's breeze and hold the girl's hand so tight that she pulls away. I am instantly depressed and short of breath. The heat of my body disorients my thoughts, and I can't speak.

"What's the matter?" she asks.

"I…I know a little bit about that feeling is all," I manage to mutter.

Actually, I know too much about that feeling. No, I don't make up fake profiles online to fulfill a romantic or egotistical fantasy, but I can relate to *Catfish* in another way. I have a sibling with severe mental disabilities who for most of his life has had self-injurious behaviors and cannot communicate beyond basic needs or through the imitation of others.

***

This is the story of my experiences with a sibling who has severe mental disabilities portrayed through an autoethnographic lens. Autoethnographies provide scholarship through author reflexivity and cathartic storytelling. Although quantitative research and generalizability is typically preferred in the social sciences (Anderson & Middleton, 2014), qualitative methods—specifically autoethnographies—make sense of difficult experiences by empowering authors and audiences to confront challenging realities (Wall, 2006). These accounts provide not only a release for the author but are also a reflection of the institutions that situate and shape identity (Dillon, 2012). Thus, a key strength of autoethnography lies in its ability to provide rich understandings of contextualized experience. Using Ronai's (1992) layered account methodology, I am able to display a lived and multiperspective reality that is reflected through "emotion, systematic introspection, self as subject and object, fantasies, abstract theoretical thinking, and statistics . . . a layered account makes accessible to the reader as many ways of knowing as possible" (p. 397). Although some forms of inquiry —like surveys and questionnaires—may provide a gauge for objectively measuring my difficulty in expressing this subject, they cannot contain the people, places, and events that contextualize the pain and happiness of living with and wondering about a sibling with severe mental disabilities.

***

It is January 15, 2016, one day before I end my winter break and fly back to my new home in the South to begin my second semester of my doctoral pursuit. My dad, my mom, my brother, and I are walking from the gastroenterologist's office to the blood laboratory at a prominent hospital in Philadelphia, Pennsylvania. Nathaniel, my brother, had a good checkup, as usual, which means he was well-behaved and let the doctor look at him without physically attacking himself or others in the room. For some reason, he likes to show off and be nice and courteous to doctors, even volunteering to open his mouth for a look at his throat or pulling up his sleeve to have his blood pressure checked. Despite the positive checkup, it is yet another reminder that we are still no closer to finding out why he is in pain.

"Doctor, we don't know what ails him, but we do know that when he hits his head, he is in pain," my mother would say.

"Let's try a different medication," said the female doctor.

These words have been repeated so many times by so many doctors in New York, Philadelphia, and in Baltimore that I sometimes feel it would be more appropriate for us to wear a shirt with them emblazoned on it, explaining to the gawkers everywhere that we don't like it when he hits his head, either. We are not the only family to experience this, though. Green, Darling, and Wilbers (2013) confirmed what every family with disabled children already knows: No one knows nothing. Excuse the double negative, but it is appropriate for my frustration. In studies compiled from 1960 to 2012, Green et al. (2013) found that receiving no diagnosis or a delayed diagnosis for a child with a disability was a continual theme in responses from parental caregivers. Furthermore, Resch et al. (2010) revealed through focus groups that parents of the disabled were either turned away or shuttled between professionals in an endless cycle of bewilderment. Medical professionals are sometimes just as baffled as families are when it comes to diagnosing or caring for someone with a disability.

While my dad goes to get coffee for us and my mom is scheduling another appointment, it is just Nate and I waiting in line at the blood lab. It is exceptionally busy, and we have to stand outside the immediate room in a hallway where the hospital's occupants walk by. I assume the ready position behind him and lightly hold his arms in hopes of intercepting an unexpected fist to his head. As Nate waddles back and forth (he cannot sit or stand still, ever) and tosses his toy ball up and down in a rhythmic state (which cannot be duplicated by anyone in our family), each passing person stares. Some do the classic stare that we all do—once caught staring, you quickly look away but give one more glimpse before passing by. Others smile and nod at me as if to say, "You are commendable for taking care of someone with special needs." It always feels like more than a few, however, stare as though they have never seen someone with Down syndrome, autism, or who wears a helmet for protection from themselves. I understand my brother is not the norm, but it infuriates me to see these reactions. Expressing anger is a delicate act, and I have not been good at it, to say the least. In this way, Nate and I are very similar: although our physical and mental capabilities are strikingly different, our emotional expressions are poorly developed, animalistic, and relationally damaging. Autoethnographies address areas like these that are often difficult to express or even access because we have been socialized to repress them (Ellis, 2004). Thus, by confronting why I cannot communicate about my relationship with Nate, I may be able to understand why it is that we cannot as a society appropriately handle sensitive issues like disability and stigma.

***

The United States has displayed a historically ambivalent attitude toward individuals with mental disabilities (Dinitz, Dynes, & Clarke, 1969; Lippman, 1972). Beginning in the middle of the 19th century, the U.S. began institutionalizing the mentally handicapped with the intention of improving mental hygiene (Davis, 1938). A major shift in attitudes soon formed, though, after rehabilitation largely failed and society felt threatened by the release of the mentally disabled into the general public (Schutt, 2011). Pity for the disabled increased, however, so much so that "funny farms" were built as the "idea grew that the retarded should be viewed as innocent victims of fate or parental sin, and that instead of schooling, loving care and protection should be best bestowed upon them" (Wolfensberger, 1975, p. 28). An increase in funding for Medicaid coupled with advances in psychiatry in the 1950s and 60s, though, allowed the government to fund outpatient community health centers and group homes to care for the mentally disabled in a more social atmosphere (Rodger, 2002). Unsurprisingly, this was met with reluctance, as one Northeastern newspaper editorial casually noted in the mid-1970s: "Like prisons, homes for the retarded, and waste disposal facilities, power plants have become unwelcome, however necessary in many communities" (Sarason & Doris, 1979, p. 104). Deinstitutionalization, however, brought the disabled back into residential areas and into group homes for increased social interaction and development in the late 20th century.

Disability, then, is not just a physical or mental issue but a societal one that continually displays how we interpret the "imperfect." For famed sociologist Erving Goffman, a physical imperfection represented *stigma*, or a mark that is "deeply discrediting" (Goffman, 1963, p. 3). Individuals with intellectual and cognitive disabilities follow a similar fate (Mercer, 1973). The mentally disabled are not only identified for their stigma but are evaluated negatively for it, which aids in the "perpetuation of the social classes" (Farber, 1968, p. 19). Indeed, Smith (2007) showed that stigma is a communicative reality initiating from a mark (physical or ideological) of the disabled, a receiver's reaction to the mark, and a labeling and storing of stigma attitudes that reinforce group membership. In other words, "the labeling process brings attention to the group's stigma, stresses that this is a separate social entity, and helps to differentiate the stigmatized group from the normal" (Smith, 2007, p. 469). This is exactly how I feel in public situations with Nate. I am keenly aware of his disability, but I'm even more aware that others are aware.

***

"You hold this side and I'll hold the other," my mom said, as we both crammed into Nate's full-sized bed for another night. Since his cataract surgery, it is imperative that he does not touch his eyes in order for them to heal properly. This is a serious problem, though, because Nate has self-injurious behaviors. Just saying "self-injurious behaviors" embarrasses me because hurting oneself just doesn't make sense, and I can't believe that my brother does it, and I can't stop it. I then get depressed and wonder whether this process is even worth it. Do I actually want to submit this to a journal to be judged? Autoethnographers call this double victimization because after divulging sensitive and exhaustive material about one's life, the author is often scrutinized for not conforming to classic methodology or conventional storylines of what learned readers want (Ellis, 2004). However, I remind myself to be brave and go forward because it is the purpose of an autoethnography to "open up old wounds but also manifest the energy to heal them completely" (Custer, 2014, p. 9).

Nate will typically attack himself with an open hand or closed fist. It strikes his ears, temples, cheeks, or the outside of his eyes repeatedly. When he is out of sight, which is extremely rare and admittedly negligent, his attacks on himself can sound like his famous ball juggling. This can cause confusion, which exhausts us in making sure it is not the worst-case scenario. I cannot take the ball away from him, though. He loves it and will not go anywhere without it. In this regard, he is like the rest of the men in the family. I can recall my grandmother on many occasions claiming that my father "could always be heard in the neighborhood dribbling a basketball." I keep the tradition going by squeezing a tennis ball in my car, and Nate is our sports-balls insurance salesman—he incessantly hides them under furniture all around the house just in case disaster strikes and one is lost.

We can take no chances with him after this surgery, though. His eyes must heal properly, and that requires us to sleep with him for a few weeks to make sure that he does not hit them. The mental and physical toll this takes on our family is immeasurable. It is ever-present, and to remedy this, I have proposed tying his hands behind his back. Seriously. I call it tough love, but my mom considers that proposal extremely cruel. Once, when I did tie his hands (my mom wasn't home), he started to bang his head against anything near him, including bedposts and doorknobs. I have a suspicion that he did this in part to show me that I couldn't stop him from doing what he wanted to do. Our Irish stubbornness even resides in Nate, I guess. I think my mom eventually considered tying his hands, too. I knew this not because she said so but because I could see the exhaustion on her face.

"We have to do something," I said, defeated.

***

Individuals who have self-injurious behaviors (SIB) like Nate typically cannot communicate why they do what they do, which makes understanding SIB so frustrating and saddening. The most common forms of SIB are head banging, pulling out one's hair, hitting one's head with a hand, ingesting inedible objects, and self-scratching and biting (Tureck, Matson, & Beighley, 2013). Symons, Devine, and Oliver (2012) call them "one of the most distressing and intractable problems in the field of intellectual disability" (p. 421). Some consequences of SIB are bruises and bleeding to the face, teeth dislodgement, and even blindness (Hyman, Fisher, Mercugliano, & Cataldo, 1990). To compound this, Nate also has Down syndrome and autism spectrum disorder, or as my mom calls it, "the double whammy." While research shows that SIB can be minimized through functional communicative therapy that replaces harmful behaviors with prosocial behaviors (Boesch, Taber-Doughty, Wendt, & Smalts, 2015), our attempts to get Nate to say "no," clap his hands, or point to pictures when we miscommunicate have produced little effectiveness over the last 20 years.

Nate's SIB could come at any moment, but they were usually triggered by something in his environment. Usually these situations stemmed from too much stimuli for him to respond to, such as strangers wanting his attention, obligations to open presents that are wrapped tightly, turning off music or TV, bypassing McDonald's on our trips, waiting to eat food that had to cool, or receiving too many questions from those who didn't understand that he cannot understand. I cringe at the thought of these public moments. I don't mind holding Nate at all to protect him, myself, or others. I hate others seeing me do it. It somehow reflects that my family and I did something wrong, or that we couldn't overcome this, and we have to resort to the extreme. Researchers call this affiliated stigma which negatively affects siblings and parents of the stigmatized more than other nondisabled individuals (Davis & Salkin, 2005; Werner & Shulman, 2015). A friend of mine once remarked after seeing Nate in arm splints that he "couldn't imagine what you deal with." To be honest, it felt good to just talk about it. The simple act of sharing is what most caregivers of the disabled are looking for, yet so rarely find (Faw & Leustek, 2015).

***

It is my sophomore year of college at Temple University in the fall of 2005, and one of my friends is coming from my hometown of the Lehigh Valley to pick me up for a road trip. We are off to see my best friend at the University of Maryland for the weekend, and it is a trip I had been looking forward to for a while. After surviving freshman year and securing a sense of adulthood with an off-campus apartment, I felt more and more like I was coming into my own. I had spent so much time caring for and worrying about Nate prior to college that I was taken aback that I could actually have my own life in college. I sometimes felt like I had to make up for lost time, and so I did what I thought every college kid was supposed to do—party. Even back in high school, on the rare occasion that I did get to party, I had to go all out because I never knew how much time I would have around others. Between caring for Nate and the watch of an overprotective mother, there wasn't much time for social interaction.

The trip was supposed to be a joyous occasion, yet I was thinking of someone who couldn't enjoy these same moments. Throughout the night, I drank more and more as we went from house party to house party. The beginning moments of meeting new people is always fun for me, and I think this stems from my lack of social interaction growing up. On this night, though, the excitement began to wane. As I continued to drink, I started to get angry, and then I got sad. I was thinking about Nate. I was thinking about his blindness. Prior to the trip, my parents told me over the phone that he hit himself so many times that he detached his retina. They said the school didn't watch him (years later they won a settlement against the school district, but that can't give him his eye back). While on a bus heading back to my buddy's apartment, I started to cry uncontrollably. For so long, I had felt like scholar and author Ann Bauer, who had an autistic child with violent tendencies. She said she "could not accept what was happening. I could not write about it; I could not speak of it. Not even my closest friends knew what was happening inside my life" (Bauer, 2009, p. 1). This time, however, I could not hold it in anymore.

"It's not fair," I screamed. "It's not fair!"

My two friends did the best they could to console me, but I couldn't stop crying. I couldn't stop thinking about the cruelty of it all. I told them that if God created Nate, who is already limited in every imaginable way, why add one more limitation? I kept picturing Nate looking at me and smiling, bouncing his ball, and laughing at me as I yelled at a basketball game on TV. I kept picturing Nate and me singing anything from Big Poppa by Notorious BIG to Jingle Bells at Christmas. I kept picturing Nate and me going out to the park, or to eat, or to anywhere that wasn't his isolated room. He loves those moments—he'll wait at the bottom of the steps when he knows we are all going out together. I love those moments too. We are the best of friends, and I can't fully explain it, but he listens to me and always behaves. He never hits around me anymore. I can only interpret this through friendship. I take care of Nate—bathe with him, eat with him, dress with him, brush teeth with him, watch TV with him—but I also talk with him. I find little catchphrases that I punctuate with a laugh, like "oh, baby," "bullshit," "Are you a big boy?" and others whose meanings have become symbolic of our relationship over the years. Baumeister and Leary (1995) showed that the desire to have close relationships is innate. Human survival depended upon people loving one another, and, over time, this learned activity became instinctual. Unfortunately, I was not there for Nate that horrible day. I sometimes wonder if instead of hitting himself, he wanted me to take him out or sing him a song. I sometimes wonder if he uttered those catchphrases that day but there was no one there who could understand him.

***

As he would get older and move through puberty, the self-injurious behaviors took a more drastic turn: Nate started hitting others. Children with intellectual disabilities are known for their obsessive behaviors, and when something was out of place or startled the order, Nate would flip. He has cleared restaurant and kitchen tables, broken glass, ruined furniture, pulled hair, dug his nails into us, and made my family bleed for trying to restrain him. In rare cases, such as the 2009 death of Kent State political science professor Trudy Steuernagel at the hands of her autistic son, the reality is unimaginable. To this day, my parents are hesitant to grab him during an episode where he starts hitting himself or clearing an area. They are too afraid of him. When he was in attack mode on himself or others, I felt so embarrassed and enraged that I would immediately pick Nate up through a headlock and throw him on his bed or shove him in a corner very forcefully. There is no way for me or Nate to deal with this verbally, so I'm connecting with him through physicality. I think this may actually have worked, though. I'd get so enraged when he would hit that I would immediately grab his head, jerk it back, and yell, "I've had it with you!" Consequently, he would immediately flinch at the sight of me when he began to hit, place his hand on his chin, and lifts his head upwards to mimic me. He'll also clasp his hands together in front of me, almost as if to say, "Look, I'm behaving."

***

Communication studies' night classes in graduate school are a real treat for me. The topics encompass a wide variety of issues ranging from the important (race relations) to the nerdy (rhetorical analyses of superheroes). Tonight's discussion in *Introduction to Graduate Research* involves a criticized new form of scholarship called autoethnography. Ethnographies are a hallmark of qualitative research because they describe rich scenes of action and grant the public access to cultures that are sometimes hard to reach or understand. Autoethnographies, however, are different in that while they still describe a scene in rich detail, it is nonetheless a scene contained within the author's subjective world. So while ethnographers have people and artifacts that readers can validate, autoethnographers have just themselves as validation. This does not strike me as responsible scholarship.

These concerns were on full display in class tonight as we reviewed Dillon's (2012) autoethnography of fatherhood in academe. I couldn't believe what I was reading. Everything fit together so perfectly. As he explained the struggles of being a parent and a graduate student, he then seamlessly transitioned into—you guessed it—scholarly literature telling us how hard it is to do both of those things! Even more surprising, most of my class loved it. I kept my mouth shut as one by one everyone agreed with its significance.

"It's so well-written," described one older student.

"I didn't know work like this was considered scholarship," said another.

Most graduate courses take place at night, which means students and professors can already be drained from a long day. On nights like this, when everyone seems to be in agreement, it is very tempting to just let this subject resolve itself based on its own momentum—to quote George Costanza—so we can go home and avoid a lengthy conversation. But it is moments like these when graduate school is most fruitful because it questions metatheoretical assumptions on the nature of reality, knowledge, and ethics. We may not think it, but challenging methodology makes you a scholar, and I can't keep my mouth shut tonight.

"I didn't like it," I said during a brief moment of silence. "It's too convenient."

"What is convenient about it?" asked my professor.

"I mean, he's saying whatever he wants to say. He could claim anything he wanted to and then find literature to back it up, and I don't think it's a worthy topic."

"What do you mean it's not worthy?"

"It just sounds like he's telling us how hard he works and how hard it is to have a family while working for a career. What am I missing? Aren't we all doing that right now?"

I really took offense to this study. I mean, he thinks he has it rough? Think about not having the mental or physical capabilities to even enter into a "struggle" of upward mobility, the toll that takes on the loved ones who want nothing more than the best for their family, and the struggle to communicate this in a society that seems ignorant or willfully blind to its existence.

***

Although I lambasted Dillon (2012), I couldn't deny his writing. It was engrossing and human. It had struggles and acknowledgements of imperfection, and, above all, it wanted to communicate them. That is what stuck with me weeks later. For all of our "objectivity" as scholars, the one thing we are dying to hear from others—especially superiors in the classroom—are their feelings during communication challenges, and autoethnography brings that to the forefront. I could have studied Nate in so many different ways, but almost all of them would have situated him as the subject, yet we know it is foolish to think that understanding Nate can only be accomplished by studying Nate. By deciding to finally tackle my reluctance on communicating about him, I found that he resides in me not just because I love him as my brother but because he is what makes me human. He may not have been what we asked for, but he is what we received. Without him, I wouldn't know the highs and lows of humanity. I wouldn't know how to treat people who are not like me, and I wouldn't know what it is like to truly love someone for who they are rather than what you want them to be.

***

I've never been more proud of a piece of scholarship than I am with this autoethnography. To be fair, though, it remains a questioned methodology; despite performing it at The Western States Communication Association in 2017 where a few audience members cried and hugged me afterwards, faculty judges at a recent research symposium at my university appreciated the storytelling but wanted me to advocate for change in the areas of disability and stigma. They said it needed that ending, and while I appreciate their recommendations, I was, in fact, advocating. I was advocating—like others before—that an autoethnography is not only worthy of scholarship but it also advocates that others confront their own insecurities and share some deeply traumatic experiences. Catharsis is real, and hopefully this piece communicates to others that the struggles they have learned to repress do not have to stay that way. Reflexive storytelling showcased in autoethnography "frequently stirs the self-reflection of listeners, a powerful by-product of this research inquiry" (Chang, 2008, p. 53). If I had not read Dillon (2012) and disagreed so vehemently, I never would have gone down this path. I hope someone reads mine and has a similar experience.

As for my relationship with Nate, there are still issues. As my parents get older, they recognize that Nate will need future care when they are gone. I have volunteered for this, but they now know—because of my willingness to finally communicate about the past—that I may not have had the easiest time growing up, and they feel that my own family should not have to take care of Nate. Having met a wonderfully caring and loving woman in my own life, however, gives me hope that this will not be a problem. My girlfriend read this story before ever meeting Nate, and she has been along for the ride ever since. There has been a potential breakthrough in Nate's SIB, too, as the growing wave of medicinal marijuana in America prompted my parents to look into getting some for him. For almost a year now, Nate has been taking liquid drops once a day, and we have seen a tremendous change in behavior and demeanor. He is more social, goes out in public with a care worker from the state on a daily basis, and is less volatile around guests. I've noticed a change in myself, too. Subconsciously, I realize that I probably left home to get away from Nate and pursue my own life. I feel like I have done that now, and after telling this story, I just want to go back to having Nate in my life.

REFERENCES

Anderson, J. A., & Middleton, M. K. (2014). Epistemological movements in communication: An analysis of empirical and rhetorical/critical scholarship. In P. Gehrke & W. Keith (Eds.), *A century of communication studies: The unfinished conversation* (pp. 82–108). New York, NY: Routledge.

Bauer, A. (2009, March 26). The monster inside my son. *Salon*. Retrieved from http:/// www.salon.com/2009/03/26/bauer_autism

Baumeister, R. F., & Leary, M. R. (1995). The need to belong: Desire for interpersonal attachment as a fundamental human motivation. *Psychological Bulletin, 117*(3), 497–529.

Boesch, M. C., Taber-Doughty, T., Wendt, O., & Smalts, S. S. (2015). Using a behavioral approach to decrease self-injurious behavior in an adolescent with severe Autism: A data-based case study. *Education & Treatment of Children, 38*(3), 305–328. doi:10.1353/ etc.2015.0012

Chang, H. (2008). *Autoethnography as method*. Walnut Creek, CA: Left Coast Press.

Custer, D. (2014). Autoethnography as a transformative research method. *The Qualitative Report, 19*(21), 1–13.

Davis, K. (1938). Mental hygiene and the class structure. *Psychiatry, 1*, 55–65.

Davis, C. S., & Salkin, K. A. (2005). Sisters and friends: Dialogue and multivocality in a relational model of sibling disability. *Journal of Contemporary Ethnography, 34*(2), 206–234. doi:10.1177/0891241604272066

Dillon, P. J. (2012). Unbalanced: An autoethnography of fatherhood in academe. *Journal of Family Communication, 12*(4), 284–299. doi:10.1080/15267431.2012.686945

Dinitz, S., Dynes, R. R., & Clarke, A. C. (1969). *Deviance: Studies in the process of stigmatization and societal reaction*. Oxford, England: Oxford University Press.

Ellis, C. (2004). *The ethnographic I: Methodological novel about autoethnography*. Lanham, MD: Altamira Press.

Farber, B. (1968). *Mental retardation: Its social context and social consequences*. Boston, MA: Houghton Mifflin.

Faw, M. H., & Leustek, J. (2015). Sharing the load: An exploratory analysis of the challenges experienced by parent caregivers of children with disabilities. *Southern Communication Journal, 80*(5), 404–415. doi:10.1080/1041794X.2015.1081978

Goffman, E. (1963). *Stigma: Notes on the management of a spoiled identity*. New York, NY: Simon & Schuster.

Green, S. E., Darling, R. B., & Wilbers, L. (2013). Has the parent experience changed over time? A meta-analysis of qualitative studies of parents of children with disabilities from

1960 to 2012. In B. Altman & S. Barnartt (Eds.), *Research in social science and disability* (pp. 97–168). West Yorkshire, England: Emerald Group Publishing.

Hyman, S. L., Fisher, W., Mercugliano, M., & Cataldo, M. F. (1990). Children with self-injurious behavior. *Pediatrics, 85*(3), 437–441.

Lippman, L. D. (1972). *Attitudes toward the handicap: A comparison between Europe and the United States*. Ann Arbor, MI: University of Michigan Press.

Mercer, J. R. (1973). *Labeling the mentally retarded*. Berkeley, CA: University of California Press.

Resch, J. A., Mireles, G., Benz, M. R., Grenwelge, C., Peterson, R., & Zhang, D. (2010). Giving parents a voice: A qualitative study of the challenges experienced by parents of children with disabilities. *Rehabilitation Psychology, 55*(2), 139–150. doi:10.1037/a0019473

Rodger, D. (2002). Deinstitutionalization: Why a much maligned program still has life. *Scientific American, 287*(6), 38.

Ronai, C. (1992). Multiple reflections of child sex abuse: An argument for a layered account. *Journal of Contemporary Ethnography, 23*, 395–426. doi:10.1177/089124195023004001

Sarason, S. B., & Doris, J. (1979). *Educational handicap, public policy, and social history*. New York, NY: Free Press Publishing.

Schutt, R. K. (2011). *Homelessness, housing, and mental illness*. Cambridge, MA: Harvard University Press.

Smith, R. A. (2007). Language of the lost: An explication of stigma communication. *Communication Theory, 17*(4), 462–485. doi:10.1111/j.1468-2885.2007.00307.x

Symons, F. J., Devine, D. P., & Oliver, C. (2012). Self-injurious behavior in people with intellectual disability. *Journal of Intellectual Disability Research, 56*(5), 421–426. doi:10.1111/j.1365-2788.2012.01553.x

Tureck, K., Matson, J. L., & Beighley, J. S. (2013). An investigation of self-injurious behaviors in adults with severe intellectual disabilities. *Research in Developmental Disabilities, 34*(9), 2469–2474. doi:10.1016/j.ridd.2013.05.022

Wall, S. (2006). An autoethnography on learning about autoethnography. *International Journal of Qualitative Methods, 5*(2), 1–12.

Werner, S., & Shulman, C. (2015). Does type of disability make a difference in affiliate stigma among family caregivers of individuals with autism, intellectual disability or physical disability? *Journal of Intellectual Disability Research, 59*(3), 272–283. doi:10.1111/jir.12136

Wolfensberger, W. (1975). *The origin and nature of our institutional models*. Syracuse, NY: Human Policy PR.

CHAPTER 30

"You Don't Have to Be Superwoman!"
Navigating Professional and Chronic Illness Identities in the Family Business

Anne Kerber – *Minnesota State University, Mankato*

ABSTRACT

Under the best of circumstances, how family members communicatively negotiate the intersections of work and home life is fraught with tension. Running a family business, or being one of the 5.5 million American enterprises where multiple family members participate or have controlling interests, complicates matters further. Family businesses create unique communication dynamics that blend the deeply personal work of maintaining relationships with the depersonalized tasks required for organizational success. Yet, such configurations can be disrupted by internal and external stressors, as well as other variables that challenge the organization's stability. This fictionalized case study explores how the members of a small, family-run business grapple with the uncertainty presented by a leader's chronic health condition. The case highlights the intersections of family, organizational, and health communication issues, especially related to understanding the business as a system, managing professional identity, dealing with the stigma surrounding chronic illness, setting and maintaining privacy boundaries, and providing and receiving social support.

The intersections of work and home lives present salient concerns for most families (Wang & Repetti, 2013). On the one hand, economic realities require individuals to work in exchange for resources (e.g., salary, healthcare) that enhance a family's quality of life. Yet, the effort required to secure these resources can be detrimental to family relationships. The boundaries between work and home spheres has become increasingly permeable as organizations demand more of their employees' time and energy to support managerial interests (Russell, 2013; Wieland, 2011). Although the family is considered "the crucible of society," it is often discursively positioned in competition with paid work (Vangelisti, 2013, p. ix). For example, corporate discourses have steadily colonized the personal realm in recent decades, increasingly linking an individual's identity and sense of worth to their career (Deetz, 1992). Because family and work are both highly esteemed cultural institutions, individuals experience tensions for negotiating a "balance" between them. Such tensions can be consequential for personal well-being and relationships. A case in point: Even when self-described workaholics acknowledge the impact of their habits on family relationships, their ability to change can be complicated by financial needs (Russell, 2013). Research also indicates that workers carry job stresses home with them, sparking increased conflict within or social withdrawal from family relationships (Wang & Repetti, 2013).

COMMUNICATING IN A FAMILY-RUN BUSINESS

Family-run businesses, or enterprises where multiple family members participate or have controlling interests, add further complexities to the intersections of work and home (Knapp, Smith, Kreiner, Sundaramurthy, & Barton, 2013). An estimated 5.5 million family businesses, ranging from small firms to large, multinational organizations, collectively contribute an estimated 60% of the United States' gross domestic product (Sundaramurthy & Kreiner, 2008). These organizations blend the deeply personal work of family with the depersonalized tasks required to meet expectations for productivity, efficiency, and other measures of success (Knapp et al., 2013; Sundaramurthy & Kreiner, 2008). In doing so, family-run businesses create unique relational arrangements and pressures. Family members who work together must communicatively negotiate and maintain boundaries "to avoid negative spillover from the emotion of the family into the business and from the stress of the business into the family" (Knapp et al., 2013, p. 333). These individuals may also experience tensions between individuation and belonging as they reconcile personal roles, ambitions, decision-making practices, and values with those of the greater familial and organizational collectives (Hall, 2012). For instance, communication among family members who work together may become strained if an individual is unable or unwilling to meet others' performance expectations. Yet, family businesses also offer important benefits, such as perceptions of motivation, commitment, and trust. These characteristics are essential for developing social capital and long-standing relationships with internal and external stakeholders (Neubaum & Voordeckers, 2018). Additionally, the interconnections between family and business may foster the creation of *voluntary kin*, as long-term associates without blood ties can come to be treated as extended family (Braithwaite et al., 2010).

Researchers have similarly approached the study of families and businesses as systems, reflecting how communication within them is more than the sum of individual relationships. Both families and businesses encompass broader patterns of interaction, as well as collective responses to internal and external stressors, and other variables that affect overall functioning (Pecchioni & Keely, 2011; Poole, 2014; Vangelisti, 2013). Given the interdependence of relationships in both family and organizational systems, one member's health can be a specific variable that influences ongoing interactions, represents an actual or potential threat, or exemplifies challenges to the system's stability (Pecchioni & Keely, 2011).

This case study explores the relational dynamics within a small, family-run business as members communicate about a specific health challenge—a leader's diagnosis of multiple sclerosis. Although the story is fictionalized, it is based on interview data I collected exploring the identity work of professionals living with chronic health conditions. From these stories, I drew a composite sketch of the everyday challenges individuals face as they make choices regarding whether (or not) to share information regarding their health status, partake in (un)supportive interactions, and maintain a professional image.

THE CHRONIC ILLNESS CONTEXT

The term "chronic illness" refers to any condition that lasts for more than one year, requires ongoing medical management, and/or limits an individual's daily activities (Centers for Disease Control and Prevention [CDC], 2017). This definition's breadth means a diverse array of physical and mental health conditions (including, but not limited to, heart disease, diabetes, cancer, rheumatoid arthritis, fibromyalgia, depression, and unexplained recurring pain) are considered chronic. Estimates suggest that more than 60% of American adults experience at least one chronic illness, and 25% have two or more conditions (CDC, 2017). The prevalence of chronic illnesses is expected to continue increasing due to demographic shifts (e.g., the aging of the Baby Boomer generation) and improved disease management (McGonagle & Barnes-Farrell, 2014).

Adapting to the Chronic Illness Identity

Although chronic illnesses have significant physical and mental implications, how they are experienced varies widely. Unlike acute illnesses, chronic illnesses are rarely fully cured, and do not follow a linear progression from diagnosis to treatment and recovery (Checton, Greene, Magsamen-Conrad, & Venetis, 2012). Rather, the symptoms and severity of a chronic illness are characterized by a high degree of variability and uncertainty. Some forms of multiple sclerosis, for example, steadily become more debilitating over time, while others vacillate unpredictably between periods of relapse and remission (National Multiple Sclerosis Society, 2018). The visibility of chronic illnesses also varies. Although there could be some physical manifestations of a chronic health condition (e.g., a limp), others are invisible (e.g., chronic pain; Defenbaugh, 2013). Chronic illnesses can also take a mental toll, as individuals cope and learn to live with the "new normal" imposed by a diagnosis (Hayden, 1993, p. 264). Charmaz (1991) described how chronic illnesses are often viewed as disruptions to life narratives, spurring individuals to (re)consider and seek to maintain control over their identities, goals, and future plans. Coping with a chronic illness is also a relational experience, as people turn to family and friends for physical care and social support following diagnosis (Pecchioni & Keely, 2011). However, there are risks to sharing information about health status in the workplace.

Concealing and Revealing Chronic Illness Identity at Work

Cultural roles socialize us to behave in specific ways when we are sick. Ill individuals are typically expected to step out of social roles (e.g., working, parenting) for a brief period of time to seek treatment and regain a state of good health (Charmaz, 1987). Such norms are aligned with acute illnesses, where cures are anticipated if the patient follows prescribed treatment. Not only do chronic health conditions deviate from expectations regarding recovery, most individuals must eventually attempt to resume their social roles. Chronic illness thus represents a stigma, or an attribute inscribing a spoiled or tainted identity (Goffman, 1963). The stigmatization of illness identities is especially prevalent in the professional sphere, where chronic health issues depart from social norms surrounding productivity and ideal working bodies (McGonagle & Barnes-Farrell, 2014). For example, "bad days" may include flare-ups of physical pain and/or cognitive difficulties that temporarily render a worker unable to perform his or her job. Ongoing medical care and health maintenance can be viewed as disruptive to a worker's regular schedule. Even when a chronic illness does not constrain the ability to work, its presence becomes a source of anxiety as the worker (along with peers and supervisors) must grapple with the condition's uncertainties and future implications.

Given such stigma, it is unsurprising most people use a range of communicative strategies to conceal or minimize illness identities in the workplace. First, individuals may hide or avoid disclosing information about their health status with supervisors and colleagues to minimize threats to their professional identity (Butler & Modaff, 2016; Myers, 2004).

Although concealing health status may be one way to protect professional identity, a second tactic involves strategically revealing this information. In some circumstances, individuals may disclose a chronic illness as a means to negotiate necessary accommodations, manage anticipated or perceived discrimination, or to seek and receive social support from their colleagues (McGonagle & Hamblin, 2014). Communication privacy management theory (Petronio, 2002) suggests individuals and their colleagues must negotiate privacy boundaries following a disclosure. Like families themselves, the members of a small family business may "coordinate regulation of this information in a unified manner," establishing a collective privacy orientation that shapes norms for how, where, and with whom a person's health status is concealed or revealed (Caughlin, Petronio, & Middleton, 2013, p. 322). Following disclosure, a third communicative strategy for minimizing illness identity involves face-work, or the projection of a desired identity during interactions with internal and external stakeholders in the workplace (Goffman, 1955). For example, a chronically ill person may participate more intensely in work to increase others' perceptions of their competence and fend off pity. Such overperformance is characteristic of what Charmaz (1987) called the "supernormal social identity," where a person is focused on achieving or maintaining a preferred professional status in spite of their illness (p. 287). Moreover, face-work creates reciprocal commitments for how others should respond to identity maintenance strategies during interactions (Goffman, 1955). For instance, coworkers or family members who notice physical manifestations of a person's chronic health condition may purposefully avoid bringing it up, or will do so in ways to save the other's face.

KELLY'S STORY

Kelly is the senior director of Stone Strategies, a family-run public affairs and communication consulting firm founded by her father, Tom. Although Tom remains the firm's president, he began transitioning many of his leadership duties to Kelly two years ago in preparation for retirement. Kelly frequently jokes that she has been getting ready to take over the family business since she was 10 years old, when she began "helping" in the office by stuffing envelopes and filing paperwork. It was through the firm that Kelly discovered her professional passion, and she has only stepped away from the business once—to earn her undergraduate degree. More than 25 years later, her work ethic and internet marketing savvy have been instrumental in helping Stone Strategies expand to a staff of 15 associates.

Although Kelly feels mentally ready to lead the business, her physical health can be another story. Approximately five years ago, Kelly was diagnosed with multiple sclerosis (MS), a disease caused when the immune system attacks and damages parts of the body's central nervous system, such as the brain and spinal cord (National Multiple Sclerosis

Society, 2018). The diagnosis itself was not surprising. Kelly had experienced telltale symptoms, such as unexplained fatigue and reoccurring numbness and tingling in her hands and arms. She learned her disease followed a relapsing-remitting course, meaning that her symptoms may unpredictably get worse for a few weeks, and then will get better or disappear for months at a time. Kelly is grateful that she only currently experiences flare-ups two or three times per year, usually when she is under stress or not getting enough sleep. Even when she does have bad days, her medication seems to be keeping her MS mostly manageable for now. But, she can't help but wonder what will happen if (or when) her symptoms get worse. Specifically, she worries about what her MS means for the future with her spouse, Jason, and their three young children. As her family's primary breadwinner, Kelly is also concerned about how MS will impact her work at Stone Strategies.

Although Kelly has confided in some of the firm's associates who have been "in the trenches" with her for years, she chooses not to share her health status with junior staffers and current or potential clients. "Dad was such a strong leader. I need people to believe I can fill his shoes," Kelly often thinks, "It is tough enough to convince people that a woman with a family can prioritize her career. I can't give anyone another reason to think I can't do this." However, keeping her health information private and perceptions of her professional reputation intact proves to be a challenge in a close-knit business.

Preparing for the New Business Pitch

"9:30 already? Ugh!" Kelly winced as she checked her watch before opening the doors to Stone Strategies. She had been up late the night before, polishing a new business presentation she would be delivering later in the day. Given the meeting's importance, and knowing that the lingering fatigue of a recent flare-up meant she needed to carefully manage her energy, Kelly had allowed herself a precious extra half-hour of sleep. But, it made her morning routine hectic. There were kids to wake and get on their way to school, lunches to make, and a dog to feed—not to mention, getting herself ready for the day. "It's a miracle I'm here before noon," Kelly grumbled inwardly. But she nevertheless paused to greet to Kim, the firm's receptionist, before striding quickly down the long hallway to her office.

"Good morn-," Sandi, her father's executive assistant started to greet her absentmindedly, but then immediately jumped up when she noticed Kelly fumbling with her office keys. "Here, let me help," she offered, taking the keys and opening the door. As both women entered Kelly's office, she added in a low whisper, "Still a bit of numbness in that hand?"

"Thanks. Um, yeah," Kelly admitted reluctantly, "It's definitely getting better, though."

"Good." Sandi said, watching Kelly carefully as she hung up her coat and purse. "You know, I just saw an article about a promising clinical trial at Mayo Clinic. I'll print it and leave it on your desk, if it's something you want to look into."

"Thanks, Sandi. I'd appreciate that," Kelly smiled, "I'm grateful for any help, as long as you aren't trying to get me to eat kale!" Such motherly concern might have been annoying from anyone else. But Kelly considered Sandi, the firm's very first hire more than 25 years ago, more of a beloved aunt and confidant than an employee. Because of their deep bond, Kelly didn't mind when Sandi noticed her bad days or offered assistance. Kelly tried so hard to be "normal" in front of most of her other colleagues, which made it nice to have someone she could be real with. It also helped that, unlike others, Sandi offered useful information, too. Since her diagnosis, Kelly had gotten used to people offering inappropriate and unsolicited forms of advice. Most of the time, she chalked it up to people being under-informed about MS. But, the frequent "have you tried?" questions were still exasperating. "Especially kale," Kelly thought, "Why do they always want to know if I've tried kale? If eating one miracle food would really stop my MS, don't you think I would have done that already?"

"Kale? Disgusting! I would NEVER!" Sandi laughed and shook her head. "Okay—so, in terms of the serious stuff, your father will be here in an hour to rehearse the Meyer & Sons new business pitch. I've put together last month's billing files for you to review in the meantime. They just need your signature. And, I have a few time-off requests from the junior associates requiring approval. Specifically, there's one from Jessica I'd like you to take a look at."

"Again?" Kelly rolled her eyes. Jessica was a 20-something associate who had only been with Stone Strategies for a year. Despite the firm's generous leave policy, she had already exhausted her earned paid time off. It wasn't Jessica's work performance that worried Kelly. In contrast, Jessica had already developed a reputation for being a strong contributor. Following her own diagnosis, Kelly had learned the Americans with Disabilities Act only requires employees to disclose a chronic illness if they required reasonable accommodations to perform their core job functions. But the increasing frequency of Jessica's absences made Kelly wonder if she could legally ask what was going on. "Definitely something to check into with our corporate counsel," she noted.

"Yes," Sandi pursed her lips, "She says it's for a couple of medical appointments next week. But she also called in sick once last week, and is wondering what she should do about those hours." She noticed Kelly's growing look of irritation. "Hey, I'm just the messenger here. Is there anything I can do to help, or should I set up time for the two of you to talk?"

"Thanks, Sandi," Kelly flashed a chastened smile, "I don't mean to get annoyed—I know I should be more empathetic here. I just know that even when I was first diagnosed, I went out of my way to organize my appointments and treatments so they wouldn't get in the way of work. And, I mean, there's been a lot of times when I haven't felt good. But, I rough it out and make sure the work gets done. I don't always understand why that's so hard for other people."

"You can do it because you are your father's child! And a typical overachieving oldest child, too!" Sandi laughed, then paused. "But we don't know Jessica's story. She seems like a good associate, and is coachable. She just might learn a thing or two from hearing your health story." She looked at Kelly meaningfully, "Don't forget that you don't always have to be superwoman, too, young lady! I don't actually remember the last time you actually took a sick day. Even superheroes need their rest, you know!"

"You're right," Kelly sighed. "I'll talk to her. The last thing I need is for Jessica to go blabbing to the other junior associates about my MS issues, though—especially before Dad retires. But, I also don't need her complaining that she's being treated unfairly, as that could set up some morale issues with the team. Can you set up a meeting later this week?"

Planning for an Uncertain Future?

"Knock knock," Kelly swiveled in her chair almost immediately when she heard her father's voice boom behind her. "Nice work today," Tom appeared in her office doorway, "We nailed that new business presentation, and that's thanks to you, kiddo."

"Thanks, Dad," Kelly beamed. "The team worked really hard on this one."

"Yeah, we did good," Tom sat down in the overstuffed chair facing Kelly's desk. "But this was special, Kel. We've been aiming to land the Meyer & Sons account for a long time. And that presentation was really your show the whole way. The Meyers loved it, too."

"Oh yeah?" Kelly leaned forward with anticipation, "Any word?"

"Not yet," Tom smirked at his daughter's excitement, "But I bet Cal will have a thing or two to say on the golf course tomorrow morning. You should join me. We need to start grooming your golf game anyway—the country club is where a lot of business decisions get made in this town. And, the physical activity just might help keep your muscles moving."

"Um, yeah, NO, but thanks Dad." Kelly laughed, then became serious. "I've never been much of a golfer, and I don't think it's a good idea to advertise my MS. I would hate for potential clients to be concerned that I'm healthy enough to represent them."

"I get that, Kelly, I really do. And I know people see you as an industry leader," Tom said thoughtfully, "I just know how the game is played. You're going to have to find other ways to rub elbows with people to drum up new business."

"Oh I know," Kelly sighed, "That's why I'm volunteering for the PTA, the Hospital Board of Directors, and the Arts Council. I mean, I have to live up to your 'pillar of the community' reputation!"

"Ouch," Tom winced, "That's too much, Kel. You have a family to consider and shouldn't be the only one out there doing all this stuff for us."

"Do I have a choice?" Kelly exclaimed. "I seem to remember you doing all this stuff when I was younger!"

"That's true," Tom relented, "But to be frank, I was a man. It was also a different era, with different expectations for how I spent my time. And I didn't have MS. I don't mean to be rude or step on your toes, Kelly, but we don't know how everything is going to play out. And, that's a tough thing. Have you given any thought to taking a partner like we discussed?"

Kelly was flabbergasted, "DAD! You know I have a perfectly capable spouse who handles the family stuff, not unlike what Mom did. And as for the MS, do you really think I'm going to let the occasional numbness get in my way?"

"Stop." Tom held up his hands, halting Kelly momentarily. "I'm not saying anything about how you and Jason do things, so let's take that off the table. I just know you're handling a lot, and your doctors have told you to be careful about stress. My concern is that if you don't take on a partner, it's going to be too much. Not that you can't do the work— you're a brilliant consultant and leader. But, physically, it could be too much down the line. And, that could mean downsizing. You have a lot of employees, and their families, counting on you. We've worked too hard to build Stone Strategies over the years. I just think we need a plan to ensure the business stays strong down the line, no matter what."

DISCUSSION QUESTIONS

1. What makes talking about chronic illness in the workplace so difficult? What kinds of communication skills or scripts might be necessary to discuss chronic illness while minimizing stigma?
2. Families and workplaces are often studied as systems. Based on the case study, what evidence do you see for how Stone Strategies operates as a system?
3. Put yourself in Kelly's shoes: Would you share information about your health with Jessica? What are the potential risks and benefits of disclosing this information?
4. Reflect on Kelly's conversations with Sandi and Tom. What evidence do you see of her concerns surrounding her professional identity? What kinds of face-work strategies does she use to protect her desired status? How do their responses support or threaten her face?
5. Why do you think Kelly appreciates Sandi's social support but finds support from others to be unhelpful? Based on your experiences, what makes support beneficial or not? How might the support you receive influence future decisions to disclose health information?
6. Existing research suggests that communicating in a family-run business could create ethical challenges by blending personal and professional relationships. What are some of the potential ethical implications that emerge from Kelly's conversations with Sandi and Tom?
7. What role do gendered relational expectations play in Kelly's conversations with Sandi and Tom?

REFERENCES

Braithwaite, D. O., Bach, B. W., Baxter, L. A., DiVerniero, R., Hammonds, J. R., Hosek, A. M., … Wolf, B. M. (2010). Constructing family: A typology of voluntary kin. *Journal of Social and Personal Relationships, 27*, 388–407. doi:10.1177/0265407510361615

Butler, J. A., & Modaff, D. P. (2016). Motivations to disclose chronic illness in the workplace. *Qualitative Research Reports in Communication, 17*(1), 77–84. doi:10.1080/17459435.2016.11 43387

Caughlin, J. P., Petronio, S., & Middleton, A. (2013). When families manage private information. In A. L. Vangelisti (Ed.), *The Routledge handbook of family communication* (2nd ed., pp. 321–337). New York, NY: Routledge.

Centers for Disease Control and Prevention. (2017, June 28). *Chronic disease overview.* Retrieved from https://www.cdc.gov/chronicdisease

Charmaz, K. (1987). Struggling for a self: Identity levels of the chronically ill. *Sociology of Health Care, 6*, 283–321.

Charmaz, K. (1991). *Good days, bad days: The self in chronic illness and time.* New Brunswick, NJ: Rutgers.

Checton, M., Greene, K., Magsamen-Conrad, K., & Venetis, M. K. (2012). Patients' and partners' perspectives of chronic illness and its management. *Families, Systems, & Health, 30*, 114–129. doi:10.1037/a0028598

Deetz, S. (1992). *Democracy in an age of corporate colonization: Developments in communication and the politics of everyday life.* Albany, NY: SUNY Press.

Defenbaugh, N. L. (2013). Revealing and concealing ill identity: A performance narrative of IBD disclosure. *Health Communication, 28*, 159–169. doi:10.1080/10410236.2012.666712

Goffman, E. (1955). On face-work: An analysis of ritual elements in social interaction. *Psychiatry, 18*, 213–231. doi:10.1080/00332747.1955.11023008

Goffman, E. (1963). *Stigma: Notes on the management of a spoiled identity.* New York, NY: Simon & Schuster.

Hall, A. (2012). *Family business dynamics: A role and identity based perspective.* Cheltenham, England: Edward Elgar.

Hayden, S. (1993). Chronically ill and "feeling fine": A study of communication and chronic illness. *Journal of Applied Communication Research, 2*, 263–278. doi:10.1080/00909889309365371

Knapp, J. R., Smith, B. R., Kreiner, G. E., Sundaramurthy, C., & Barton, S. L. (2013). Managing boundaries through identity work: The role of individual and organizational identity tactics. *Family Business Review, 26*, 333–355. doi:10.1177/0894486512474036

McGonagle, A., & Barnes-Farrell, J. (2014). Chronic illness in the workplace: Stigma, identity threat and strain. *Stress & Health, 30*, 310–321. doi:10.1002/smi.2518

McGonagle, A., & Hamblin, L. (2014). Proactive responding to anticipated discrimination based on chronic illness: Double-edged sword? *Journal of Business & Psychology, 29*(3), 427–442. doi:10.1007/s10869-013-9324-7

Myers, K. (2004). Coming out: Considering the closet of illness. *Journal of Medical Humanities, 25*, 255–270. doi:10.1007/s10912-004-4832-0

National Multiple Sclerosis Society. (2018). *What is MS?* Retrieved from https://www.nationalmssociety.org/What-is-MS

Neubaum, D. O., & Voordeckers, W. (2018). Documenting the "family effect" on family business research. *Family Business Review, 31*, 238–239. doi:10.1177/0894486518774980

Pecchioni, L., & Keely, M. (2011). Insights about health from family communication theories. In T. L. Thompson, R. Parrott, & J. F. Nussbaum (Eds.), *The Routledge handbook of health communication* (2nd ed., pp. 363–376). New York, NY: Routledge.

Petronio, S. (2002). *Boundaries of privacy: Dialectics of disclosure.* Albany, NY: State University of New York Press.

Poole, M. S. (2014). Systems theory. In L. Putnam & D. K. Mumby (Eds.), *The SAGE handbook of organizational communication* (3rd ed., pp. 49–74). Los Angeles, CA: SAGE.

Russell, L. D. (2013). Reconstructing the "work ethic" through medicalized discourse on workaholism. *Journal of Applied Communication Research, 41*, 275–292. doi:10.1080/00909882.2013.825046

Sundaramurthy, C., & Kreiner, G. E. (2008). Governing by managing identity boundaries: The case of family businesses. *Entrepreneurship Theory and Practice, 32*, 391–591. doi:10.1111/j.1540-6520.2008.00234.x

Vangelisti, A. L. (2013). Preface. In A. L. Vangelisti (Ed.). *The Routledge handbook of family communication* (2nd ed., pp. ix–xi). New York, NY: Routledge.

Wang, S., & Repetti, R. (2013). After the workday ends: How jobs impact family relationships. In A. L. Vangelisti (Ed.), *The Routledge handbook of family communication* (2nd ed., pp. 409–423). New York, NY: Routledge.

Wieland, S. M. B. (2011). Struggling to manage work as a part of everyday life: Complicating control, rethinking resistance, and contextualizing work/life studies. *Communication Monographs, 78*(2), 162–184. doi:10.1080/03637751.2011.564642

Family Communication Perspective: An Application of Emotion Regulation Theory

Corey Jay Liberman – *Marymount Manhattan College*

ABSTRACT

The time has come for Charley to disclose some very important, health-related information to her cousin, Hailey. How will she do it? Using the key ideas embedded within Gross's (1998) emotion regulation theory, the two mutually negotiate this difficult situation and shed light on the salience of emotion management.

CASE STUDY

If you have ever had to tone down your sarcasm to adapt to a new social partner, cease your laughter during a solemn religious event, create more interest in an otherwise monotonous conversation, or seem more amused following a magician's act, you have engaged in the process of what has become known as emotion regulation. According to Gross (1998), emotion regulation can be defined as "the processes by which individuals influence which emotions they have, when they have them, and how they experience and express these emotions" (p. 275). This chapter focuses on the emotion regulation processes and practices adopted by an individual when she suddenly learns that her cousin has been diagnosed with end-stage mesothelioma. The chapter first introduces an overview of emotion regulation theory, inclusive of the original process model. Next will be the case study, detailing the disclosure that transpired between cousins, Charley and Hailey. The chapter concludes with a discussion linking the case study back to the major tenets of emotion regulation theory, explicating how the communication of emotion between the two social agents produced an effective social encounter.

Emotion Regulation Theory

It becomes evident, based on even a cursory review of the communication literature, that the field is interdisciplinary. That is, although communication is a field in itself, it borrows from other academic fields and disciplines (namely those within the social sciences). The theory undergirding this chapter, emotion regulation theory, is a prime example of the idea that communication is, at its very core, interdisciplinary. Even though emotion regulation research is commonly framed within the rubric of cognitive/behavioral psychology, it extends to other branches and to other related fields. Even Gross (2015), who most consider to be the father of the theory, claimed that "the field of emotion regulation emerged in the mid-1990s and has been gathering steam ever since" (p. 1). However, 17 years earlier, Gross (1998) argued that "research on emotion regulation originated in development psychology [by]…Gaensbuaer, 1982" (p. 271). And in a publication four years later, Gross (2002) then claims that "the study of emotion regulation has roots that go back over a century to early psychoanalytic theorizing about the nature of psychological defenses" (p. 281), citing the work of Sigmund Freud. Research on emotion regulation then finds its way into the social psychology (Gross & John, 2003), clinical psychology (Bariola, Gullone, & Hughes, 2011), family psychology (Chen, Lin, & Li, 2012), abnormal psychology (Ramsden & Hubbard, 2002), and communication (Cupach & Olson, 2006) literatures. As such, emotion regulation can be, and has been, viewed from many different perspectives.

Before detailing the theory, it is important to define what is meant by emotion and emotion regulation. Much like any terms, these are extraordinarily difficult to define, as such definitions need to be macro enough for inclusion of variables, though micro enough for purposes of empirical measurement. Gross and Levenson (1993) offer what is perhaps the most useful definition of emotions, when they describe them as "biologically based reactions that organize an individual's responses to important events … [which] unfold over a relatively brief time course … are malleable … and have components in the domains of physiological response, subjective experience, and expressive behavior" (p. 970). Breaking this definition down a bit, an emotion is a reaction to some stimulus (i.e., happiness as a result of getting news about having won the lottery; fear associated with riding on a forthcoming airplane; sadness associated with having to say goodbye to a friend who is leaving on vacation), which [oftentimes] has a short duration, and which ultimately results in some bodily response (i.e., increased heart rate, dilation of pupils), coupled with some overt action (i.e., smile, frown, clenched fist). It is quite important to realize that the overt action is a direct function of the emotion in question, solidified by Koole's (2009) claim that "emotions are often portrayed as irresistible forces that exert a sweeping influence on behavior" (p. 4). It is here that communication enters into the discussion. Communication becomes the social tool necessary for the behavioral manifestation of the emotion in question. There is, thus, a striking difference among "having anger," "being angry," and "doing being angry," where the former two involve the psychological processes of emotion creation and the latter involves the communicative process of emotion performance.

According to a review by Shaver, Schwartz, Kirson, and O'Connor (2001), there are over a 100 tertiary emotions that can be communicated by social actors during their interactions with others. Regarding emotion regulation, Koole (2009) offers the most parsimonious definition, when he argues that it "involves changes in emotional responding" (p. 6). The key word here is "changes." That is, assume that one finds a joke humorous, but also knows that she should not laugh because doing so would be in bad taste. The social action, or communication, of non-laughter, given the foregoing definition, would be a cognizant change in an emotional response—the laughter triggered by the humorous joke would be suppressed by some other emotion, such as surprise, dejection, shame, sadness, or distress. An additional definition that warrants inclusion here, especially given the nature of this chapter's case study, is that offered by Sheppes et al. (2014), when they claim that this process involves "the choices individuals make as to how they should regulate their emotions in a particular context when regulation is warranted" (p. 163). While the regulatory process is, indeed, warranted in certain cases (i.e., suppressing one's anger toward his parental unit during confrontation), it might very well be unwarranted in others (i.e., promoting joy to celebrate the unity of two newlyweds). All three of the aforementioned definitions (including the one offered by Gross, 1998, at the start of the chapter) seem to have one overarching claim in common: that social actors have the ability to control, or regulate, the communication of their emotions. Given this argument, it is likely that developmental and cognitive psychologists interested in emotion regulation would argue that regulation occurs due to social actors' abilities to "turn emotions on" in certain contexts and "turn emotions off" in others.

What, then, is emotion regulation theory? In short, the theory argues that there are rewards associated with regulating, or controlling, one's emotion(s) in certain social situations. As Gross (2015) explains, there is oftentimes a direct, event–emotion relationship, meaning that something, specifically, triggers the onset of the emotion in question. For example, an individual is not just amused, surprised, or frustrated. Rather, some event, some person, or some social exchange produced the emotion. However, sometimes the emotion is not the one that should be communicatively produced, which is where emotion regulation enters the discussion. For purposes of the forthcoming theoretical explication, assume that an individual (Jason) wants to regulate his emotion of fear associated with riding a rollercoaster, so as to reduce the likelihood of emotional contagion linked to his younger cousin (Bradley). In this example, if Bradley has an inclination that Jason fears riding the rollercoaster, there will be an increased likelihood that Bradley, too, will be overcome with fear … and that neither will ride.

According to emotion regulation theory, the first important claim is that one's decision to regulate emotion is what Gross (2015) calls *activation of a goal to influence the emotion trajectory*. One's conscious decision to engage in emotion regulation is predicated on the achievement of a goal that such regulation can produce. In this example, the goal is to regulate fear to produce more courage, which will, in turn, hopefully influence both Jason, himself, and Bradley to ride the rollercoaster.

The second important claim, according to Gross (2015), is that emotion regulation *can be intrinsic and/or extrinsic*. An emotion regulatory behavior is said to be intrinsic to the extent that it helps regulate one's own emotion(s) and, thus, has egocentric effects. In the previous example, Jason regulating his fear of riding a rollercoaster might very well increase his own likelihood of riding because the emotions of confidence, comfort, and bravery outshine his fear. An emotion regulatory behavior is said to be extrinsic to the extent that it helps regulate another's emotion(s), thus having altercentric effects. Again using the previous example, Jason's regulation of fear might help Bradley's bravery and intrepidity.

A third important claim is that, oftentimes, *individuals will try to up-regulate positive emotions and down-regulate negative emotions*. Social actors will try to increase the communicative manifestation of emotions such as hope, amusement, pride, love, and joy (Frederickson, 1998) and decrease the communicative manifestation of emotions such as anger, shame, sadness, envy, and hatred (Kuppens, Realo, & Diener, 2008). Interestingly, sometimes individuals will try to up-regulate negative emotions and down-regulate positive emotions, resulting in the 2 × 2 matrix illustrated by Gross (2015)—increasing and decreasing both negative and positive emotions. Although one might ask why an individual would ever want to suppress a positive emotion and manifest a negative emotion, the answer lies in the contextual nature of communication and social interaction. Assume, for example, that Gillian gets the greatest news of her life on the same day that Sara gets the worst news of her life. According to this theory, if the two are in a mutually beneficial relationship, it would behoove Gillian to regulate her positively-valenced emotion of joy, at least when in the same physical confines as Sara, so as to not produce the negatively-valenced emotion of jealously or, even worse, hatred. Regarding the communication (or up-regulating) of a negative emotion, examples of social protest are tantamount to this: suppressing the communication of anger and hatred would be a social disservice in this context.

Three additional qualities linked to emotion that warrant attention, all of which are mentioned in Gross's (2015) overview of emotion regulation theory, are the intensity of emotion, the duration of emotion, and the quality of emotional response. Regarding *the intensity of emotion*, individuals, according to the theory, are able to control the quantitative output of some manifested emotion. For example, one can decide to become more emotionally saddened following a funeral or less emotionally angered after finding out that her favorite sports team lost to its biggest rival. In terms of *the duration of emotion*, social actors have the ability to regulate the length that the communication of the said emotion lasts. For example, one can communicate anxiety about the results of a nonroutine blood test, yet also control this emotional elicitation so that it is not perpetual and ever-present. Similarly, one can communicate love about a significant other, but can regulate the manifestation of this emotion so as to not do so in the presence of those who might oppose the relational communion (i.e., an ex-partner). Finally, *the quality of emotional response* forces individuals to reconfigure or reframe the way that a particular emotion, communicated in a particular context, is encoded. For example, one can psychologically convince herself that there is nothing abnormal about laughing in a moment that likely predicts sorrow or that being overcome with sympathy in a moment that would have otherwise produced the emotion of rage is the norm.

Before turning to the case study, it is important to note that, as a result of one's ability to regulate his/her emotion(s), there exist several emotion regulation strategies, as part of what Gross (1998) calls his process model. According to Gross (2015), "the process model of emotion regulation makes the prediction that different emotion regulation strategies … should have different consequences for how a person feels, thinks, and acts, both immediately and over the longer term" (p. 7). The first strategy of emotion regulation is called *situation selection*, wherein one will actively choose to engage in, or withdraw from, a social context that will promote the manifestation of a preferred, desirable emotion. For example, to increase the likelihood of proactively producing the emotion of happiness, one will choose to spend his birthday at his favorite restaurant, with his closest friends, and order his favorite menu items. In addition, to reduce the likelihood of producing the emotion of loneliness, one will not stay home, by herself, on a weekend evening to watch her favorite situation comedy.

The second strategy of emotion regulation is called *situation modification*, which entails altering the likelihood of emotion emergence by changing the contextual parameters. For example, assume that Daniel knows that although Maurice is not very astute at playing poker (which, if brought up in conversation, might produce the emotion of embarrassment), he is quite an effective canasta player (which would likely produce the emotion of pride). Using the situation modification strategy, Daniel, adopting the altercentric perspective mentioned earlier, would be able to highlight Maurice's superior knowledge and gameplay of one card game, while masking his inferiority complex associated with the other.

The third strategy of emotion regulation is called *attentional deployment*, which involves the purposeful delay (or distraction) of one's emotions. In other words, this strategy enables one to devote her emotional energies toward a positively-valenced emotional event and/or cognitively block herself from a negatively-valenced one. For example, assume that on the same day that Leona earns stellar marks on her report card, she also learns that she did not land the lead role in the school play. According to the theory, she will, in order to regulate her emotions, deploy her attention to the emotion providing most reward (her report card) and distract herself from the emotion providing most psychological pain (the news about her school play).

The fourth strategy of emotion regulation is called *cognitive change*, which entails the active process of reframing the situation creating the emotion altogether. For example, assume that Alexis just received news that she did not make the varsity basketball team. Rather than viewing this as a problem ("I am not a good player"), she could reframe this as an opportunity ("This will provide me a chance to become a better player and make the team next year").

The fifth, and final, strategy of emotion regulation is called *response modulation*, which involves, according to Gross (2015), "directly influencing experiential, behavioral, or physiological components of the emotional response after the emotion is well-developed" (p. 9). For example, assume that Ella is overcome by the psychological effects linked to the recent breakup with her boyfriend, Brayden. She might very well turn to therapy or yoga or rid herself of relational keepsakes (or a combination thereof) in an effort to modify her emotion of sadness.

As dictated in the great majority of the extant literature (see Naragon-Gainey, McMahon, & Chacko, 2017, for an extensive review), the physical, social, mental, cognitive, and relational rewards linked to regulating emotions are vast. When speaking about the underlying motive for emotion regulation, Koole (2009) perhaps puts it best when he argues that "emotion regulation is driven by people's needs to experience hedonically rewarding states, which consist of low levels of negative and high levels of positive emotion" (p. 18). And if, as Williams, Morelli, Ong, and Zaki (2018) argue (and support), individuals are able to control (regulate) their own emotions, and the emotions of their interpersonal partners, social agents do, to some extent, have agency over emotional manifestation. However, as will be seen in the forthcoming case study, it is oftentimes more difficult than it seems. Even adopting Koerner and Fitzpatrick's (2002) "relational schema model" of family communication, wherein one's cognitive knowledge of being in a family relationship with a social alter comes to predict behavior (it is likely much easier to disclose bad information to someone if this someone is a familial member), this case study demonstrates how difficult both family communication, and emotion regulation, can be. It is never easy to hide, mask, and/or purposefully create emotions while in interaction with others. However, the importance of doing so must not be underestimated, nor undervalued. As will be highlighted, one's ability to socially regulate his/her emotions, especially in the face of the disclosure of what one might call "bad news," could very well be the difference between relational (and communicative) success and failure.

The Case Study

Charley and Hailey, first cousins, had been very close since the age of five. They had grown up two streets away from each other and found a similar interest in the same things: dance, theatre, and singing. All the way through high school, these two were joined at the hip. Although they look nothing like each other physically (Charley has brown hair and stands at 5 feet 10 inches and Hailey has blonde hair and stands at 5 feet 4 inches), their social network of friends would call them the "inseparable twins." However, at the end of their high school tenure, they found themselves separated for the first time in their lives, as Hailey decided to attend the University of Delaware and Charley decided to attend the University of Wisconsin. They vowed, at the start of freshman year, to do whatever was within their collective power to retain their strong relationship. One of their routinized, relational customs was seeing each other each fall semester, for the University of Wisconsin's homecoming weekend—what many students consider to be a pinnacle of the social experience at UW.

Hailey had just arrived at the campus and, as usual, could not wait to see her cousin, despite the fact that they had spoken every night since they last saw each other (and even FaceTimed the morning of her flight). Everything about this homecoming weekend in Madison, Wisconsin, seemed to be the same as it had been for the past three years. The Badgers football team was nationally ranked in the top 15 (with a record of 5–1). It had already snowed four times and the campus had a steady stream of white glossed across its streets. Midterm exams were nearing, and the collective stress could be seen, heard, and felt among the college students. Yet three things were quite different this year. First, Charley had a steady, quasi-serious boyfriend for the first time since her junior year of high school. Unfortunately, Hailey had no idea whether or not this was going to impact her forthcoming weekend. Would he be joining them for much of it? Would his role in her life come to affect her relationship with Charley? Would Hailey get along with him? Second, this would be the last homecoming for the two of them and, thus, the social ritual would be coming to an end. Charley was going to be graduating and attending graduate school at Columbia University's Department of English and Comparative Literature. She has been reading at a high school level since third grade and has had a love for historical fiction, and, thus, decided to pursue a master's degree. Hailey, on the other hand, will be graduating with a degree in fashion marketing. Third, and most importantly, in addition to this being a social visit, Charley also needs to inform Hailey of some news that she recently received from her oncologist.

After picking Hailey up at Dane County Regional Airport, and after she had brought all her luggage back to her apartment, Charley took her to a local restaurant, the Tornado Steak House. They had a very normal, blasé conversation about life, boys, college, the future, and family. During dinner, at a point that Charley framed as opportune, she decided that it was time to disclose something important to her cousin.

Charley: Hails . . . as you likely remember . . . I told you a few months ago that I was feeling . . . well . . . not 100% . . . remember???

Hailey: Of course . . . you thought that you were pregnant.

Charley: Right . . . exactly.

Hailey: Charley . . . you are pregnant!!!

Charley: No . . . Hailey . . . relax, girl. I am not pregnant.

Hailey: Phew . . . I have no idea what I would have done . . . or said. I was about to throw this entire salt-shaker at you . . . or at least a small pinch of it.

Charley: Well . . . I kind of wish I was pregnant.

At this moment, it was clear that the nonverbal communication of both Hailey and Charley was disclosing some pertinent information. On the one hand, Hailey's facial reaction was one of shock and it was clear that she was anticipating some bad news. On the other hand, Charley's verbal tone, in conjunction with her facial gestures (i.e., raised eyebrows, somewhat squinted eyes), was predictive of forthcoming disappointment.

Charley: I saw Dr. Phillips this past Wednesday . . . you know . . . the cute one. When I told him of my symptoms, he did a hundred different tests. You remember that line from the Sopranos? Well . . . he did Catscans and Dogscans. He then sent me to what is called an oncologist, which is a doctor who specializes in cancer.

Hailey: Cancer??? Charley . . . you are kidding me!!!

Charley: So, I went to see Dr. Nussbaum . . . who was great . . . she is so amazing.

Hailey: Well what did she say???

Charley: Hailey . . . I have something called mesothelioma. It is a type of cancer. It is weird…most likely found in men and men who work in conditions with asbestos and not those who grew up in living conditions like mine. Like ours. It is also more likely to happen in people much older than me. But when I started asking all of these questions…asking the question why . . . why me . . . she said that it is also because of genetics. That someone in my family might have had the gene for it. Like the way that your dad has diabetes, I guess. Or that it could just happen . . . because . . . well . . . just because.

Hailey began to cry, immediately and fervently, and crossed to the other side of the table and put her arms around the neck of Charley. She grabbed her tightly and, although the combination of tears and sadness clearly became an obstacle for her verbal elocution, she told Charley that she loved her. Charley did not respond and her facial expression was as blank as a poker player with a straight flush in her hand. Their conversation continued, yet at a much closer proximity, now that the two were sitting next to each other.

Hailey: Charley . . . I am so, so, so, so, so sorry . . . I just don't know what . . .

Charley: Hails . . . do not say that . . . I know that this is hard . . . for both of us . . . trust me . . . it was extremely hard for me to figure out how to say this to you.

Although her tears were beginning to subside a bit, Hailey was still crying, shocked and frightened by the news that she had just been provided.

Charley: Please try not to cry. I have been crying for the past 24 hours and it has not done me any good. Do you remember that whole "grant me the serenity to accept the things I cannot change, the courage to change the things I can, and the wisdom to know the difference" thing that Mrs. Connell taught us back in the day?

Hailey: Yes . . . of course . . . I still use that damn thing.

Charley: Well . . . this is something that I cannot change. Something that I have to live with. Something that I have to deal with. It is at the final stage. I know that this sounds bad, but I do not have all of the bad symptoms. Right now, it is still just shortness of breath and abdominal pain and fatigue.

Hailey: Are you able to get surgery? I know that some people with cancer are able to get surgery. That is what my uncle did . . . I think.

Charley: No. The cancer has spread throughout my body and I am too far along to get the surgery.

Once Hailey hears this, she is again brought to tears, as she decodes this information as though there is nothing to do but wait for death. This time, however, her tears become contagious as Charley, too, begins to sob. This lasts for roughly 30 seconds, during which time Hailey is nonverbally hugging and coddling her best friend. Afterward, Hailey asks an extremely salient question that then points the discussion in a different direction, albeit subtly.

Hailey: So . . . what is there to do?

Charley: Well . . . the doctor said that chemo, radiation, and surgery are all out. These are, according to her, all too risky . . . given the stage of cancer here. We are going to look into experimental treatments and trials, but this, too, might be risky. But we will see.

Hailey: Charley . . . we will get you through this. I will be here for anything and everything that you need. Remember that time when I told you that I had a bedtime of 11:00 p.m. and then you convinced your mom that you should be able to stay up for an extra hour . . . and she let you? But then your mom checked with my mom and found out that I had bent the truth . . . and I had a bedtime of only 10:00 p.m . . . and we both got grounded?

Charley: Of course . . . how could I forget???

Hailey: That was the first time that we ever really got in trouble . . . together.

Charley: Yup.

Hailey: But that was also the first time that we were there for each other . . . and it has never stopped. I will be there for you for this. Anything that you need. I am here.

Charley: Even if I need you to come to Wisconsin to bring me a Rainbow Loom bracelet . . . like the ones that we used to make as kids?

Hailey: OMG . . . do you remember those??? We used to spend hours and hours and hours making those. I think we thought we were going to go into business or something. LOL!!!

Charley: Yes. And you were so detail oriented.

Hailey: Hey . . . I just wanted to be sure that I could market them to the right people. After all . . . I am in fashion marketing!

Charley: I love you, Hailey.

Hailey: I love you too, Charley.

Hailey: What do you say we go to Chili's tomorrow night . . . just . . . because???

Charley: Absolutely . . . but you are paying!

DISCUSSION QUESTIONS

1. Based on your understanding of emotion regulation theory, did Charley and Hailey effectively manage their emotions during their interaction? If yes, explain why. If no, explain what they could have done differently.

2. According to the chapter, there exist five emotion regulation strategies. Explain which strategies Charley and Hailey used during their interactions and whether, to what extent, and why these seemed to work.

3. One of the claims made in the chapter is that emotion regulation is goal driven. What were the goals of emotion regulation for both Charley and Hailey? Were these goals achieved for both individuals?

4. Did the fact that Charley and Hailey were cousins make the process of emotion regulation more difficult or did it make the process easier? Please explain your answer here.

5. After having read the chapter, what makes the regulation of emotion so important? What makes the regulation of emotion so difficult? Please explain your answer here.

REFERENCES

Bariola, E., Gullone, E., & Hughes, E. K. (2011). Child and adolescent emotion regulation: The role of parental emotion regulation and expression. *Clinical Child and Family Psychological Review, 14*, 198–212.

Chen, F., Lin, H., & Li, C. (2012). The role of emotion in parent-child relationships: Children's emotionality, maternal meta-emotion, and children's attachment security. *Journal of Child and Family Studies, 21*, 403–410.

Cupach, W. R., & Olson, L. N. (2006). Emotion regulation theory: A lens for viewing family conflict and violence. In D. O Braithwaite & L. A. Baxter's (Eds.), *Engaging theories in family communication: Multiple perspectives* (pp. 213–228). Thousand Oaks, CA: Sage.

Frederickson, B. L. (1998). What good are positive emotions? *Review of General Psychology, 2*, 300–319.

Gross, J. J. (1998). The emerging field of emotion regulation: An integrative review. *Review of General Psychology, 2*, 271–299.

Gross, J. J. (2002). Emotion regulation: Affective, cognitive, and social consequences. *Psychophysiology, 39*, 281–291.

Gross, J. J. (2015). Emotion regulation: Current status and future prospects. *Psychological Inquiry, 26*, 1–26.

Gross, J. J., & John, O. P. (2003). Individual differences in two emotion regulation processes: Implications for affect, relationships, and well-being. *Journal of Personality and Social Psychology, 85*, 348–362.

Gross, J. J., & Levenson, R. W. (1993). Emotional suppression: Physiology, self-report, and expressive behavior. *Journal of Personality and Social Psychology, 64*, 970–986.

Koerner, A. F., & Fitzpatrick, M. A. (2002). Toward a theory of family communication. *Communication Theory, 12*, 70–91.

Koole, S. L. (2009). The psychology of emotion regulation: An integrative review. *Cognition and Emotion, 23*, 4–41.

Koole, S. L., & Rothermund, K. (2011). I feel better but I don't know why: The psychology of implicit emotion regulation. *Cognition and Emotion, 25*, 389–399.

Kuppens, P., Realo, A., & Diener, E. (2008). The role of positive and negative emotions in life satisfaction judgement across nations. *Journal of Personality and Social Psychology, 95*, 66–75.

Naragon-Gainey, K., McMahon, T. P., & Chacko, T. P. (2017). The structure of common emotion regulation strategies: A meta-analytic examination. *Psychological Bulletin, 143*, 384–427.

Ramsden, S. R., & Hubbard, J. A. (2002). Family expressiveness and parental emotion coaching: Their role in children's emotion regulation and aggression. *Journal of Abnormal Child Psychology, 30*, 657–667.

Shaver, P., Schwartz, J., Kirson, D., & O'Connor, C. (2001). Emotional knowledge: Further exploration of a prototype approach. In G. Parrott (Ed.), *Emotions in Social Psychology: Essential Readings* (pp. 26–56). Philadelphia, PA: Psychology Press.

Sheppes, G. Scheibe, S., Suri, G., Radu, P., Blechert, J., & Gross, J. J. (2014). Emotion regulation choice: A conceptual framework and supporting evidence. *Journal of Experimental Psychology, 143*, 163–181.

Williams, W. C. Morelli, S. A., Ong, D. C., & Zaki, J. (2018). Interpersonal emotion regulation: Implications for affiliation, perceived support, relationships, and well-being. *Journal of Personality and Social Psychology, 115*, 224–254.

CHAPTER 32

"What Do You Expect from Me?": Family and Marital Coping after a Breast Cancer Diagnosis

Andrea Meluch – *Indiana University South Bend*
Maria Hannah – *Indiana University South Bend*

ABSTRACT

Cancer diagnoses are stressful, atypical events for families. When a family member is diagnosed with cancer, the nature of family relationships often transform as a result. The additional stress and uncertainty that accompanies cancer treatments may also create or intensify family conflict and leave the individual diagnosed with cancer without necessary support. This case study illustrates the negative toll of a cancer diagnosis on marital and family interactions. In particular, the case focuses on how the relationship between a married couple, Camille and Brad, and their family members changed in the aftermath of Camille's cancer diagnosis. Camille and Brad's story highlights the uncertainty, stress, and conflict that many families experience when someone they love is receiving cancer treatment. Further, the case study also demonstrates common communication behaviors, such as topic avoidance, that family members exhibit when they are dealing with cancer.

CASE STUDY

A cancer diagnosis is a stressful event that is not typical or expected by both the individual who is diagnosed or their family (Segrin & Flora, 2005). People who are diagnosed with cancer often experience negative psychosocial effects related to their diagnosis, such as feelings of uncertainty, depression, isolation, and hopelessness (Charmaz, 1983, 1995; Helgeson & Cohen, 1996; Mathieson & Stam, 1995). Family relationships are also altered by a cancer diagnosis. When a family member is diagnosed with cancer the family may, or may not, adjust their communication with each other. Past research has identified various aspects of family and marital communication that are impacted by a cancer diagnosis (Donovan-Kicken & Caughlin, 2010; Goldsmith, Miller, & Caughlin, 2007; Venetis, Magsamen-Contrad, Checton, & Greene, 2014). In particular, families may experience conflict, topic avoidance, and/or changes related to members' social support needs when a loved one is diagnosed with cancer.

Apart from obvious health risks an individual diagnosed with cancer faces, families may experience changing family dynamics in the wake of a cancer diagnosis. Cancer severely disrupts the everyday lives of families. That is, prior to a cancer diagnosis, family members have specific roles and responsibilities related to maintaining their family structure. However, when an individual becomes incapacitated because of a cancer diagnosis, family structures change. For example, the ways that family members maintain their relationships with one another are often disrupted by a cancer diagnosis. Family members may experience difficulty expressing emotions, demonstrating intimacy, and/or facilitating productive dialogue when cancer causes instability in their everyday lives (Donovan-Kicken & Caughlin, 2010). Although family members may be very concerned about how the individual diagnosed with cancer is feeling, they often avoid discussing cancer. Topic avoidance may occur because a spouse or family member is simply unsure of the reactions the individual who is diagnosed may have when discussing their thoughts and emotions related to their cancer diagnosis (Goldsmith et al., 2007; Venetis et al., 2014). Ultimately, some family members choose to avoid discussions about the cancer diagnosis altogether.

While attempting to make sense of their new reality after a cancer diagnosis, family members may experience increased conflict because of misunderstandings and miscommunication regarding expectations. Expectations range anywhere from tangible tasks, like household chores and assisting with transportation, to cognitive efforts, such as active listening, expressing empathy, and taking on the role of the courageous family member despite obvious fears. The expectations individuals have of their family members also has a critical impact on families dealing with a cancer diagnosis. Largely, the expectation to unconditionally support a family member with cancer can be taxing on family, and caregivers may experience negative mental and physical effects (Kirchoff, Yi, Wright, Warner, & Smith, 2012). Further, if certain expectations are unmet, caregivers may feel an intense amount of failure, fatigue, and eventual burnout (Olson, 2015). Finally, people diagnosed with cancer may begin to feel like a "burden" on their family because of the many needs that they must rely on their family members to now fulfill (Olson, 2015).

All families experience stress in their daily lives. However, a cancer diagnosis creates a type of stress that is particularly difficult for families to cope with. The following case study illustrates the experience of one family coping with a breast cancer diagnosis. In particular, many of the communicative issues identified in the research related to family and marital dynamics are explored throughout this narrative.

The Results Are Incomplete

Camille Tillerson had had an extremely busy few months. Her daughter, Annie, had recently gotten engaged. To help save up for the upcoming wedding costs, Camille decided to pick up extra shifts at work. Camille's husband of 27 years, Brad, had also been busy at his construction job. Despite the added stress of the wedding, both Camille and Brad were looking forward to their only daughter's wedding. Even with everything Camille had going on in her personal and professional life, she made sure to keep her scheduled doctor's appointment. She had scheduled a wellness checkup with her doctor before all of the wedding commotion and briefly considered cancelling last minute, but still made the effort to go.

Camille sat uncomfortably on the paper lining the exam table in her doctor's office. Her doctor, Dr. Fairhurst, knocked on the door lightly and then entered the room. "How are you doing today, Camille?" she asked as she put her laptop down and sat on the stool.

"I'm good," Camille replied.

"Good," Dr. Fairhurst said. "Before we do the exam and get you on your way, I noticed you are due for a mammogram, so I am going to put the order in for one. You can call and set it up after our appointment."

Camille nodded and then answered all of Dr. Fairhurst's questions. After she finished up with her appointment, Camille went to Dr. Fairhurst's receptionist and picked up the information for scheduling a mammogram.

A few weeks later Camille went in for her mammogram. After her mammogram she felt a little soreness and tenderness and winced as she sat down on the couch that evening. Brad noticed that she was in pain. "You okay?" he asked.

"Yeah, just a little sore after the mammogram today," she said.

"Did they find anything?" he asked.

"It usually takes a few weeks to get the results, but the doctor didn't feel a lump or anything during the exam so I'm not worried."

Later that month, Camille's cell phone rang. She saw that it was her doctor's office phone number and answered. "Is this Camille?" Dr. Fairhurst asked.

"Yes," Camille replied.

"I have the results of your mammogram and, well, … the results are incomplete, and I am going to order an ultrasound. I don't want you to get too concerned yet, but I do want to follow-up."

Camille was a little annoyed that she had to set up an additional appointment. She was very busy planning her daughter's wedding and had another hectic month coming up at work. Having worked as a nurse for the past 12 years, Camille had a feeling that the incomplete findings were probably due to a cyst, which she knew was a common reason for an incomplete result. When Camille went home that evening, she told Brad about the call.

"I don't even know if I'm going to schedule the ultrasound. It's probably nothing," she said.

"Oh, you'd better go back," Brad replied. Camille decided he was probably right and made the follow-up appointment for the ultrasound.

During the ultrasound Camille looked at the screen intently. As soon as she saw the tissue, her stomach dropped. She knew that it was not full of fluid like a cyst would be and right then realized that it was probably cancerous. After the ultrasound was over the doctor ordered a biopsy, but Camille already knew what the results of the biopsy would be. "*How am I going to tell Brad?*" she thought to herself as she walked out of the hospital. When she got in her car, she pulled out her cell phone and dialed Brad's phone number.

"Hey, there," he answered.

"Hi, it's not good," she responded.

"What did they say?" he quickly replied.

"They need to do a biopsy, but I can tell it's not a cyst. I know the results are going to come back and show that it's cancerous," she said. She could feel her eyes starting to tear up and a lump rising in her throat.

"It's okay, it's okay," Brad said on the other end of the phone. "We don't know for sure yet and you're going to be okay," he said.

Camille tried to relax and breathe. "Are you okay to drive home?" Brad asked.

"Yes, I'll be fine," she said.

"Okay, I'll talk to you later," he said and hung up.

Shouldn't He Want to Come with Me?

Camille's biopsy confirmed her breast cancer diagnosis and she was quickly referred to a surgeon for the lumpectomy. Camille sat in her kitchen looking at her already full calendar and questioning how she was going to fit the doctor's appointments, surgery, likely radiation and possibly chemotherapy in with everything else they had going on. Camille knew that her health was the priority but felt extremely guilty that this had happened while planning for Annie's wedding. Undergoing breast cancer treatment was definitely not how Camille had envisioned planning her daughter's wedding. Just as Camille was starting to feel completely overwhelmed looking at the calendar, Brad walked into the kitchen.

"Do you want to go with me to the surgical consultation?" Camille asked.

"Do you need me to go?" Brad replied as he looked in the refrigerator. Camille was troubled by his response. "*Shouldn't he want to go with me?*" she thought to herself.

"I mean, it is just a consultation, so you don't have to be there to drive me home or anything," she said.

Brad grabbed a can of soda from the refrigerator and brought it over to the kitchen table. "It's just a busy time of year with the crew. You know we have a bunch of jobs coming up and since I will already have to take off work for the surgery, I just don't think I should take additional days that are not completely necessary right now."

Camille understood his logic, but still felt like he should want to go with her. She nodded, but Brad could see that she was displeased. "Can't you ask Annie or your mom to go with you?" he said. Camille did not want to worry her daughter or her mom any more than they already were. Camille felt that Annie already had a lot on her plate with the wedding planning and her mom was 78 years old and had her own health issues. "I don't want to trouble either of them," Camille said. She then called the surgeon's office and scheduled the appointment.

"You're Going to Need Chemo"

During Camille's consultation, the surgeon thoroughly explained the biopsy results. "Everything looks really good," he said. "I don't think the cancer has gone into your lymph nodes yet, which is good because you will probably only need the lumpectomy and a little radiation." Camille asked a few questions about the recovery. She felt better after meeting with her surgeon, but still was nervous.

The following week Brad drove Camille to the surgical center for her lumpectomy. Camille's mom and Annie had offered to come to the hospital too, but Camille did not want Annie to take any extra time off work and felt that the hospital was too far for her mom to drive to on her own. The surgeon met with Camille and Brad before the surgery. He told them that they would let Brad know what they found after the surgery and then come back to talk to Camille more when she was alert.

When she woke up from the surgery, Camille felt cold and her mind was muddled. She noticed that the nurse Brad brought into the room but was still too groggy to talk to him. When she was finally awake, she looked over at Brad expecting him to have a comforting expression. Instead, he looked scared and tired.

"What did they find?" Camille asked.

"The doctor said that it was in a node and you're going to need chemo and stuff," Brad said. Camille was upset and asked Brad more questions, but he was not sure how to answer them. He just shook his head and said, "I don't know."

"Did you tell Annie and my mom?" Camille asked.

"Your mom called while you were still out and I told her that you were going to need chemo. I texted Annie and let her know you were out of surgery," he said.

Camille was later discharged from the hospital. She was exhausted and scared of what was ahead of her. Brad did not say anything on the drive home. After Camille got comfortable on the couch, she looked at her cell phone and noticed that she had four missed calls from her mom and several text messages from Annie.

"Are you okay?" "What did they find?" "Mom, text me back!" Annie texted. Camille knew Annie was worried, but she did not have the energy to respond.

"Can you text Annie and tell her what the surgeon said?" Camille asked Brad.

"I thought it would be better coming from you since you are the nurse," Brad responded.

"I'm tired and I don't have the energy to deal with her questions right now, but I can tell she's freaking out. Can't you just text her for me?" Camille snapped.

Brad sighed loudly, agreed to text Annie, and walked out of the room. Camille knew she was being difficult, but she also felt like Brad was not being helpful.

Feeling Like a Burden

Camille hated that she needed someone to drive her to and from her chemotherapy appointments and that she was unable to work throughout the treatment. She felt utterly useless and like she did not have any control over her life. Most days Camille's mother drove her to the appointments. Brad tried to drive her when he could, but his work schedule was making it difficult for him to help Camille as much as she needed. Annie also tried to help take her to the appointments, but Camille knew Annie's vacation and sick time were really limited and she hated being dependent on her daughter for rides. For the first time in her adult life, Camille truly felt like she was a burden on her family. Even though her mother was retired and able to help out, she hated having her mother drive her anywhere and having to depend on her so much. Camille felt like it was time for her to take care of her mother, not the other way around.

Camille's mother was also trying to help Camille out around the house, which was making Camille feel even worse. Her mother had come over to cook and clean up several times, but Camille found her mother's help distracting and stressful. One afternoon, Camille decided she had had enough of her mother's help when her mother had gotten a stool out of the garage to try to clean the top of the refrigerator. Camille watched as her mother was struggling with the stool and almost fell down.

"Mom, you're going to fall and then I'm going to have to take care of you!" Camille exclaimed. "Can't you just sit down and spend time with me?"

"I'm just trying to help you," Camille's mother said before climbing down and taking a seat at the table. After that incident, Camille decided she would just tell her mother that she was doing better and didn't need any help around the house. It was too stressful for Camille to worry about her mother getting hurt trying to help her. However, without her mom's help, the house quickly became a mess.

A few weeks later, Camille sat on the couch a day after her latest round of chemotherapy treatments. She had very little energy to do anything and to make matters worse, she could barely lift her arms. Camille's doctor had recently diagnosed her with lymphedema, a swelling in her arms that occurred as a side effect to the lumpectomy. The swelling constricted her movements, which made it difficult to do everyday activities like cooking and cleaning. Camille tried to relax, but all she could think about was that the carpeting needed vacuuming, the dirty dishes were piled up in the sink, there was a layer of dust that was covering what seemed like every inch of the furniture in the house, and that she badly needed to run to the grocery store so that they had food in the house. Camille was frustrated that she could not do anything, but was also upset by the fact that Brad did not seem to care that it felt like their life was falling apart.

Brad came home from work later that evening and sat down next to her. "How was your day?" he asked as he flipped through the sports channels on television.

"It was fine," Camille said. "I wish I could get some of this cleaning done, but I'm having trouble doing much."

"Don't worry about it," Brad said. "If things don't get done it is no big deal. All you need to focus on is getting better."

"I guess you're right," she replied.

"What do you want me to make for dinner?" Brad asked.

Camille could feel the anger building up as she stared at him since she felt like he should be the one to plan the meals. "I don't think we have much. We haven't made it to the grocery store yet this week," she said.

Brad just shrugged his shoulders. "No big deal. I'll just make a peanut butter and jelly sandwich. Do you want one?"

"I'm not hungry," Camille said as she shook her head.

"Okay, well I can always make you one later," he said before getting up and walking into the kitchen. "I'll run to the grocery store this weekend. Let me know what you need me to get." Camille knew he was trying to help as best he could and felt guilty for getting upset with him.

The Wrong Expectations

The following Saturday, Camille and Annie got together to work on wedding planning. Camille was feeling a little better and looking forward to helping her daughter. She felt like she had not been able to do as much as she would have liked since the diagnosis and was ready to pitch in.

"Thanks for coming with me today, mom," Annie said as walked out of the floral shop. "How are you feeling?"

"I'm doing a little better today. Honestly, it just feels good to get out of the house a little," Camille said.

They then walked over to the car and drove to their favorite sandwich shop to get a quick lunch. Camille ordered a bowl of soup but was having trouble eating very much. Annie asked her if she wanted something else to eat, but Camille told her that she was fine.

"I'm worried about you, mom," Annie said. "You've lost so much weight already. Is dad cooking things you like?"

"You know your father," Camille said.

"Dad really needs to make sure you get the right nutrition right now. I found this article online that said a healthy diet can contribute to your recovery."

"I'm fine. Your father is doing his best and I'm getting through everything."

"Okay, but I don't want you to feel like you can't ask me for help if you need it. I can come over and cook you dinner this week if you want?" Camille felt touched by her daughter's offer, but also felt like she did not want to ask too much of anyone.

Annie dropped Camille off at home later that afternoon. Brad had asked her how everything went, but she could tell he was not very interested in wedding planning other than how much everything was going to cost. "Well, I'm glad she's happy," Brad said after Camille explained to him the type of floral arrangements they had picked out.

"The wedding feels like it is coming up so fast. With everything going on, it just feels like a lot right now," Brad said.

Camille was a little annoyed since she did not feel like he had done anything to help plan for the wedding. "Well at least you're not the one expected to do anything," Camille replied.

Brad looked back at her and grimaced. "I'm expected to pay for a lot of it," Brad snapped.

"We're both expected to pay for it. It just would be nice if you helped out a little more with planning since I can't do as much."

"Honestly, what do you expect from me? I'm doing the best I can. I've taken you to all of your appointments that I could. I'm helping out around the house. I'm worried about you, but I'm tired and stressed too," Brad said.

Camille felt guilty for having made him feel like he was not helping. "*Maybe I have the wrong expectations*," Camille thought to herself.

"I'm sorry. I did not want to make it seem like you were not helping," Camille said.

Brad apologized and then went out to the garage. It felt like their entire life was falling apart. Camille was scared about the cancer, but she and Brad did not talk about "what ifs." At the same time, Camille did not feel like Brad was doing everything she needed from him. Camille felt tired and sat wondering what she could do to make things better.

DISCUSSION QUESTIONS

1. How did Camille's cancer diagnosis affect her family?
2. In what ways did Camille's family provide social support to her throughout her cancer treatment? In what ways were her expectations of support left unmet?
3. Did Camille and her family seem to talk about her cancer diagnosis or avoid the topic? What does topic avoidance say about the family's coping with an uncertain diagnosis?
4. How did Camille's feelings of being a burden influence her communication with her family members?
5. How did Brad express caregiver stress?

REFERENCES

Charmaz, K. (1983). Loss of self: A fundamental form of suffering in the chronically ill. *Sociology of Health and Illness, 5,* 168–195.

Charmaz, K. (1995). The body, identity, and self: Adapting to impairment. *The Sociological Quarterly, 36,* 657–680.

Donovan-Kicken, E., & Caughlin, J. P. (2010). The multiple goals perspective on topic avoidance and relationship satisfaction in the context of breast cancer. *Communication Monographs, 77,* 231–256.

Goldsmith, D. J., Miller, L. E., & Caughlin, J. P. (2007). Openness and avoidance in couples communicating about cancer. In C. S. Beck (Ed.), *Communication yearbook 31* (pp. 62–115). New York, NY: Lawrence Erlbaum Associates.

Helgeson, V. S., & Cohen, S. (1996). Social support and adjustment to cancer: Reconciling descriptive, correlational, and intervention research. *Health Psychology, 15,* 135–148.

Kirchhoff, A. C., Yi, J., Wright, J., Warner, E. L., & Smith, K. R. (2012). Marriage and divorce among young adult cancer survivors. *Journal of Cancer Survivorship, 6,* 441–450.

Mathieson, C. M., & Stam, H. J. (1995). Renegotiating identity: Cancer narratives. *Sociology of Health & Illness, 17,* 283–306.

Olson, R. E. (2015). Exploring identity in the 'figured worlds' of cancer care-giving and marriage in Australia. *Health and Social Care in the Community, 23,* 171–179.

Segrin, C., & Flora, J. (2005). *Family communication.* Mahwah, NJ: Lawrence Erlbaum Associates.

Venetis, M. K., Magsamen-Conrad, K., Checton, M. G., & Greene, K. (2014). Cancer communication and partner burden: An exploratory study. *Journal of Communication, 64,* 82–102.

CHAPTER 33

"My Mom Has Been Gone for A While, But She's Still Alive…" Communicating As a Child of a Parent with Alzheimer's Disease

Aimee E. Miller-Ott – *Illinois State University*

ABSTRACT

Alzheimer's disease accounts for a significant number of dementia cases in the United States. The disease causes devastating physical, psychological, and relational losses for the person suffering from the illness and those in the person's social and familial networks. Children of parents with the disease are particularly vulnerable to mental and physical illness as a result of stepping into a caretaker role for the parent, even when the role is more informal in nature. In this case study, siblings Michael and Avery discuss their family's experiences with their mother's Alzheimer's disease. Through their conversation and flashbacks to previous interactions with family members and strangers, Michael and Avery highlight family members' common struggles with the illness, including identifying as children of a parent with Alzheimer's, coping with the impact of the disease on their family, managing their mothers' private health information, reacting to others' perceived insensitive comments about the illness, responding to stressors, and seeking support.

BACKGROUND

More than 5 million Americans live with Alzheimer's disease, and by 2050, that number may increase to 16 million (Alzheimer's Association, 2018). Presently, there is no cure for this disease. Alzheimer's disease affects the person diagnosed with the illness and creates chaos in the family system (Karner & Bobbitt-Zeher, 2005). Specific to Alzheimer's disease, family members with the illness become "nonparticipating, nonrelational, noncommunicating, dependent" individuals (Karner & Bobbitt-Zeher, 2005, p. 552). Scholars have focused on the physical, mental, relational, and psychological strain that caring for a parent puts on a child (Kruk, 2015; Stoeckel & Weissbrod, 2015). However, even family members who are not the formal caretakers struggle with escaping "the everyday challenges of communication when it comes to interacting with the [person]" (Bute, Donovan-Kicken, & Martins, 2007, p. 236). One particularly challenging aspect of the disease is the experience of ambiguous loss; in this context, a family member is physically present yet psychologically absent (Boss, 2009). Ambiguous loss stems from knowing that the parent will never be the same and experiencing uncertainty about the family member's quality of life and future (O'Brien, 2017). Family members of people with Alzheimer's disease also experience changes to their master, interactional, and personal identities (Tracy, 2013) when they become children of parents with the disease (Miller-Ott, 2018).

In this case study, the two main characters, Michael and Avery, are siblings who have a mother with Alzheimer's disease. Through their living room conversations, and their flashbacks to previous interactions with others, we get a glimpse into their struggles with communicating with family members, changes to their identities, concerns about maintaining appropriate levels of privacy about their mother's illness, and family stressors.

Note: Many of the following experiences and struggles of having a parent with Alzheimer's disease illuminated in this case study reflect actual word-for-word transcript excerpts provided by participants in Miller-Ott (2018). I wish to thank the participants for their honesty and openness in sharing their struggles with me.

CASE STUDY

TODAY
(At their parents' house)
"These are all so sad!" Avery said as she stared at the tablet screen.

"But they're true!" Michael replied.

"Yeah but they are all so depressing," Avery explained.

Michael looked out the window and then back to his sister. *Their mom was in the other room, and yes they were talking about her, but it's not like she knows what's going on anyway,* Michael thought to himself.

Avery didn't know what else to say. For months now, her brother has been spending hours on social media every day trying to figure out what to do about their mom, looking for a glimpse of hope in a very sad time. He visits online support group after online support group, reading stories that people post about their parents with Alzheimer's. So depressing was right! But it was their reality, and it didn't help to wallow in their own self-pity. *I mean, look at our mom!* she thought. *She doesn't even know her own name, let alone ours. It's too late for help now!*

1 YEAR AGO
(In the doctor's office)

It had happened all so fast. One day they were in the doctor's office with her talking about how she was having a hard time coming up with her words, which was really embarrassing for her considering her whole professional life was spent in a college classroom, teaching others how to communicate.

"So who used to handle money for the family?" the doctor asked, to gather more information about what was going on at home.

"I have always done it," Vicky, their mom, answered quickly.

"Mmm, okay," he responded, taking notes. "And are you still doing that now?" the doctor asked.

"Yes I am."

As the doctor added to his notes, Michael and Avery looked at each other with shock on their faces. Avery felt sick to her stomach. Was their mom really just outright lying to the doctor? Avery looked at her dad, who quickly turned away. Michael's eyes started to fill with tears.

"Mom, that isn't true! You don't pay the bills anymore. Dad and I do!" Avery spoke up, trying to stay focused and logical. But Avery was fuming now. They had spent the last 10 minutes correcting everything their mom was telling the doctor, and their dad wasn't being of any help. He just sat there. Does she make her own food? Mom says yes, they all know that isn't true. Does she shower every day? Mom says yes, they all know that it's only if they tell her to and even then it's usually a fight. *Why are we having to correct everything she says?* Avery thinks to herself.

TODAY
(At their parents' house)

They had no idea that a year later, she would not have a concept of time, or words, or coherent thoughts, or really anything that made sense to anyone not in her head.

"God, remember the doctor's appointment a year ago? We were stuck in that tiny room and mom was just lying to the doctor, and we had to speak up and contradict everything that she said?" Avery recalled.

"Oh man, she was so pissed off at us!" Michael responded.

"Yeah but someone had to do it. He was trying to diagnose her, for God's sake, and she was just making stuff up. We never would have gotten anywhere if we had let her keep lying."

"But remember how mad dad was at us?" Michael asked, eyes open widely.

"He still is. I think he still brings it up sometimes," Avery recalled, shaking her head.

"He was just in denial," Michael interjected.

"Are you saying he isn't still in denial?" Avery asked.

"I mean, not as much… hopefully… I think he just misses her, like we all do," Michael said.

"Of course! But even after bringing in Molly to care for her…"

Michael interrupted, "Well I'm sure it's hard watching a nurse, who really is just a stranger, take care of your wife because she screams and tries to hit you every time you help. Can you imagine?" Michael couldn't, actually. Thankfully he had his wife Laura and his daughter Maddie, although things had gotten tense at home.

3 DAYS AGO
(At Michael's house)

"But she had to lie to her grandma!" Laura yelled at Michael in the middle of the kitchen.

"It wasn't lying. It was just being super nice to mom and not making her feel bad," Michael explained as he choked up thinking back to this situation with his mom and daughter.

"Come on Michael, Maddie knows that your mom doesn't have seven brothers…"

"But I didn't want her to correct my mom. Do you know how bad that would make my mom feel?" Michael implored.

"What about your daughter? She's so confused about grandma and why she's so different now, it doesn't make sense to any of them, and what are we supposed to tell them? Grandma used to know you but now she doesn't?" Laura takes a long pause, not sure of the reaction she will get to what she's about to say next… "Maybe, well, I just think that we need to talk about maybe not having her around your mom anymore. I mean, do you really want her to remember her grandma like that?"

TODAY
(At their parents' house)

Michael shook his head to get that fight out of his mind. For now he had to focus on what to do next for his mom, even if that meant staying in a fight with Laura for a few more days.

He turned to Avery, "So Uncle Jim has been texting me and asking if he can come see mom. The last time we talked to him about her, she was doing much better. I think he might be really mad that we haven't kept him in the loop more."

Avery replied angrily, "If Uncle Jim cared that much, he would come see her more often or call or just ask how she's doing! My God, we are doing all of the work with mom, calling doctors for her, hiring the nurse, getting her medications, just hanging out here … and then we have to take care of our own families and carve out time for our own careers! Dad is useless because he's either outside working in the yard or watching TV and still doesn't admit that she's gone…"

Michael tried to interrupt but she kept talking, which is typical when she gets into these tirades about the rest of the family.

"And if anyone in our family wants to come hang out with her or take her on a walk or just try to talk to her, then they will see how she is doing." Avery drew in a deep breath after finishing her monologue. She was so tired of having these conversations about family members who act like they care but just want to make themselves feel better.

"But don't you remember that dad asked us to keep everyone informed?" Michael asked.

"That was after he told us not to tell anyone!" Avery retorted.

Michael continued, "But then we got him to change his mind, so let's let everyone know how bad it's gotten and that they might want to come see her before we move her into the nursing home." He then said, "And Uncle Tony did come by last week to see her."

"And don't you remember how pissed off we got?" Avery asked.

1 WEEK AGO
(At their parents' house)

"You will never believe what Uncle Tony just texted me," Avery said to Michael. They were two hours into going through their parents' belongings in the attic. They had come to the realization a few weeks ago that once their mom moved into the nursing home, their dad might want to sell the house and live closer to her.

"Why is Uncle Tony even texting you in the first place? Aren't you fighting because he pretty much ignores mom?"

Avery explained, "Yeah but then last week he said he wanted to come over this week and bring her some old family photos to look through. He thought it would help her remember, like she had amnesia or something!"

"So what he did write?"

"Get this. He said, 'Wow, Vicky is doing great! I can't even tell she has Alzheimer's!'" Avery said in a high-pitched incredulous voice.

"What?" Michael called back at her. What nerve he had to say that. He clearly has no idea what is going on. *Maybe it was his attempt to make us feel better*, Michael thought.

Avery continued, "Screw him! Seriously, if she doesn't have Alzheimer's, then what does he think we are spending our days dealing with here? And if she isn't sick, then why isn't he coming around much anymore?"

TODAY
(At their parents' house)

Michael crossed the room and looked at his mom, who was staring out the front window of the house, murmuring to herself.

"Well it's not like it's any better when it's a friend. My favorite was when her old friend Nicole came by and took her for a walk. Remember she was like, 'Oh she's just getting old. This is what happens when you get older!'" Michael added.

"Right, it was like, 'Um, okay I didn't realize that getting older meant forgetting who you are, who your kids and husband are, not knowing how to feed yourself, and not making any sense when you talk!'" Avery put her hands on her head and shook it back and forth. She'd had a headache for what felt like six months. This was just all so stressful, trying to do the right thing for everyone. Should the family know? What should she do for their mom? Is dad okay? Is Michael spending his time trying to find a solution to everything? It's really hard when Michael thinks he can fix their mom by reading ideas online!

"Yeah it's like everyone thinks we are making it up!" Michael said, taking Avery out of her own thoughts. He took a breath and continued, "Well… at least they haven't made fun of her as far as we know."

Avery had a puzzled look on her face. She asked with a sarcastic tone in her voice, "What are you talking about? Who would do that?"

He hesitated telling his sister because he didn't know what she'd say. He thought she might get mad that he ever got involved in the first place. He knew that she'd think he was too emotional about this whole situation. Michael stopped for a moment, and suddenly he was back to a couple of days ago at the gym when just the word "Alzheimer's" set him off.

2 DAYS AGO
(At the gym)

Michael was packing his bag after spending an hour working out at the gym. *There's nothing like a good workout and a game of basketball to help me forget about mom for a little while*, he thought to himself. As he sat down to take a breath before returning to work, his attention shifted to a group of guys who took over the court after he and his friends finished playing. One of them missed what he considered to be an easy layup. Another of the guys called to him, "Did you forget how to play?" Another one then added, "What is it, Alzheimers's already?" Overhearing this, Michael felt like he had been punched in the gut. He got really mad and for some reason, in a way that typically wasn't like him, he wanted to fight them. Michael took a deep breath to calm down as he could feel his face turning red. But it didn't work. He found himself getting up and walking onto the court.

"Dude, what are you doing? No dress shoes on the court!" one of the men yelled at Michael as he approached them.

Ignoring the guy's question, Michael called, "I don't appreciate that comment. My mother has Alzheimer's!"

The men each looked at each other and starting apologizing to him. Michael wasn't in the mood for their expressions of "I'm sorry, man," so he walked away but not before turning around again and calling back at them, "Well you don't know how many people suffer from it!" He was shocked by how upset and loud he was. It was completely out of character for Michael. He then grabbed his bag from the bleachers and walked out of the gym.

TODAY
(At their parents' house)

At the end of Michael's story, they both looked at each other for what seemed like ten minutes but was really only a few seconds. Finally, Avery sat down at the end of the couch and laughing, said, "I'm not sure if this conversation is making us feel better or worse!" She paused, rubbing her temples, and then continued by taking the subject back to their uncles, "Okay, first, we need to figure out what are we going to do about telling everyone in the family about how she's doing."

Michael paused for a moment and then said, "I don't know. Maybe it's selfish or just because I want to protect her. I get that we have to keep people updated but I just don't see the need for them to hear all of the details. She doesn't control what people think of her anymore so it's our job to make sure that everyone else remembers her in a certain way."

Avery jumped in, "Or that basketball players don't talk smack about her!"

"Okay, that's not fair. I know they weren't talking about *her* but her illness was the punchline." Michael hesitated bringing up what he was reading online because his sister thought it was goofy to spend time looking for help on social media. But he just had to share this. Maybe she would start to understand that they weren't alone in figuring this whole thing out. He'd be happy if she just even seemed upset one time and wasn't always in a logical mode, "I just read a story on a Facebook post that a guy took his dad with Alzheimer's to a football tailgate and his dad was acting like he does and people assumed that he was drunk. They started taking pictures of him and laughing because they thought he was wasted, that he was so hilarious. And the guy who posted this wrote that he thought it was great that people were involving his dad, but then as it kept going, he started thinking, *Wait they're mocking him and it's not funny.*"

Avery clasped her hand over her mouth. "Oh my God, that's awful. Can you imagine? What would you do?"

"Probably punch them," Michael joked.

"What is up with you thinking of punching people?! Who are you?"

Michael replied, "Out of control, clearly! I can't help it. It's like they're talking about mom without actually talking about mom."

Avery changed the subject from his story, mainly because she questioned in her head, *How can I respond to that?*. She continued, "Going back to the uncles again, I don't have a lot of time to sit around and call everyone, not with everything else going on in my own life. My God, I haven't seen my husband in two nights, and I feel like I haven't slept in weeks."

"Well this is so hard. I mean, it's mom!" Michael asserted.

"Well it's kind of our…" Avery trailed off, hoping that Michael hadn't picked up on what she was about to say.

But he had. Michael stood from the spot where he was sitting opposite Avery on the couch and snapped back, "What does that mean?"

Avery hesitated because of the look on her brother's face. "You know what I mean. She sits in front of us but she's not there."

"Avery, don't," he said as he pointed his finger at his sister. He then paused, took a deep breath, and looked away.

They both waited to talk for a while. They had gotten used to silence, especially when around their dad who didn't want to talk about anything.

Avery started again and tried to break the ice. "Okay, we've gotten serious again. Let's go back to talking about you punching guys playing basketball!" She smiled, trying to get a smile from her brother in return. But considering that he wasn't even looking at her, she could only imagine the angry look on his face.

She walked up to her brother and put her hand on his shoulder and explained in a soft voice, "I just meant, *our mom*, the one who we knew, who raised us … she's gone. And she's been gone for a while."

Michael remained facing the other side of the room. "I understand what you're saying, but she's still here. She's alive; it's not like she's dead. And you know, even though it's like we've become the parents, we have to respect her and be loyal because she did so much for us. We're her kids and we have to protect her, we have to help her through this."

Immediately, Avery questioned, "But what's on the other side, what are we helping her through?"

"We're helping her through the rest of her life! Without us, she can't do much on her own. Remember dinner a couple of months ago?"

2 MONTHS AGO
(At an Italian restaurant near their parents' house)

Michael and Avery decided to take their mom and dad out for dinner. They hadn't been to a restaurant since their mother's illness had progressed, but they had to get out of the house and be around other people. They were all going stir crazy! Within a few minutes of being at the restaurant, their mother grew very agitated. She started asking questions about the menu that didn't quite make sense and got angry when they wouldn't order her food that wasn't on the menu. She snapped at the server, loudly telling her to "go away!" People started staring at her. She was clearly ill, but no one around them knew what was wrong with her.

Michael had read about an idea online to make papers that look like business cards that tell people that their mother has Alzheimer's and give some tips on how to best interact with her. So he pulled a card from his wallet, walked up to the server who was preparing their drinks, and handed her a card.

When he got back to the table, Avery asked, "Tell me that you didn't just give that woman one of those cards? We never agreed to do those!"

Michael just looked at his sister and nodded his head, then looked away.

Avery said quietly but angrily, "So you still don't think that it was weird, almost inappropriate, to just out of the blue, be like, 'Hey random server who I don't know and will likely never see again, just a heads up, my mom has Alzheimer's?'"

At the same time, the server came back with their drinks. She smiled and handed their mom her water, and then asked everyone what they wanted to eat. When talking to their mother, she asked her directly but then looked at Michael who ordered for his mom. She then walked away.

Michael responded quietly, "Well it worked. She was very sweet to her."

Avery snapped back, also quietly, "Well now she feels bad for us! And I hate that."

"I have to make a quick call," Michael said as he stood up and walked from the table, first nodding at Avery for her to follow. Avery was close behind him.

"Hey," Michael said sternly to Avery when they got around the corner near the bathrooms, "at least we get to go to dinner and it's not awful so far, and people know what's going on. Without this, she can't do anything or go anywhere. Do you think she'd want to be like that?"

Avery quickly responded, "She doesn't even know whether she's here or at home!"

He took a long pause without responding. They both walked back to the table and finished their dinner.

TODAY

(At their parents' house)

"Yeah that was fun," Avery said sarcastically. After a long pause, she asked, "Wanna hear a funny story?" trying to connect with her brother.

"Sure," he replied unconvincingly.

"Well, I didn't tell you this before, but last time I took her out in the car—I mean this was months ago—I told her to put her seatbelt on and you know what she said?"

"No idea."

"She told me to f-off!" Avery said with a smile on her face.

"She did not!" Michael shook his head, "No way!"

"Yes, she certainly did."

"When did she start speaking like that? I've never heard her say that!" Michael laughed along with his sister.

They locked eyes and sat down on the couch again, only after both looking back at their mom in the other room.

"You know what I miss?" Michael asked, sadness in his voice.

"What? Her cooking, since you can't cook?" Avery laughed.

Michael responded, now smiling, "Not funny! No, I miss calling her. I don't know if you know this but before she got sick, anytime I was in the car for more than 15 minutes, I would always call her. We would talk about so much. But once she started to get sick, I found myself avoiding calling her... I mean, you remember, talking to her became a mess." Michael's throat tightened.

Avery added, "I know, I remember when that got really bad. Every conversation became a one-way conversation. The only way we could talk would be if I prompted it, if I was the engager in the conversation and asked all of the questions."

Michael recalled, "Yeah, then I think after that is when she started withdrawing. Remember she started getting really quiet around us, around Maddie? It was so hard to interact with her at all!"

Avery said, "I know. It's hard on us and on dad and of course on mom every day. And it's hard on our families and I mean, I can't remember the last time my head was actually into work while I was *at* work."

Michael added, "I feel like I'm a dad to my kids and a dad to our mom. Did you ever think we would be in this situation where we're making these big decisions and taking care of our own mom?"

Avery paused for a few moments before responding, "I pictured taking care of her as she got older, but only when she was otherwise healthy. Nothing like this..." She trailed off but then added, "You are doing a good job finding some helpful information online even though I make fun of you for always being on your computer."

After pausing, Michael said, "Okay, so *only* because you brought it up, there *is* one page I found recently that gives advice to others about interacting with people who have a parent with Alzeheimer's. And it's kinda cool because the advice is based on what other people like us are experiencing or have experienced…" He tried to read his sister's face with little luck. But she was looking at him and had a half smile on her lips, so he assumed she wasn't completely against him sharing what he'd found. He walked across the room and grabbed his tablet from the table. He logged in and started scrolling to find the page. When he did, he started reading, "So like, for instance, this says to avoid using the disease as a joke, like those guys at the gym. You know, and it says to be thoughtful because the parent's illness influences how the kids see themselves, and the kids want people to acknowledge and validate what they are going through… kind of like we were mad at Uncle Tony and Nicole for telling us that mom was fine when we are spending all of this time knowing that she's *not* fine and how it's turned our lives upside down too!"

He looked up smiling, and saw that his sister was now crying.

"You okay?" He asked her.

"I am. We'll be okay, she'll be okay. It's not how I thought things would play out as we got older. I'm just glad that people are recognizing that what we are going through is hard and that people want to talk about it."

"Absolutely."

After a long pause, and after wiping the tears from her face, Avery smiled and said, "Well now that we've solved all of our problems looking online …" she winked at her brother and continued, "Wanna go hang out with mom?"

DISCUSSION QUESTIONS

1. What communication changes and/or challenges did Michael and Avery seem to encounter during their mother's diagnosis and through the progression of her illness?
2. In what ways did their talk reveal experiences of ambiguous loss?
3. In what ways did they seem to experience changes and threats to their identities in their recollection of communication with their mom and with others?
4. On what stressors did both children reflect in their conversation with one another?
5. What issues of disclosure and privacy about the illness are evident in their conversation?

REFERENCES

Alzheimer's Association. (2018). *Quick facts about Alzheimer's disease*. Retrieved from https://alz.org/

Boss, P. (2009). The trauma and complicated grief of ambiguous loss. *Pastoral Psychology, 59*, 137–145.

Bute, J. J., Donovan-Kicken, E., & Martins, N. (2007). Effects of communication-debilitating illnesses and injuries on close relationships: A relational maintenance perspective. *Health Communication, 21*(3), 235–246.

Karner, T. X., & Bobbitt-Zeher, D. (2005). Losing selves: Dementia care as disruption and transformation. *Symbolic Interaction, 28*, 549–570. doi:10.1525/si.2005.28.4.549

Kruk, B. (2015). 'I can't bear the thought that he might not recognize me': Personal narratives as a site of identity work in the online Alzheimer's support group. *Communication & Medicine, 12*, 273–286. doi:10.1558/cam18453

Miller-Ott, A. E. (2018). "Just a heads up, my father has Alzheimer's:" Changes in communication and identity of adult children of parents with Alzheimer's disease (Epub ahead of print). *Health Communication*. doi:10.1080/10410236.2018.1547676

O'Brien, M. (2017). Ambiguous loss in families of children with autism spectrum disorders. *Family Relations, 56*, 135–146.

Stoeckel, M., & Weissbrod, C. (2015). Growing up with an ill parent: An examination of family characteristics and parental illness features. *Families, Systems, & Health, 33*, 356–362. doi:10.1037/fsh0000140

Tracy, K. (2013). *Everyday talk: Building and reflecting identities* (2nd ed.). New York, NY: Guilford Press.

CHAPTER 34

Confronting the Master Narrative of Starting a Family: Infertility, Miscarriage, and Mother-Daughter Social Support

Shaye Morrison – *University of Missouri*
Haley Horstman – *University of Missouri*

ABSTRACT

Lucy and Jason just got married and are eager to start their family. Lucy has always dreamed of settling down, getting married, and having a baby right away. Plus, her parents, Maria and Dennis, are constantly asking about when they will have a grandchild. After a few months of trying to get pregnant, Lucy decides to visit the doctor for a checkup and is diagnosed with endometriosis, a medical condition that may inhibit her ability to conceive. Later, Jason also visits the doctor and is diagnosed with fertility problems, rendering their chances of conceiving without medical intervention nearly impossible. Lucy and Jason always assumed they would follow the family master narrative and be able to grow their family biologically and without much trouble, so they are shocked and disappointed. After a lot of talking, they decide to seek fertility treatment. As the two embark on the journey of fertility treatment, they struggle with how to tell friends and family, and what it means for their idea of parenthood. Just when Lucy was beginning to feel defeated and alone, her mom Maria confesses a family secret that will bring the two closer than ever.

CASE STUDY

Lucy had dreamed about her wedding ever since she was a little girl. She pictured herself wearing a beautiful white dress, walking down the aisle of a magnificent church, and staring into the eyes of a perfect (and good-looking!) man as she said her vows. Just a couple of decades later —at precisely the age of 26—her dreams came true. Her wedding day was perfect. The church was beautiful, the guests had a great time, and her family members all got along with her new husband's family.

The morning after their wedding, while her husband Jason is in the shower, Lucy sits on the porch with her coffee and lets everything soak in. She reminisces about Jason and her relationship. It started during her sophomore year of college after they met at a student government meeting, and then they dated through the rest of college. Their friends would make comments to them about getting married; everyone *knew* they were going to. Everyone was excited, but no one was shocked, when they got engaged. They followed the courtship canonical narrative (Langellier & Peterson, 1993), wherein two heterosexual people meet and date in their early twenties and then get married soon thereafter. Their wedding day was the ideal start to a beautiful life that she and Jason were going to create together. Lucy was surprised that several wedding guests asked her when she and Jason would start having kids. She didn't mind the questions though—her biggest aspiration in life had always been to be a mother. She told them that they had planned to start trying to have kids right away! Maybe they'd be lucky enough to have a honeymoon baby!

Six months later…

Lucy and Jason have been trying to get pregnant since the wedding. At first, they were having sex when they wanted to and keeping it pretty casual. They told each other that "it will happen when it's supposed to happen." Privately, though, Lucy was getting sadder and more disappointed every month when she got her period. She secretly started tracking her cycles and trying to schedule sex during her ovulation times. Even though it had only been six months, Lucy expected to get pregnant right away, just like her mom did. She started to become worried that something was wrong—she didn't feel like it should take so long for a healthy couple in their mid-twenties to become pregnant.

Lucy feels very lonely, like she has no one to talk to about her disappointment and frustration over not being pregnant yet. It seems like everyone she knows, including her mom and a few of her girlfriends, got pregnant on their honeymoon or right after, so she is embarrassed to talk about her issues (Frost, Bradley, Levitas, Smith, & Garcia, 2007). All she wants is to have a "normal" family that starts at a "normal" time. Lucy doesn't realize it, but she is adhering to the master narrative of birth (Horstman, Anderson, & Kuehl, 2017), which involves a quick conception, a healthy pregnancy, and an uneventful birth. The fact that her story is not aligning to the master narrative is stressful to Lucy (Japp, Harter, & Beck, 2004). She knows she has to do something about it.

During dinner one night, Lucy tells Jason that she is thinking about making an appointment with her OBGYN to discuss the fact that she hasn't conceived a baby yet. She wants to get a check up and make sure everything is okay. Jason seems surprised. It's only been six months. He assures Lucy that everything is fine. By all accounts, Lucy is at the epitome of health—she is young, eats fresh fruits and vegetables, works out with a personal trainer several times a week, enjoys destressing by running, and doesn't smoke or drink excessively. So, how could anything be wrong with her?

Jason tells Lucy that she just needs to stop worrying and relax. Everything will happen in its own time. He reminds her that his parents had trouble conceiving at first because they put too much pressure on themselves. Frankly, Jason finds it a little premature that Lucy is so fixated on having a baby rather than just enjoying marriage. He doesn't understand why it's such a big deal to her. Lucy leaves the conversation unsettled, and wonders if Jason might be right, that she is worrying for no reason. She decides not to make the OBGYN appointment, at least for now.

Through the next couple of weeks, Lucy tries to broach the topic of having a baby with Jason. He reassures her that everything is okay and their baby will come any day now. He sometimes walks out of the room as he is saying that. Lucy knows Jason is trying to help, but she also knows that he is getting annoyed with her worrying. Every time she tries to talk about a baby, he seems to brush off her concerns about it. After a while, she starts to feel like he's not supporting her (Faw, Harvey, & Feng, 2018; Xu & Burleson, 2001). He doesn't understand how she's feeling. He hasn't always wanted to be a parent like she has.

Later that week…

Lucy has been avoiding talking with her mother, Maria, about this problem. Maria had such an easy time getting pregnant and Lucy is afraid that Maria will blame her for not being pregnant yet. However, Lucy's mom is her best friend and they talk about everything (Harrigan & Miller-Ott, 2013). Just like Maria and her mom Delores, Maria and Lucy talk on the phone every single day and know everything about each other's life (Miller-Day, 2004), so it feels strange not to talk with her about this. It's also difficult to make sense of it all; Lucy feels like she has no one to talk with about this (Brier, 2008)! *It would be much easier if people actually talked about infertility*, Lucy thinks.

The next day, Lucy decides just to call her mom and tell her she's having trouble getting pregnant. Maria says she could tell something was wrong; Lucy had been on edge lately. Lucy tells Maria that she's starting to think she should go to the doctor for a checkup. Maria remarks that it's a good idea and tells Lucy (for what feels like the hundredth time) how easy it has been for all the women in their family to get pregnant. That's enough to convince Lucy to see a doctor.

The next week…

During the OBGYN appointment, Lucy describes how she and Jason have been trying to conceive for the last six months, and that she feels that they should be pregnant by now. The doctor responds by telling her that everything will be fine and that it is normal to take up to a year to conceive. Lucy feels dismissed by this comment (Leite, Makuch, Petta, & Morais, 2005). Even though the doctor didn't ask if she had any symptoms of infertility, she describes how she had always experienced incredibly painful and irregular periods. This information finally convinces the doctor that Lucy should have some tests conducted. Lucy is comforted by the fact that the doctor decides to run the tests because it means that he does believe there may be a problem with her. This reassured Lucy a bit that she would have the medical support needed if the tests indicated any fertility problems (Willer, 2014).

After going through several steps of testing, pelvic exams, ultrasounds, and a few minimally invasive procedures, the doctor confirmed his original suspicion and diagnosed Lucy with endometriosis (i.e., a painful condition where uterine tissue grows outside the uterus; Mayo Clinic, 2018). Although her doctor makes it clear that this does not make her infertile, it would make conception more challenging. He advises Lucy and Jason to continue trying to naturally conceive for another six months, and to come back for an additional evaluation if there is no progress. The doctor reassures Lucy that she can likely eventually have a biological child, and that he will help explore all treatment options if it should come to fertility treatments. Overall, she appreciates the support and feels comforted that the doctor is so confident that she will eventually get pregnant (Willer, 2014). Additionally, she is relieved that her dreams of having a biological child can remain intact—she couldn't stomach the thought of telling her husband they would never have "children of their own," reinforcing the dominant master narrative that biological children are best (Suter, Baxter, Seurer, & Thomas, 2014).

When Lucy gets home and tells Jason about her endometriosis, she is surprised at how nonchalant he is about the news. Rather than asking Lucy how she feels about the diagnosis and what it means for the future of their fertility, he just tells her it will be fine and they can go back in six months if needed. Lucy is hurt by Jason's lack of support. She wants him to be more empathic and concerned about this potentially life-altering problem (Linden & Vodermaier, 2012). She becomes even more enraged when he brings up a recent HuffPost article he read about how stress is bad for conception, so she should relax.

Lucy starts to believe that Jason thinks this is all her fault, and that she is overreacting. Little does she know Jason thinks he is being empathic and supporting her emotions. Yet, Jason is struggling with his identity as a man, and fears that maybe there are problems with him too. He doesn't have any friends who have gone through this before, so he doesn't know what to think about it, let alone how to talk to Lucy about it (McCreight, 2004).

Two months later…

Jason and Lucy are heading to dinner at her parents' house. Typically, they enjoy these dinners, but they know that as soon as they walk through the door, Dennis and Maria will ask for an update on their pregnancy status. Unfortunately, their report is that nothing has changed. Lucy began feeling a little bit better because she thought that Jason was *finally* starting to worry too. Unbeknownst to her, Jason actually felt like she was obsessing over her ovulation and pestering him about going to the doctor too. He began dreading intimacy with his wife, and their sex life went from spontaneous and fun to feeling like an extra job (Luk & Loke, 2015).

Just as predicted, upon walking into the house, Dennis immediately asks Jason when he will be getting a grandchild. Although Jason laughs it off and says, "We're working on it!" he is thinking that it may never happen. Ever since Jason was introduced to the family, it was clear that grandchildren were expected. Both Dennis and Maria came from large families and wanted their children to continue that tradition. (Un)luckily for Jason, Lucy is the first of their children to get married, so the pressure to fulfill this master narrative was mounting. As dinner continued, Maria and Lucy began talking about a recent article Lucy saw that certain changes in diet may reduce the likelihood of endometriosis becoming more severe. Maria reaffirms that children should be Lucy's main priority and that she should be willing to try anything that might help. *Of course her mom will make Lucy try one of those crazy diets, instead of just letting this happen naturally*, Jason thought. After dinner, both Lucy and Jason feel an increased sense of pressure from Dennis and Maria to quickly have (biological) children to build their family (Jordan & Revenson, 1999).

A few days later…

It's been nine months since the wedding, and Lucy is still not pregnant. Jason is starting to feel that his wife and in-laws think that maybe it's his fault. It's like they think he can't uphold his obligation to fulfill Lucy's destiny of becoming a mother. So, mostly just to prove them wrong, he decides to go to the doctor and get his fertility tested.

During the appointment, he finds out that his sperm count is very low. This means that he and Lucy will need to meet with a fertility specialist and likely undergo some more advanced procedures if they want to conceive a baby. This diagnosis is hard for Jason to stomach. He feels that his worst fears are coming true! *Everyone was right*, he thought. *I'll never become a father, and I can't give Lucy what she so desperately wants. What kind of a man does that make me?* This all feels threatening to his masculinity (Medved, 2016).

When Jason tells Lucy about his diagnosis, she is very understanding and supportive, as she always is (Jordan & Revenson, 1999). She reassures him that they will find a good doctor and figure out their options, and they will do whatever is necessary to have a baby "of their own."

Two weeks later...

During the meeting with the fertility specialist, Jason and Lucy are informed that their chances of natural conception are nearly impossible due to both of their medical diagnoses. Although the doctor doesn't directly tell them they are infertile, the conversation is focused on alternative ways to have a baby, including in-vitro fertilization (IVF), intrauterine insemination, surrogacy, and adoption. This is so much information to process, so the doctor tells them to talk about it and come back in a week to discuss their chosen treatment plan.

When Jason and Lucy get home, they are overwhelmed by all the information they just received and how quickly they need to make a decision. After a long conversation, they decide that the most important thing for them is to try to have a biological child. So, because their doctors say the route with the highest chance of effectiveness is IVF, they're going to try it. With that decision comes a variety of interpersonal struggles for Jason and Lucy.

Jason is concerned about the moral objections his family will have. His parents are Catholic and have always said that "everything will happen in God's timing." Jason knows that if he tells them about his and Lucy's decision to undergo IVF, they will tell him that he shouldn't interfere with God's timing. They will likely have other concerns about creating life through science, rather than through God. Because his parents have always made their decisions based on their Catholic beliefs, he is scared that they won't support his and Lucy's IVF decision. At the same time, he feels uncertain about the status of his own religious grounding. Both he and Lucy are healthy and have always engaged in safe health practices, and he doesn't know who else to blame for their circumstances than God (Steuber & Solomon, 2008).

Lucy, on the other hand, is more concerned with her personal identity (Steuber & Solomon, 2008). She knows her parents just want grandchildren and will support whatever she needs to do to make that happen. However, Lucy doesn't know anyone who has undergone IVF and is scared of what her friends will think. She knows that they won't understand how hard this is for her physically, emotionally, financially, and relationally, and she's scared she will be left dealing with her emotions alone. Deep down, she is scared of always having to explain and defend her decision to other people (Bute & Vik, 2010). All of a sudden, Lucy feels that even though this decision may lead to fulfilling her master narrative dream of having biological children, she and Jason will receive judgment for not doing it the *right* way.

Lucy and Jason share their concerns with each other to try to understand each other's reservations with IVF. Jason leans forward, grabs Lucy's hand, and says, "It must be really lonely to think that you can't even talk with your friends about this." Lucy feels validated and supported. This conversation helps them realize that they can count on each other for support, and that they *are* attacking this challenge as a united front. Overall, they agree that they will face a variety of challenges as they begin telling people about their struggle to conceive and their decision to undergo IVF. Talking about their perspectives with one another really helped them to feel supported and satisfied in their relationship, helping to ease the fear of what was sure to be a long and stressful road to having a baby (Horstman & Holman, 2018).

Although they were nervous, Lucy and Jason were firm in their decision to undergo IVF and decided they needed to tell their families. As expected, Lucy's parents support their IVF decision, and are elated that they are one step closer to becoming grandparents. Jason's parents come around too and understand that Jason is doing what he needs to do to support his wife and grow their family. Lucy and Jason are grateful for the support of their families as they begin the preparations to start IVF treatments.

One month later…

After a month of doctor appointments and research, Lucy and Jason are finally ready to start IVF. The only thing standing between them and starting their family is learning how to give Lucy the shots. She asks her mom to come to an appointment to learn how to give her shots in case Jason is ever out of town. After the appointment, Maria tells Lucy that she "never knew how invasive the treatments were." She says she admires Lucy for her bravery to undergo this treatment and for her openness about their infertility struggle. Maria said that she wishes people were open about these experiences when she was Lucy's age because it would have helped her too. Lucy is happy that her mom recognizes that this is a challenging experience but is confused about what her mom is referring to. Maria has always talked about how important having a family is and how her and Dennis loved being parents soon after their marriage.

A week later…

Lucy calls Maria at their "usual time," 5:30 p.m. Lucy feels bad that she's never in a good mood when she talks with her mom anymore. She tells her mom that her dreams to get pregnant seem to be getting further and further away, and she hopes this first cycle of IVF will work. It's so frustrating that Maria was able to get pregnant right away and she can't!

Maria pauses and takes a deep breath. "Mom, what's going on? Things seemed weird when you left the doctor last week, and you're acting strange now. Are you not on board with Jason and me doing IVF?" says Lucy. Maria proceeds to tell her daughter that two months after she got married to Dennis, she had a miscarriage. She was "only" six weeks along, but it was still really tough. They have kept the miscarriage a secret because "no one really talked about those things back then" (Brier, 2008). It happened before they told their families that they were expecting, and after all this time she was embarrassed that it was covered up (Frost et al., 2007).

Lucy is immediately very angry with her mother for keeping her miscarriage a secret. "Why the heck haven't you told me about this, especially since you knew we've been having such a hard time getting pregnant?!" she yells. Lucy feels betrayed and hurt. She felt that her mother put all this pressure on her to have kids right away. She believed their story about it being so easy to have a baby, when in reality it wasn't true!

Maria says she understands why Lucy is angry. "It's just that when we got married, people believed it was your fault if you miscarried, like you did something wrong. And for a long time, I believed that too. I carried around the guilt and shame for so many years, thinking that I could have done something to save my baby," she said. Maria explained that her pregnancy loss was the reason she was so protective of Lucy and her brother. "But I've always loved you so much because you're my 'rainbow baby,' Lucy," said Maria. "You're the baby that came after the storm."

At this, Lucy softened to her mother. It all began to make sense. She started to understand why family was so important to her parents—they lost a child at an early age. Her brother and her had always been the most important things in their parents' lives; they attended their every dance recital, drama performance, and soccer game. They were great parents and valued the lives of their children, and their children's future children. Even though she knew they made each other crazy sometimes, her mom was excited to continue the legacy in their family of grandmothers, mothers, and daughters being best friends (Miller-Day, 2004).

Although it was a tough conversation, it brought Maria and Lucy closer together. Lucy finally felt like someone understood her deep desire to have kids and the lengths she would go to in order to make it happen. In the end, Lucy was glad that Maria would be there to support her through her fertility treatments and any challenges that lay ahead.

DISCUSSION QUESTIONS

1. Lucy and Jason both talk about the pressure they feel to have a baby and their concerns about how people might judge their decision to undergo IVF. How do they each understand the master narrative about having children? In other words, how does their decision to undergo IVF support or contradict what they were told about having a family?

2. Overall, the master narrative in Western society is that biological children are best (Suter et al., 2014). Critique this narrative. Why do you think it exists? What types of families might this narrative marginalize? How can we change this narrative?

3. How do you see the interactional sense-making behaviors of *engagement*, *turn-taking*, *perspective-taking*, and *coherence* (Koenig Kellas, 2005) in Lucy and Maria's conversation about the miscarriage?

4. How do Lucy and Jason differ in the ways they give and expect to receive social support? What factors might contribute to their different expectations of received social support and their different styles for providing support? How might the topic of infertility influence this?

REFERENCES

Brier, N. (2008). Grief following miscarriage: A comprehensive review of the literature. *Journal of Women's Health, 17*, 451–464. doi:10.1089/jwh.2007.0505

Bute, J. J., & Vik, T. A. (2010). Privacy management as unfinished business: Shifting boundaries in the context of infertility. *Communication Studies, 61*, 1–20. doi:10.1080/10510970903405997

Faw, M. H., Harvey, J., & Feng, H. (2018). A replication of Xu & Burleson's "Effects of sex, culture, and social support type on perceptions of spousal social support: An assessment of the 'support gap' hypothesis in early marriage". *Communication Studies, 69*, 314–325. doi:10.1080/10510974.2018.1464043

Frost, J., Bradley, H., Levitas, R., Smith, L., & Garcia, J. (2007). The loss of possibility: Scientisation of death and the special case of early miscarriage. *Sociology of Health & Illness, 29*, 1003–1022. doi:10.1111/j.1467-9566.2007.01019.x

Harrigan, M. M., & Miller-Ott, A. E. (2013). The multivocality of meaning making: An exploration of the discourses college aged daughters voice in talk about their mothers. *Journal of Family Communication, 13*, 1–18. doi:10.1080/15267431.2013.768249

Horstman, H. K., Anderson, J., & Kuehl, R. A. (2017). Making sense of the role of a doula in childbirth: Implications for the U.S. master birth narrative. *Health Communication, 32*, 1510–1519. doi:10.1080/10410236.2016.1234537

Horstman, H. K., & Holman, A. (2018). Communicated sense-making after miscarriage: A dyadic analysis of spousal communicated perspective-taking, well-being, and parenting role salience. *Health Communication, 33*, 1317–1326. doi:10.1080/10410236.2017.1351852

Japp, P. M., Harter, L. M., & Beck, C. S. (2004). Overview of narrative and health communication theorizing. In L. M. Harter, P. M. Japp, & C. S. Beck (Eds.), *Narratives, health, and healing: Communication theory, research, and practice*. Mahwah, NJ: Lawrence Erlbaum Associates.

Jordan, C., & Revenson, T. A. (1999). Gender differences in coping with infertility: A meta-analysis. *Journal of Behavioral Medicine, 22*, 341–358. doi:10.1023.a:1018774019232

Koenig Kellas, J. (2005). Family ties: Communicating identity through jointly told family stories. *Communication Monographs, 72*, 365–389. doi:10.1080/03637750500322453

Langellier, K. M., & Peterson, E. E. (1993). Family storytelling as a strategy of social control. In D. K. Mumby (Ed.), *Narrative and social control: Critical perspectives*. Newbury Park, CA: Sage.

Leite, R. C., Makuch, M. Y., Petta, C. A., & Morais, S. S. (2005). Women's satisfaction with physicians' communication skills during an infertility consultation. *Patient Education and Counseling, 59*, 38–45. doi:10.1016/j.pec.2004.09.006

Linden, W., & Vodermaier, A. (2012). Mismatch of desired versus perceived social support and associated levels of anxiety and depression in newly diagnosed cancer patients. *Support Care Cancer, 20*, 1449–1459. doi:10.1007//s00520-011-1228-3

Luk, B. H., & Loke, A. Y. (2015). The impact of infertility on the psychological well-being, marital relationships, sexual relationships, and quality of life of couples: A systematic review. *Journal of Sex & Marital Therapy, 41*, 610–625. doi:10.1080/0092623X.2014.958789

Mayo Clinic. (2018, July 24). *Endometriosis*. Retrieved from https://www.mayoclinic.org/diseases-conditions/endometriosis/symptoms-causes/syc-20354656

McCreight, B. S. (2004). A grief ignored: Narratives of pregnancy loss from a male perspective. *Sociology of Health and Illness, 26*, 326–350. doi:10.1111/j.1467-9566.2004.00393.x

Medved, C. E. (2016). Stay-at-home fathering as a feminist opportunity: Perpetuating, resisting, and transforming gender relations of caring and earning. *Journal of Family Communication, 16*, 16–31. doi:10.1080/15267431.2015.1112800

Miller-Day, M. A. (2004). *Communication among grandmothers, mothers, and adult daughters: A qualitative study of maternal relationships*. New York, NY: Taylor & Francis Publishing.

Steuber, K. R., & Solomon, D. H. (2008). Relational uncertainty, partner interference, and infertility: A qualitative study of discourse within online forums. *Journal of Social and Personal Relationships, 25*, 831–855. doi:10.1177/0265407508096698

Suter, E. A., Baxter, L. A., Seurer, L. M., & Thomas, L. J. (2014). Discursive constructions of the meaning of "family" in online narratives of foster adoptive parents. *Communication Monographs, 81*, 59–78. doi:10.1080/03637751.2014.880791

Willer, E. K. (2014). Health-care provider compassionate love and women's infertility stressors. *Communication Monographs, 81*, 407–438. doi:10.1080/03637751.2014.940591

Xu, Y., & Burleson, B. R. (2001). Effects of sex, culture, and social support type on perceptions of spousal social support: An assessment of the "support gap" hypothesis in early marriage. *Human Communication Research, 27*, 535–566. doi:10.1111/h.1468-2958.2001.tb00792.x

CHAPTER 35

Managing Uncertainty and Making Decisions in the Context of Dementia

Anne M. Stone – *Rollins College*

ABSTRACT

This case study explores family relationships, managing uncertainty, and making decisions in the context of dementia. In particular, sources of uncertainty family members may experience and communication strategies commonly reported in the literature for managing uncertainty are explored through the experiences of four people—Peggy, a 74-year-old woman and her three children, Michelle, Amy, and Edward. Michelle and Edward are proximal caregivers, living only miles away from their mother while Amy lives abroad. The challenges of providing care for an aging parent from each of their perspectives as well as conflicts that often arise when navigating new roles as caregivers are highlighted. Overall, this case uses Brashers' (2001) uncertainty management theory to frame and understand common familial experiences associated with a diagnosis of dementia. Discussion questions at the end encourage readers to consider the role of communication in managing uncertainty in a caregiving context.

CASE STUDY

According to the Alzheimer's Association (2018), 50 million people worldwide are living with Alzheimer's disease with estimates of 76 million people being diagnosed by 2030. This common form of dementia is not a normal part of aging and influences relationships far beyond the patient–provider dyad. Many online testimonials as well as scholarly articles, (Stone, 2013; Stone & Jones, 2009) provide evidence that Alzheimer's disease is experienced not only by the person diagnosed but by their family and friends as well. This case examines the myriad communication challenges families face when a parent is diagnosed with Alzheimer's disease. The case begins with conversations about symptoms noticed, the diagnosis, and appropriate next steps for care that occur between the parent and adult children. Brashers' (2001) uncertainty management theory serves to highlight the experiences of uncertainty associated with changing roles of family members, navigating healthcare and treatment decisions around moving into a nursing home and taking medications, disclosure, and family conflict.

Peggy is a 74-year-old woman who lives in her two-storey home in England where she raised three children after her husband passed away 50 years earlier. She has recently had trouble with her memory but has not told anyone about her symptoms. Her oldest daughter, Michelle, who lives a few miles from Peggy, checks in on her frequently and has noticed some changes in her mother's behavior. For example, when Michelle came to visit her mother on a Saturday afternoon, Peggy asked if she could make her breakfast and then scolded Michelle for not going to school. Michelle corrected her mother saying, "Mom, it's Saturday afternoon and I haven't been in school for 20 years. Are you feeling okay?" Peggy brushed her off saying that she was just joking … that of course she is feeling okay.

Michelle continued to be troubled by this interaction and decided to call her younger sister Amy who lives in New York—a five-hour time difference. She waited until later that night because she wanted to wait for Amy to get off work. It was 11 p.m. in England and 6 p.m. in New York. Amy picks up the phone when she sees her sister's phone number and greets her sister saying, "How are you? What's new?" as she always does when her family calls. Typically, there's nothing new and they chitchat about family, but today Amy can tell Michelle is worried about something. Michelle responded, "Well… mom's acting strange." She went on to describe her earlier experience and her mother's confusion about the time, day, and year. Amy started to laugh saying, "I'm sure she was joking." Michelle: "Well… that's actually what mom said. Do you think I'm overreacting? I haven't told anyone else because I don't want to worry them unnecessarily."

Amy: "Oh no! Don't tell Edward. You know how he'll react."

Amy is reflecting on an experience a few years ago when their brother Edward decided to tour nursing homes thinking that it wasn't safe for their mother to go up and down the stairs to her bedroom after she suffered a fall. Peggy didn't want to leave her home and she recovered quickly, so Michelle and Amy were able to convince their brother not to pursue it further but Amy knows her brother is uneasy about their mother living alone.

Amy asks Michelle to keep her in the loop. When her mother fell years ago, Michelle and Edward decided it was better not to tell Amy until after their mother had had a few days to recover in the rehabilitation facility and was back at home. Amy was furious but her siblings thought they were just protecting her. Amy remembers Edward telling her, "You have your own kids to worry about. And you're all the way in New York…. what could you do about it anyway?!"

A few months later Michelle drops by her mother's house to discover the gas stove on with no flame. The entire house smells of gas and Michelle finds her mother sitting outside collecting wood for the fireplace. Michelle wonders what would have happened if she had arrived later and her mother had actually lit the wood in the fireplace. For Michelle, this is the moment when she decides to call Edward.

Michelle: "Edward, I need to talk to you about mom. I think she needs more help. I think there might be something wrong."

Edward: "What do you mean? What's going on?"

Michelle: "I'm at the house and she's really confused. She left the gas stove on with no flame and went outside to collect firewood. Why would she light a fire on such a warm day? Why didn't she notice there was no flame on the stove?"

Edward: "You know what it sounds like, right? For the last year she has been more and more forgetful."

Michelle: "I know. I just don't know what to do. I mean she was fine last week."

Michelle highlights what so many adult children experience when they notice symptoms of dementia in a loved one. As other researchers have described, experiences of uncertainty are common in the context of dementia and Alzheimer's disease. Stone and Jones (2009) described the utility of the model of the sources of uncertainty that Brashers et al. (2002) outlined including medical, personal, and social sources. However, Stone and Jones, and other researchers, found that while the general sources of uncertainty fit with the categories medical, personal, and social, the specific experiences of uncertainty are distinct for various illness contexts. For adult children with a parent diagnosed with dementia, medical sources of uncertainty include: unknown etiology of illness, variable symptom patterns, complex treatment decisions, and lack of information about prognosis. In this case, it's clear that the conversations Michelle is having with her siblings may be focused on the medical forms of uncertainty, particularly relevant to the variable symptom patterns. Not all people with dementia exhibit the same symptoms and most people, with or without a diagnosis of dementia, exhibit the most common symptom, forgetfulness, from time to time. It is important to note that variable symptom patterns make it difficult for caregivers, especially informal caregivers like Michelle, to provide adequate care. Her comment about her mother being "fine" last week reminds us of the complexity of caregiving. Periods of perceived normalcy where a parent is lucid make caregivers question previous experiences and plans for treatment.

Michelle: "Well, before we go any further, let's schedule an appointment with the doctor."

Michelle schedules an appointment with Peggy's doctor for the following week. During the week preceding the appointment, Michelle and Edward make an effort to spend more time with their mother. They observe her behaviors and, for the most part, nothing stands out to them. Edward decides they need to speak directly to their mother about their concerns.

Edward: "Mum, how are you feeling these days?"

Peggy: "Fine. Good. Why?"

Michelle: "Mum, remember the day I came by and the gas stove was on with no flame? What happened that day?"

Peggy: "I don't know what you're talking about."

Michelle: "You were getting ready to light a fire even though it was quite warm outside and the house smelled like gas."

Peggy: "You know I get cold easily. And there must be something wrong with the stove. Maybe I need a new one. I'm fine."

Edward: "We know you feel fine and we're so glad but we're concerned about your forgetfulness. Will you go to the doctor and talk to her about some of the things we've noticed? Will you allow us to join you?"

Peggy is reluctant to let her children attend the appointment with her. She has always been a strong, independent woman and does not like the idea of anyone having to take care of her but she agrees to allow Michelle to attend the appointment with her.

Although there is no test that can confirm a person has Alzheimer's disease, Peggy's doctor can make a likely diagnosis based on the answers she provides to a series of questions and the results of physical and neurological exams. One of the tests was the Alzheimer's clock draw test which screens for dementia (Agrell & Dehlin, 1998). Peggy's doctor gives her a blank piece of paper and asks her to draw a clock by hand. Some other versions of the test present patients with a series of blank clocks and asks them to draw hands to show a particular time. Peggy begins to draw a circle. Then, she starts to write in the numbers.

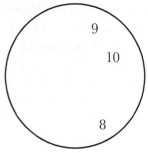

As Agrell and Dehlin (1998) describe, "clock drawing (with a score range of 1–5) is strongly correlated with the Mini Mental State Examination (MMSE) in patients with various cognitive dysfunctions" (p. 399). Peggy's doctor is concerned when she sees the clock drawing. Coupled with the other exams, the doctor believes that Peggy is exhibiting symptoms consistent with Alzheimer's disease. Michelle looks at her mother in disbelief. She didn't realize, as this test indicates, that her dementia is categorized in the middle stages. Peggy's doctor begins to outline her options including a prescription for Aricept.

This is a moment that many adult children with a parent exhibiting symptoms of dementia experience—a moment when their uncertainty is quelled by the apparent certainty of a diagnosis. This calls into play new sources of uncertainty related to treatment. Stone and Jones (2009) described the uncertainty that both patients and family members experience given that there is no cure for Alzheimer's disease. There are, however, a variety of pharmaceutical and nonpharmaceutical options. The pharmaceutical option Peggy's doctor offers has been widely recommended. Birks and Harvey's (2006) review of drug trials provides evidence that people who take Aricept have improved cognition compared to those who were not taking the medication.

Despite evidence of medication efficacy, adult children experience uncertainty about whether or not the medications do in fact help. One participant in Stone and Jones' (2009) study highlighted this uncertainty saying, "How do you know? I have no base. I don't have Dad 1 and Dad 2—one's taking [medications] and the other one isn't" (pp. 680–681).

Michelle's first call after the appointment is to Edward. Edward and Michelle talk for a long while about a range of topics and conclude that they should include their sister Amy in this conversation. They're still unsure about their mother's prognosis and have questions like: "How is this going to progress?" "How long is this going to take?" Researchers (Sperling et al., 2011) have outlined the typical progression of Alzheimer's disease but have consistently noted that each person will experience the disease differently.

In addition to the range of experiences of uncertainty tied to the medical concerns associated with caregiving, adult children with a parent experiencing symptoms of Alzheimer's disease also report experiencing uncertainty related to their changing role. As participants in Stone and Jones' (2009) study described, adult children often experience a reversal of roles where they take on decision-making responsibilities that are typically ascribed to parents. One participant in Stone and Jones' study said:

> And so, you're put in the position of making decisions for your parents that you're not used to doing. You become the parent in many ways. And it actually gets easier as the disease gets worse. Because you truly, at one stage, you almost become like parallel. You're on equal footing because you're having to do caregiving things, but it's hard to explain. Before it was the parent-child relationship, even though you're both adults there's still certain things. And then it gets closer and closer and then all of the sudden you're the parent and they're the child.

This is a struggle for Michelle, Edward, and Amy as they discuss what the most logical next step might be from what felt like a very limited number of options: either someone moves in with mom and accepts caregiving responsibilities, they find a way to pay for a formal caregiver to move in with mom, or they place mom in a dementia care facility. Then there was the conversation about medication. And finally, the question of patient autonomy. With a disease that impairs a person's cognitive function, how much can you rely on the individual, in this case Peggy, to make logical decisions?

Amy was furious that her siblings did not tell her about the doctor's appointment. Michelle and Edward tried to explain that they were just trying to protect Amy from the worry they know she would experience but Amy still felt betrayed.

In addition to medical and personal sources of uncertainty, adult children also report experiencing social sources of uncertainty including ambiguous relational implications (Stone & Jones, 2009). Familial caregivers who live far away may be able to actively care for their loved one, via telephone, email, and sometimes in-person visits. However, Cagle and Munn (2012) reported that "many remotely located family members and friends may feel they are not meeting their caregiving obligations. Falling short of one's perceived caregiving responsibilities, whether appraised by one's self or others, can lead to these intense feelings of regret, remorse, and insufficiency" (p. 702). Caregivers who live far away from their loved one may have work commitments which prevent them from traveling to see their loved one and this does not allow the caregiver to speak to their loved one face-to-face about his/her present state or to observe their loved one in person. Additionally, long-distance caregivers have "high levels [of] stress and dissatisfaction, perhaps because they receive less information than those able to see what is occurring firsthand" (Cagle & Munn, 2012, p. 703).

Amy begins to question what her role should be given the difficult decisions they are making as a family. Like participants in Stone and Jones' (2009) study, this case highlights the challenges siblings face in defining their roles as caregivers. In most cases, proximal family members assume most of the caregiving role pertaining to their loved one with Alzheimer's disease. Negotiating these roles and communicating about the upcoming treatment and care decisions is often fraught with uncertainty as families work to adapt to their new circumstances. To manage her uncertainty, Amy begins searching for information online and encourages her siblings to do the same.

A quick Google search yields over 47 million results. She begins with the first link to the Alzheimer's Association where she begins to learn about the incidence of Alzheimer's disease. From there, she continues to scroll through the pages and pages of websites and eventually finds a blog that highlights the experiences of a daughter caring for her mother at home. The blog gives Amy a perspective on in-home care that she had not considered. As a long-distance caregiver, Amy would never be able to provide in-home care for her mother and the blog described the experience of isolation felt by the caregiver for a parent.

Amy thought about Michelle, the most likely candidate in the family if in-home care was the option. How would Michelle's life change? What would be the financial concerns if Michelle had to quit her job? What are the relational implications (family and otherwise) for Michelle? And for Amy, how would she communicate with her siblings about the information that she found? How might she organize it so that she could easily share it with others?

The decision of whether to keep a parent at home or move him/her to an assisted living facility is widely acknowledged as a challenge. Given the uncertainty associated with this decision, considering the options and the implications of those options on the different parties involved is key. One common way to manage uncertainty is through information seeking (Brashers, Goldsmith, & Hsieh, 2002). Drawing from Wilson's (2000) definition of information behavior, Hogan and Brashers (2009) proposed that information behavior should be more broadly conceptualized beyond information seeking and avoiding to focus more specifically on information acquisition, information handling, and information use. As Hogan and Rintamaki (2006) suggested, there are a variety of strategies for handling information ranging from memorizing information to using organization articles, pamphlets, and notes in physical or online filing systems.

Amy decides to email her siblings some of the articles she's reading online and asks them to take a look and call the following day. When Edward calls, Amy is not surprised that Edward found some similar sources. They know that based on Peggy's symptoms, her doctor's recommendations, and everything they are reading online, it's time to look at options for assisted living. This requires more online research. Amy offers to continue to do research online since she won't be able to actually visit any of the locations. Michelle and Edward agree that this will be the best way to keep Amy involved in the process. Michelle and Edward decide that their next step is to have the conversation with their mother about moving.

Michelle and Edward arrive at Peggy's house—their childhood home—for dinner. Peggy is making their favorite, chicken with roasted potatoes and leeks. As they finish dinner, Edward begins the difficult conversation.

Edward: "Mum, we have something we want to talk to you about."

Peggy: "Oh, what is on your mind?"

Edward: "How have you been feeling since your doctor's appointment? Have you thought at all about what the doctor said?"

Peggy: "Not really. I mean we all get older, right? We all forget things. I'm fine most of the time."

Michelle: "Yes mum, we know you're fine. You're still you but we're worried about you being on your own. What would have happened if I hadn't come over that day when the gas was leaking? What if you had lit the fire?"

They continued their conversation, going back and forth, expressing concerns and Peggy trying to reassure that nothing was wrong. In the end, Peggy agreed to consider moving. She acknowledged that it is getting harder for her to get around the house and that she likes the idea of having some company during the day. Michelle and Edward tell Amy that after their conversation they know that it will be important to find an assisted living facility that allows for a great deal of autonomy for their residents. Amy describes one location, not far from where Peggy currently lives, that has staged care.

DISCUSSION QUESTIONS

1. What sources of uncertainty do adult children experience when a parent is diagnosed with dementia? What are some communication strategies for managing uncertainty?
2. Much research has examined reasons for concealing and revealing health-related information. What happens when family members have different rules for concealing and revealing?
3. What role should a geographically distant adult sibling play in medical decision making for a parent with dementia?
4. How is conflict managed in the presence of uncertainty?

REFERENCES

Agrell, B., & Dehlin, O. (1998). The clock-drawing test. *Age and Ageing, 27*, 399–403.

Alzheimer's Association. (2018). *Alzheimer's & Dementia: Global Resources*. Retrieved from https://www.alz.org/global/overview.asp

Birks, J., & Harvey, R. J. (2006). Donepezil for dementia due to Alzheimer's disease. *Cochrane Database of Systematic Reviews*, (1), CD001190. doi:10.1002/14651858.CD001190.pub2

Brashers, D. E. (2001). Communication and uncertainty management. *Journal of Communication, 51*, 477–497. doi:10.1111/j.1460-2466.2001.tb02892.x

Brashers, D. E., Goldsmith, D. J., & Hsieh, E. (2002). Infomration seeking and avoiding in health contexts. *Human Communication Research, 28*, 258–271. doi:10.1111/j.1468-2958.2002.tb00807.x

Cagle, J. G., & Munn, J. C. (2012) Long-distance caregiving: A systematic review of the literature. *Journal of Gerontological Social Work, 55*(8), 682–707. doi:10.1080/01634372.2012.703763

Hogan, T., & Brashers, D. (2009). The theory of communication and uncertainty management: Implications from the wider realm of information behavior. In T. Afifi & W. Afifi (Eds.), *Uncertainty, information management, and disclosure decisions: Theories and applications* (pp. 45–66). New York, NY: Routledge.

Hogan, T., & Rintamaki, L. (2006). *The information work associated with taking medications: A qualitative study of U.S. veterans receiving treatment for HIV disease*. Paper presented at the Association for Library and Information Sciences (ALISE), San Antonio, TX.

Sperling, R. A., Aisen, P. S., Beckett, L. A., Bennett, D. A., Craft, S., & Fagan, A. M. (2011). Toward defining the preclinical stages of Alzheimer's disease: Recommendations from the National Institute of Aging- Alzheimer's Association workgroups on diagnostic guidelines for Alzheimer's disease. *Alzheimer's & Dementia, 7*(3), 280–292. doi:10.1016/j.jalz.2011.03.003

Stone, A. M. (2013). Dilemmas of communicating about Alzheimer's disease: Professional caregivers, social support, and illness uncertainty. *Journal of Applied Communication Research, 41*, 1–17. doi:10.1080/00909882.2012.738426

Stone, A. M., & Jones, C. (2009). Sources of uncertainty: Experiences of Alzheimer's disease. *Issues in Mental Health Nursing, 30*(11), 677–686. doi:10.3109/01612840903046354

Wilson, T. (2000). Human information behavior. *Informing Science, 3*, 49–55. doi:10.28945/576